BADGE TO BADGE

365 Days of Encouragement for First Responders
and Those Who Support Them

Brad Green

ISBN 978-1-0980-9330-3 (paperback)
ISBN 978-1-0980-9331-0 (digital)

Christian Faith Publishing, Inc.
832 Park Avenue
Meadville, PA 16335
www.christianfaithpublishing.com

Printed in the United States of America

Chaplain Brad Green's devotionals are specifically written to encourage first responders in their relationship with God, and to deepen their faith in His word. Brad's years of experience as a faithful, servant-based police officer is the basis of his devotions. More importantly, the messages are an expression of his life as a Christian husband, father and one who faithfully endured a full career in public service. The spiritual parallels he uses of those incidents and God's word are direct and will give first responders great hope that God is with them as they face a multitude of career challenges, while balancing the importance of life outside of the job.

I pray that these devotionals will find their way into the hands of first responders who continue to serve their communities with courage, honor, dedication, and faithfulness.

—Chief Tom Gazsi
Los Angeles Port Police

Retirement from law enforcement is somewhat a misnomer. Retired Officer Brad Green is still on the job, working to help those in the first responder community. Devotion to a job is admirable, however, devotion to faith is a necessary element to help the men and women of the first responder calling to sleep at night. Chaplain Brad Green has that devotion. Take God's words as relayed through Chaplain Brad and know there is peace in this world that can surpass all our earthly understanding. Be assured that those painful memories will pass by letting the words of this devotional touch your heart and soul.

—Chaplain Mike MacIntosh, D.Min, D.Div
San Diego PD, Newport Beach PD,
Rancho Santa Fe Fire Rescue

Brad Green is one of the strongest men I have ever known. His strength is not just physical, it is spiritual. He has a heart for both the hurting and the courageous men and women who put on a uniform every day just like he did for years. I admired the way he fathered his three girls and I aspired to be like him: a compassionate man of character. In the darkest hours of my life, Brad supported me, encouraged me, and stood by me like no other friend, and I believe he will do the same for you. That was when I discovered he was an excellent writer. I still have the letters and notes he wrote me through that difficult time of abandonment and betrayal.

Now everyone can benefit from his wit and wisdom in this fascinating book of inspiration for first responders. Brad communicates truth from scripture to the reality of the front lines of crisis in a way that anyone can appreciate and enjoy. I strongly endorse this wonderful work of Brad Green as well as the man who wrote it.

—Stephen Arterburn
Author and founder of NewLife Ministries

Like you, my husband Ken and I admire and respect our nation's law enforcement officers, EMTs, and firefighters. And with our country in so much turmoil right now; with terrorism, natural disasters, and riots, our First Responders are being stretched to the limit. And I'm not only referring to the numbers in their ranks—these brave Americans are battling stress and discouragement. This is why I am 100 percent behind *Badge to Badge*, a new devotional book written by Brad Green. My friend Brad is perfectly qualified to encourage First Responders—as a former police officer and pastor, he is expertly gifted to offer guidance and courage to our beleaguered frontline responders. If you have a loved one who serves in emergency services, this is the *perfect* gift to bolster their spirits and energize their commitment to the cause. I give *Badge to Badge* a double thumbs-up!

—Joni Eareckson Tada
Joni and Friends International Disability Center

I have enjoyed reading Brad Green's devotionals for many years. They are well-written, succinct, and encouraging. Brad's experience as an elite athlete, career law enforcement officer, pastor, and parent of daughters with medically challenging issues has prepared him to speak calm encouragement into the lives of people who live on the edge as first responders. When you read Brad's writings you are hearing the voice of someone who has not just survived but thrived in the midst of crisis. Brad gets it and will help you keep doing what you do with courage, strength, and joy.

—Dave Rolph
Senior pastor, Calvary Chapel Pacific Hills

Brad Green is what you would call, "a cop's cop." He worked in patrol, traffic, vice, hostage negotiation, defense tactics instruction, and more during his twenty-one years of service with the Newport Beach Police Department. But Brad is also a pastor, with a heart for first responders. He cares about them, and he knows what it's like to walk in their shoes. He has written a new book full of encouragement from one first responder to others serving in law enforcement, fire, medical services, and the military. This book will ground you in Scripture, encourage you, and point you to Christ. I recommend this new book by Brad Green to you.

—Greg Laurie
Senior pastor, Harvest Christian Fellowship

As a law enforcement first responder, Brad Green has gained a first-hand, up close, and personal understanding of the human condition. Continually on the frontlines of adversity, showing up to help others in their worst moments and sharing some of the most memorable experiences with his brothers-in-arms; Brad has accumulated a career of recollections that he utilizes to dispatch truths as they relate to the spiritual battlefield. You will find yourself drawn into the events he relays and will come away with a clearer perspective about knowing God and making Him known.

—Chad Williams
Former Navy SEAL

God used Brad in my life as a conduit to Jesus while we played football together at the University of Southern California. He was, and remains, thoughtful and discerning. Brad pulls experiences from his life and law enforcement career into his writings that will stimulate your thought and faith.

—Anthony Munoz
NFL Pro Football Hall of Fame 1998

I would like to recommend to you the life and gleanings from a man who knows what it's like to see God work in his life. It is exciting enough to have success in one area of life, but Brad Green has found himself being used by God in many areas over the years that have uniquely qualified him to write this perennial devotion.

Brad is no stranger to Jesus' command to "Love they neighbor." In doing so, he has served his God, nation, community, and his family faithfully. His effectiveness in these areas has distinctively qualified him to speak into our lives.

I trust that you will receive much from this devotion and I pray that you would add it to your daily walk with God.

—Pastor Jack Hibbs
Senior pastor, Calvary Chapel Chino Hills

I first had the opportunity to know Officer Brad Green when I became a chaplain with the Newport Beach Police Department. Then as I joined him on, "pastoral ride-alongs," I realized that he was a committed Christian man who loved to serve in ministries. Some years ago, when he began sending out his weekly Badge to Badge devotions, it became apparent that he had an ability to put together great spiritual thoughts focusing on and relating to first responders. As he has now put together these devotions in a book, I am sure they will encourage many in their relationship with Jesus Christ.

—Don McClure
Pastor, Calvary Chapel

I've known Brad Green for over forty years and consider him a great friend who has walked through the thick & thins of life with me. Over four decades of trusting and following God in his marriage, his parenting, his friendships and his various career paths are represented in the powerful lessons of God in this book.

In Brad's *Badge to Badge* devotional, he provides an awesome tool to help seek the wisdom of God to jump start each day of the year.

I love the way each day's message includes a brief truth from the Bible, a compelling real-life story from Brad's life (as a first responder, athlete, father, husband) and a practical "thought for the day" that helps focus us on God's presence and power in the midst of every situation we are in.

Brad's ability to tell a captivating story and tie it into a truth from the Word of God inspires me to turn the page and see what he and God want to share with me to start out the new day!

I highly recommend Badge to Badge for anyone wanting to develop a daily rhythm with God to combat the chaos of the world, the darkness of the enemy and provide you with supernatural peace.

—Allen Pugh
CEO of Rhyno Corporation

Chaplain Brad Green has taken his real-life experience as a police officer and chaplain and applied it to the alarm bells of every first responder. His insight into biblical truth, challenges us to adopt faith into our daily lives, whether we are responding down the street with red lights and siren, or at home away from the job.

—Greg Newland
Captain II, LA City Fire Department (retired)

Life can be incredibly difficult. Those of us who have been called to serve the medical needs of others get a front row seat to many of the tragedies this world has to offer. The full effects of that exposure can only be truly understood by those in our same professional circle. Thankfully, Chaplain Brad Green has drawn from his own experiences in law enforcement to invoke the hope that a faith in Jesus Christ can bring during our darkest moments. He simultaneously strikes just the right balance between God's unapologetic truth, and His unending love for us. In his own unique way, Brad is able to communicate the very words needed for any first responder who longs to be reminded of God's goodness and purpose for their life. Regardless of the events that your calling leads you to, the devotions found in this book will allow you to overcome any circumstance as you continue to selflessly serve others in need.

—Maria Santana
Adult critical care registered nurse

To Terri, Kara, Tayler, and Paige. Your love has always given me the best reason to get up and face the day no matter what the circumstances. To David, Lucius, and Nala, for continuing to bring meaning, joy, and purpose to my life.

To first responders, who every day redefine the word "hero" by their daily sacrifice for others.

To Dorothy Helfer, without whose support this book would not have been possible.

*Greater love hath no man than this, that a
man lay down his life for his friends.*

—John 15:13

*Down these mean streets a man must go who is not himself
mean, who is neither tarnished nor afraid...
He is the hero, he is everything.*

—Raymond Chandler

INTRODUCTION

In spring of 2007, I was in the police station walking through the Administration Division section. As I passed Captain Tom Gazsi's office, I stuck my head in to say hello. Captain Gazsi had been my first field training officer when I joined the force in 1990. He was a man of God who was not shy about his faith in Jesus Christ and had been instrumental in creating the chaplain's program at the department. We had a brief discussion about the program due to my involvement as its sworn officer liaison. I had been involved with several others in generating the rules and requirements for the program and had sat on the oral board as we interviewed potential applicants. After a few minutes of conversation, Captain Gazsi looked at me intently for several seconds and said, "I think you should be one of our chaplains." The statement took me by surprise, but my answer was immediate. Since I was familiar with the applicant rules for chaplains, I reminded the captain that in order to serve in the program, it was a requirement to be ordained in an established religious denomination. There were several more seconds of quiet before he broke the silence and told me to "go take a seat outside and close the door on your way out." Now, I didn't want to be paranoid, but when a supervisor asks you to wait outside and close the door behind you, that usually doesn't end well. I spent the next several minutes going over our conversation in my mind, wondering if I had said anything to offend him, or to get myself in trouble.

After several minutes of nervous waiting, Captain Gazsi opened the door and asked me to come inside and take a seat. He walked behind his desk, sat down, looked up at me, and with a smile on his face, he said, "Dave Rolph will ordain you." Dave is the senior pastor at Calvary Chapel Pacific Hills and was one of the chaplains in our program. Captain Gazsi went on to state that he and some of the other chaplains had seen something in me that led them to believe that it was God's plan for me to be ordained and serve NBPD as a chaplain. I was stunned. I tried to think of all the reasons why I didn't deserve this "field promotion" and how I wasn't qualified for the job. I was a young adult at Calvary Chapel during the Jesus revolution era of the 1970s, and I had great respect for the pastors who had helped me while I was there. How could I possibly be worthy of this honor? Well, the short answer was I wasn't, but I had heard the quote many times in my life, "God doesn't call the qualified, He qualifies the called." Despite my doubts, I was not about to refuse to walk through an obvious open door in my life by turning down an opportunity to serve the citizens of Newport Beach, or the men and women of our department.

In 2009, I started to write a devotional to encourage Newport Beach police officers, and *Badge to Badge* was born. Over the next ten years, the list of those requesting the devotional grew to include people from other law enforcement agencies, as well as civilians who just liked the first responder stories. I was then urged to publish a book to encourage all first responders with God's word. This book is that attempt.

I pray that the devotions you find here will encourage and inspire you to have a closer relationship with God. One thing all first responders have in common is a bunch of stories to tell. I think these devotional stories will, at times, make you laugh, cry, encourage you, exhort you, and you will be convicted along with me, as I reveal the truth about my experience and struggles as a law enforcement officer. Know this, as I wrote these devotionals, I was always preaching to myself. I pray as you read them you will be convinced that we are all in this life together, sharing the same hopes, dreams, disappointments, and difficulties.

The work of a first responder has always been difficult, but at no time has it been like it is now. In the book of Esther, we read the account of a young Jewish girl whom God used to save her people. God's word tells us that Esther became a queen for "such a time as this" in the history of the Jewish nation. I pray that these devotions will be used in a small way to encourage all first responders, and the people who care about them, for such a time as this in our country's history.

DAY 1

*Trust in the LORD with all thine heart; and lean
not unto your own understanding. In all thy ways
acknowledge Him. And He shall direct thy paths.*
                                          —Proverbs 3:5–6

Hang On or Let Go?

One late night when I was on the bicycle patrol team, I was riding with a partner in the area of the Mariner's Mile (Coast Highway between Dover and Newport Boulevard). We were in a dark part of the restaurant district at about Tustin and the highway when we noticed a group of three men seated in a car parked on the north curbline. We silently rode up to them and were able to look inside the car without their knowledge of our existence. We saw nothing unusual at first, but we made contact and spoke with the occupants of the vehicle. Due to the late hour, the closed businesses in the vicinity, and, frankly, the "creepy factor" our conversation with them gave us, we asked them if they would step out of the car so that we could talk further. All the subjects were wearing loose, bulky clothing. The law allows us to perform a quick pat-down search in that situation for officer safety reasons. As I put my open palm on the front right waistband of one of the subjects, I immediately felt a flat, hard object. From my training and experience, I knew exactly what it was. The thin metal handle of a semiautomatic pistol had a very distinct feel. So did the knot in my throat as I realized what we were dealing with.

I had one of two choices to make at that moment. Do I push him away, draw my gun, and hope that he couldn't get to his weapon before I got to mine, or do I keep hold of the gun with all my might until I could pull it from his pants and then draw my weapon? In that instance, I decided to keep hold of the gun and thought, well, at least if we fight for it, I will have no doubt that lethal force would be acceptable. It turned out to be the best option. I was able to remove the gun, shout to my partner, and we successfully took all three men down at gunpoint. After the arrest, we found an additional gun and duct tape in the vehicle. It turned out that they were in the car planning a takeover robbery of one of the restaurants across the street when we happened upon them.

Sometimes, it is hard in this life to know what to do. Do we hang on to things or let them go? Does God want us to persevere and keep trying, or change course and let loose of our current situation? Either one could be in His perfect will. So here is the answer: I don't know.

When confronted with a choice, pray for wisdom, read God's word, and do all you can to obtain a clear direction on which way to go. Sometimes a clear answer doesn't come, so just do your best, and make a choice. If that choice didn't work out, pursue the other option.

I wish I could tell you that knowing God's will for your life is an exact science. We would all like it if we knew that doing A, B, and C, is what we needed to do every time to get God's clear direction. But sometimes we need to seek Him, lean not on our own understanding, and take an action in order for God to reveal to us His perfect will for our lives.

Thought for the Day

Hold on or let go? Acknowledge Him, read His word, then make a move. He will direct your path.

DAY 2

*For the Holy Spirit will teach you in that
very hour what you ought to say.*

—Luke 12:12

Ministry of Presence

S everal years ago, I responded to a suicide call on the east side of
town. Officers had been dispatched to a suspicious man seated
in a car in the parking lot at a local park. As officers approached his
vehicle, the subject pulled out a gun, put it to his head, and shot
himself. The wound was fatal, and he was pronounced dead at the
scene. My job that night as a chaplain was not to comfort the victim.
That was not possible. The victim's family was not at the scene, so I
couldn't assist them. My sole purpose that night was to support the
officers who had just witnessed a suicide. Police officers must often
handle death scenes where individuals have taken their lives, but it
is rare that they witness a suicide in real time. That is traumatic for
anyone, even for seasoned, trained police personnel.

I didn't do anything special that night regarding the officers
at the scene. I stood and talked with them as they conducted their
investigation. I let them tell me whatever they wanted to about what
they had seen, and their part in the call. It wasn't until weeks later
that I was told what my being there had meant to the officers. They
said that just my mere presence let them know that the incident was
viewed by their supervision as a difficult situation. This allowed the
officers, especially the younger ones, to not feel ashamed or worried that they were emotionally affected by what they had seen. It
gave them permission to process their feelings and know that they

were not alone in what they were dealing with. Normalizing such emotions is the key to stress management in processing any critical incident. Officers need to know that if they are having difficulty in what they had experienced, they were having normal reactions to an abnormal situation. In the chaplain world, this type of help is called the ministry of presence. We don't have to say the right thing, or come up with any detailed plan to help. We just need to be there! In fact, saying too much can often be the wrong thing to do.

If you are ever called on to help someone through a situation of loss or grief, just your presence alone can speak more to them than anything you might say. When I am on my way to minister in a difficult situation, my prayer isn't "Lord, help me to say the right thing," it is, "Lord, help me to not say the wrong thing." God's word tells us that the Holy Spirit will guide us on what to say in the hard discussions of our life. The good news is that He will often lead us to say nothing at all!

Thought for the Day

The ministry of presence can be more powerful than eloquence in the moment.

DAY 3

*In peace I will both lie down and sleep; for you
alone, O Lord, make me dwell in safety.*

—Psalm 4:8

Safety Skid

One night I was working in a two-man DUI car on the west side of Newport Beach. It was in December, and our assignment was to locate and arrest individuals who were driving under the influence of drugs and/or alcohol. It was a target-rich environment at that time of year due to the numerous holiday parties in the area. My partner and I stopped to do some paperwork in a cement-paved lot located across the street, from the Arches restaurant, just north of the Coast Highway on the west side of Old Newport Boulevard. We were parked facing the street so we could see vehicles that made the northbound turn from the highway onto Old Newport. Sometimes drivers rounded the corner at an unsafe speed and struck the raised center median located at the intersection. Our training and experience taught us that intoxicated drivers often exhibited this lack of control.

Our position and expectations turned out to be prophetic. As we watched the intersection, we saw a red Porsche convertible (top down) race around the corner and hit the center median at a high rate of speed. The impact was so intense that it flattened and shredded off all four of the car's tires! Somehow, the vehicle was able to negotiate a partial right turn and skidded onto the paved lot where we were parked. Now sliding on the drums of the Porsche's wheels, the car continued to move toward our unit which was located about forty yards away. I don't know if the driver still had his foot on the accelerator, or if it was just the car's forward momentum, but the vehicle continued to slide northbound. As the car slowed down, it passed by our open driver's side window with the sickening sound of grinding metal on cement in the air. The driver, who still had his hands on the, now useless, steering wheel, locked eyes with us only a few feet away as he crept by with an expression of horror on his face. It could not have been scripted any better if it had been in a movie. I exited my car and approached the vehicle with the rhetorical question of the evening, "Do you think you were going too fast?" The surprising thing was that he was only guilty of a vehicle code violation and had not consumed any alcohol that night!

Have you hit a curb and knocked the wheels from your life? Do you feel that you are skidding along with no real idea of where your final destination will be? It might be time to take your hands off your life's useless wheel, and let God slow you down and bring you to a safe place. It doesn't matter if you are in a situation of your own making, or if the circumstances were out of your control. God can safely start you on the process to rebuild your life. But first, you must stop! Stop trying to run everything. Stop trying to figure everything out. Stop using the world's wisdom and standards to make your decisions and stop leaning on any person or thing other than Jesus Christ and His word to you.

Thought for the Day

If you trust in Him, He will control the direction and destination of the wreck you might have made of your life.

DAY 4

And being in agony, He prayed more earnestly. Then His sweat
became like great drops of blood falling down to the ground.

—Luke 22:44

Stage Fright

Not long after I became a chaplain for the Newport Beach Police Department, I was asked to give my first public invocation. We were swearing in a new chief of police, and I was asked to pray for him. That might not sound too intimidating to you, but I knew what it meant, and more importantly, I knew who would be there. I was still an active sworn officer at the time and had been to many of these ceremonies in the past. I knew that all the supervision of my department would be there. Also, many chiefs of police from neighboring cities and counties would be in attendance. In addition to that, a good number of my peers and coworkers would also be present. I had never met our new chief until that afternoon, and how I performed would be his first (or last) impression of me. Are you sweating yet? I was.

I was introduced and walked to the podium to pray. When I turned around and faced the audience, I saw that several other individuals I knew had just walked in. Pastor Greg Laurie of Harvest Christian Fellowship and Harvest Crusade fame; Pastor Dave Rolph from Calvary Chapel Pacific Hills and the Balanced Word radio program; pastor, author, and educator Mike MacIntosh from the megachurch Horizon Fellowship in San Diego; and Don McClure of Calvary Chapel who was well-known as the elder statesman of prayer. Each one of these men had written a book on prayer (or could have) and represented the who's who for influential pastors in the Southern California area. I was wearing a weapon at the time and briefly thought about using it on myself. Well, I got through it and was told that I did a decent job despite the intimidating audience in attendance that day.

Do you know that God also knows firsthand what it is like to be afraid? The above verse in Luke describes an event that happened at the Garden of Gethsemane the night before Christ's crucifixion. Jesus had just prayed out in anguish, "*Father, if it is Your will, take this cup away from Me: nevertheless not My will, but Yours, be done*" (verse 42). He knew not only the manner of His impending death, but also that He was about to take on the punishment for the sin of the entire world, past, present, and future. As Jesus continued to pray, He started to sweat so heavily that it was like large drops of blood. That is fear, greater fear than I've ever known. And despite that fear, God the Son bowed to the will of God the Father, died on that cross for our sin, rose again, and now sits in glory in heaven.

God's word says, "*For we do not have a High Priest who cannot sympathize with our weakness, but was in all points tempted as we are, yet did not sin*" (Hebrews 4:15). Jesus knows what it is like to be hungry, thirsty, tired, betrayed, and, yes, afraid.

Thought for the Day

Don't let your fear stop you from believing in, serving, and obeying God. He understands your fear and will help you through.

DAY 5

A time to cry and a time to laugh. A time to grieve and a time to dance.
—Ecclesiastes 3:4

A Time to Cry

Several years ago, I was called out to the scene of a suicide at a local park. A distraught male had gone to the park, sat on a bench, put a revolver to his head, and pulled the trigger. The shot went through and through and killed him instantly. The damage it caused was exactly like many of the other suicides by handguns I had seen over the years, small entry wound, large exit wound. There was no note left in the area, so we had no immediate idea as to why he had taken his life.

The sergeant at the scene had requested a chaplain because of a female witness at the park. She had seen the man walk to the bench, sit down, and then heard the shot. She turned around just in time to see him fall from the fatal self-inflicted wound. She now was sitting in her car crying and was unable to stop. I spoke with her and told her that her actions were natural considering what she had just witnessed. This kind of response can be defined as a normal reaction to an abnormal event. I asked her to look at the officers who were there working the scene. I told her that somewhere inside each of them, they wanted to do the same thing that she was. They were just not allowed to because of their jobs. Then I asked her, "So who is the healthy one here?" Of course, that rhetorical question was meant to reassure her that her tears were normal, and that this was an appropriate time to cry.

As a first responder, you will see many horrific things during the course of your career. You will work through each event in a professional manner, controlling the scene, gathering evidence, documenting information, and comforting witnesses. And when the incident has been cleared, you will get back in your unit and move on to the next call. The nature of your work does not usually allow you the time to grieve that is allotted to the public you serve. I have seen this lack of grief time result in relationship losses, alcohol abuse, and physical illnesses. Willing exposure to these possible negative effects is part of what makes first responder true heroes.

Take some time after your shift to allow yourself to grieve for the pain, fear, injustice, violence, and death that you have seen. I know that you don't want to go there, but I assure you it will help you in the long run. Listen to an ex-officer who is on the other end of an archive of difficult mental images. If you take the time to process these events now, you will come out better on the other side of your retirement.

Thought for the Day

There is a time to cry and grieve. Take the time.

DAY 6

*I waited patiently for the Lord to help me, and
he turned to me and heard my cry.*

—Psalm 40:1

Waiting

I am not a very good flier. You might not be able to tell that I am uncomfortable from my demeanor, but my calm appearance belies what is going on inside me. It isn't that I am panicked or claustrophobic in any way, I am just uncomfortable from the time we lift off until the time our wheels return to the tarmac. I try to distract myself by reading or watching a movie which at times can help, but I have resigned myself to the fact that I am just not comfortable in the air. Air travel is about waiting, and I guess I am not a very patient person.

The Christian life, at times, is a lot about waiting. In order to develop our character, or to use us to fulfill His plan, we often have to wait for the answers to our prayers.

The above verse in Psalms tells us a few things about God and our part in the process of answered prayer. It appears that it is our part to cry out to God for help and wait patiently for His reply. "Wait patiently," that sounds a lot like the same character trait that is developed at airports where we experience check-ins, security checks, delayed flights, cancellations, and lost luggage. It is what we endure in order to get to our final destination.

To be honest, I don't like it when God wants me to learn patience, but it appears to be a requirement in order for me to be obedient and realize His will in my life. Fortunately, this short verse gives us two promises that reveal God's part of the equation as an answer to our patient endurance. *"He turned to me and heard my cry."* What a great promise as a payoff to patience. The God of the universe will take the time to turn to me when I pray and see my anguish. But He goes beyond a mere notice of my issue. The final three words in our verse tells us that He will "hear my cry." That means more than just an auditory recognition, it means he really listens to us. It is a lot like the old saying from the 1960s when you wanted someone to know that you really understood them, "I hear you, man!"

If you are waiting today for an answer from God in your life, cry out to Him, He will turn to you, and He will hear your cry.

Thought for the Day

> *Wait on the Lord; Be of good courage, And He shall strengthen your heart; Wait, I say, on the Lord!*
> (Psalm 27:14)

DAY 7

*I will lift up my eyes to the hills—From whence comes
my help? My help comes from the LORD,
who made heaven and earth.*

—Psalm 121:1–2

Backup

One day we were dispatched to a call of a violent individual on the beach. He was physically confronting citizens, and had either some sort of drug on board, or was having a severe psychotic break. The male suspect was large in size, and to make matters worse, he was exhibiting superhuman strength due to his current psychological or chemical state. Tasers were unsuccessfully deployed, and it took at least eleven officers to subdue him. In the end, the suspect compound fractured his own arms in an effort to get free from the handcuffs that had been placed on him.

I know what officers feel when they confront a dangerous suspect. I have had that sense of relief when I heard the sirens of my backup coming from all around the city. It was always good to know that help was on the way.

If you are a follower of Jesus Christ, God has your back in this life, and as great as the sound of a siren can be, it can't compare to an almighty God who is always right there for us in times of trouble. If you have a personal relationship with Jesus Christ, then all the promises in His word are yours to stand on. In Jeremiah 29:12, the Father tells us, "*Then you will call upon Me and go and pray to Me, and I will listen to you.*" What a great promise! The almighty God of the universe will listen to us. Listening denotes an active involvement in our lives that shows more action than merely hearing what we say.

Thought for the Day

Next time we are in a spiritual, emotional, health, or financial fight for our lives, just remember our backup is only a prayer away.

DAY 8

But as it is written: "Eye has not seen, nor ear heard,
nor have entered into the heart of man the things which
God has prepared for those who love Him."

—1 Corinthians 2:9

Unbelievable Future

Have you ever wondered why "alternate world" movies are so popular? Movies like *Avatar, Harry Potter,* and *The Lord of the Rings* offer views of worlds where, at their best, are exciting, peaceful, and without the troubles that we experience in our everyday lives. The characters have long lives, powers that we do not, and live in magical lands without pollution where there seems to be answers for all illness and financial need. Studies found that after the release of *Avatar,* depression and suicidal thoughts increased among those who had viewed the movie. Apparently, some individuals longed for the alien world of Pandora over their own.

The above verse in 1 Corinthians promises us that we have not heard about, seen, or even imagined the thrilling things that God has planned for those who have given their lives to Him. I'm not certain as to all that our Lord has planned for us, or exactly what heaven will be like. I do know that God has placed that longing for a better world in our hearts. We are encoded with a desire to see heaven and to be with our creator.

The minds of man created the alternate worlds that we see in movies today. I am excited to know that the best human fiction ever crafted won't come close to the unbelievable place that God has prepared for me. For me it gives new meaning to the verse, "*To live is Christ and to die is gain*" (Philippians 1:21).

Thought for the Day

The destination that God has planned for us is a far better place than Pandora, Hogwarts, or the Shire.

DAY 9

He said to him, "I too am a prophet as you are, and an angel spoke to me by the word of the LORD, saying, 'Bring him back with you to your house, that he may eat bread and drink water.'" (He was lying to him.) So he went back with him and ate bread in his house and drank water.

—1 Kings 13:18–19

Cell Phone Reception

Police officers dislike nothing more than when victims talk on their cell phone while we are attempting to interview them. It slows the process by introducing competing, incorrect information into the situation. It is also disrespectful to the officer and clearly shows the low esteem they have for law enforcement.

An account found in 1 Kings 13 tells of a prophet that had been sent by God to warn King Jeroboam. The prophet was ordered by God to go directly home after speaking with the king without stopping. He was admonished to *"not eat bread, nor drink water, nor return by the same way you came"* (verse 9). We can see from the above passage that someone else contacted the prophet and told him that an "angel" had given him orders that were in direct opposition to what God had said. Unfortunately, the prophet disobeyed God and believed the lie that was told to him. He chose to listen to that competing, incorrect information, and paid for that mistake with his life in verse 24.

God speaks to us every day through His word, the Bible. In its pages is contained not only the message of salvation, but also information we can use to restore broken relationships, avoid emotional pain, sustain us in times of trouble, and live generally happy, healthy lives. But so often, we listen to competing voices who tell us to follow a path not directed by God. And like the prophet above, we do so to our own detriment.

The Bible is the inerrant word of God and can give us clear direction as to what is best for us. Pastor Greg Laurie has a great answer to all those who ask him what he does when he reads something in the Bible that he doesn't agree with. He tells them, "I change my opinion!" THAT'S RIGHT! Either God is our Lord, or He is not. If we esteem His direction in our lives, we will follow His word whether we agree with it or not.

Thought for the Day

Let's commit to listen to Him and ignore the competing voices who will only lead us to destruction.

DAY 10

But God said unto him, thou fool, this night thy soul shall be required
of thee: then whose shall those things be, which thou hast provided?
—Luke 12:20

Ready or Not

I was once dispatched to check on the welfare of an elderly resident
who lived alone. As a police officer, I often got calls like this that
turned out to be a result of some sort of miscommunication. I usually found the person at their residence and informed them that a
relative was attempting to make contact.

The out-of-town reporting party for this incident told Dispatch
that she had not been able to reach her seventy-year-old aunt by telephone for three weeks. Having been around the block a few times
on calls like this, that didn't sound good. When I arrived at the residence, I received no response to my repeated knocks at the door. I
could hear that a television was on inside of the apartment and found
the front door closed but unlocked. As I pushed the door open, I was
hit by the strong stench of a dead body. If you have ever experienced
that smell, it is easy to identify, and I had a pretty good idea of what
I was about to find. As I pushed the door all the way open, I saw
the subject of the call. She was seated on a chair next to her dining
room table about fifteen feet away. Three weeks was about right for
the advanced stage of decomposition that I observed, and the body
appeared to be melting into the chair and carpet beneath it. This
was another one for the cop mental video archive. There were folded
clothes on a table next to her and a laundry basket with additional
clean clothing inside. It looked as though she had been in the middle

of doing her laundry when she started to not feel well. She then sat down and quickly passed away. As I entered the residence, the first thing that went through my mind, other than "I don't want to do this anymore," was "I wonder if she knew she was dying when she sat down in that chair?"

When I made the death notification to the niece, I found that this woman's passing was unexpected. She had been doing well recently and had given no sign that the end of her life was near. I'm sure that as she went about her business that day, watching TV and folding laundry, she had no idea that she would be so quickly ushered into eternity.

So it is for all of us. We might have decades left to live or only minutes. Heaven is a prepared place for prepared people. It is not our default destination. God's word says that the gospel was written *"that ye may know that ye have eternal life, and that ye may believe on the name of the Son of God"* (1 John 5:13).

Thought for the Day

As first responders, we have to confront life-threatening situations all the time. If this were your last minute, hour, or day on earth, would you be ready?

DAY 11

In the fear of the Lord there is strong confidence,
and His children will have a place of refuge.
—Proverbs 14:26

Daddy

In addition to tithes and contributions, attendees at Harvest OC Church often put prayer requests written on preprinted cards into our offering. As an associate pastor, it was my responsibility to pray for these petitions to God on behalf of those who are going through difficult times in their lives. Due to the sensitive nature of some of the requests, I destroyed them after I had prayed for them so that their pleas will remain confidential between them, God, and myself.

One week, I received an anonymous request that I could not discard after I had prayed for it. It was from a child, as was evident by the unsteady penmanship and the simple word structure of the request. It was written on behalf of "Daddy" and documented this child's simple prayer: "I pray for my dad to come home and for God's word in his heart and peace in his heart. Amen." My heart broke as I tried to imagine the backstory of this little one's pain that would cause such a request to be written.

I often counsel couples who are determined to break up their marriages despite God's prohibition and commands. I have heard before "the children will be better off without all the arguing and fighting between us." That might be true, but there is a better alternative: STOP FIGHTING! I think that many couples in their selfishness don't stop to consider the pain and suffering they leave behind them as they seek to resolve their own, often self-induced, pain. The prayer request that this child wrote documented the fear and emptiness left in the heart of a child who has been abandoned by their earthly father. I prayed that this feeling of abandonment would not be erroneously transferred to this child's heavenly Father, who would never leave or forsake them, and in whom they would always have a place of refuge.

That prayer card is still on my desk. I know that someday, in the middle of a husband's rant about how he can't take his wife and family anymore, I will be able to slide it across the desk to help him realize the full ramifications of his desired actions. At least I pray that it will.

Thought for the Day

Children need that place of refuge. Don't take it away from them.

DAY 12

And from Jesus Christ the faithful witness, the firstborn from the dead, and the ruler over the kings of the earth. To Him who loved us and washed us from our sins in His blood.

—Revelation 1:5

Paid For

Being a football player on a full ride (athletic scholarship) is pretty great! Among other perks, the student is given a form that is used to register for classes or to buy class materials at the bookstore. All they have to do is show the form and their debt is paid. As easy as this might seem, that form does not come without a great cost. The endless hours spent conditioning, practicing, traveling, and rehabilitating from injury can take quite a physical toll.

You may not have been given a full scholarship to college, but God has something far greater than free tuition to offer you. Through the blood of Jesus Christ which was shed for you by His death on the cross, you can be given complete payment for your sin and an eternity in His presence. You don't have to do anything to earn it, and you don't need a form to obtain it. It is a free gift God has offered to you at a great personal cost to Himself. John 3:16 says, *"For God so loved the world that He gave His only begotten Son; that whosoever believes in Him should not perish but have eternal life."* All you have to do is ask for it.

If you have never officially invited Jesus Christ into your life, why not do it now. Just say the following simple prayer and God will hear you.

> Lord I know I am a sinner, and that I've sinned against you.
> I believe that you died on the cross to pay the price for my sins.
> I turn from that sin now and in the best way I know how,
> I give my life to you. Lord come into my heart, take control of my life and make me the kind of person you want me to be. Lord thank you for loving me, for saving me, and for giving me hope and a future with You.

Thought for the Day

If you prayed that prayer and meant it, you now know what it is like to have a full-ride scholarship!

DAY 13

*By that will we have been sanctified through the offering
of the body of Jesus Christ once and for all.*
—Hebrews 10:10

Easy Renewal

Several years ago, I saw that my driver's license was about to expire. I had not received a notice in the mail and thought that I had not qualified for an automatic renewal. That meant that I would have to go stand in a long line at the DMV, take a written test, and get a new picture taken. The new picture was probably the worst part. But then it came! The DMV sent me a letter that stated I could renew my license online! No test, no picture, no long lines, and no surly government workers. It was easy, and I received my new license in the mail a short time later.

The above verse was written by the apostle Paul to those in the new church who were struggling with the old laws and traditions of their previous Hebrew faith. Under that law, they had been required to bring yearly sacrifices to the high priest who would offer them to God as a covering for their sin. As new believers, Paul wanted them to know that they were free from that requirement. Now instead of picking out a spotless animal to sacrifice, hauling the animal to the temple, standing in line to see the priest, and repeating that process every year, they could simply ask God for forgiveness directly due to Christ's blood sacrifice on the cross for them, once and for all. There was no need to bring offerings that merely covered their sins for the previous year, but now the price for their transgressions had actually been paid for on a continual basis if they brought those sins to God in prayer through Jesus Christ.

If you want to experience God's forgiveness today, it is as close as a prayer away. God's word says that "*if we confess our sins, He is faithful and just to forgive us our sins and to cleanse us from all unrighteousness*" (1 John 1:9). There is no need for you to do anything more than to ask God for that forgiveness and do your best to turn from your sin. One of my favorite quotes says, "The moment I confess the transgression in my heart, even before the words can come out, God has already forgiven me." Isn't that a beautiful picture of how eager God is to forgive us and to set us whole and right before Him?

Thought for the Day

You don't have to stand in a hot, dirty, and crowded line to be renewed. You just need to ask God through Jesus Christ, and forgiveness will immediately be sent to you wherever you are!

DAY 14

Write this letter to the angel of the church in Philadelphia.
This is the message from the one who is holy and true,
the one who has the key of David. What he opens, no
one can close; and what he closes no one can open.
—Revelation 3:7

Painted Doors

My daughter participated in theater for many years and performed in numerous musicals, plays, and concerts. Elaborate scene designs were usually a regular part of these productions, and the set designers would create realistic-looking rooms that were complete with windows and doors. Many doors on set were functional, allowing the actors to open and walk through them as the scene required. Many, however, were just realistic-looking replicas complete with hinges and knobs. They looked like real doors, but they could not be opened or used no matter how hard the actor would try. The key was to know the real doors as opposed to the fake ones.

After accepting Jesus Christ as our Savior and Lord, finding His will for our lives should be one of the greatest pursuits of the Christian life. Sometimes many "doors" present themselves to us as we seek to find direction in life. The problem is that many of these doors look real and seem to be viable alternatives for us to follow. But when we try the handles, we quickly find that the door is shut tight and unable to be opened.

Determining God's will for our lives always begins with His word. Most of what we need to know to make wise decisions is directly covered by scripture. But there are times when we will need to pray about our circumstances, in order to find His direction. As long as we are not in violation of God's clear word, we can't go to the Bible to determine exactly which job we should take, who we should marry, or what house to buy. We will need to examine God's open and closed doors in our lives to help us. Since that is the case, it is great to know that if we seek Him, the open door He wants for us will not be able to be closed. It is also comforting for us to know that He can keep doors closed in our lives that could be harmful to us.

Thought for the Day

Don't waste any time trying to pull open a fake door that looks real. Seek God's will and walk through the open doors that He has prepared for you. If it is His will, they will never be shut.

DAY 15

But if you do not do so, then take note, you have sinned
against the LORD; and be sure your sin will find you out.
—Numbers 32:23

Failing Grade

During my first semester at USC, I was approached by an assistant coach who was supposed to "help" me with my academic scheduling. He told me that there was a one-unit PE class that I did not have to attend, but if I showed up on the day of the final, I would get a passing grade. I knew this was wrong and something that God didn't want me to do. I signed up for the class anyway. After all, what could happen, right?

When I walked up to the classroom on the day of the final, the door was locked, and I saw a notice taped to the door. It said the final had been rescheduled for the week before and I had missed it! I got an F in the class. There wasn't much I could do about it. After all, who could I complain to about not getting my free, undeserved grade? I had to accept the fact that I was an NCAA athlete who got an F in PE! I knew right away that God had orchestrated the whole thing to teach me about the consequences of my dishonesty. It was, in fact, one of the greatest lessons I learned while in college. From that point on, I never listened to the advice of anyone associated to the team when it came to my academic scheduling. God, in His love for me, had taught me a great "one-unit lesson." When I graduated in 1980, I had earned every unit it took to get me there. But I still have that F on my official record to this day.

If you are being tempted to go in a direction that you know is against His will for your life, stop now. We may think it is no big deal or that no one will ever find you out, but the above verse in Numbers tells us that we are wrong. God just might, because He loves us, allow our actions to be discovered to stop us from future pain. It is not that God will reveal all our sins to the world, but I believe that habitual sin, if not repented, will eventually be found out.

God's word says that *"in Him we have redemption through His blood, the forgiveness of sins, according to the riches of His grace"* (Ephesians 1:7). If you are about to do something you know you shouldn't, stop now. If you are involved in something you know you should not be, stop and repent (turn away from it). Let God's forgiveness protect you before He is forced to revel your sin to the world in order to keep you from further hurting yourself.

Thought for the Day

Don't get caught with a failing grade because of an attempt to maintain a sin in your life. Turn from it now before it "finds you out."

DAY 16

And the Lord restored Job's losses when he prayed for his friends.
Indeed, the Lord gave Job twice as much as he had before.

—Job 42:10

Obedience in Loss

The first car I ever owned was a 1967 Ford Mustang convertible. What a car that was! I have many great memories of driving around town with friends, top down, enjoying the numerous sunny days offered in Southern California. Unfortunately, I drove that car into the ground in a span of two years. By the time we turned it in, they only gave my dad $100 on the trade-in. I wish I had that car back now. With minimal restoration, it would be worth a lot of money. It has been said by car enthusiasts that "we spend our adult years trying to buy back the cars we gave away in our youth." I have to agree with that.

Job experienced many losses in his life. Family, finances, and health were all taken from him during the heavenly test initiated by our adversary Satan and allowed by God. In addition to all that was seized from him, Job had friends who falsely accused him of sinning and causing his own problems. God's word says that despite all that happened to Job, he did not *"sin nor charge God with wrong"* (Job 1:22). By the end of the book, we have Job coming out of his trial victorious. And when Job had prayed for his false accusers, God restored what he had lost twofold!

I wish it could be said about me, that I did not "sin nor charge God with wrong," during the trials of my life. Unfortunately, I have done my share of shaking my fist at heaven from time to time. But there is still hope for those of us who are imperfect. God restored Job, not only because he did not charge Him wrongly, but also because, after all he had been through, he obeyed God and prayed for those friends who had falsely accused him! Was it difficult for Job to pray for those who had added weight to his already torturous situation? I don't know, but either way, Job did what God said and he was restored.

We might not be a Job, but we can act like him. Jesus commanded us to love our enemies! Pray for those who persecute us (Matthew 5:44). If we are obedient to Him in this matter, God can restore the things we had lost by clinging to our own anger and hurt.

Thought for the Day

Don't give away your restoration. Forgive and just obey.

DAY 17

*So it was when the Philistine arose and came and
drew near to meet David, that David hurried and
ran toward the army to meet the Philistine.*

—1 Samuel 17:48

Giants

As first responders, we often find ourselves running toward what
everyone else is running away from. It's our job to confront
the people and situations that the rest of the world tries to avoid.
It takes a special person to demonstrate that kind of courage every
day. David was that kind of person. "The Philistine" that the above
verse speaks of was Goliath. He was nine feet, nine inches tall and
probably weighed over five hundred pounds. The coat that he wore
was about one hundred and sixty-seven pounds, and the tip of the
spear he used weighed 20 pounds. I'd say that if I had a physical
confrontation with Goliath on a call, he would be a candidate for a
Taser deployment, less lethal rounds, pepper spray, the kitchen sink,
or anything else I could think of to throw at him. David didn't have
any of those resources. He was a young shepherd boy who did not
have a very impressive stature even by the standards of that day. All
David had were five smooth stones and an unshakable faith in God.

It has often been said that it is not "who" we are that counts in
this life, but "whose" we are. God's word tells us that "*if God is for us,
who can be against us?*" (Romans 8:31).

I don't know who or what the "Goliaths" are in your life. It
could be a financial situation, a health problem, a personal relationship, or an addiction of some sort. The good news is that the God

who helped a boy kill a giant is still here to offer you the same kind of power and victory over your circumstances. If you have accepted Jesus Christ as your Savior and Lord, you can stop running away from your problems and start to run toward them.

Thought for the Day

If the God of the universe is "whose" you are, you can become an army of one.

DAY 18

*The grass withers, the flower fades, but the
word of our God will stand forever.*

—Isaiah 40:8

Mail Call

When I became a police officer, I was assigned a mailbox that was located in a small room just outside of our briefing area. The box was keyed and looked exactly like what you might expect to see at the post office if you rented a PO box. We would get all kinds of correspondence from outside the department as well as from within. Of course, like with all things cop, the mailboxes offered the perfect prank opportunity.

Before briefing, an officer would grab the contents of their box without looking at it and place the items on a table in the briefing room. It wasn't until after all their beat partners had seen their mail that they discovered they had, "somehow," been placed on a scrapbooking mailing list or were now the proud recipients of *Seventeen Magazine*. I remember one officer who was put on a mail order bride interest list and could not seem to cancel the subscription.

Prayer is the way we communicate with God. God's word says, *"Then you will call upon Me and go and pray to Me, and I will listen to you"* (Jeremiah 29:12). Prayer might be how we communicate with God, but His word is how He talks with us. That is why it is so important to read the Bible every day to give Him the opportunity to reveal His truth, direction, and encouragement to us. It is like a direct correspondence from God being placed in our mailbox daily. Unlike some of the mailboxes at the PD, everything that is delivered from Him will be good and true for our lives. Second Timothy 3:16 tells us, "*All Scripture is given by inspiration of God, and is profitable for doctrine, for reproof, for correction, for instruction in righteousness.*" I think we all do a lot of talking to God, but do we listen to what He has to say in return?

Thought for the Day

You don't have to worry that someone else will sign you up for something that is not in your own best interest. Subscribing to God's word is always in your best interest!

DAY 19

The generous will be made rich, And he who
waters will also be watered himself.

—Proverbs 11:25

Happiness

It seems to be the goal of just about everyone to find happiness in their lives. They look for the right career, the right relationship, the right place to live, and the even the right hobby, all in an attempt to find true contentment.

As a police officer, I often had to investigate the deaths of many affluent people who had unfortunately died as the result of a suicide. Many of these individuals seemed to have it all (or at least most of it anyway), but that didn't stop them from sinking into a despair that led them to that leap, pill, rope, or gunshot.

Wanting to be happy is not a bad thing in and of itself. It isn't the wanting of it as much as it is the method we use to get it.

The above verse in Proverbs gives us the key to the best way to receive true happiness in our lives. It isn't about what we do for ourselves as much as it is about what we do for others.

A recent study conducted by UC Riverside psychology professor Sonja Lyubomirsky concluded the following: "After rigorous review on the therapeutic benefits of positive emotion, my colleagues and I found widespread support for the notion that people with a tendency toward depression can help themselves by helping others or otherwise introducing positivity into their day-to-day lives."

God knows this, and He said so in His word. Acts 20:35 states that "*it is more blessed to give than to receive,*" Galatians 6:7 tells us that "*whatever a man sows, that will he reap also,*" and Mark 10:44 says, "*And whoever of you desires to be first shall be slave of all.*"

Do you want to beat depression and be first in line for the happiness and joy that God's word promises you? Start serving others! It could be at church, or at work, or even in your own family. God made us, and He knows the right combination of actions and circumstances that will make us happy. It is the exact opposite of what the world tells us, and it involves giving rather than receiving.

Thought for the Day

Happiness should not be a goal; it should be a result.

DAY 20

*"These things I have spoken to you, that in Me you may
have peace. In the world you will have tribulation; but
be of good cheer, I have overcome the world."*

—John 16:33

Lasting Peace

In 1984, our oldest daughter Kara was born with severe cerebral
palsy and a serious heart condition. The surgeons were able to
save her life, but she was left with physical, neurological, visual, and
hearing impairments that are still with her to this day. As a twenty-
seven-year-old first-time father, I was immediately thrust into the
world of special needs which is an exclusive club that I never wanted
membership in. It was a dark time of discouragement and disappointment for us.

I can remember many mornings that I had about three seconds
of peace. You see, it was for those few seconds after opening my eyes
from a complete sleep that I forgot what it was I had to face that day.
But it would come flooding back as I became completely awake. As
hard as that was, I was thankful for those three seconds whenever
they would come. They seemed like glimpses of perfect peace compared to what we were going through. Time went on, and those few
seconds grew to minutes, then hours, and after many operations,
when her condition stabilized, we experienced days of relative peace.

Today I can truly say that things have turned around. Now I
might experience three seconds of anxiety about Kara's future, followed by peace for the rest of the day. This is true even though her
situation is still uncertain and could turn south at any given moment.

This didn't happen through my own self will, or some positive thinking program, but through a conscious decision to choose God's word over my own feelings. He is in control and has given my wife and me the *"peace that surpasses all understanding"* that is promised in Philippians 4:7.

The only certain thing about our future is that we will have tribulations and difficulties. But we can still have peace knowing that He is in charge and that He has overcome this world. As a follower of Jesus Christ, you can access that peace by obeying His word (Bible study), asking for it (prayer), and by fellowship with other believers (church).

Thought for the Day

Let God's peace in to your life. It might start with only seconds, but He promises to make it grow as you continue to follow Him.

DAY 21

*For the time is coming when people will not endure sound
teaching, but having itching ears they will accumulate
for themselves teachers to suit their own passions.*

—2 Timothy 4:3

A Closer Look

After a midwatch shift (3:00 p.m. to 3:00 a.m.), I got a ride home from one of my partners who had worked with me that night. While traveling northbound (N/B) on Jamboree Road, we saw a police unit with its overhead lights on stopped alone at the east curbline just south of San Joaquin Hills Road. It appeared as though one of our guys had finished up on a car stop and was still at the side of the road doing paperwork. The light controlling our N/B traffic was red, and my partner decided it would be "funny" to blow the red light and startle our unwitting officer. It was a safe bet that the officer would be a rookie since they usually worked night shifts early in their careers. He would call out the stop, and when he approached the car he would be greeted by two laughing off-duty cops who had probably been his training officers. I know it might seem like a stupid game to play, but there was no real danger on a deserted road at 3:30 a.m. My partner approached the red light and went through it at about thirty miles per hour. There was only one problem. The color of the police unit was the same as our agency, but as we passed by, we could see that the marking on the door was from the University of California at Irvine (UCI) police. Why was he working so far into our city? Well, the subsequent car stop was not as humorous as we planned. It took several minutes to convince the UCI cop that we were really two idiot veterans from Newport Beach who had just ended our shift.

Sometimes it is hard to wade our way through the differing theological presentations made by various churches today. Many seem to be saying the right things and appear to be committed to the gospel of Jesus Christ, but upon closer inspection, they turn out not to be what we first thought they were.

So how do we separate then "the wheat from the tares," so to speak? Our passage in 2 Timothy warns us of those who will not listen to sound doctrine and instead hear only what they want to. God's word has been, is now, and will always be the only true litmus test as to the authenticity of any church we attend. If the teaching at your church waters down, is at odds with the clear word of God, or only teaches the things that people want to hear, leave that place!

If we don't look closely, we can do something stupid and allow ourselves to get caught up in unscriptural teaching.

Thought for the Day

Read, memorize, follow the word of God, and insist that the leaders of any church you attend does the same.

DAY 22

For all have sinned and fall short of the glory of God.
—Romans 3:23

Sure Sin

As a police officer, I "interviewed" (the politically correct term for *interrogated*) people almost every day. I would often inquire as to their previous arrest history without knowing what it was at the time. I would never ask "Have you ever been arrested?" Instead, I would ask, "When was the last time you were arrested?" It was a subtle difference, but the first question encouraged them to answer, "Never," while the second presupposed that I had accurate knowledge of their past criminal record, which "encouraged" them to be truthful. It was just a quick way to cut to the chase.

When it comes to the question of our actions, God's word never asks us "if" we have sinned. The above verse in Romans states that the answer to that question is "Yes, you have!" All of us have sinned and come short of God's glory. In the event that someone claimed they had not sinned, scripture covers that as well in 1 John 1:10, "*If we say we have not sinned, we make Him a liar, and His word is not in us.*" And just in case we don't realize it, calling God a liar would definitely be placed in the category of sin!

Romans 6:23 spells out both the punishment and cure for our sinful condition. *"For the wages of sin is death, but the gift of God is eternal life through Jesus Christ our Lord."* We have all sinned against God, separated ourselves from Him, and deserve what is coming to us. But the good news of the gospel is that Jesus paid the price for our sin by His death on the cross. Now, instead of the death sentence we have earned, we can have forgiveness and eternal life through Jesus Christ if we accept Him as our Lord!

Thought for the Day

Have you ever sinned? Sorry, when was the last time you sinned? Ask and be forgiven.

DAY 23

*If we confess our sins He is faithful and just to forgive us
our sins and to cleanse us from all unrighteousness.*

—1 John 1:9

The Weight

I had a BB gun as a boy. I used to shoot at targets, dirt clods, and the like in the backyard of my parents' home. One day, I got the idea to shoot at something else. I saw that birds often came down to the lawn in our backyard to eat worms and seeds from the grass, and I thought I might like to shoot one. I was at the young age where I hadn't really thought through the consequences of my actions and just imagined that I would be "hunting." I upped my chances of attracting a bird to the lawn by placing bread crumbs at one end of the yard. I then positioned myself about twenty yards away in a prone position on the lawn. After several minutes, an average-size bird flew down to the lawn to take the bait. I raised my BB rifle and pulled the trigger. To my great surprise, I hit my target. I now know shooting a bird is an animal cruelty crime, but I wasn't aware of the penal code at the time. My problem was that I didn't kill the bird with the first shot.

I watched as the bird flapped helplessly on the ground at the other end of the yard. I stood there for a second as the weight of what I had done to this innocent creature sunk in. I was also horrified by the thought of what I had to do next. I moved over to the bird's location in what was the longest twenty-yard walk of my life. I could not let the bird suffer, so I stood over the animal, pumped my gun, and delivered the fatal shot from about one foot away. I was grief-stricken. I owned many guns in my childhood and on into adulthood, but I could never get myself to actually go hunting. I think that incident will stay with me for the rest of my life, and I must have made the unconscious decision to never shoot a helpless thing again. Helpless thing, that is. I was prepared to do what I had to as a cop.

Sin is a lot like that. Satan can convince us to do many things that we do not fully realize the consequences of until after we have pulled the trigger. All we can do then is stand involuntarily by and think, "Why did I say that, why did I go there, why did I do that?" But it is too late, and the deed is done.

Fortunately, we serve a God who loves us enough to come to earth in human form and pay the price for the sins we have committed. We now can do more than simply stand there in regret for our actions. The above verse in 1 John tells us what we need to do next, "confess."

I asked God to forgive me for killing that bird on that afternoon so many years ago, just as I have asked Him many times since to forgive me for other offenses. I am glad that because of my decision to make Jesus the Lord of my life, I can be cleansed from "all unrighteousness." Not because of what I have done, but because of what He has done for me.

Thought for the Day

Jesus took the weapon of sin from me and bore the weight of my blame.

DAY 24

*You keep track of all my sorrows. You have collected all my tears
in your bottle. You have recorded each one in your book.*

—Psalm 56:8

Bagpipes

Just after I retired from the police force, my wife and I lived in
a high-rise apartment for several years. A couple times a year, I
could hear bagpipes playing from the hotel parking lot next to where
we lived. Their players gathered en masse to prepare for some sort
of annual competition in the area. Dozens of individuals played
throughout the day as they practiced a variety of songs. My wife loves
to hear them and was pleasantly surprised each time they showed up
next to our building. I do not feel the same way.

You see, to me, the bagpipes have a completely different meaning. I have heard them play "Amazing Grace" at each first responder
funeral I have ever attended. It is a tradition for police, fire, and lifeguard departments alike. They have for me a sad connotation of pain
and loss. It is odd that the song "Amazing Grace," which they sing at
church, does not affect me. It is just the sound of those bagpipes that
choke me up. My reaction started in 1995 when my beat partner,
NBPD Officer Bob Henry, lost his life on duty. For me, the feelings
associated with that day, combined with the events I have experienced since then, and what I knew I would experience in the future,
all come flooding to my consciousness when I hear that instrument
play. Because of what I experienced in law enforcement, I know that
something about me has changed, and this is one of those things.

There are not too many people who tear up, in a sad way, at the sound of a musical instrument.

We all have our own individual triggers for sorrow. Some might be so obscure that others will find them odd. When we feel that no one can possibly understand what we have been through, we need to remember that we serve a God who has recorded all of our sorrows. He has kept track of and collected all our tears.

God's word promises us that we will have trials and tribulations in this world. But for the believer in Jesus Christ, He has also made a great promise for our future. *"He will wipe every tear from their eyes, and there will be no more death or sorrow or crying or pain. All these things are gone forever"* (Revelation 21:4). Those specific tears that He has collected throughout our lives, the ones He has recorded in His heart, they will be wiped away forever. Someday I may love the sound of bagpipes, not yet, but someday.

Thought for the Day

It is comforting to know that the sorrows specific to each of us will be taken care of in eternity if we have chosen heaven as our final destination.

DAY 25

*My little children, let us not love in word, neither
in tongue; but in deed and truth.*

—1 John 3:18

Walk the Walk

One of the things that we learn in police work is to make quick, accurate evaluations of people. We do this by taking nothing at face value. We don't believe what subjects say as much as what their actions show.

We often see athletes interviewed on TV after a competitive event. I have seen many give the credit for their victory to their "Lord and Savior, Jesus Christ." I love it when they do that, and I am blessed by their witness. Unfortunately, sometimes I later read about their family problems, infidelity, criminal behavior, or substance abuse. It would seem that they talked a good game for the Lord, but their deeds did not match their words.

As first responders, it is often hard to keep our spiritual and work lives consistent. We are pulled in many directions by negative influences both inside our departments and out on the street. If we are not vigilant, we can also become guilty of failing to show our faith in Christ by "deed and truth." We become good at the "talking" rather than the "doing" when it comes to our faith.

It has been said that "we need to witness for Christ, and when necessary, use words." I think that both actions and words are import-ant in order to show God's love to the world.

Thought for the Day

Let's do all we can to not only talk the talk, but walk the walk, when it comes to our witness for Him.

DAY 26

Being confident of this very thing, that He who has begun a good work in you will complete it until the day of Jesus Christ.
—Philippians 1:6

Under Construction

When Harvest Christian Fellowship was in the process of building a new church in Irvine, California, they called it Harvest OC 2.0. The building provided almost three times the space of our old location.

It was fun to drop by the new remodel to see the progress that had been made. During one visit, I saw that the workers had framed the back wall of the main worship space. For the first time, I could visualize the size and dimensions of the new sanctuary and saw just how great a space it would be. We had many volunteer days at the new church as we worked hard to clear the inside of the building for construction. But there is nothing like watching the professionals make something of an area by use of their precise plans. They know exactly where they are headed, and I'm sure they can visualize the completed project, well before a layman like me.

Do you know that God has a precise plan for you? He is the ultimate contractor who can build you up by using His perfect design for your life. You may think you have done things to thwart that possibility, but just like a talented workman, He can take a structure that looks worthless, and perform a miracle remodel on it. And just like any building contractor, He only needs one thing to get started: your approval of the project!

Frank Lloyd Wright was one of the most famous and successful architects of the twentieth century. The structures that he designed are still considered to be some of the most innovative and unique buildings ever erected. If he was still alive and came to me and said, "I want to design and build a house for you. There is only one catch. You have to let me build whatever I want to." Considering his past history and the products that he had put out, I don't think I would hesitate to give him my approval on that deal!

So, when we consider God's past record and some of the astonishing products He has put out, why do we hesitate to let Him take over the building project of our lives? Ephesians 3:20 says, "*Now to him who is able to do exceedingly abundantly above all that we ask or think, according to the power that works within us.*" His plan for our lives is better than anything we can ask or think!

Won't you let Him take over the construction of your life so He can complete the work in you that He so wants to do?

Thought for the Day

Does God have your project approval?

DAY 27

*Declaring the end from the beginning, and from ancient
times things that are not yet done, Saying, "My counsel
shall stand, and I will do all My pleasure."*

—Isaiah 46:10

Certain Future

When I was young, I played junior All-American football from ages nine to thirteen. I remember a conversation I had with one of my classmates in junior high. She wasn't a fan of football and didn't have much good to say about the sport. She asked me if I planned to get a scholarship to play in college someday. To tell you the truth, I hadn't really thought that far ahead in my life, but I answered, "Sure." She then told me of an article she read that stated football was not a good bet to count on to pay for a college education. She even had the statistics memorized that claimed there was only one chance in thousands that I would be good enough to get a football scholarship. I really don't know what her point was other than to discourage me from the sport. Fast forward seven years after I had finished two seasons at Orange Coast Community College, I had the head line coach at the University of Southern California in my coach's office holding out a Rose Bowl ring and asking, "Do you want one of these?" I guess I beat the odds. While I played for the Trojans over the next three years, I sometimes wondered if my fellow classmate had remembered what she said, and if she knew how wrong she had been about me.

Even though some might have had doubts about my future, God knew all along where I was headed and what I would someday become. Our verse in Isaiah 46 tells us that God knows "the end from the beginning," and sees things that "are not yet done." Notice He does not say, "The beginning to the end," but rather the other way around. I think that God wanted to stress the point that He already knows how all things will turn out in the end.

We might get anxious sometimes, wondering what our lives have in store for us. In those moments, we need to remember that the uncertainties of our lives are only a mystery to us. God knows where we are headed, and the great news is that we can totally trust Him with that future.

God must have smiled just a little when I was told of my poor chances to have my education paid for by a sport. I think that He is still smiling a little when we express our concerns about the events in our lives yet to come.

Thought for the Day

Let's trust in the One who knows our story to the end.

DAY 28

For I know the thoughts that I think toward you says the LORD,
thoughts of peace and not of evil, to give you a future and a hope.
—Jeremiah 29:11

Tag, You're It

I think sometimes we spend a lot of our time running from God's
will in one way or another. It is almost as though we fear His plan
for us and feel that if we give our lives completely to Him, He will
send us to be a missionary in the Congo. But the Bible says that
God's plan for our lives is designed to give us peace, a hope, and a
future.

I heard of a young boy whose home was near a psychiatric institution. He was warned by his mother to never walk home past the
establishment. One evening when it was getting late, the young man
had a decision to make. He could either get home on time and take
the direct route to his house by the institution or take a different
route and get in trouble for being late. He chose the path by the hospital in violation of his mother's wishes. As he neared the location, he
saw a male jump the fence and start to run toward him. The frightened youth ran away as fast as he could, but soon the man closed
in on him. After running for quite a distance, he fell to the ground
in complete exhaustion. When he looked up, he saw the large male
standing over him. The man touched the boy on his shoulder and
said, "Tag, you're it," before running away.

God's will for our lives won't be what we fear. He made us with
specific talents, desires, and abilities that are unique to His plan for
us. When I played football at USC, my teammates would express

worry that if they submitted their lives to Jesus Christ, He might want them to give up football and become missionaries. I told them that anything was possible, but that I didn't think God made them six feet, six inches tall and three hundred pounds to send them to Africa! Their mission fields turned out to be in the NFL.

As followers of Jesus Christ, we will only be truly happy when we let go and follow God's will for our lives. Will you decide to completely follow him today? It is up to you.

Thought for the Day

Tag, you're it.

DAY 29

*Repent, then, and turn to God, so that your sins may be wiped
out, that times of refreshing may come from the Lord.*

—Acts 3:19

Damage That Disappears

Several years ago, I was in the garage when I looked out onto the
street through one of the square windows that line the top of my
garage door. My wife had just taken my car to run an errand and was
supposed to be out of the neighborhood. Instead, I saw her standing
in the street in front of our house with a concerned look on her face.
When I went out to see what had happened, she told me that when
she backed out of our driveway, she had struck a car parked across the
street. There was minor damage to both cars, but mine had taken the
worst of it. I would like to claim victory for my actions toward my
wife, but the best I can say for myself is that I didn't say anything stupid. In fact, I didn't say anything at all, nothing stupid or encouraging. Sometimes that can be worse than yelling. The next day, I took
my car in to get an estimate for the repair work. After three days, I
got a call from a technician at the repair shop who advised me that
my car was ready. When I went to pick it up, I examined the dented
area on my car and was happy to see that it looked as if it had never
been in a collision at all. All evidence of any damage had been wiped
away from my car as if the accident had never occurred.

The above verse in Acts 3 tells us that we can have the sins in
our lives "wiped out." If we will repent and turn to God, He will
repair the damage that sin does to our lives in such a complete way
that, as far as He is concerned, it will look like the sin never occurred

at all. And in addition to our erased sin, God promises a time of refreshing that will come from Him.

One of the biggest concerns I see over and over again in counseling is the inability for Christians to truly embrace and believe in the promises of God's forgiveness. We seem to have more of a problem wiping our own sin from our consciousness than God does. Romans 5:8 tells us, "*But God demonstrates his own love for us in this: While we were still sinners, Christ died for us.*" God knew the damage each of us would do to ourselves through our sinful actions even before we were born. And knowing that, He still chose to die on the cross and take on the penalty earned by our sin. All we have to do is accept His actions on our behalf and hand over the ownership of our lives to Him. The cost of this eternal insurance plan is pretty hard to beat. It is free!

You may feel dented up and damaged by the actions of your life, but that is not what God sees. If you have accepted Jesus Christ as your Lord and Savior, you have been repaired in such a way that, to God, it looks like you have never sinned at all. All those dents, scratches, and brokenness in your life will have been erased due to the power of Jesus and his sacrifice for you on the cross.

Thought for the Day

All of us have collided with sin that has caused damage to our lives. Let God smooth out the areas of destruction through Christ's atoning work on the cross for us. If we accept that, it will look like the damage never occurred.

DAY 30

So we do not lose heart. Though our outer self is wasting away, our inner self is being renewed day by day.
—2 Corinthians 4:16

Reverse Aging

One day, I went to a local restaurant that I hadn't been to for several years. I thought I would make a change from my normal routine and get my lunch salad at a different eatery. I walked up to the cashier and placed my order. She rang up my purchase and told me the price. She then leaned in and, with a smile on her face, whispered, "I gave you the senior discount." Now, I hadn't asked for it, and I had no idea as to the age threshold needed to receive this honor. I was torn between being excited about the discount and insulted at her automatic determination that I qualified!

I would like to think that the COVID-19 mask I was wearing had something to do with her quick calculation of my "seniorness," but probably not. I had to come to grips that, in the eyes of some, I am an elderly man in need of a financial break. Now I am not sure if I am going to buy food there regularly for the cost savings, or never go inside the establishment again! Probably the former. After all, 10 percent is 10 percent.

In the 2008 movie *The Curious Case of Benjamin Button*, the lead character, played by Brad Pitt, got younger and younger throughout his life. He started off as an old man and ended up dying as an eighty-four-year-old infant. The above verse in 2 Corinthians gives us encouragement that as we grow older, we can experience the same kind of reverse aging process. As our bodies "waste away," our inner self can be renewed day by day.

It has often been said that "you are only as old as you feel." If this is true, I'm 105! I can be encouraged, however, that through the Holy Spirit, I can be renewed in my Christian walk daily. And when my time on this earth is over, I can have the great assurance that even though my body has wasted away, my spirit and zeal for God can be young and fresh.

Thought for the Day

Our youthful attitude for God need never be discounted regardless of our physical age.

DAY 31

That if you confess with your mouth the Lord Jesus and believe in your heart that God has raised Him from the dead, you will be saved.

—Romans 10:9

Entrance Pass

As a Southern California boy, I have gone to Disneyland more times than I can remember. Originally, we used to purchase ticket books that contained a pass to get into the park, along with ride tickets that had the alpha labels A, B, C, D, and E. Of course, the E tickets were for the best rides. I have one of those ticket books on my desk from 1963. The feature rides on the E ticket then were Submarine Voyage, Monorail, Matterhorn Bobsleds, and the Jungle Cruise. Back then, there were no Pirates of the Caribbean, Haunted House, Space Mountain, or even It's a Small World. Eventually they stopped using tickets altogether and just required the purchase of an entrance pass.

Disneyland might have changed their entrance pass requirements over the years, but heaven has not. Our above verse in Romans tells us the only way to attain eternal life is through confessing Jesus Christ as Lord. Jesus Himself confirms this in John 14:6 when He said, "*I am the way, the truth, and the life. No one comes to the Father except through Me.*"

The world might have come up with many ways to get to heaven including, works, self-enlightenment, or repeated phrases and actions. But all of those entry methods will be rejected at the eternal ticket office of judgment. Only your all-access Jesus pass will get you in.

Thought for the Day

Order your eternal pass now. Accept Jesus as the Lord of your life, and you will have an assured place in the true magic kingdom.

DAY 32

Peace I leave with you, My peace I give to you; not as the world gives do I give to you. Let not your heart be troubled, neither let it be afraid.

—John 14:27

Panic Under Pressure

Scuba diving can be an exciting but sometimes dangerous activity. You might think that the biggest hazard while underwater comes from the sea creatures you may encounter or by simply running out of air. Those could be problems, but they seldom occur and result in any injury.

When a scuba tank is filled, it contains oxygen and nitrogen which are normally found in the air we breathe. That air is condensed with pressure into a relatively small scuba tank. One of the results of breathing pressurized air is that an increased amount of inert gases will be passed into the body. The longer a diver is underwater, and the deeper they descend, the more that one of these gases, nitrogen, will be assimilated into the bloodstream.

This is not usually a problem if the diver allows time for a gradual ascent allowing the nitrogen to be breathed out by a process which has been termed as degassing. If a diver has been deep enough, for long enough, it might take them some time to ascend to the surface while making safety stops along the way. If he comes up too quickly, the nitrogen in his bloodstream will bubble out due to the sudden pressure change and result in what is known as the bends. This is a dangerous and painful condition that could result in permanent disability or death and requires a decompression chamber to alleviate. The key to not getting "bent" is if something unusual occurs underwater, do not panic and rush to the surface.

I think we can sometimes panic under the pressure of our lives and forget that we serve an all-powerful God. We might feel that we are deep under because of our problems and that we have been there too long to see any solution. But if we panic now and start to move down a path that is against God's word, it will only lead to disaster.

The above verse in John records Christ's promise to us to give us peace. He makes it clear that the world will offer us a false direction to obtain peace that will fail. But if you put your faith in God and His plan for your life, you will always be taken in the right direction no matter how dire the circumstances seem. God's word says, *"Trust in the LORD with all your heart, And lean not on your own understanding; In all your ways acknowledge Him, And He shall direct your paths"* (Proverbs 3:5–6).

Thought for the Day

Don't get so bent up about your problems and swim off in a desperate direction. Trust God, He will not fail you!

DAY 33

Watch therefore, for you do not know what hour your Lord is coming.
—Matthew 24:42

Fair Warning

As a patrol officer, the first thing I would always do after an unusually difficult field contact was to call my watch commander. I would telephone in if I felt that he might receive a complaint about me from a citizen who was not happy with how I had handled a call. My watch commander was thankful to get a heads-up as to the possible complaint, the name of the subject involved, and the full story of what had really happened. Supervisors were always grateful to receive this warning so they could prepare a coherent response before the call even came in.

God's word has many things to tell us about His love for us, His desired direction for our lives, as well as cautions about future events and what our reactions to them should be. The above verse in Matthew gives us one of those warnings. From what we see in the world today, the return of our Lord might be imminent. But having been a believer for almost sixty years, I have heard this claim many times before. The truth is that we just don't know when Jesus will come back again or when He will rapture His church. Mark 13:32 confirms this by stating, *"But of that day and hour no one knows, not even the angels in heaven."*

Most of the time, warnings are given to keep us from something bad in our lives. The United States surgeon general places warnings on cigarette packages to tell us of the dangers of smoking. There are labels on almost all cleaning products that attempt to keep us from ingesting them or using the items against their intended use. The warning that Jesus is coming back might be bad news for some, but great news for others! For believers in Jesus Christ, the warning of His second coming is like telling us to be ready to win the lottery. For others, it might foretell of the worst day of their lives. It all depends on what you have done with Jesus Christ in your life now. Is He your Lord and Savior? Have you committed your life to Him by accepting His payment on the cross for you? If the answer is yes to those questions, the warning of Christ's return is a joyous promise, not a caution of impending doom.

Since we have received the warning that He is coming back, what are we to do until then? Luke 12:43 tells us, *"Blessed is that servant whom his master will find so doing when he comes."* We are to keep busy doing God's work and will, until we see Him again, whenever that may be.

Thought for the Day

Jesus has called in the heads-up of his return. Are you ready?

DAY 34

Your ears shall hear a word behind you, saying,
"This is the way, walk in it," Whenever you turn to
the right hand or whenever you turn to the left.

—Isaiah 30:21

Obvious Answer

When I was working as a uniformed police officer, we routinely responded to calls for assistance at residences throughout the city. On one such call, I walked up to the front door of the house and knocked to make my presence known. When the resident answered the door, I introduced myself, and told her I had come in response to her request. She said to me, "How do I know that you really are a police officer?" Since I was in full uniform, with a badge, gun, radio, and traditional black wool police garb, and had a black-and-white Newport Beach Police unit parked behind me, I thought that the question was a little odd. I provided her with Dispatch's phone number and suggested that she call to confirm that the department had sent me to her residence.

I never found fault with people checking my credentials when I was working undercover. I thought it was a good idea to confirm the identity of the six-foot-two, 230-pound long-haired bearded guy standing on their porch. But a cop in full uniform was a little too cautious. Either I was who I appeared to be, or it was a spectacular hoax. I think that the answer to my identity was obvious.

We often counsel people who have questions about their lives, and what direction God wants them to take. I have found that usually, during the course of our conversation, they inevitably answer their own question, and already know what action they should take according to God's word. The answer was obvious. They just have to do it.

There are some situations in our lives that might need counsel and mediation on God's word in order to resolve. But most of the time, the answers are pretty apparent. It is not a matter of solution identification, but obedience to the obvious answer.

Thought for the Day

When difficulty comes knocking at our door, recognize the answer from God's word that is standing right in front of you.

DAY 35

*As far as the east is from the west, so far hath he
removed our transgressions from us.*

—Psalm 103:12

Global Forgiveness

This is one of my favorite verses in the Bible. It not only shows us God's forgiving nature, but also, it speaks to His scientific and geographical intelligence. God chose to use an "east from west" reference when referring to how far He had removed our sins from us. Why not north from south? If you start at the South Pole on the globe and travel north, you will eventually reach the North Pole. If you continue to move in the same line of travel, you will come full circle back down to the South Pole again. So, the distance between north and south on the globe can be measured as half the circumference of the earth. That is a great distance, but a fixed one.

Now if you start at any point on the globe and move in an eastbound direction, you will never come to a point where you start to travel westbound. The distance between east and west cannot be calculated and has no limits. God sent this message of forgiveness to man centuries before we even knew that the world was round. There is no limit to His forgiveness!

God's word says *that "for all have sinned and fall short of the glory of God"* (Romans 3:23). Whether you are a criminal in the street or the officer who arrests him, we all need God's forgiveness for something in our lives. Isn't it reassuring to know that God has a never-ending supply of what we need most? And for those who will accept Jesus Christ as their Savior and Lord, He offers this unlimited forgiveness at the right price: it's free!

Thought for the Day

Do you want a clean slate and a fresh start in life? God is just waiting to give it to you.

DAY 36

*Then He will answer them, saying, "Assuredly, I say to you, inasmuch
as you did not do it to one of the least of these, you did not do it to me."*
—Matthew 25:45

Milk Saucer

God's word calls on us to treat those in need as if they were Jesus
Himself. We usually define a need as some sort of monetary
or material assistance. I think that the definition of "those in need"
might go a little further than that. We all have difficult people in
our lives. They might be that coworker or family member whom we
would rather avoid than spend time with. God calls on us to treat
these people the same way that we would treat Jesus Himself, which
means that we are to talk to, listen to, and give our time to them.
Man, can't I just give them some money or something! This is a hard
one!

There is an exception to this. There are some people in our lives
whom we need to limit our time with. They are those toxic types
who bring us down with their verbally abusive, gossiping, or negative
personalities. I don't think that God calls on any of us to endanger
our spiritual walk or mental health by spending a lot of time with
these people. Then there are those who are in the odd category that
we can show Christ's love to with just a little extra time and attention.

As first responders, we have learned that we represent our entire
service community to those whom we come in contact with. I might
be the only cop, firefighter, nurse, or military personnel they will
ever talk to. I need to be thinking, "What will they think about first
responders in general by my actions?" So, it is with the "least of these"

types of people in our lives that we need to be thinking, "What will they think about God from my actions toward them?"

Thought for the Day

I know we are all afraid of putting out the saucer of milk and attracting the cat that might never go away, but that is what God calls us to do.

DAY 37

We are pressed on every side by troubles, but we are not crushed. We are perplexed, but not driven to despair. We are hunted down, but never abandoned by God. We get knocked down, but we are not destroyed.
—2 Corinthians 4:8–9

Hard Knocks

I've never been knocked out. That is quite an accomplishment considering that I played football for many years at the Pop Warner, high school, and college levels. I can't really tell you why. I was certainly hit hard enough to make me lose consciousness. Some would say that I have a genetically structured anatomy that assisted me in this ability to take a blow. Do you suppose that is what people have meant when they called me thickheaded? Probably not, but I choose to believe that. Maybe my belief in that delusion is prima facie evidence that the numerous blows I took to the head over the years really did have an adverse effect on me. It has been said that you lose ten thousand brain cells with every hard blow you take. If that is true, I think I am one head slap away from a cerebral flat line.

Even though I never lost consciousness due to a blow, I was hit off my feet more times than I can remember. Getting knocked down isn't much of a problem. Even the best players in the world unexpectedly go to the ground during a game. In fact, I believe it would be impossible to play without getting knocked off your feet at some point. It isn't going down that is the issue, it is staying down.

The above passage was written by Paul in his letter to the church in Corinth. He was giving them an accurate, honest picture of what the Christian life is like. We will experience pressing troubles, perplexing situations, be hunted, and flattened by life. But the good news for the believer in Jesus Christ is that we will not be crushed, driven to despair, abandoned, or destroyed. God promises us that we may get knocked down, but we will never be knocked out.

If you are going through a time of hardship and stress in your life, know that God is always with you. You may feel hopeless, defeated, and knocked down. But know this, if you will just get up and keep moving in your Christian walk, God will be there to help you. God's word says, "*What then shall we say to these things? If God is for us, who can be against us?*" (Romans 8:31).

Thought for the Day

You may find yourself on the ground at times in life, but you won't be out of the game. Stand up and see what God has for you next.

DAY 38

But in my distress I cried out to the Lord; yes, I prayed to my God for help. He heard me from his sanctuary; my cry to him reached his ears.
—Psalm 18:6

Instant Response

As first responders, we rely on our radio communication systems. But even in this digital age, those devices can sometimes let us down. In Newport Beach, as I am sure it is in every city, there are dead zones that don't allow for clear radio communication. If you have ever been caught in a fight at zero dark thirty in a remote location, you know the sinking feeling when Dispatch is unable to read your garbled transmission attempt. It is devastating to need help, ask for it, and to be uncertain if your request was heard.

In the above verse in Psalms, David cried out in distress to the Lord. But unlike the spotty function of our earthly communication systems, David declared, *"He heard me from His sanctuary; my cry to Him reached his ears."*

In the book of Daniel, we read of another account where the heavenly system for answered prayer is revealed. The angel Gabriel told Daniel, *"The moment you began praying, a command was given. And now I am here to tell you what it was, for you are very precious to God"* (Daniel 9:23a).

Isn't that a beautiful statement? "The moment you began to pray!" Sometimes God's delayed answers to prayer, or His seeming denial of a request for our own good, will be interpreted as deafness on God's part. It might be honest for us to ask the question, "Lord, why won't You answer me," but it is never accurate for us to think, "He doesn't even hear me!" GOD HEARS EVERY PRAYER!

As an omniscient God, He knows all things, and hears all prayers whether they are from His people or not. But to those of us, who confess Jesus as Lord and have accepted His payment for our sins through His death on the cross, we can be assured that He not only hears us, but also just like Daniel, He will start to answer "the moment you begin to pray."

Thought for the Day

You never have to worry that you are in a prayer dead zone if you are a follower of Jesus Christ.

DAY 39

Finally, dear brothers and sisters, we urge you in the name of the Lord Jesus to live in a way that pleases God, as we have taught you. You live this way already, and we encourage you to do so even more.

—1 Thessalonians 4:1

Walking the Line

As police officers, we always refer to codified law in order to make decisions on the job. Whether it is the penal, vehicle, health and safety, or the business and professions code, we will use specific sections to determine if a suspect has violated the law. Sometimes we make our decisions based on an interpretation of the code in the light of current case law, and other times, action will be clear as a result of well-established precedent. Either way, there will be a line drawn that will help us to determine if a law has been broken and if we can arrest the suspect for that violation. It seems that many of the people that we contact will constantly try to get as close to that line as possible without actually stepping over it. In short, their lives are centered around figuring out how much they can get away with.

A lot of us live our Christian lives like that when it comes to seeking God's will. We will search the scriptures to see if our activities are specifically covered in its pages, and if they violate His word. Our lives seem to be centered around getting as close to the world's standards as possible without "crossing the line."

I think it would be better if we stopped looking for definitions and loopholes in scripture and ask ourselves one simple question: "Would it please God or not?" Doing God's will is not a matter of interpretation of the law and minutiae; it is as easy as doing what He wants us to.

Thought for the Day

Let's stop walking as close as we can to the world's line and start simply trying to please God.

DAY 40

*And they sang a new song with these words "You are worthy to take
the scroll and break its seals and open it for you were slaughtered,
and your blood has ransomed people for God from every tribe and
language and people and nation. And you have caused them to become
a Kingdom of priests for our God. And they will reign on the earth."*

—Revelation 5:9–10

A New Song

Several years back, Harvest OC Church hosted "the Epic Worship
Team Event". It was a one-day conference for the equipping, fellowship, worship, and personal refreshment of musicians who led
worship in their individual churches. I had the opportunity to stand
in the back and listen to a thousand-seat sanctuary full of worship
leaders sing in unison to the Lord. Now, as much as our typical congregation sings enthusiastically every Sunday, the sound of all those
worship leaders singing was much different than what I normally
hear in that room. I am sure that God loves whatever joyful noise that
is made to Him, but my earthly ears could tell the difference between
the singing I usually hear in church, and the perfectly in-tune beautiful sound that I heard on that day. It took my breath away and gave
me a small glimpse of what a heavenly choir will sound like. Maybe
someday God will give people like me the ability to sing on key (a
miracle for sure) when I stand before Him.

The above verse in Revelation tells of a future celestial scene
where a new song will be sung declaring the worthiness of Jesus due
to His sacrifice on the cross for our sin. I am sure that this chorus will
be unlike anything we have heard before. In fact, I am certain that all

the songs and proclamations we hear in heaven will be unbelievable. It makes me anxious to get there in God's perfect timing.

There will be many things about heaven that will be incredible. First Corinthians 2:9 tells us, "*But as it is written: "Eye has not seen, nor ear heard, nor have entered into the heart of man the things which God has prepared for those who love Him.*" I am so glad to have that complete assurance as to what my eternal future holds. If you do, also, rejoice in that fact. If you do not, make that decision about your future today!

Thought for the Day

What we will see and hear in heaven is up to our obedience and surrender now.

DAY 41

Surely your goodness and unfailing love will pursue me all the days of my life, and I will live in the house of the Lord forever.

—Psalm 23:6

Wanted

After my second season in junior college, I started to get heavily recruited by several teams in the Pacific 10 Conference (now the Pac-12). I narrowed it down to four schools, Arizona State, Cal Berkley, Stanford, and USC. It was a pretty heady time for me. I came home one night and found Bill Walsh (the then Stanford coach and the future Hall of Fame 49ers coach) sitting in the living room with my parents! I can tell you that it is a great feeling to be wanted, recruited, and chased after.

Do you realize how much God wants you? He came to this earth in the form of a man and died a horrific death for you (Romans 5:8). He has pursued you to offer you the free gift of salvation, a gift that we cannot earn on our own (Romans 6:23). And His love will continue to pursue you all the days of your life so that you can be with Him for eternity (Psalm 23:6). He will continue to knock on the door of your heart and life and encourage you to open it to Him (Revelation 3:20–21).

If you are a believer in Jesus Christ and have already made Him the Lord of your life, this truth should make you unbelievably thankful for God's incredible grace and mercy to you. If you have not yet invited Jesus into your heart and life, then you should be honored that the God of the universe wants you and is pursuing you to live for eternity with Him!

You may never have felt wanted in your life, but God's word says that he is actively pursuing you to be on the greatest team that the universe has ever seen.

Thought for the Day

All you have to do is say yes to His free gift. Now how is that for a heady recruiting story?

DAY 42

As for God, His way is perfect; The word of the Lord is proven; He is a shield to all who trust in Him.

—Psalm 18:30

Ball Control

As a lineman for the University of Southern California football team in the late 1970s, I was privileged to play with a Heisman Trophy award–winning tailback, Charles White. As we learned our blocking assignments, our coaches made one thing perfectly clear to all of us in the trenches. Charlie was the Heisman winner, and we were not. When we blocked a defensive lineman, we were to take him straight off the ball and not in any specific direction. Whenever we took an opponent to one direction or another, our coaches would always say, "So you are going to pick a side and tell our Heisman Trophy winner where he is supposed to run? Let's let him decide, okay."

How often do we take a side in our decisions or attempt to tell God which way we think He should take us? If we have truly given the control of our lives to Jesus Christ, we need to let Him retain possession of every aspect of our lives. For us to take back that control makes about as much sense as a lineman wrestling the football away from a running back as he passes by. I guarantee that no progress could have occurred if we had attempted to do that to Charles White. Compared to him, we were slow, had no moves, and would fumble the ball anyway.

Thought for the Day

Is there any area in your life that you are trying to wrestle back from God? Let Him carry the ball, it is the only way you will successfully gain ground in the Christian life.

DAY 43

*Even before he made the world, God loved us and chose
us in Christ to be holy and without fault in his eyes.*
—Ephesians 1:4

Undeserved

When I walked around the church on a Sunday morning, I was
often met by the familiar greeting, "Morning, Pastor Brad!"
At that time, I had been an associate pastor at the church for seven
years, but I have to admit, I never really got used to the sound of that
salutation. I spent four decades being called a variety of other names.
In football, we were known by our last names, so "Hey, Green" felt
normal. It was the same while I was a cop by my peers and supervisors, although I would have to say I was often called many less-than-
kind names by some suspects I had come into contact with.

In my personal life, I have been called either Dad, honey, or
just plain Brad. So, the moniker of pastor seems to me to be somewhat strange and undeserved. I know the great respect I have for the
knowledge and position of those whom I call pastor, and I wonder
how it came to be that I earned this title. Well, the truth is I did not
earn it, it was just given to me. I know that there is not a time when I
am with other believers that I'm not in the presence of someone who
knows more about God's word, or who demonstrates a better example of an authentic Christian life than I do. So why am I a pastor? I
don't know, God just called me to be one, and He convinced someone in church authority to ordain me. If they came to their senses
tomorrow and took it all back, I would understand, and just go back
to being regular Brad, the ministry volunteer and church attender.

It might not make complete sense to us, but if we have accepted Christ as our Savior and Lord, God calls us by a different name than we had before. We might have been Mary or Bill, or "Hey, you" in the past, but when we turn our lives over to God through accepting Christ's death on the cross for us, we are given the name son or daughter by the almighty God of the universe. And on top of that, the above verse in Ephesians tells us that we become "without fault in his eyes."

As a follower of Christ, you have been adopted into the family of God, been given an honored role in that family as a son or daughter of the King and have been forgiven to the extent that when the King looks at you, He sees only the perfection of Jesus. And unlike the fleeting titles of this world, "child of the king" has been written into the Lamb's Book of Life with the blood of Jesus that cannot be erased. John 10:28 tells us the words of Jesus Himself when he says, *"And I give them eternal life, and they shall never perish; neither shall anyone snatch them out of My hand."*

So, when the King calls you son or daughter and sees you without fault through Jesus, just do what I did every Sunday when someone says, "Morning, Pastor Brad." I smile and answer back as if I deserved the title.

Thought for the Day

We might not deserve to be viewed as faultless, but we are through Jesus's sacrifice for us.

DAY 44

I am the LORD, and I do not change.

—Malachi 3:6a

Changeless

I recently bought five old hymnals on eBay. They are all dated between 1852 and 1869. That would have made their publishing at the time of the Civil War! The owners of the books signed their names inside with the unique penmanship of that day. I don't know who these men were, but you can't help but think about where they lived, and what their relationships with God were like.

When you read the songs in the books, you can see the praise of God in the words printed there. Sure, they have an older English slant to them, but they give honor to God in a very similar way that our worship songs do today. And why shouldn't they? The God they are singing about is the same yesterday, today, and forever.

I love the above verse in Malachi! God does not change. His love for us, His promises to us, and His patience with us are the same today as they were in the distant past. When we counsel new believers, that is one of the first things we tell them. Now that you have accepted Jesus as your Savior and Lord, all the promises in God's word belong to you. They are there for you to read and rely on. His word will never change just as God Himself never does.

Thought for the Day

You can count on God's promises. They are the same yesterday, today, and tomorrow.

DAY 45

*Having then gifts differing according to the grace
that is given to us, let us use them.*

—Romans 12:6a

Talents

I played center for my entire football career. That included five years of Pop Warner, four years of high school, and five years of college. Snapping the ball became so automatic after thousands of practices and games that I didn't even have to think about it. There was one thing about being a center that I could never seem to do, the long snap. I don't know if my arms were the wrong length, or my neck was too short to be able to look back between my legs, but I could never master the art of snapping the ball back to the punter with the zip that was required. That was unfortunate for me because the player who took over the long snap duties for my college team made a career out of it. He played for the Rams for several years and was well paid for that single ability.

Christians will often not be satisfied with the gifts they have been given by God. They see others' talents and wish that they could switch skills with them. I have to admit that I sometimes think that when I watch our worship team and see them play their instruments with such ease.

God has given us each the gifts and talents that He wants us to have. He didn't make a mistake or run short on the ability list and give us the only thing left. He paired a specific gift with you. The above verse in Romans says these gifts are given to us with only one requirement on our part, "let us use them!"

No matter what gifts and abilities God has granted you, you will only be held responsible for one thing, to use those talents for His glory.

Thought for the Day

We can make a ministry career out of a single ability God has given us as long as we use them!

DAY 46

But someone will say, "You have faith, and I have works." Show me your faith without your works, and I will show you my faith by my works.

—James 2:18

Dead or Alive?

When I worked undercover as a vice investigator, I did not look like a cop. The long hair (then blond), goatee, and casual clothing made me unrecognizable as a law enforcement officer. In all the undercover stings I participated in, I was never burned as an officer during the actual operation.

The above passage is from one of the most difficult passages found in scripture. Verse 17 had just told us that "faith without works is dead." But then in verse 18, we get a little clarity when James states, "*I will show you my faith by my works*." We know that we are saved by faith and not works (Ephesians 2:8–9), so what does the "dead" designation mean in verse 17? The New Living Translation helps us understand when it reads, "So you see, faith by itself isn't enough. Unless it produces good deeds it is **useless**."

James was not saying that works are what saves us, but rather they show if the salvation we confess is genuine. (i.e., I will show you my faith by my works). There are many who claim to be believers in Jesus Christ, but the true commitment to the Lord is exposed by their works or lack thereof.

As an undercover cop, I might have not looked like a law enforcement officer, but my communication, and the swift arrest of those involved in illegal transactions, showed that I was one. I was a cop the entire time, but my actions revealed what and who I really was. If I never took any action, no one would have ever known I was an officer, and even other cops could have doubted if my credentials were real.

If you have truly accepted Jesus Christ as your Lord and Savior, you are saved by that faith and the works in your life will show that you are. If we are living a life with no visible fruit for God, we are either in a backslidden state, or never really turned our lives over to Him in the first place. So, who ultimately decides which one? That is for God to judge.

Thought for the Day

Only by our actions can we prove to others that we are dead or alive in Him.

DAY 47

*Be angry, and do not sin; do not let the sun go down
on your wrath, nor give place to the devil.*

—Ephesians 4:26–27

Righteous Anger

During the football season of my junior year in high school, we played against another local team. We lost the game, big, just as we usually did. I don't remember exactly why, but I was extremely angry that game. I was on the verge of a fight with the other players on almost every down. In short, I was out of control. It is a miracle that I didn't get thrown out of the game, but my actions definitely drew the attention of my line coach.

The next week in practice my wise old coach developed a plan to "help" me. He told some other players to hit me late on every chance they could and to start fights with me. Well, the practice went as you might think, and I was swinging and punching most of the time. Not too bright, considering that it never hurts to get punched in a metal face mask by a hand. The puncher always loses that battle. By the end of practice, they all stood smiling and I was exhausted. I learned a valuable lesson that day that took me through to the end of my football career. Being out of control would never make me a better football player, and it would only hurt my team. I am proud to say that in the many years that followed, at both the high school and college level, I did not lose control again, and I was never flagged for unsportsmanlike conduct in a game or practice.

Anger is not always a sin. We know that Jesus himself became angry with the money changers in the temple as described in Matthew

21. Sometimes people hurt us, and our anger at them might be justified. It isn't the anger that is the problem; it is how we handle it and what we do about it that can result in sin. The above verse in Ephesians tells us to go ahead and be angry, but do not let those emotions fester inside of us. If we do that, we are giving the devil a place in our lives.

So, if we are hurt, we might get angry, but we need to immediately give the situation to God and let Him take care of it.

Thought for the Day

Don't throw punches that will only end up hurting yourself. Give the problem to Him.

DAY 48

"Do not lay up for yourselves treasures on earth, where moth and rust destroy and where thieves break in and steal.
—Matthew 6:19

Eternal Savings Account

In my career as a police officer, I took many reports that documented the loss of various treasures people had "laid up" for themselves here on this earth. Bicycles, jewelry, gold, electronics, pets, vehicles, and even the copper gutters and downspouts on the exteriors of homes were just some of the items that were routinely taken. I came across many victims who had put their possessions in the proper perspective and did not seem overly distraught about their loss. Some, on the other hand, seemed devastated with the theft of even the smallest item. And what was most interesting to me was that many times, those with the most financial wealth seemed to be the ones most bothered! Not always, but often.

The above verse in Matthew warns us to not place our stock in the material things this world can offer. No matter how much we acquire, it will someday be stolen, lost, or will deteriorate. Nothing we have will last forever, and our ownership of it usually won't even last during our lifetime.

Matthew 6 tells us what our focus should be. Verse 20 says, *"But lay up for yourselves treasure in heaven, where neither moth nor rust destroys and thieves do not break in nor steal."*

Heaven is the only place that can guarantee perfect storage for our valuables. What we give, how we treat others, and whom we share our faith with are only a small sample of treasures that we can "send ahead," and that will last an eternity.

Of course, you can only receive the use of this secure facility if we have opened up a savings account. And how do we sign up for these heavenly banking benefits? We must confess Jesus Christ as Lord of our lives. If you have not done that, start your tally right away. If you already have a relationship with Him, keep adding to that existing balance!

Thought for the Day

Open an account and start laying up treasure at the main branch today.

DAY 49

You will show me the path of life; In Your presence is fullness of joy; At Your right hand are pleasures forevermore.

—Psalm 16:11

Pathfinder

There is a path in life that God says will lead to "fullness of joy." It is not hard to find, we just need to know where to look.

One night, while working on the Balboa Peninsula, I investigated a battery where a suspect had struck a victim and fled the area. Fortunately for me, he left numerous clues as to his whereabouts. During the altercation, the barefoot suspect had kicked a cement parking stall divider and had cut his big toe. I knew this because I could see the small circular blood spots on the sidewalk that indicated he had been injured. Once my partner arrived on the scene, we had little trouble locating him. We just followed the blood spots down to the bay, around the corner to a residence, and then up the stairs located on the outside of the building. The suspect was hiding at the top of the stairwell with his right toe still bleeding. He might have got away if we hadn't known what we were looking for.

God is clear about the path we need to follow in order to obtain a life of fullness and joy. Jesus said, "*If you love me, keep my commandments*" (John 14:15). It is just that simple. We do what He says to do, and we avoid what He says not to do. The Bible gives us all we need to know in order to find the path that God wants us to take in life.

Thought for the Day

If we read His word (another one of His commandments) and do what He says, we will be able to "connect the dots" of the Christian life and His plan for us.

DAY 50

No longer do I call you servants, for a servant does not know what his master is doing; but I have called you friends, for all things that I heard from My Father I have made known to you.

—John 15:15

Famous Friends

I know a lot of famous and talented people. I am neither, but God has brought many well-known individuals into my life. Whether it is through my connection to football or my association with law enforcement chaplaincy, I have many friends who are household names in the athletic and ministry communities. Sometimes they come up in my conversations with others, and I always get the same surprised and doubtful question. I'm often asked, "Are they a friend of yours?" with a special emphasis on the word "friend." I'm not acquainted with them because of anything I am or have done. God has just brought them into my life for His purposes which are unknown to me.

It is even more remarkable that Jesus calls us His friends. Can you imagine that? The almighty God of the universe loves us so much that He wants to be more than our Savior; He wants to be our friend. There is nothing we have done or could do to earn this honor; it is just the nature of God's grace to give us what we really don't deserve.

As much as Jesus wants to be involved in our lives, He will not force us to have a relationship with Him. It is our choice to invite Christ into our hearts and lay hold of the promises that God's word, the Bible, offers us.

Today you may feel betrayed by friendships that you thought you could count on. Jesus Christ has good news for you; He wants to be your friend. He will never let you down, talk bad about you, use you, or turn His back on you. You can reach Him day or night, and He will always be there to help you. He knows all, owns all, is all powerful, and promises to answer you whenever you call on Him.

Thought for the Day

Jesus is the best kind of famous friend to have!

DAY 51

For God so loved the world that He gave His only begotten Son, that whoever believes in Him should not perish but have everlasting life.
—John 3:16

Obvious Guilt

I used to own a Boston terrier named Butler, who always seemed to be getting into some kind of mischief. One day, I walked out of the kitchen and found him seated quietly in the living room next to a coffee table. As he sat there motionless, an unusual thing for him, he stared at me with a frozen look on his face. I know that some experts say that dogs live in the here and now and don't feel guilt or remorse about their actions, but it was obvious that this little guy had done something that he knew he wasn't supposed to. I believe that if he could, he would have been whistling a distracting tune in an attempt to avert my attention from the area. I walked over to the coffee table and found a chewed-up apple core underneath that Butler had retrieved from the kitchen trash when I was out of the room.

In spite of what the world might say, the fact that we are all sinners is not such a hard sell. We all know what we are, in spite of our best efforts to claim otherwise. I think that people attempt to deny their sin not because they don't believe that it exists, but because they just don't know what to do with it once it has been revealed. Fortunately for us, God knew exactly what to do.

The above verse in John is arguably the Bible's most famous passage. It encapsulates the entire theme of God's word into one simple sentence, and states that we can have forgiveness and eternal life through Christ's sacrifice on the cross. Romans 6:23 tells us of our situation and its solution, *"For the wages of sin is death, but the gift of God is eternal life through Christ Jesus our Lord."*

We have been separated from God by our own sin. He saw that separation and decided to pay the price for us because He loved us and knew that there was no way we could accomplish that task on our own. There is no need to ignore, attempt to cover, or deny our sin. If we accept His free gift of forgiveness, that debt can be completely paid for.

Thought for the Day

We don't have to sit with a guilty look on our face when God has already done the cleansing work in us.

DAY 52

Your word I have hidden in my heart, That I might not sin against You.
—Psalm 119:11

Go-to Moves

I studied martial arts for many years, and I had to learn hundreds of moves in order to earn my belt rankings. It always seemed odd to me that whenever a physical confrontation came my way on the job, I always resorted to only a handful of "go to" moves that worked best for me. It turned out that it wasn't the amount of moves that I knew, but my proficiency with the few that I used.

We are encouraged in Psalms to memorize God's Word. It is the key to a victorious Christian life as we battle the difficult situations and temptations that will inevitably come our way. It is also vital to be grounded in His promises to us so that we can share His plan of salvation with others.

The Bible is a big book, and it can sometimes seem like a daunting task to learn what we need to know in order to use the scriptures with authority. One of Satan's biggest lies to us is that we don't know enough, "just yet," to be effective in our testimony for Him.

There is great power in the Bible because it is the inspired word of God. Just a little bit of knowledge can go a long way when we consider that it is given to us by the almighty Creator of the universe. If you want to get started, just memorize John 3:16, Romans 10:9, and Revelation 3:20. They are three verses that can be lethal in their effectiveness when combined with your personal testimony.

We have the rest of our lives to learn God's word. We don't need to be biblical scholars in order to share our faith with others. Just a few words spoken by the power of the Holy Spirit can be more effective than many years of secular study.

Thought for the Day

Learn your "go to" scriptures and let the Holy Spirit do the rest.

DAY 53

*And I saw the dead, small and great, standing before God, and
books were opened. And another book was opened, which is
the Book of Life. And the dead were judged according to their
works, by the things which were written in the books.*

—Revelation 20:12

Miranda Rights

**You have the right to remain silent. Anything you say may
be used against you in court. You have the right to an attorney,
before and during questioning. If you cannot afford an attorney,
one will be appointed free of charge before questioning if you
want.**

The above phrases have been a part of every American police
officer's life since the Warren Court's decision, which required
them, was made in the late 1960s. They were instituted to make sure
that each defendant understood their rights before talking with law
enforcement about the incident that they had been arrested for.

Our rights in an American court of law are similar to what we
will have in God's eternal court of judgment. God's word says that
everything we have said or done has been recorded and could be used
against us. If it ended there, each of us would be found guilty because
of our sin and we would receive a death sentence. But fortunately,
we, too, will have the right to an attorney who will plead our case
for us.

If we accept Jesus Christ as our Savior and Lord, He will be our
advocate before a Holy God and will effectively defend us and keep

us from the Great White Throne of Judgment as described above. This will not be due to our innocence, but because of His sacrifice on the cross for us. None of us could afford this type of representation ourselves, but just as in the Miranda Warning, we can be appointed it free of charge if we want. God's great gift to us, the condemned, is the free gift of forgiveness that Christ paid. But we can only receive this gift if we ask for it.

No one in their right mind would go to court without competent counsel, especially if the highest priced, best qualified attorney in the universe was available free of charge.

Thought for the Day

We will never know when our ultimate day in court will come. It could be in the next decade or the next minute. Don't get caught in front of the judge without effective representation.

DAY 54

Then Joseph's master took him and put him into the prison, a place where the king's prisoners were confined. And he was there in the prison. But the LORD was with Joseph and showed him mercy, and He gave him favor in the sight of the keeper of the prison. And the keeper of the prison committed to Joseph's hand all the prisoners who were in the prison; whatever they did there, it was his doing.

—Genesis 39:20–22

He Is Able!

Joseph is one of my favorite biblical characters. He was a young man who was sold into slavery, wrongfully accused of a crime, and thrown into the pharaoh's prison. This was not a place of civil rights and appeals; it was the last stop before an unknown future. But even in Joseph's darkest hour, God was with him. He gave Joseph favor with the warden of the prison and brought about circumstances that led to his freedom and rise in power. By the time God was done, Joseph was second-in-command in all of Egypt.

It's not that I like the story of Joseph because I think that I will become second-in-command of anything someday. The only place where I am second-in-command is at home, just ask my wife! The story of Joseph gives me great hope that God can overcome any circumstance that I might find myself in and bring me out victorious on the other side. I need that hope!

God has a plan for our lives. We might not be able to see past our present situation, but fortunately for us, God has better eyesight than we do. He can see our future with even better clarity than we can see our past, and God has the unlimited power we need to make

His plan for our lives happen. No matter how improbable the circumstances are, God is able.

Thought for the Day

It doesn't make any difference if your problem is financial, physical, relational, or emotional, God can enter that situation and work it out for His glory! But in order to initiate His rescue plan, you must first put your total trust in Him.

DAY 55

But when Rehoboam was firmly established and strong, he abandoned the Law of the Lord, and all Israel followed him in this sin.
—2 Chronicles 12:1

Leading Position

Many years ago, I was feeling particularly bad after a failed attempt to promote. I had done well enough in all areas of the sergeant's exam but fell short in what we called the beauty contest. That was the department evaluation where all the supervisors would give you anonymous ratings which provided their personal opinion of your fitness to lead. I passed, but my score was average, and it placed me too low on the list to be realistically considered for promotion.

I started to read some positive written materials in an effort to console myself. I opened a book, and my eye was immediately drawn to a line at the bottom of the page that read, "You don't need an official position to lead." This statement has meant a lot to me over the years as I sought to make a difference in the lives of those at my department.

The above verse in 2 Chronicles tells of King Rehoboam who was the son of the famous Solomon. As wise as his father was, Rehoboam was foolish in his decision-making and leadership ability. He not only abandoned the laws of God personally, but he also led all of Israel to do the same.

Whether you are a king or a commoner, you are a leader. You can be an example for God at your workplace, with your friends, or in your personal family relationships. The question is not "if" you can be a leader, but rather, "what type" of leader you will be. Rehoboam decided to forsake God and took a whole country down with him. How many times have I seen someone provide poor leadership and destroy the moral of their department, the self-confidence of their subordinates, and the strength of their family relationships.

No matter where you find yourself today, God wants you to be a leader at some level. Be remembered as a person who lifted others up and brought them to righteousness rather than someone who dragged others down and encouraged them to do evil.

Thought for the Day

You don't need an official position to lead.

DAY 56

Be sober, be vigilant; because your adversary the devil walks
about like a roaring lion, seeking whom he may devour.

—1 Peter 5:8

Weak Points

It is hard getting old. As time passes, my list of orthopedic challenges gets longer. Some are from many years past, while others are more recent.

Several years ago, I had a bad flu. It was one of those that makes your body ache all over. I noticed, however, that the areas that hurt the most were the joints where I had severe injuries in my past. My surgically repaired knee, which had not given me much trouble in recent years, throbbed as I lay there in bed. It is funny how viruses attack the weak points of your body almost as if they knew exactly where to make you hurt the most.

Satan, our enemy, does the exact same thing. When he wants to bring us down, he will often go directly to areas in our lives where we have experienced difficulty or failure in the past. He knows exactly what has the best chance of tripping us up and bringing us down.

There is an old saying, "Forewarned is forearmed." If we know something difficult is coming, we can prepare ourselves for its arrival. When I had that flu, I knew there was no new damage to my knee. It was just a problem based on an old injury and a new virus. For that reason, I could easily rest knowing that it was temporary and "this, too, shall pass."

The above verse in 1 Peter warns us that our adversary, Satan, is like a roaring lion searching around for something to eat. And just like lions, he will seek out the weak animals in a herd so that he can attack them with greater success. But if we are familiar with Satan's plans, and know God's word, we can fight off his attempts to make us fall or be fearful about the weak points in our lives.

James 4:7 tells us, "*Therefore submit to God. Resist the devil and he will flee from you.*" God's word encourages us to do two things to defeat Satan's attempts to hurt us. First, submit and obey God, and secondly, resist! Then we are promised that he will flee from us.

Thought for the Day

When that same old pain comes to you, realize who it is, and rest assured that he will run if you resist and obey.

DAY 57

There is therefore now no condemnation to those who are in Christ Jesus, who do not walk according to the flesh, but according to the spirit.
—Romans 8:1

Suspect ID

Several years ago, a body was found floating in the bay in Newport Beach. When the female victim was taken from the water, a butter knife was found protruding from one of her eyes. The knife had passed through the eye and into her brain, causing her death. Our bay had been used by the murderer(s) as a dump site, and the actual murder scene was later determined to have been in a neighboring city. The detectives on the case immediately recognized that the crime involved a great amount of passion and hatred for the victim. Most real murders, unlike made-for-TV movies, are not that hard to figure out. Detectives generally begin with those closest to the victim and work their way out in the investigation. In this case, they found that the daughter and her "not liked by Mom" boyfriend had committed the crime.

Most of the time, the spiritual attacks in our lives are just not that hard to figure out either. Sure, it may be possible that the Holy Spirit is convicting us of sin, but that is usually followed by positive encouragement by God for us to do the right thing. Romans 8:1 tells us that, "*There is therefore now no condemnation to those who are in Christ Jesus.*" So, if you have sinned and confessed that sin to God, and you still feel condemnation about it in your life, it is the usual suspect, Satan, who is responsible.

First John 1:9 states that, *"If we confess our sins He is faithful and just to forgive us our sins and to cleanse us from all unrighteousness."* I love the word "cleanse" in this verse. To me it means an active hard scrubbing of an item to get it clean. It's not a "rinsing off" or a "wiping down" of something, but a deep cleaning that speaks of a permanent removal of the impurities.

Thought for the Day

Don't allow yourself to get confused about the identity of the suspect who causes your feelings of condemnation. It isn't hard to figure out. Ask for forgiveness, receive it, and move on.

DAY 58

*Do not be deceived, God is not mocked, for
whatever a man sows, that he will reap."*

—Galatians 6:7

Intended Consequences

When I was an associate pastor, I did a lot of counseling. I have learned that almost all the situations I dealt with have their roots in the person's direct disobedience to God's word, otherwise known as sin. This is not unusual, but the counselee's reaction to the revealed transgression can be. Some see their offense, eagerly repent, and start a renewed effort to obey God's commandments for their lives. But there are others who understand that their actions are against God's word, do it anyway, and say, "I'll just take the consequences." They believe that because God has been merciful with them in the past, He will overlook their purposeful actions of disobedience. In short, they want to sin more than they want to please God.

The Bible is a book that documents God's love for us and His far-reaching grace and mercy in our lives. Romans 5:8 tells us, *"But God demonstrates His own love toward us, in that while we were still sinners, Christ died for us."* God's word also tells us, *"For the Lord disciplines those He loves, and He punishes each one He accepts as his child"* (Hebrews 12:6). So which is He? A God of love or the stern father? The answer is both!

God loves us and wants the best for our lives. When we sin, He is right there encouraging us to recognize our actions and to ask for forgiveness (1 John 1:9). But when we choose to deliberately disobey

His commands, God, for our own good, will apply discipline in order to redirect us back into a position where He can continue to bless us.

God's word gives us firm warnings to those who choose to disobey God's will purposely and continually. The above verse in Galatians states, "*Do not be deceived, God is not mocked, for whatever a man sows, that he will reap.*" If we continue to go against God's commandments for our lives, we do so at our own peril and our actions will not be without consequence.

I don't know about you, but I want to be in the place of compliance in my life where God can put me in a position to receive his blessings. I want to be known by God for instant repentance and obedience, not for selfish action and disobedience. If you ever fought with a sibling as a child while riding in a car, you are familiar with the statement often made by an exhausted parent when they said, "Don't make me come back there!" This is a warning that will either be followed by changed behavior, or a punishment.

Thought for the Day

Don't make God come into your life with a corrective action. Repent quickly and continue to receive His blessing.

DAY 59

*For he will conceal me there when troubles come; he will hide me
in his sanctuary. He will place me out of reach on a high rock.*

—Psalm 27:5

A Safe Place

In the city of Newport Beach, the police, fire, and lifeguard departments have a great relationship. PD officers view each firefighter,
paramedic, and lifeguard as a brother from another mother, so to
speak, and we have always worked well together. We have a comradery that can only be built by years of standing together during unbelievable tragedies. Almost every time we were dispatched to the latest
horrific scene, we found one another there in different capacities or
another. It is an unusual bond that cannot be explained to anyone
who has not experienced it.

Many times, in my law enforcement career, I needed a place to
stop to eat, use the restroom, or just get out of my unit for a while.
Twelve hours of driving in circles can be tedious. On the west side of
the city, it was Lifeguard Headquarters, and on the east side, it was
any fire station in my area. At those places I found safety, peace, and
acceptance from my fellow first responders who all knew how much
it meant to just get away from the pressure cooker for a while. As I
write this, I just realized that I never officially thanked the fire and
lifeguard personnel who were, and still are, so giving to us police officers. They allowed us to make unofficial police substations of their
workplaces. You will never know how much it meant to us to have a
place to go when our PD building was so far away. Thank you, and I
hope that this acknowledgment finds its way to you all.

The above verse in Psalms was written by King David who expressed a similar praise to God about his feelings of gratitude and protection in the sanctuary of God. I am so thankful for my church and what it has given to me. Church should be a place where we can go, not to be closer to God because He is everywhere, but to feel safety, peace, and acceptance from God and his people. It should be a place where, just for a few hours, we can worship, learn, have fellowship, and, spiritually, recharge after a long week.

It is difficult to enter the first responder ranks. The selection process is brutal, and only a few make it through. Not so with the church of God! Jesus said, "*Come to me, all of you who are weary and carry heavy burdens, and I will give you rest*" (Matthew 11:28). Notice it says, "ALL OF YOU who are weary," and that is all of us.

Thought for the Day

Don't let a bad past experience or false perception keep you from the place of safety and rest that you so desperately need. Go to church, be with God's people, and let Him hide you from the troubles of this world.

DAY 60

*For the word of God is quick, and powerful, and sharper
than any two-edged sword, piercing even to the dividing
asunder of soul and spirit, and of the joints and marrow, and
is a discerner of the thoughts and intents of the heart.*

—Hebrews 4:12

Weapons

L aw enforcement is a gun culture. I always carried several with me
when I went on duty each shift. I had a rifle and shotgun in my
police unit, in addition to the one or two handguns I carried on my
person. I practiced with all those weapons so that I would be proficient in using them. In fact, carrying a gun became so natural to me
that I thought of them in the same way as I did my flashlight, cite
book, or any other piece of standard gear.

Of course, when I had to unholster my gun and point it at
somebody, the weapon immediately took on a deadly serious meaning as I had to make split-second judgments whether or not to pull
the trigger. If someone was intent on killing me or someone else,
I was prepared to, and still am for that matter, stop them in any
way they forced me to. Thankfully, I never had to do so and ended
my career like the vast majority of police officers without shooting
anyone.

God's word is often likened to a sword (Ephesians 6:17). At the
time the above passage in Hebrews was written, the sword was the
premier weapon of the old world. It was sharp, accurate, and deadly.
No soldier would have thought about going into battle without a
sword to protect himself and defend others. We know from the above

passage of the effectiveness of God's word, stating that it is "*sharper than any two-edged sword, piercing even to the dividing asunder of the soul and spirit.*" But a weapon is only of value if someone can and is willing to use it. That is why it is important to memorize scripture and practice with this primary weapon that God has given us. If I hadn't known how to rack and load the guns I used on the job, their only defense value would have been if I threw these weapons at someone.

Thought for the Day

Get familiar with God's word and how to use it as a weapon against the enemy. Don't get in a situation where your only option would be to throw your Bible at the problem.

DAY 61

Then they came to the place of which God had told him. And
Abraham built an altar there and placed the wood in order: and he
bound Isaac his son and laid him on the altar, upon the wood.

—Genesis 22:9

BBQ Faith

The above verse chronicles Abraham's great faith in God. He
was instructed to travel with his son Isaac to a remote location
where he would be required to take the young man's life by sacrifice.
Isaac was the son of Abraham's old age. He had waited 100 years for
him! Isaac was the son in whom God had promised to create a great
nation. Abraham's faith in God was so great that he believed God
would keep His promise to him even if it meant raising Isaac from
the dead.

If we only see Abraham's actions in this account, we miss
another great example of faith. We usually think of Isaac as a small
boy who went with his father totally unaware of the intent of the
trip. But if we do the math on the Genesis timeline, we can see that
Isaac was somewhere between his late teens and midtwenties, and
that Abraham was around 120 years old! At Isaac's age, he was in
the prime of his physical condition. The biblical account also tells
us that Isaac was the one who carried the wood up the mountain for
the sacrifice. It would not have taken much for Isaac to overpower a
120-year-old man. Isaac could have looked at the knife, the rope, the
wood, and the Wizard lighter fluid, and said, "Forget you, old man,
sacrifice yourself!" But verse 9 says, "*And he bound Isaac his son and
laid him on the altar, upon the wood.*" It is obvious that Isaac's faith in

God and his father was pretty special because he allowed himself to be bound and laid on that altar.

God wants you to make a sacrifice today. Not by taking a life for Him, but by giving a life to Him, <u>YOURS</u>! Maybe for you it is about giving Jesus Christ the control of your life for the first time. If you have already done that, maybe the faith sacrifice He wants from you is the rededication of all the areas of your life to Him.

Because of his faith, God provided Abraham with a ram to take Isaac's place. Because of His love for us, God came to this world in human form through the person of Jesus Christ to take our place.

Thought for the Day

The only faith He requires from us now is to believe in that sacrifice and give the control of our lives to Him.

DAY 62

Many will say to Me in that day, 'Lord, Lord, have we not prophesied in Your name, cast out demons in Your name, and done many wonders in Your name?' And then I will declare to them, 'I never knew you; depart from Me, you who practice lawlessness!'
—Matthew 7:22–23

Unexpected Presence

One day, during my time as an associate pastor, I walked into the green room that is to the rear of the sanctuary stage. The green room is where the musicians congregate prior to going out to perform. As I passed an office located there, I looked into the open door and saw a male talking with one of our pastors. It only took me a fraction of a second to recognize the man as Vincent Furnier, the front man for hard shock rock band Alice Cooper. In fact, Alice Cooper had been the name he had become generally associated with, so much so that people thought it was his actual name. He has such a distinct look that I could recognize him anywhere, even without his traditional theatrical makeup and clothing. As a high schooler in the 1970s, who could ever forget his greatest hit, "School's Out."

To say that I was surprised to see Alice Cooper standing behind stage at church would be an understatement. Fortunately, I passed by without flinching, and continued on with my duties, thinking, *Well, that's the last person I expected to see here today.* I had read that "Alice" had become a born-again Christian and was vocal about his faith in Jesus Christ. So, his presence in a church should not have been a total surprise to me.

From the above verse in Matthew, it is evident that there will be many people who will rely on their works in this life to get them into heaven. They might be able to recite a long list of accomplishments for God, thinking that they had tipped the balance of the heavenly scales in their favor, and that their effort will assure them a place in God's kingdom. But Jesus's response to them will reveal the truth of their faith by stating, "I never knew you; depart from Me." They had demonstrated a faith that looked genuine but had never actually turned the control of their lives over to Him.

On the other hand, there will be many people in heaven that we did not expect to be there. Their lives might have not been as showy, or successful from a typical Christian standpoint, but their faith, though small, was genuine. It has been humorously stated that there are three things that will be a surprise to us when we get to heaven: those who are not there whom we thought would be, those who are there whom we didn't think would be, and that we, ourselves, are there!

If you have lost a friend or loved one who never seemed to show a true faith in Christ, have hope. You never know what a person truly believed in their heart or at the last second of their lives. I have often preached the gospel to a person lying in a coma in a hospital room. I talked with them as though they could hear me. Science tells us that is true for some and have documented cases where people said they heard everything around them while seemingly comatose.

Thought for the Day

Don't be shocked by who you see or don't see in heaven. Fortunately for us, God is the righteous judge who knows all things, including who should really be there.

DAY 63

*Do not be afraid of sudden terror, nor of trouble
from the wicked when it comes.*

—Proverbs 3:25

Sudden Terror

I t has been said that police work can be defined as "hours of sheer boredom punctuated by moments of sheer terror." If you have been in law enforcement for any time at all, you know the meaning of "sudden terror." One minute, you can be driving down the street on a peaceful weeknight patrol shift, and the next minute, you are in a wild pursuit or in a confrontation with an armed subject.

David, the author of the above verse, knew a little bit about terror and being pursued by the wicked. He had to go into hiding when King Saul sought to take his life. Yet his trust in the Lord was unshakable.

All first responder careers are definitely more of a marathon than a sprint. We will have our moments of terror throughout our time on the job. It is great to know that God will always be with us in those moments and will never forsake us.

Thought for the Day

Don't fear the terror of the wicked, God is greater.

DAY 64

"For I am the Lord, I do not change; Therefore you are not consumed, O sons of Jacob.

—Malachi 3:6

Changes

Years ago, I attended the Orange County North versus South All-Star football game at Dick Tucker Field in Costa Mesa, California. I was there to watch a friend's son play wide receiver for the North team. As I sat in the stands, a young man seated in front of me turned around and asked, "Did you play football?" I told him that I had, and he then asked me, "Did you ever play in this game?" I answered, "Yes, I did," and waited for the question that I knew was coming, "When did you play?" It was the first time I ever had to actually say it out loud, "Thirty-five years ago tonight." The look of shock on this young man's face said it all. That number seemed so long ago to him that I'm sure he was wondering if we had helmets "back then," or if we had just kicked the king's head around as they did in the Middle Ages. He was also surprised to find that I had once been an offensive lineman. Considering my current size when compared to today's three-hundred-pound standard, I'm sure it didn't make any sense to him. Not only am I not what I used to be, but also I never was what they are now.

Time passes, things change, we decline, but isn't it good to know that the God we serve never does? He is the same today as He was yesterday, and as He will be tomorrow. He is the same God who created the earth, parted the Red Sea, healed the sick, and rose from the dead in the person of Jesus Christ. He is the same God who can hear your prayers and has the unchanged ability to respond to your situation, no matter how dire your circumstances may seem. God has only one requirement to obtain this assured admittance into His presence. If you have turned the control of your life over to Him and accepted Jesus Christ as the Lord of your life, you have access to an unchanging God in this life as well as in the next.

Thought for the Day

Our abilities may change over time, but God's never will; He is just as strong and ready to play today as He has ever been.

DAY 65

I will instruct you and teach you in the way you
should go; I will guide you with My eye.

—Psalm 32:8

Talk to the Hand

Early in my law enforcement career, I was sent to search for an attempted murder suspect on the east side of the city. He had shot the victim in the man's home before fleeing the scene. The suspect was still at large, and the crime resulted in the deployment of numerous officers to the area.

As I walked down the sidewalk in front of a residence about a block from the crime scene, a man approached me from the porch of an adjacent house. He said to me, "I just shot someone." It was quite a surprise to have the suspect that we were all looking for walk right up to me so that I could arrest him. As I stood with him in the front yard of the residence, I called out to one of the senior officers who was walking down the middle of the street with a long rifle in his hands. He continued to look down the street and placed his hand, palm out in my direction (a talk to the hand motion), and continued to walk northbound. Apparently, he was so focused on his mission to find the suspect that he didn't have time to back me up with the arrest of the very man that he was so intently looking for.

Sometimes we do the same thing to God as we attempt to navigate through the problems in our lives. We are so focused on our plan that we don't see that He is standing in plain sight, calling out to us with the answer to the very problem that we are struggling with. We may even hear His voice, but we continue to walk in the direction that we want.

The above verse in Psalms states that God is eager to instruct and teach us in the way we should go. All we need to do is to be willing to listen to Him through his word, through the Holy Spirit's leading, and through wise counsel. God loves us and only wants the best for our lives.

Thought for the Day

Don't make God "talk to the hand" as He calls out to you with the answers to your problems.

DAY 66

Yea, though I walk through the valley of the shadow of death, I will fear no evil; For You are with me.

—Psalm 23:4

Death Valley

Many years ago, we were in the West Oceanfront alley responding to a "shots fired" call. We all know that most of these calls in Newport Beach will be either firecrackers, or a car backfiring. When I arrived on scene, I became immediately aware that this one was different. There were spent 9 mm casings all over the pavement in the alley. It was obvious that a shooter had been there and might still be! As we searched the alley from breezeway to breezeway, and trash can to trash can, I briefly looked up to the sky and noticed that it was one of those incredible pitch-black star-filled nights. I knew we were in a position that would leave us completely vulnerable if the shooter was still there and decided to target us next. I remember thinking, *Well, at least I got to see that incredible night sky one last time.*

For the accountants and office types of the world, that kind of thought has probably never crossed their minds while they are at work. But we know that it is part of the first responder's job and will always be as we continue to protect others.

The truth is that when we are in situations like this, we are never alone. God promises that even though you walk through the valley of the shadow of death, He is there.

Thought for the Day

I don't need to tell you that this world is a dangerous place and becoming more so all the time. But if you put your trust and faith in Jesus Christ, He will always be by your side.

DAY 67

*"I am leaving you with a gift—peace of mind and heart. And the peace
I give is a gift the world cannot give. So don't be troubled or afraid.*
—John 14:27

Peace Near the Fire

A couple of years ago, I agreed to perform a wedding for my niece
in Norman, Oklahoma. The ceremony was conducted outside at
a beautiful rustic old train depot in the center of town. The building
and surrounding grounds made for one of the coolest venues where
I have officiated a wedding. There was one problem. The depot was
located next to a functioning train track that was still in regular use.
Every thirty minutes or so, a train would literally come barreling
through the location about thirty yards from where the altar had
been set up. Due to the length of the trains, it would take several
minutes for the cars to clear the area and for the accompanying noise
to subside. If I didn't time my ceremony correctly, there could be a
long pause in the proceedings as we waited for the noise to end. To
make matters worse, I tried to time the space between the train's passing and was unable to get a definite "quiet window of opportunity." I
have to say that I didn't feel much "peace of mind and heart" during
the service. I am not usually known to go long, but I think that was
the shortest, fast-talking ceremony in Norman, Oklahoma, history!

Sometimes the circumstances of our lives can seem chaotic and
unsettling. We may feel like a freight train of trouble comes barreling
by us at sporadic intervals that can ruin our peace as we wait for the
other "shoe of adversity" to drop. The above verse in John records

the very words of our Savior as He spoke to an anxious crowd. "I am leaving you with a gift—peace of mind and heart."

So how do we access this unlikely peace? C. S. Lewis wrote, "If you want to get warm you must stand near the fire...If you want joy...peace, eternal life, you must get close to...the thing that has them." And according to the second half of our verse for the day we find who has the peace we seek, "And the peace I give is a gift the world cannot give. So, don't be troubled or afraid."

Thought for the Day

Stand near the fire, get close to Him, read His word, do what it says, and warm yourself with His peaceful truth.

DAY 68

*Diverse weights and diverse measures, they are
both alike, an abomination to the Lord.*

—Proverbs 20:10

Even Justice

**I will never act officiously or permit
personal feelings, prejudices, animosities, or
friendships to influence my decisions.**

The above statement is found in the Law Enforcement Officer's
Code of Ethics, and it is our pledge to dispense justice in an
even and fair manner. During my career as a police officer, I was
always impressed by the way my fellow officers treated those whom
they came into contact with. Regardless of the subject's economic,
social, or racial differences, I saw them demonstrate the same due
diligence when it came to investigating crimes or providing other
police services. Of course, there was the rare exception, but the positive contacts far outweighed the negative ones despite the spin that
many in the far left and the media attempted to portray as a negative
standard in law enforcement.

God hates uneven justice. The above verse in Proverbs speaks
of the weights that were used to determine the price of goods in the
ancient world. Unscrupulous vendors would sometimes use incorrect
weights to cheat patrons from the full portion of an item that they
were purchasing. These shopkeepers would have one set of weights
they would use to buy merchandise and another to sell the inventory.
Both would look correct, but in reality, they were altered to give the

merchant an unfair advantage. Proverbs tells us that God thinks that this kind of practice is an "abomination" to Him.

I realize that I am biased in favor of police officers, but I think that this idea of total fairness is something that the United States law enforcement community has down and that the rest of the world might need to catch up with. In no other job are employees video recorded, scrutinized, and evaluated as in American policing. If we are unfair in our administration of justice, we can be prosecuted, criminally, federally, civilly, and departmentally. There are few other careers where the consequences of injustice can be so severe, and the level of success so great.

Thought for the Day

God hates diverse weights. He loves first responders.

DAY 69

*My eyes are on all their ways; they are not hidden from
me, nor is their sin concealed from my eyes.*

—Jeremiah 16:17

Obviously Broken

During my senior year at the University of Southern California, we were playing a day game in our home stadium, the Los Angeles Coliseum. I was on the sideline when one of our defensive players, Chip Banks, ran off the field and walked over to me. Chip was a great linebacker for us who went on to be a four-time pro bowler and played for the Cleveland Browns, San Diego Chargers, and the Indianapolis Colts. When Chip removed his helmet, I noticed that he had his right hand over his nose. As he lowered his hand, he said to me, "Does it look bad?" I then saw that Chip's helmet had been forced down during the previous play and had broken the bridge of his nose. Broken noses were not uncommon, but this break had left Chip's nose looking like, well, I guess there is no other way to say it, like a pig's snout! It took all I had to not let the expression on my face reveal my true reaction when I told him, "It's not so bad, man, you're all right."

We might be able to hide the sin from those around us, but nothing can be hidden from God. You might say that it is as plain as the broken nose on your face! The good news is that our sin is not a surprise to God. He knew us before the world began. He knew everything about us and was well aware of every last thing we would do or say in our lives. God did not walk around the corner for a minute only to return to be shocked by what we had done. And here is the unbelievable news, He loves us anyway! Romans 5:8 tells us, *"But God demonstrated His own love towards us, in that while we were yet sinners, Christ died for us."*

The apostle Paul had many sins in his past that could have made it hard for him to believe God could really forgive and love him. But this is what he wrote in Romans 8:38–39, *"For I am persuaded that neither death nor life, nor angels nor principalities nor powers, nor things present nor things to come, nor height nor depth, nor any other created thing, shall be able to separate us from the love of God which is in Christ Jesus our Lord."* *"For I am persuaded."* Paul, with all his past, had been convinced by God that the plainly evident sin in his life could be forgiven, and that God loved him in spite of it.

Have you been persuaded, really persuaded? Are you convinced that your clearly visible brokenness can be seen and forgiven by God?

Thought for the Day

Forgiveness is not about what you feel, or how you look, it is about what Jesus did on the cross for you. Surrender your life to Him and let him convince you.

DAY 70

O LORD, You have searched me and known me. You know my sitting down and my rising up; You understand my thought afar off. You comprehend my path and my lying down, And are acquainted with all my ways; For there is not a word on my tongue, But behold, O LORD, You know it altogether. You have hedged me behind and before, And laid Your hand upon me. Such knowledge is too wonderful for me; It is high, I cannot attain it.

—Psalm 139:1–6

Father Knows Best

Handcuffs are a standard piece of law enforcement equipment. They are usually placed on defendants after they have been arrested. But sometimes it is required to restrain distraught individuals for their own safety. Police officers have been forced to handcuff the loved ones of recently deceased subjects, one or both verbal combatants in domestic situations, and individuals experiencing some sort of medical emergency. Many were released after the situation had stabilized and when they no longer posed a threat to the responding officers.

God loves us, and sometimes we need to be restrained for our own protection. He may close the door on what we perceive as a golden opportunity in order to keep us from a negative future that only He can see. He may allow a seemingly difficult situation into our lives with the intent to guide us in a direction that we had never considered. Or God might simply say no to a request that He knows is not in our own best interest.

It is never a good idea to fight after you have been handcuffed. I've seen suspects give themselves significant injures by struggling against the restraints that had been placed on them.

Thought for the Day

Don't get hurt fighting a constraint that God has placed in your life. He knows you and He loves you. Your Father always knows best.

DAY 71

You will keep Him in perfect peace, Whose mind is stayed on
You, Because He trusts in You. Trust in the LORD forever,
For in YAH, the LORD, is everlasting strength.

—Isaiah 26:3–4

Leap of Faith

When I was on duty, I trusted my partners. I placed my life in their hands many times, and as I write this devotional, I still have a pulse, so I guess we can assume that they never let me down. Trust is vital to any organization or relationship. In Steven Covey's book *Speed of Trust*, he states that trust not only raises the moral and positive atmosphere of a work environment, but it also has an "economic benefit." Organizations that have a high level of trust built into their culture will experience increased productivity resulting in greater operational and financial rewards.

In God's economy, the word "trust" is used to encourage His followers to have faith in Him. The Bible defines faith as "*the substance of things hoped for, the evidence of things not seen*" (Hebrews 11:1).

In the movie *Indiana Jones and the Last Crusade*, we see this type of faith demonstrated when the main character took a "leap of faith," in order to cross the gorge to find the Holy Grail. He stepped out into what appeared to be a certain fall to his death, only to discover that the situation was not as he thought. A camouflaged bridge had been there the whole time that would lead him safely to the other side.

At first, trusting in God can be a difficult thing. We are asked to step out into the unknown and frightening areas of our lives. But the more we do, the more we realize that God is faithful and will always be there for us. Isaiah 41:10 tells us, *"Fear not, for I am with you; Be not dismayed, for I am your God. I will strengthen you, Yes I will help you, I will uphold you with My righteous right hand."*

Does God want you to step out into the unknown today in some area of your life? If you have faith in your partners, how much more can you trust in a God who loves you so much that He came to earth in human form and died for you on the cross?

Thought for the Day

Step out in faith, and God will reward you with a bridge to the other side of your problem.

DAY 72

Also I heard the voice of the Lord, saying: "Whom shall I send,
And who will go for Us?" Then I said, "Here am I! Send me."
—Isaiah 6:8

Go Where?

Nothing is more rewarding in the life of a Christian than to be used by God. Many of those who have committed their lives to the Lordship of Jesus Christ will have no problem saying, "Here am I! Send me." They might even have a few good ideas as to where God should send them and exactly how they should be used.

As police officers, we always like to be in the middle of the action. I don't know any cop who doesn't want to be at the termination of a pursuit where they can see the suspect taken into custody. This tendency is why most departments have limits on the number of vehicles that are allowed in a pursuit. If they didn't, the entire shift would be at the scene. As much as I wanted to be in the action, I can't tell you how many times I was given an assignment on the perimeter of the incident where my job was to direct traffic or lay down flares. I knew that what I was doing was important, but listening to the radio traffic far from the scene was not where I wanted to be.

It is easy to say, "Send me Lord," until we get an assignment that we don't like. We might say to ourselves, "But, Lord, I want so badly to be used by You" and we have another job or ministry in mind. If we are to call Him Lord, we have to realize that the plan for the direction of our lives isn't settled by a democratic vote. He should have the final word in whatever we say or do. If God's will for our lives makes us unhappy, it is only an indicator that we are not seeking

Him at that moment. I have to admit that I've been disappointed plenty of times by that failed promotional process, specialty selection, or unfulfilled ministry desire. But God knows what is best for us, and it is our job to obey His orders according to His timing no matter how we may feel about them. Don't let Satan tempt you into thinking that God doesn't know what He is doing or that He doesn't care about you.

Thought for the Day

> *For I know the thoughts that I think toward you, says the Lord, thoughts of peace and not evil, to give you a future and a hope.* (Jeremiah 29:11)

DAY 73

For He shall give His angels charge over you,
To keep you in all your ways.

—Psalm 91:11

Invisible Guardians

When I was in the Investigations Division, I worked with an undercover team whose task was to trail an infamous child molester. He was the main suspect in a cold case involving the murder of a thirteen-year-old boy. The subject was a resident in our city, and we wanted to make sure that he did not repeat any of his suspected, or confirmed, past criminal activity.

As we followed him around the city, it was a little creepy to watch him interact with various young men in a "flirting fashion." They were blissfully unaware of who they were talking with even though we all knew exactly what he was capable of. His actions just skirted around his parole restrictions at the time, and there was nothing we could legally do to stop him.

But the truth is that those young men were not in any real danger. We were there invisibly, and silently watching every move the suspect made. It would have been a dark day for him if he had tried anything. A large group of armed angry men would have descended on him immediately.

Our assignment finally ended when the district attorney put together a case and charged him with the murder mentioned earlier. He was found guilty and was given a sentence of death. In May of 2012, he avoided final judgment, on this earth anyway, when he committed suicide in his jail cell at San Quentin prison.

The above verse in Psalms tells us that God has his angels invisibly, silently watching over us. They are there to protect us and to keep us according to God's will. Now I must admit that I don't always understand that will, but God promises us that He loves us and that He is in control.

Thought for the Day

It is good to know that God's angels have our back even when we can't see that they are there.

DAY 74

For My yoke is easy and My burden is light."
—Matthew 11:30

Weighed Down

I used to be a regular mountain bike rider. I sold my bike years ago when I moved to a place that did not have any access to off-road options. When I moved back to Mission Viejo, I wanted to take advantage of the hilly terrain found in the area. To vary my workout, and because I missed riding, I bought a bike again. I decided to ride the streets near my home. After all, they were not nearly as challenging as the mountain paths I used to tackle. On my first ride, I found that was not the case. I had great difficulty riding up the steep hill that led to my home. The term "great difficulty" was not really sufficient for what I experienced. "Almost died" was more accurate. I had to resign myself to the fact that I was getting older and I just could not do what I used to be able to do.

After several weeks of "difficult" rides, I took a closer look at the bike I had purchased. I weighed it and was surprised to find that it was forty-three pounds. That was a good twenty pounds heavier than my old mountain bike! I also realized that where I used to have eighteen gears, I now only had seven. I decided to go back to the store and buy an inexpensive mountain bike. It was still heavy, but it had one big difference, twenty-one gears! I went back to the before-mentioned steep hill and tried again. I found that with the right gearing, I made it up the hill without an issue. So, it wasn't my declined fitness level or my age that was the problem. I had the wrong equipment for the job.

The above verse in Matthew records Jesus's words to those who had labored their entire lives under the weight of the law. Jesus had good news! They could now let Him take on the burden of their sin. The problem they had up to that point was the inaccurate belief that through the law they would be able to lift the weight of that sin from their own lives. But that is not what the law was about. Galatians 3:24 tells us that "*wherefore the law was our schoolmaster to bring us unto Christ, that we might be justified by faith.*" The law was there to show them the impossibility of earning their own salvation. It was all about what Jesus did for them through His death and resurrection, and their faith in that completed work.

Now if we place our faith in Him, then Christ's words, "*My yoke is easy and My burden is light,*" can become a reality in our lives too. We no longer have to fight under the weight of sin when our redemption has been purchased for us by Jesus. If we are believers in Jesus Christ, and if we have already dedicated our lives to Him, we can rest in His promise to us of an easy yoke and a light burden.

Thought for the Day

Jesus has already purchased the right equipment to give us eternal life and to get us up the hills of this life. We need to live like we believe that truth, then there won't be any place He cannot take us to.

DAY 75

You will know them by their fruits. Do men gather
grapes from thornbushes or figs from thistles?
—Matthew 7:16

Actions, Not Words

As a police officer, I had to make quick decisions that had serious
consequences for others. When I was in the middle of a field
investigation, I would often be confronted with a variety of varying
accounts of an event that had just occurred. It was sometimes hard
to weed through the conflicting statements to get to the truth. I had
to be reasonably convinced of what had really happened, especially
when an arrest could result. I cannot tell you how many times an
individual's actions would lead me to the truth of their guilt in spite
of their seemingly sincere denials. Whether it was their past record,
involuntary physical tells, or their general attitude, I often learned
more about their guilt through their actions over their words.

Andrew Carnegie, the great nineteenth-century industrialist
and philanthropist, was quoted as saying, "As I grow older, I pay less
attention to what men say. I just watch what they do." If I have any
one piece of advice for Christian singles and their search for a spouse,
it would be to take heed of these words. The above verse in Matthew
tells us that *"you will know them by their fruits."* That is, regardless of
what they say, the actions of their lives will tell you the truth.

Anyone who wants to date a member of the opposite sex can say
wonderful things and might even be able to "white-knuckle" their
actions for a while to match those words. But eventually their true
self will come out. They might claim to be a born-again, committed

Christian, but will they read God's word and pray with you regularly? Did they attend church as God's word commands even before they knew you, and would they continue to do so even in your absence? Are they committed to honor God and maintain sexual purity until they are married? Are they reliable people of their word, and are they willing to put others' needs before their own desires?

This is not just for single people but also for any other type of relationship in our lives. When the Bible tells us that we are not to be "*unequally yoked together with unbelievers*" (2 Corinthians 6:14), it should have implications as to whom we get into business with, whom we have as our closest friends, or whom we look to for advice and counsel. We need to watch what they do and not just listen to what they say. If we followed that advice, it would have an effect on all our future relationships. It could even have an effect over who we vote for!

Thought for the Day

Actions speak louder than words. Are you watching?

DAY 76

We give no offense in anything, that our ministry may not be blamed.
—2 Corinthians 6:3

Weird Words

Ten-thirteen to 10-19 for 10-45? If you are a civilian or not on a police department who uses the 10 code, you would have no idea that the above radio transmission would be generated to ask Dispatch if it was clear for an officer to come to the station for an equipment problem. We use codes to shorten our transmissions, clarify our messages, and to keep our activities private from those outside of law enforcement. To us, they have a useful purpose, but to others, these codes make no sense at all. If I were to talk to everyone in police code, I would be viewed as weird, creepy, and possibly a little deranged.

At times, believers can get involved with code talk in our personal lives. Whether we are talking to churchgoers or unchurched people, we tend to use Christianese, which can be confusing to those who are not familiar with it. Sometimes this is done unintentionally, but at other times, it is done to sound more spiritual to those around us. We all know those who "amen," "brother or sister," and "praise the Lord" themselves into the weird category that serves to push people away from God and hinder true and honest communication with others.

What's wrong with talking normal? Whether it is about our relationship with Christ or to fellowship with other believers in the church, why do we feel that we need to use strange vernacular to get our points across? First Corinthians 9:22–23 tells us, "*To the weak I became as weak, that I might win the weak. I have become all things to all men, that I might by all means save some. Now this I do for the gospel's sake, that I may be partaker of it with you.*"

As a former athlete and police officer, I have had to navigate secular language for the majority of my life and have done so with various levels of failure and success. It can be difficult for the Christian not to get sucked into improper communication as we strive to become "all things to all men." But just as we know that the use of profanity can hurt our testimony for Christ, we need to know that sometimes the use of Christianese can result in the same thing.

The answer to this problem starts in the same way as any other desired change in our lives, with prayer. We need to ask the Lord to help us to communicate with others in the most effective way possible without becoming an offense to His purposes. Then we just need to be ourselves!

Thought for the Day

You don't need to use a vocabulary of weird words to reach others for Christ.

DAY 77

This is good and pleases God our Savior, who wants everyone to be saved and to understand the truth. For there is only one God and one Mediator who can reconcile God and Humanity—the man Christ Jesus. He gave his life to purchase freedom for everyone.

—1 Timothy 2:3–6

Bible Audit

When I was in college, there were two ways to get credit for a class. You could either receive the standard letter grade, or you could take the course "pass/fail." Taking the class pass/fail would mean that you fulfilled the minimum requirements needed to have received a C grade or better. That was okay if you got a C, but not so good if you would have received an A. Of course, there were some who would just "audit" the class. This meant that a student would attend class without being officially signed up for it. They would not have to take tests or complete all the assignments and would not receive any credit on a school transcript. Their sole purpose for attending would be for self-enrichment and academic exploration.

I have seen many nonbelievers who treat the Bible that same way. They read it to receive self-enrichment and to conduct moral exploration. In times of trouble, they may even quote it in an attempt to claim a specific promise for their lives. Romans 8:28, "*All things work together for good,*" is such a verse. People who have not made Jesus Christ the Lord of their lives will incorrectly believe it is a universal promise that God is working to make the bad things that happen to us work out for the good for all people. That is actually not true. The first half of Romans 8:28 does say that "*all things work together for good*," but the second half of the verse qualifies that statement by adding, "*For those who love God and are called according to His purpose.*" And what is the purpose of God in this life? First Timothy 2:3–6 tells us, "*This is good and pleases God our Savior, who wants everyone to be saved and to understand the truth. For there is only one God and one Mediator who can reconcile God and Humanity—the man Christ Jesus. He gave His life to purchase freedom for everyone.*"

If you have not confessed Jesus as the Lord of your life, and received His free gift of salvation, the Bible is simply a collection of good words and uplifting stories. The promises it contains do not apply to you. You are just auditing the course of this life and will receive no credit for your effort in eternity. But if you have turned over the complete control of your life to Jesus, then all the promises, benefits, and peace available for this life and the next, documented in God's word, belong to you.

Thought for the Day

Receive Jesus now and take this life for credit that will be placed on your eternal transcript.

DAY 78

And which of you by worrying can add one cubit to his stature? If you then are not able to do the least, why are you anxious for the rest? Consider the lilies, how they grow: they neither toil nor spin; and yet I say to you, even Solomon in all his glory was not arrayed like one of these. If then God so clothes the grass, which today is in the field and tomorrow is thrown into the oven, how much more will He clothe you, O you of little faith? And do not seek what you should eat or what you should drink, nor have an anxious mind. For these things the nations of the world seek after, and your Father knows that you need these things. But seek ye first the kingdom of God, and all these things shall be added unto you.
　　　　　　　　　　　　　　　　　　　　　　—Luke 12:25–31

Unfunded Loan Payments

These words that Jesus spoke to His disciples two thousand years ago are just as true today as they were then. God knows our needs and has promised to provide for us if we seek Him first. I've learned from personal experience that this is easier said than done. I've been a Christian for fifty-seven years, and I still struggle with worry sometimes. The more I experience in this life, the more God has convinced me that He is faithful, and His word is true. When I look back on all the things that I chose to worry about, I realize two things: God was always there to meet my needs in His perfect timing, and most of the things I was so anxious about never ended up happening anyway. They say that worry is like making payments on a loan before it is funded. I've found that worry has been a colossal waste of my time.

God loves you, knows your needs, and has a plan for your life that can only be realized if you have accepted Jesus Christ as your savior and Lord. As you read this today, God is lining things up for you, bringing people into place, and has the resources needed to answer your prayers. God is able, but it is our choice to trust in Him or not.

Thought for the Day

As a fellow traveler down the senseless road of worry, let's choose, just for today, to believe that He will provide for us. Let's not start making payments on that loan just yet.

DAY 79

*These were more noble than those in Thessalonica, in that
they received the word with all readiness of mind, and
searched the scriptures daily, whether those things were so.*

—Acts 17:11

Check the Credentials

When I was working undercover, I wore civilian clothing. From
my grooming standards (or lack of them) at the time, it was
hard for anyone to believe that I was a police officer. I often contacted subjects who doubted that I was in law enforcement. Even
though I had my badge and identification with me, witnesses and
victims often called into the station to confirm that there really was
an officer named Brad Green who worked for the Newport Beach
Police Department. I was never bothered by their doubt and felt it
was a good idea for them to confirm who I was.

The above verse in Acts talks about those who heard the gospel
and searched the scriptures daily, whether those things were so. They
didn't just take the word of what a teacher had told them about God
and His purposes for their lives.

That's as good of an idea now as it was then. If you are attending
a church whose doctrine seems to veer away from the plain simple
truths found in God's word, leave! I have seen too many lives ruined
by a false loyalty to a location over adherence to His word. Always
test what you are being told by what you read in the Bible.

Thought for the Day

Don't take anything at face value; always check their credentials via the word of God.

DAY 80

The beloved of the Lord shall dwell in safety by Him;
and the Lord shall cover him all the day long.
—Deuteronomy 33:12

Thank You, Lord!

I had a roommate at USC who was also on the football team. Myron was a large blond-haired Viking type who was extremely strong. He once had his picture taken holding a motorcycle off the ground (right hand on the front fork and his left hand on the rear suspension) for a lightweight bike advertisement. The only misleading thing about the ad was that the motorcycle wasn't that light.

One day at practice, I was sent over to help with the defensive line. It was a one-on-one tackling drill where there was a defensive lineman, an offensive lineman, and a running back. The drill was designed to simulate a running play and help the defensive lineman practice shedding a block and making a tackle. When it was my turn, I went against my roommate Myron. When the ball was snapped, I hit Myron and grabbed the outside of his right shoulder pad. As I pulled his right shoulder in toward me, I pushed out with my left hand on his left shoulder. This is an old offensive line trick that some would call holding, but as a slightly undersized Trojan lineman I called it survival! The twisting motion took Myron by surprise, and he went straight to the ground. As the running back went by, he tapped Myron on the helmet just to add insult to injury. The legendary USC defensive coach Marv Goux ran over to Myron, kicked him, and yelled, "What are you doing on the ground!" I got back in line and waited for my next turn up. I saw Myron count back to see where my place in line was. I then watched as he slipped into the same spot in his line so he could be my next opponent. I knew what this meant. Revenge was imminent.

You see, Myron wore these red leather Everlast sparring gloves for hand protection. He had become an expert in their use, and I had witnessed their effectiveness on numerous occasions. It looked like a broken nose, or at least a bloody one, was in my immediate future. As I ran to the line coach, Goux looked at me, smiled, and said, "Get out of here." I've never been so thankful to return to the offensive line drills at the other end of the practice field.

We can always be thankful to God for his protection from the things we see coming, and from those that we don't.

Thought for the Day

We have no idea how many "bloody noses" God has kept us from.

DAY 81

Nor is He worshiped with men's hands, as though he needed anything, since he gives to all life, breath, and all things.

—Acts 17:25

Deep Diving

Underwater visibility varies greatly depending upon the weather, marine life, and topography of the area you are diving in. As a scuba diver, I spent most of my time at Catalina Island where the visibility was better than on the surgy Southern California coast. But even on its best day, the visibility at Catalina is no better than 40 to 50 feet. When you are diving within the first pressure atmosphere (33 feet), you can usually see the surface from the bottom and are shallow enough to come up quickly in the event of an emergency, like running out of air! Deep diving is a little trickier.

I have dived on the shipwreck of the Valiant many times. The Valiant is a pleasure yacht that burned and sank off the coast of Catalina in 1930. Due to the slope of the ocean floor, the bow (front) of the ship is in about 70 feet of water and the stern (back) rests at about 110 feet. This is considered a deep dive that requires more training and preparation. At that depth, you enter the third and fourth pressure atmosphere where nitrogen buildup and decompression become issues. Due to how far I went down, I spent more time getting back to the surface because of the required safety decompression stops than the 15 minutes of bottom time I was allowed due to the advanced depth.

There are several things that strike you when you are 110 feet underwater. First, you can't see the surface, not even close. This is where some succumb to claustrophobia and panic (not good). At that depth, you also realize that there is no easy way out if a problem arises and shooting straight to the surface could be lethal. And lastly, when you realize that you are currently the slowest thing floating in this "no man's land," the theme music from Jaws pops into your head.

Sometimes we can feel so far under the surface of life's problems that we can see no way out. We think that no matter which way we swim, our problems will only get worse. But if we have given the control of our lives to Jesus Christ, we will have an endless supply of what we need to survive regardless of the size of our problems or the depth of our despair. We need to have faith in Him because He is the one who gives us our very "*life, breath, and all things.*"

Thought for the Day

Let's commit ourselves to rest in the middle of our problems even when they seem to have no answer. You will never run out of air if you put your trust in Him.

DAY 82

Now the two angels came to Sodom in the evening, and Lot was sitting in the gate of Sodom. When Lot saw them, he rose to meet them and he bowed himself with his face toward the ground.

—Genesis 19:1

Run!

As I read this verse, something jumped out at me. What was Lot doing there? In Genesis 13:12–13, we see that Lot had chosen to live in the area of Sodom whose inhabitants were well-known as *"exceedingly wicked and sinful against the Lord"* (verse 13). I think that Lot went to the city to "watch the show" of wickedness that must have been a daily occurrence there.

Every July 4, the Newport Beach Police Department has full deployment due to the revelry on the west side of town. Citizens often asked me, "Why does everyone pack into our city on the Fourth, what's the big attraction?" If you have ever worked down there on Independence Day, you know the answer. Young males come for alcohol, women in bikinis, and to see the numerous arrests for intoxication, battery, and possession of contraband. It is what they call a real "party." Some people even bring their children (in strollers) to watch the general evil that goes on with the excuse of celebrating a national holiday. I felt like handing out CARs (Child Abuse Reports) to each parent I saw with a child out in the city on the Fourth.

What is it about evil that is so attractive to us? God says that it is part of our nature, it is just in our DNA (Matthew 15:19). He also provides us with the answer to the temptation evil can bring. First Corinthians 6:18, 1 Corinthians 10:4, 1 Timothy 6:11, and 2

Timothy 2:22 all contain the same word in connection with resisting temptation: FLEE!

Sometimes the only way we can avoid giving in to temptation is to not be where we might be tempted. Lot had the wrong idea. He was hanging around the city gate of Sodom. Nothing good can come from placing ourselves in harm's way. It is like continually walking near the edge of a cliff. Sooner or later, you will slip and fall into the canyon.

God's word says that *"no temptation has overtaken you except such as is common to man; but God is faithful, who will not allow you to be tempted beyond what you are able, but with the temptation will also make the way of* **escape***, that you may be able to bear it."* (1 Corinthians 10:13).

Thought for the Day

Sometimes running from the evil that confronts us can be the bravest thing we can do!

DAY 83

Now when the devil had ended every temptation, he
departed from Him until an opportune time.

—Luke 4:13

Evil Persistence

During my tenure as a police officer, we had a notorious transient who was arrested over four hundred times by our department for mostly intoxication/alcohol violations. I don't think there was an officer who had not arrested Bill (not his real name), and most like myself had taken him into custody multiple times. I first arrested Bill when I was a rookie cop in training, and had many dealings with him over the next twenty-one years. There were periods when we did not hear from him, but those times were short-lived, and Bill would always turn up again requiring police intervention of some kind. He was such a regular arrestee that I had a copy of his booking form in my posse box (metal form case) so I would not have to look up his identifying information each time I contacted him. Two weeks after I retired, I heard that Bill had passed away at a fairly young age due to the years of physical abuse he had put his body through. His choices in life finally caught up with him.

As I was reading the above passage in Luke, I read something I had not thought about before. When Jesus had endured forty days of deprivation and temptation, the devil finally left Him after his numerous attempts to entice Jesus to sin had failed. The passage said that "he departed from Him until an opportune time." The New Living Translation makes it very clear by saying, "He left Him until the next opportunity came." It was obvious that Satan was not through trying to tempt Jesus despite his failure on this one particular occasion.

The enemy will keep turning up in our lives in his continued effort to get us to fall. There might be times when our temptations seem to take a hiatus, but we can always count on them to return, in one form or another, as Satan continues his attacks on us. This will, unfortunately, be our situation for the remainder of our lives as we struggle with our own sin nature.

The good news, however, is twofold! First, Hebrews 4:15 assures us that Jesus "was in all *points* tempted as *we are.*" He knows what it feels like to be enticed to do wrong and can sympathize with our situation. Secondly, Jesus made the provision for our forgiveness when we do sin by his death on the cross. First John 2:2 tells us, "*He himself is the sacrifice that atones for our sins—and not only our sins but the sins of all the world.*" We might not be able to escape temptation and sin in this world, but as we fight to do what is right in this life, we know that we can be forgiven through our faith in Jesus and His sacrifice on our behalf.

Thought for the Day

We shouldn't be surprised when we find ourselves tempted, yet again, by the same old adversary. Fight to resist, ask for forgiveness if we fail, and rest in the assurance that Jesus understands our plight and has made provision for us before God.

DAY 84

*I will both lie down in peace, and sleep, For You
alone, O LORD, make me dwell in safety.*

—Psalm 4:8

Peace

I can be an anxious person. I don't fully understand why that is, but it is something that I struggle with at times. I know that God is in total control of my life and can be completely trusted with my future, but sometimes I still allow worry to creep into my consciousness.

Something in the above verse in Psalms struck me as I read it. *"I will both lie down in peace, and sleep."* Anyone who is a worrier knows that you can lie down and try to sleep without being able to attain any peace whatsoever.

The author of this psalm, King David, knew a lot about the possibility of anxiousness and worry. I'm sure he spent many sleepless nights in the wilderness as he fled from King Saul who planned to take David's life. But apparently, David learned to rest in God when he said, *"For You alone, O LORD, make me dwell in safety."* I'm sure that David's trust in God is one of the reasons why He said that David was "a man after My own heart." I want to be a person like that, don't you?

In his famous quote about worry, Mark Twain said, "I've had a lot of worries in my life, most of which never happened." The truth is that many of the things we are anxious about never happen anyway. The rest are in the care and control of our heavenly Father.

Thought for the Day

Let's both lie down and sleep in peace with the trust that God is watching over us.

DAY 85

And to man He said, "Behold the fear of the Lord, that is wisdom, and to depart from evil is understanding."

—Job 28:28

Fear and Avoid

As defense tactics instructors, we trained our officers about the tactics of criminals. We had video recordings of prison inmates practicing gun takeaways and restraint-hold escapes while they were incarcerated. Their purpose was to evade law enforcement custody when they were released from jail and back out on the street. Their efforts were proof positive that they had no intention of stopping their criminal activity but were looking for more effective ways to continue in it. You could say that we had a healthy respect for their capabilities whenever we contacted an ex-con on the street. It was a wise way to think.

The above verse in Job talks about how the fear of the Lord is wisdom. Does this mean we are to be terrified of God and what He might do to us? I don't believe so. But it does go further than to simply have a simple respect for God and His commandments. I think we should have a healthy fear of disobedience and the removal of God's blessing in our lives. But there is another side of the wisdom coin shown here. Not only is it wise to fear and obey the Lord, but it also shows understanding to avoid evil in our lives.

Proverbs 17:28 tells us that *"even a fool, when he holdeth his peace, is counted wise: and he that shutteth his lips is esteemed a man of understanding."* The "departing from evil" here would be to keep our mouths shut!

I have seen many people in counsel who never got the "obey God/depart evil" memo in their lives. So, I guess that according to God's word, they would be defined as unwise and without understanding.

God loves us and wants only the best for our lives. To obtain all God has for us, we need to have a respect for His word and a desire to avoid evil.

Thought for the Day

If we are truly His followers, that really is the wisest thing to do.

DAY 86

And when you look up into the sky and see the sun, moon, and stars—all the forces of heaven—don't be seduced into worshipping them. The Lord your God gave them to all the peoples of the earth.
—Deuteronomy 4:19

Misguided Worship

Gobekli Tepe, the oldest temple ever discovered by archeologists, is found in southern Turkey. It predates the pyramids by thousands of years and was built to worship the star Sirius which is commonly referred to as the Dog Star. Sirius is the brightest star in the night sky and is only 8.6 light-years from the earth. The walls of the Gobekli Tepe temple are aligned in such a way as to follow Sirius's travel across the night sky. The ancient builders of the stone shrine used it to track and worship the star as a god.

It seems that man has always been predisposed to worship the heavens as mentioned in the above verse in Deuteronomy. God warns us not to be seduced into worshiping heavenly objects and that He made them for us to enjoy, not to deify. The modern version of heaven worshippers are those who practice and believe in astrology. The belief that the alignment of the planets and stars can predict your personality, financial future, and personal relationships is somewhat accepted in today's world as anything from a fun curiosity to a serious religion.

We might not go as far as to participate in the worship of the heavens as described in Deuteronomy, but we might be guilty of other kinds of subtle idol worship. In my life, I have seen people worship money, fame, pleasure, and themselves. Some even worship things that seem good, like their family, the church they attend, or even a ministry they serve in. The truth is anything we put before God can become an idol in our lives. Deuteronomy 5:6–7 tells us, "*I am the Lord your God who brought you out of the land of Egypt, out of the house of bondage. You shall have no other gods before Me.*"

Thought for the Day

We don't have to kneel before the stars, a stone temple, or a carved image to worship an idol. Let's be careful to put Him first in our lives before anything else.

DAY 87

Yea, though I walk through the valley of the shadow of death. I will fear no evil: for thou art with me; thy rod and thy staff, they comfort me.
—Psalm 23:4

God Is Always with Us

First, I want to say God is good!

I once had a 1965 Ford Thunderbird convertible. I had issues with it and had been slowly working my way through them. I recently had the brake system worked on, replacing the master cylinder, brake hoses, and vacuum lines. I thought I had done my due diligence so that I could stop the car safely.

Well, one day, I was driving it home from church when I exited the Santa Ana Freeway at La Paz. If you know South County, the exit was bordered by a field of ice plants between the ramp and the 5 Freeway southbound traffic. As I attempted to slow my car down for the red light at La Paz road, the brake pedal went all the way to the floor. I had no brakes. Fortunately, I thought quickly and swerved my car to the left and onto the ice plant field. When I finally came to a stop, I sat in the car staring at my cellphone, trying to remember how to call AAA. As I sat there in a daze, I heard a loud pop in the area of the front right tire. When I saw smoke start to rise from the engine compartment, I quickly got out of the car and walked to a safe distance about fifty yards away. From my vantage point, I could see flames starting to rise from the hood. I immediately called the fire department who arrived a short time later.

The car was designated as a total loss two weeks later. I can't imagine what would have happened if I had made it to the busy intersection and had been unable to stop there. As it turned out, there was no traffic collision, and no injury of any kind, except for the car. I promised my wife that I would pick up stamp collecting as a hobby from that point on.

Whenever we are in trouble, or in a dangerous situation, the believer is never alone. The above verse tells us, "*I will fear no evil: for thou (God) art with me.*" What a great promise! No matter how dark, or dangerous the situation might be, God is there with us. I am certainly glad he was with me that day.

Thought for the Day

When the flames of this life threaten us, don't be afraid, God is always with us!

DAY 88

*Then you will call upon Me and go and pray
to Me, and I will listen to you.*

—Jeremiah 29:12

Straight Talk

W hen I first became a cop, there were no cell phones. At least,
we did not have the small, easy-to-carry portable devices that
we see today. If I needed to phone home, or contact anyone during
an investigation, I had to call 911 from a pay phone, and a dispatcher
would dial the number for me. This time-consuming process sometimes resulted in dropped or misdialed calls.

As followers of Jesus Christ, we do not have to go through a
two-step process in order to speak with God. The above verse in
Jeremiah informs us of one of the greatest gifts that God has given us,
direct access to Him. In Old Testament times, that was not the case.
People needed to contact God through the high priest. But if we read
Jeremiah in the light of 1 Timothy 2:5, we can see that our standing before God has changed. *"For there is one God and one Mediator
between God and men, the Man Christ Jesus."*

Through Christ's redeeming sacrifice for us on the cross, and
through His blood which he shed for us, we can now contact God
directly in Jesus's name. We no longer need to ask someone else to
talk to God for us. Whether it is a petition, prayer of forgiveness, or

even a praise, we can tell God what is on our hearts without having to ask a spiritual dispatcher to dial the call for us.

Thought for the Day

No dropped, or misdialed calls, just straight talk.

DAY 89

"God blesses you when people mock you and persecute you
and lie about you and say all sorts of evil things against you
because you are my followers. Be happy about it! Be very glad!
For a great reward awaits you in heaven, and remember,
the ancient prophets were persecuted in the same way.
—Matthew 5:11–12

Libel

As a young police officer, I made a car stop in the early morning hours on the west side of Newport Beach. The driver had failed to stop at a posted sign, and I had pulled her over for the violation. As I spoke with the subject, I saw that her pupils were dilated, she was nervous, and when I took her pulse, I found that it was elevated. These can be symptoms of drug ingestion, so I questioned her about it and searched her vehicle. I found no contraband, and when I took her pulse again, it had slowed to a normal level. I decided that she probably had larger pupils naturally, and that the other symptoms I observed where reactions due to anxiety about being pulled over by the police. I gave her a verbal warning about the stop sign violation and sent her on her way.

The next morning, I found out what the subject did for a living when I picked up the local newspaper. She was a reporter for my hometown paper and had written a story about our contact earlier that morning. I will say it was a "story" because almost nothing about what she had written had any truth to it. She accused me of actions, which if true, would have been violations of her civil rights. She quoted me as making comments that were rude and unprofessional and claimed that I had held her at the scene for more than an hour. This was at a time when we did not have video recording systems in our police units, and basically, she had carte blanche to say whatever she wanted unchallenged. The only lie that could be proven at the time was her assertion that I had kept her at the scene for an hour. Dispatched records indicated that the entire stop had taken only fifteen minutes from start to finish. If I had been able to record the stop, it would have resulted in a retraction from the paper and the termination (maybe) of the reporter. It was my first initiation to a biased media.

The above verse in Matthew warns us that as followers of Jesus Christ, we will be persecuted. People will tell lies about us in an attempt to hurt our Christian witness and, in turn, the body of Christ. We are to expect and be thankful when this happens because we will have a "great reward" waiting for us in heaven. I know that it seems a little odd to be "thankful" at times like these, but that is exactly what God wants us to do.

We have a lot to be thankful for in this country. Usually being persecuted for our faith means that we will be made fun of, or at most, lose a job. This is nothing compared to our brothers and sisters in China and the Middle East whose faith in Christ might mean the loss of their freedom, or their lives.

Thought for the Day

Expect libel, slander, and persecution, as well as the rewards that they will bring!

DAY 90

He existed before anything else, and he holds all creation together.
—Colossians 1:17

He Is in Control!

Many years ago, I was working uniformed patrol in a marked unit on the west side of town. I had just dropped off a civilian who had requested a ride home after a traffic collision. When the subject had gone inside of his residence, I exited my patrol car in order to place my gear bag back on the front passenger seat. I drove a four-wheel drive vehicle that day which had cloth seats.

Over the months, a hole had worn into the backrest portion of the driver's seat where various officers' gun butts had rubbed on the material. As I exited the vehicle, a spring from inside the seat hooked onto the cap of the magazine in my holstered duty weapon and pulled it off. The bullets from inside the magazine then fell from my gun onto the asphalt beneath the car. As one round hit the pavement, it struck a tiny pebble and discharged. The bullet came straight up and hit the back of my hand. The casing exploded, sending small pieces of shrapnel in all directions. Now if you have ever shot a gun, you know what an unbelievable occurrence this is. We drop live rounds all the time and never have such a discharge. It was truly a one-in-a-million type of deal for the primer of the bullet to hit a tiny pebble on the ground at just the perfect angle. Since the bullet was not chambered, the force on the casing went outward, and the round that struck me lost velocity. I only received a large quarter-size knot on the back of my hand, but miraculously, not one of the pieces of the exploded casing struck me, not one!

As first responders, we can take great comfort in the fact that God is in control! If we have accepted Jesus Christ as our Lord and Savior, we are not in any more danger in the middle of a storm than we are at home watching TV. Nothing can happen to us without the express permission of our almighty God.

Thought for the Day

Things in your life might seem to have spun out of control, but for those who have given their lives to Jesus Christ, He is watching over you and will hold all things together if you will only trust in Him.

DAY 91

The Lord will keep you from harm—he will watch over your life.
—Psalm 121:7

Invisible Protection

One afternoon, I was working on the west side of town near the Fun Zone. I received a call of a vehicle stuck in the sand on a stretch of beach located at the end of the Balboa Peninsula called the Wedge. When I arrived on scene, I saw a woman standing next to a car that had sunk to the top of its wheel wells in the sand. The woman had driven the vehicle an impressive distance from the street, onto the sidewalk, past a small park, and out onto the loose sand before sinking in so far that it was unable to move any further. As I spoke with the female, I quickly established that she had been the driver and was the car's registered owner. I also determined that she was elderly and in an advanced stage of dementia. She did not know who she was, where she was, or how she got there. As I attempted to locate a responsible party for her, I found out two shocking facts. One, she had a valid California driver's license, and two, she had driven her vehicle from an assisted living home in Los Angeles to Newport Beach! I could only imagine the number of turns, traffic merges, directional signs, speed limit signs, stops, and starts that this woman had to negotiate in the one-hour drive from her home to our city. It is a miracle that she didn't kill herself or someone else while en route to the place where her vehicle finally came to a stop. I often wondered how many of these types of drivers were around me without my knowledge on my daily commute.

Wherever we are, we have potential danger all around us. Some of it we can see coming, while other times we are unaware of its presence. For those of us who have given our lives to the Lordship of Jesus Christ, God is always alert to whatever situation we may find ourselves in. I came close to death many times as a police officer, and in most of those incidents, I wasn't even aware of the protection that had just been afforded me.

The above verse in Psalms tells us that God is always there, watching over our lives, keeping us from harm. I can't claim that I always know God's will, and I have questioned His protection at times when something happened to me that I didn't understand. But, through our faith in Jesus Christ, He has given us the ultimate protection over death when He paid the price for our sin on the cross. In addition to eternity, time and time again, God has protected our lives here on this earth even if we were unaware of it at the time.

Thought for the Day

As you travel through life, you don't have to be worried about what or who is driving next to you. God sees all and He is able! If you devote your life to Him, He will not let anything happen to you that is outside of His perfect will.

DAY 92

That you may be sons of your Father in heaven; for
He makes His sun rise on the evil and on the good,
and sends rain on the just and the unjust.

—Matthew 5:45

Wet Duty

As a police officer, I spent my fair share of time standing in the rain. It wasn't something that I enjoyed doing, but I couldn't stop responding to calls just because the weather was bad. I investigated traffic collisions, conducted area searches, stood on the perimeters of crime scenes, and walked a routine footbeat in what were torrential rain conditions. Usually I would have prepared myself, but there were other times when I was caught by surprise and unable to get back to my unit to retrieve my rain gear. Either way, I got soaked if the assignment kept me exposed for an extended period of time.

As believers in Jesus Christ, we are not exempt from hard times in our lives. The above verse in Matthew tells us that the rain will fall on the "just and unjust" alike. In John 16:33, we read the words of Jesus when He states, *"In the world **you will** have tribulation; but be of good cheer, I have overcome the world."* It doesn't say we "might" have hard times, or that we can have them only if we fail to follow His commandments. Christ says we "will" have times of tribulation in our lives no matter what. The good news is that He has conquered the problems of this world.

If you are experiencing a season of tribulation in your life, know that God not only sees your situation, but He also has the answer to what you are facing.

Thought for the Day

The circumstances might seem too big, the hour may seem too late, or your faith might seem too little, but God is able to wade through the storm of your life.

DAY 93

Be anxious for nothing, but in everything by prayer and
supplication, with thanksgiving, let your requests be made
known to God; and the peace which surpasses all understanding,
will guard your hearts and minds through Christ Jesus.

—Philippians 4:6-7

Active Guarding

As an intelligence officer, I was part of a team that assisted with dignitary protection. It was our job to aid various federal agencies who were responsible for the safety of diplomats, politicians, candidates, and other well-known individuals who were visitors to our city. We even aided a member of England's royal family!

Over the years, I also became involved with a pastoral protection team that was headed by a retired Secret Service agent. He had been part of Ronald Reagan's security unit, and he taught us the protocols used in presidential protection.

Guarding may seem like a passive "stand around" duty, but it most definitely is not! You are constantly searching the crowd, watching people's posture and hand motions, exchanging potential threat information with your fellow guards, and varying your tactics depending upon the size of the crowd around your subject. By the end of your shift, you are exhausted from what appeared to others to be a "no big deal, just stand there," job.

The above verse in Philippians is one of my favorites. It promises that if we ask God, Jesus Christ Himself will guard our hearts and give us a peace that passes all understanding. This is not a passive protection, but an active, dynamic defense of our hearts and minds!

He will continually work to keep the enemy's attacks away from us which would seek to rob us of our joy.

It gives me great comfort to know that if I ask Him, with thanksgiving, my Lord and Savior will be vigilantly standing guard, protecting me from worry and anxiety. This is not a human protection which can sometimes fail, but an impenetrable defense by the almighty God of the universe!

Thought for the Day

If we invite Him in, Jesus Christ will never just "stand there" as He watches over our lives.

DAY 94

*Study to show thyself approved unto God, a workman that
needeth not to be ashamed, rightly dividing the word of truth.*
—2 Timothy 2:15

What Do You Know?

Many years ago, I was recruited to play football for the University of California at Berkley. On my official trip to the campus, I was shown around by the line coach who attempted to convince me that Cal would be the best place for me to play. During one of our many conversations that day, I asked the coach a little bit about himself and his family life. When he told me that he was married, I asked if his wife was a football fan, and if she knew much about the game. In his thick Southern accent, he wrapped up his wife's football expertise in one simple statement. He said, "She don't know if a football is stuffed or pumped." Apparently, her interest and knowledge of the game were very limited.

When it comes to God's word and our relationship with Jesus Christ, can we say that we have a good working knowledge of our faith? The above verse in 2 Timothy encourages us to work hard and study so that we might understand and recognize the truth when we see it. God is not calling us all to be Biblical scholars, but rather to do our best to understand what we believe and where in God's word that truth can be found.

We will often make resolutions about things we want to accomplish or change in the months to come. Let's make a resolution to learn more about our faith and to read God's word so that we might *"be ready to give a defense to everyone who asks you a reason for the hope that is in you."* (1 Peter 3:15).

Thought for the Day

Is the knowledge of your faith stuffed or pumped?

DAY 95

My sheep hear My voice, and I know them, and they follow Me.
—John 10:27

Big Boy Voice

Just before I retired from full-time duty, I responded to a dead body call as a chaplain. A woman had died in her sleep while lying on a couch in her residence. Her twelve-year-old son, who called 911 in a panic, had found her. Not knowing that the woman was already dead, the dispatcher attempted to guide the young man through the CPR process. The incident had so traumatized the boy that he was unable to even attempt to revive his mother.

When I got to the scene, the Lord spoke to me. It wasn't in an audible voice, but I heard Him say to me loud and clear, "Go look at the body." After seeing hundreds of dead bodies over the years, I have to say that I wasn't thrilled about seeing another one to store in my mental video bank. But God told me again, "Go look at the body!" I walked in the house and stood several yards from the corpse. It was evident from the postmortem lividity (blood pool staining under the skin) that the woman had been dead for many hours before her body was found.

As I walked outside, I heard the Lord speak to me again, "He blames himself." I suddenly realized that the boy who found his mother did not have the training that I did in order to make a rough time of death estimate. As far as he knew, his inability to act during the 911 call had resulted in his mother's demise. Nothing could have been further from the truth. The coroner determined that she had passed in the early morning, four to five hours before she was found.

I was then able to talk to the boy to reassure him that he did a great job when he called 911 and that there was nothing he did or didn't do that led to his mother's death.

Have you ever had God shout at you like that? I've heard His direction through His word, I've heard a still small voice sometimes, and I heard Him shout to me as in the case above. Sometimes, He has spoken to me via circumstances in my life and other times through wise counsel.

No matter which way God chooses to speak to us, we need to listen and obey. He will not communicate to us by any certain method, and we should never expect to hear a shout. However, we should be aware and ready to move on His behalf no matter by which method He leads us.

C. S. Lewis, when speaking of pain, wrote, "God whispers to us in our pleasures, speaks to us in our conscience, but shouts to us in our pain. It is His megaphone to rouse a deaf world."

Is God speaking to you today? Has He shown you direction through His word, through the circumstances in your life, or by the wise words of others? He does not need to shout to make our need for obedience any more urgent. We need to listen to His Voice, verify it through His word, and act on what He says.

Thought for the Day

God doesn't need to use His "big boy voice" to make His direction any truer.

DAY 96

In his kindness God called you to share in his eternal
glory by means of Christ Jesus. So after you have suffered
a little while, he will restore, support, and strengthen
you, and he will place you on a firm foundation.

—1 Peter 5:10

System Restore

I recently had a problem with my computer. Somehow, it had become jammed up, and my antivirus software had stopped functioning. After attempting many different solutions, I finally used the system-restore feature and took my computer operation back to a date when I knew that everything had been working correctly. That solved the problem, and I was able to continue without any trouble.

Wouldn't it be great if we could have a "system restore" feature for our past? If we could only go back to a time before we made that bad decision, had the injury, said that thing, or went to the wrong place. The old quote that says "Hindsight is twenty-twenty" speaks of this desire to go back and change old decisions with the new level of experience that we now possess.

The great news is that if we have accepted Jesus Christ as our Lord and Savior, He can restore us to a right relationship with God. Not by anything we have done but by the free gift that Christ offers to us by His death on the cross for our sins.

Just as in the system-restore feature on our computers, we can request this renewal by asking Christ to take control of our lives. It doesn't mean that we won't have to deal with the consequences caused by our past, but through our faith in Christ, we can have a right relationship with God who will do the restorative work in us. He can heal, bring change, and give us the strength and support we need to have not only a plan and purpose in this life but also an eternity with Him when this life has ended. Whether you are asking Christ into your life for the first time, or rededicating yourself to His plan for you, He can give you a fresh start today.

Thought for the Day

Do you want a total system restore? All you have to do is ask for it.

DAY 97

Now faith is the substance of things hoped
for, the evidence of things not seen.

—Hebrews 11:1

Unknown Future

One afternoon, while I was working on the east side of town, I was dispatched to a call of a suicidal subject with a knife. As I arrived at the scene with several of my partners, we were confronted by a male who was standing at the top of an exterior staircase. He was waving a six-inch kitchen knife in his right hand and was asking us to shoot him in a classic "suicide by cop" scenario. We were standing at the base of the stairs and had sufficient distance between us to not require the discharge of our weapons. We had a supervisor on scene who was talking with the distraught male, a cover officer who was pointing his handgun at him, and I had the less-than-lethal Taser gun responsibility.

A Taser gun has a red laser targeting system that makes it easy to use. I just turned on the gun and placed the red aiming dot on the front of the suspect's upper body. It was very effective when he saw that red dot floating on his shirt. When he realized that he was not going to get his suicide wish, and that his immediate future would include a painful "whole body" spasm, he gave up peacefully.

We wish we could predict the pain in our future as easily as that red laser aiming dot. But God usually only gives us enough information to help us through to our next step. I look back on some of the hard things that my wife and I have endured, and I realize that if we had known what was coming, we might have given up too soon and missed out on some of the real blessings that God brought to us as a result of those difficulties.

The above verse in Hebrews tells us that true faith comes from a future we don't know for certain and things that we cannot clearly see. But God is in control and has a plan for everything that happens in our lives. Psalm 139:16 tells us, "*Your eyes saw my substance, being yet unformed. And in Your book they all were written, the days fashioned for me, when as yet there were none of them.*"

Isn't it a relief to know that we can completely rest in the arms of our loving God with the assurance that He has our lives planned out and will help us through an unknown future.

Thought for the Day

We don't need to worry when it seems that problems are taking their aim on our lives. God knows our future and will get us through to the other side.

DAY 98

But the Lord is faithful, and he will strengthen
you and protect you from the evil one.

—2 Thessalonians 3:3

Childproof

Since my wife and I have become grandparents, we have been reminded of the lack of safeguards in our home. Having had three daughters, my grandson is the first boy we have regularly cared for in the toddler stage of development. I am surprised by how different boys are from little girls which had been our only frame of reference until now. Once our grandson's feet hit the floor in our home, he makes a beeline directly toward whatever is most dangerous. Electrical outlets, hanging window shade chains, glass beads in our fireplace, doorjambs, cabinets that store household chemicals, burner knobs on the gas range, and small steps that he can fall from. These are just a few of the things that, at times, seem to hold more fascination for him than the baskets of toys his grandmother has bought for him. We have had to put in place many protections around the house that will give this kid a fighting chance to stay alive until he can at least learn to talk.

I am sure that sometimes God sees us in the same light as a curious, reckless child. From the minute our day begins, we can take a straight path to whatever will hurt our spiritual lives either by commission or omission. It could be what we allow ourselves to feel or think, what we see, or the places we go, all of which can be dangerous to our spiritual growth.

God has put in place many safeguards in our lives that will protect us and keep us safe. The greatest of these is His word. If we follow what it says, we will be sheltered from many of the dangers of this world. Psalm 119:11 tells us, *"Your word I have hidden in my heart, that I might not sin against You."* King David knew that the greatest protection in a believer's life is the reading and memorizing of God's word. We can also take steps to safeguard our hearts that are just as direct and practical as childproofing a home. Regulating what we see, listen to, or where we go can all do a lot to keep the danger of sin from getting close to us. And while we are doing all we can, the faithful promise found in the above verse in Thessalonians will take us even further. "He will strengthen you and protect you from the evil one."

Thought for the Day

God has already "childproofed" your life. Try your best not to run directly to the light socket of the enemy.

DAY 99

But now God has set the members, each one of them, in the body just as He pleased. And if they were all one member, where would the body be?
—1 Corinthians 12:18–19.

Thankless?

When I played football, I was a center. The job of a center is to snap the ball to the quarterback, and then block for whatever play has been called. It is an important job, without which no play could begin.

Center is also a thankless position. I would snap the ball to a famous person, who either handed the ball or threw it to another famous person. The only people who knew my name were my family, friends, teammates, and sometimes my opponents. One thing was for sure, I didn't have the speed or skill of a running back, and I could never play that position. But you know what? They didn't have the size and strength that I had, and they could never play my position. Independent of the fame that our positions gave us, we each had equally important jobs to do that brought victory to our team.

This is a lot like the body of Christ, isn't it. We each have important parts to play in our team effort to serve others and to bring people to a saving knowledge of our Lord. Some might be up front and get more recognition, while others are in the background to do quiet, less noticeable jobs.

In our above passage in 1 Corinthians 13, Paul wrote of the importance of a diverse Christian body. Verses 21 to 22 wrap it up well, "*The eye can never say to the hand, I don't need you. The head* can't say to the feet, I don't need you. In fact, some members that seem the weakest and least important are actually the most necessary."

If you are not serving at your church, it is time to get in the game. It doesn't matter what ministry you choose. If God has led you there, it will be an important one. You might be a behind-the-scenes player who is not known by anyone, or you might be asked to stand up, speak, and be noticed by all. We are each responsible to God to fulfill the positions He has asked us to do, nothing more, and nothing less. There will only be two questions that will be settled for us at judgment, "What did you do with Jesus" and "What did you do with the talents I gave you?"

Thought for the Day

Don't be so concerned about who you are in the body, but what God has called you to do for His kingdom.

DAY 100

*He has made everything beautiful in its time. He has
also set eternity in the human heart: yet no one can
fathom what God has done from the beginning.*
                                                 —Ecclesiastes 3:11

Delayed Beauty

My father was born on the island of Oahu and lived there for
many years before he came to the mainland. He brought with
him some of his culture in the form of tropical plants, which were
found in Hawaii. One such plant, which was common at our house
when I was growing up, was the plumeria. Plumerias have some of
the most beautiful fragrant flowers you will ever see. They grow quite
well in the California climate during the summer. The plant has large
green leaves and produces a wide variety of vibrantly colored flowers.

When a plumeria is blooming, it is beautiful. But, during the
winter months, it's a different story. The leaves and blossoms fall off
the plant, and all that is left are thick bare antler-like branches. It is
quite a stark difference from the exotic fragrant tropical plant that
the spring and summer seasons produce.

I can't say that I have always understood God's will. Sometimes
events that I have seen seem unfair, arbitrary, and just plain ugly. But
God's word tells us that we cannot fathom what He has done, and
promises us that He will make *"everything beautiful in its time."*

If the first time I saw a plumeria was in the winter, I would
wonder why its owners would ever want such a plant in their garden.
It wouldn't be until the spring when I saw what this homely plant

was capable of producing that I would understand it was worth the wait.

When times seem tough, don't give up before you have given God a chance to bring beauty out of the seemingly ugly times in your life.

Thought for the Day

He has made **everything** beautiful in its time.

DAY 101

*Greater love hath no man than this, that a
man lay down his life for his friends.*

—John 15:13

Sacrifice

In July of 2014, Newport Beach lifeguard Ben Carlson gave his
life during a rescue in the ocean off Fifteenth Street. It had been a
busy day for all the lifeguards, and the surf was particularly treach-
erous with big waves and strong rip currents. They had gone about
their business, as they always do, and recorded hundreds of life-saving rescues. Ben, without hesitation, had jumped into the tumultu-
ous ocean soup to save a swimmer who had become exhausted from
fighting the biggest rip of the day, which had taken him against his
will well beyond the breakers. The victim, an experienced swimmer
with fins on, had become fatigued struggling against the current, and
was in real danger of drowning. What he needed was a super swimmer, one above his level of ability. Ben was just that man.

Ben was a big wave surfer who had traveled around the world
defeating some of the toughest ocean locations known. He was the
right man, at the right time, for the struggling swimmer. Ben reached
the man and was able to give him a float just before an enormous set
pounded both of them so hard that the victim stated he was slammed
against the ocean bottom in ten feet of water. They both came up
after the first wave, but Ben did not appear after the second. I was
present when they interviewed the victim about what had happened.
I came away with two truths about the incident. The victim really
needed help, and he would have drowned without Ben's intervention.

We all waited at Lifeguard Headquarters as his fellow lifeguards scoured the surf for Ben. He was found two and a half hours later one half mile away in the water just west of the Newport Pier. Ben went in the surf that day a hero, and he came out the same way.

At the memorial service, his former pastor told us of how Ben had accepted Jesus Christ as his Savior when he was a boy. I was so glad to hear that his family could look forward to a future with Ben and that they would see him again.

Thought for the Day

No matter how turbulent the waters of our lives can be, we can always be assured of a calm eternity by putting our faith in Jesus and accepting Him as the Lord of our lives.

DAY 102

*Trust in the Lord with all your heart, And lean not on
your own understanding; in all your ways acknowledge
Him, and He shall direct your paths.*

—Proverbs 3:5–6

Exhausted

Several years ago, I went to the post office to mail a package out
of state. As I stood in line, I saw that a small bird had flown into
the lobby area. The animal was moving all around the room, flapping
its wings wildly in an attempt to find an exit to the outside. As I
watched, I saw the bird flittering from corner to corner in the room.
At times, it was just inches from finding the open door, only to fly in
the wrong direction in a panic. After several minutes of this activity,
the bird landed on a small ledge, exhausted. Some movement in the
room frightened it, and I watched as it repeated the panic behavior.
I never saw the animal find its way out before I left the post office.

Later I thought about that poor bird who had exhausted itself in
a failed attempt to find its way out of a frightful situation. I thought
of how many times I had become fearful and exhausted when I tried
to use my own resources to solve a problem rather than letting the
Lord handle it for me.

The above verse in Proverbs gives God's answer to difficult situations. We are to trust Him and *"lean not on our own understanding."*
It is then that He will direct us to the path He wants for us.

Thought for the Day

Let's not get trapped exhausting ourselves with our own direction and effort. Rest in Him and find the escape He has opened for us.

DAY 103

My Father, who has given them to me, is greater than all;
no one can snatch them out of my Father's hand.

—John 10:29

Permanent Marker

As a police officer, I was called upon to assist elderly patients who had walked away from their assisted living situations. These individuals were often unable to tell me where they lived, or to provide me with their caregiver's contact info. If their wandering were a regular occurrence, there would be things I could look for to find out where they belonged.

Of course, there was always their wallet, which hopefully contained some form of ID. But most elderly dementia patients did not have a wallet on them. Since this was often the case, their caregivers had gotten smart and wrote the person's information with a permanent marker inside the neck of their shirt. They may have forgotten who they were and were not acting in a manner that was consistent with their true self, but their person had been stamped in such a way that their identity was secure.

If we have truly accepted Jesus Christ as our Lord and Savior at one point in our lives, we have been stamped by the Holy Spirit and are labeled as His property. The above verse in John records the words of Jesus Himself as to the security of our salvation when He says, *"No one can snatch them out of my Father's hand."*

It is my belief that if you have truly given your life to Christ, God's grip on your life is so great that your salvation cannot be snatched away from your Heavenly Father. Even if you have forgotten for a time whose you are, or if you are not acting in a manner consistent with your position in Christ, the label placed across your life still reads, "child of the King."

I hope this gives great hope to those who have lost a loved one who had seemed to be in a state of rebellion when they passed, or who currently have a prodigal child, or a backslidden spouse. If they truly gave their heart to the Lord at one point in their lives, they still belong to God, and He will do whatever it takes to bring them back into a right relationship with Him. No person, thing, or act will be able to pull them out of their Father's hand.

Thought for the Day

Has He labeled you with a permanent marker made from the blood of Jesus?

DAY 104

Whenever I am afraid, I will trust in You. In God (I will praise His word), In God I have put my trust; I will not fear. What can flesh do to me?

—Psalm 56:3–4

Fear Not

I played football for many years. In spite of the way I appeared, and the success I had on the field, I have to admit something. I was always afraid. I learned to put on a brave and even sometimes frightening face to my opponents, but the truth was that I was always scared before each and every game I played in. Early on in my football career, I was afraid of getting hurt. As I grew bigger and stronger and thoughts of being hurt seemed distant to me, I was afraid of being humiliated by my opponent. And after I did get hurt, I was afraid that I no longer had the ability to play at the level that Division 1 college football required.

In all those situations, I learned to play as hard as I could even in the face of that fear. Those lessons served me well when I became a police officer, and fear became a regular companion. The stakes were a little higher than a simple injury, a bad outcome on a scoreboard, or humiliation at the hands of a superior opponent.

It has been said that the term "fear not" appears 365 times in the Bible. That is one for every day of the year! When God tells us to not be afraid, He is not necessarily making that emotion a sin and its prohibition a commandment as in "*Thou shalt not fear!*" We know that Jesus Himself experienced fear in the Garden of Gethsemane the night before His crucifixion (i.e., Father, let this cup pass from me), and we also know that He never sinned (Hebrews 4:15).

Fear can sometimes be imagined, or it can be a correct response to a dangerous situation. When a child comes to us in the middle of the night, we never ridicule them for their fears no matter how unrealistic they may seem. We comfort them, tell them we are there, and assure them that everything will be all right. When God tells us to "fear not," that is the kind of reassurance He gives to us. The kind that says, "Whatever comes in the night, real or imagined, I will always be there with you, so don't be afraid."

There are a lot of fearsome things in today's world, but we don't have to be afraid because God is always with us.

Thought for the Day

> *Be strong and of good courage, do not fear nor be afraid of them; for the LORD your God, He is the One who goes with you. He will not leave you nor forsake you.* (Deuteronomy 31:6)

DAY 105

Therefore we also, since we are surrounded by so great a cloud of witnesses, let us lay aside every weight, and the sin which so easily ensnares us, and let us run with endurance the race that is set before us.
—Hebrews 12:1

Off to the Races

One evening I was working with a partner in West Newport in the area of the Fun Zone. As we drove our unit eastbound on Balboa Boulevard, I saw an individual walking on the south sidewalk at about F Street. Well, to say that he was walking was kind of an overstatement. He was staggering. My partner who was driving at the time, pulled over to the curb, and I exited the vehicle to talk with the possibly intoxicated male. Before I could say a word to him, he turned around, saw me, and was off to the races running westbound on Balboa. If you have ever been in that part of town at night, you know one thing, it is really dark. The streetlights are very poor, and it is hard to see the ground in front of you. In addition to that, some of the sidewalks in the area were poured in the early twentieth century and are uneven and cracked.

The suspect was not running extremely fast, but due to the poor condition of the concrete I was running on, the poor lighting, and the twenty-five pounds of gear I was wearing, I was afraid I would step in a hole, trip, or otherwise injure my previously surgically repaired knee. So, I just kept a steady pace and did not allow the suspect to create any distance between us. After several blocks, I noticed that he was starting to tire more than I was (due to the onboard alcohol no doubt). As he turned the corner at B Street, I was able to push him off his feet and take him into custody without incident. Instead of a simple drunk in public charge, this genius now had an obstruction of justice violation to deal with.

It has often been said that the Christian life is like a race. Paul talked about "running the race" several times when exhorting believers to finish this life well. When I worked at Harvest Church, we have the privilege to see many people make commitments to follow Jesus Christ. Some start out with a sprint only to get tripped up along the way by some life obstacle in their path. I think the better course is to keep a steady, sure tempo going for ourselves.

The above verse in Hebrews tells us to *"run with endurance the race that is set before us."* So, the best advice I can give, as to how to run the race well, is to pace yourself!

Thought for the Day

Don't blindly sprint toward whatever direction seems right to you. Seek God's will and move in a steady, purposeful, controlled course that agrees with His word. If you do, you will reach your destination without getting tripped up.

DAY 106

We will not hide them from their children, Telling to the generation to come the praises of the Lord, And His strength and His wonderful works that He has done.

—Psalm 78:4

Godly Heritage

I recently discovered that my great-great-great-great-grandfather was a soldier in the Revolutionary War. Corporal Charles Rigg was honorably discharged after three years of loyal service under the command of General George Washington and saw action in the battles of Brandywine and Monmouth. It makes me proud that I am the direct descendant of a patriot. We need true patriots now in this country more than ever.

I was contacted by a distant cousin who was also related to Charles Rigg. She told me that she had obtained a copy of a Bible that had belonged to Charles's son, Robert. It is good to know that there was a faith in God evident in the lineage of my family. I hope to see them someday to thank them for passing down God's word over the generations, and to show them one of the results of their faithfulness: me!

You might have a long lineage of godliness in your family, or you might be the first one to even consider a faith in God. You may feel that you missed the opportunity to train up your children (Proverbs 22:6) with a knowledge of the Lord. It has been said that "the only thing worse than not obeying God today, is not obeying God tomorrow!" He is always ready to forgive you and to start to bless your future efforts for Him.

You can start a godly heritage today! No matter what your actions or inactions have been in the past, you can start to model a life of obedience to the Lord with your children, grandchildren, or friends. Nothing speaks more to others about the existence and power of God than a changed life.

Thought for the Day

Who will walk up to you in eternity to thank you for the heritage you passed down?

DAY 107

Here is the man who did not make God his strength, but trusted in the abundance of his riches and strengthened himself in his wickedness.

—Psalms 52:7

Misplaced Trust

I once responded to a dead body call at a residence in Newport Beach. When the address came across my computer screen, I immediately knew the subject of the call. He was a somewhat famous elderly rich man who had a cable TV show that I occasionally watched. He made his living in manufacturing and lived on a large estate at the north end of our city. When I arrived at the scene, I was greeted by his family, his attorney, and his personal caretaker who had last seen him alive. The cause of death was old age, and it had been expected for some time. I had never been to such a call where everyone I needed to talk with was right there at the scene. I was able to contact his personal physician on the phone, talk to all witnesses required, and get clearance from the coroner to leave the scene. I have to say it was the most organized, timely dead body call I had ever been on.

As I conducted my investigation, I observed the man lying deceased on the floor where he had fallen. The house was massive, and I saw a lot of evidence from the decor and furnishings that he had been an extremely wealthy man. I wondered then, as I wonder now, did this man have a relationship with Jesus Christ, did he have the assurance of his salvation, and was he in the presence of our Lord? Or was he like the man described in the above verse in Psalms, one who had put his trust in his riches instead of God.

You might think that all this talk of the world coming to an end is premature. I have to agree that it might be. The world may not end for many years, but your world could end at any moment. Throughout my law enforcement career, I witnessed the end in people's lives more times than I can tell you. The real question for all of us is are we ready?

For those who put their trust in God through Christ's sacrifice on the cross for them, you have an assurance of not only a plan and a purpose in this life, but also an eternity with Him when this life has ended. If not, then up to this point, you have placed your trust in something else other than God. What will God say about you? Did you make Him your strength, or did you trust in the abundance of your own riches in direct disobedience? I pray you chose the former.

Thought for the Day

Don't place your trust in things instead of the God who loves you.

DAY 108

For there is no partiality with God.

—Romans 2:11

He Plays No Favorites

Several years ago, I was standing by the Bible study sign-in table at church when someone approached me from behind and said, "I heard you have a men's study here." I turned toward the voice and noticed a large male standing just behind me to my right. I immediately recognized him as a well-known pro football Hall of Fame player who had been active in the NFL during the era I played at USC. Without skipping a beat, I said, "Hello," and greeted him by his name. He was surprised that I knew him and had so quickly, and calmly, welcomed him to the study.

Since my days at USC, I became used to being around celebrities (football and otherwise). I never, to this day, seem to get star-struck in their presence. I have learned that they are just people like everyone else, even if they have a special talent that brings them fame and sets them apart from others.

When we read the above verse in Romans, we immediately think about how God gives no special treatment to the rich, famous, and powerful of this world. That is an accurate interpretation, but we can also look at this statement from the other side of the coin, so to speak. God not only gives no special treatment to the famous, but He also gives no ill treatment to the anonymous. God loves, cares about, has a plan for, and thinks highly of us no matter what our social status, level of financial success, perceived talent, notoriety, or lack of all the above. Jeremiah 29:11 tells us, *"For I know the thoughts that I think toward you, says the Lord, thoughts of peace and not of evil, to give you a future and a hope.*" God's thoughts about us are not dependent on anything but His love for us. He wouldn't love us more, or less, if we were famous, successful, or super talented in the world's eyes. He knows exactly who we are, what we are, and what we are not, for that matter. And the incredible news for average people like us is that He is proud of us and loves us anyway!

For the believer in Jesus Christ, we will someday have a reunion with our Lord and Savior when He will say to us, "*Well done, good and faithful servant; you were faithful over a few things, I will make you ruler over many things. Enter into the joy of your Lord.*" He will say this to all who have put their faith in Him regardless of their status on earth.

Thought for the Day

He plays no favorites. All who confess to Him are His favorites.

DAY 109

He first found his own brother Simon, and said to him, "We have found the Messiah" (which is translated, the Christ).

—John 1:41

Invite Them

A few years ago, a friend of mine from church died. Art had battled renal disease for many years and was on dialysis. He finally decided to stop his treatment and let God's will for the rest of his life take its course. The last time I visited him at home, he smiled and told me that he was at peace with his decision and excited to see the Lord soon.

Art was not a great evangelist or talented spokesman for God. He was something that is more important than that. He was an "Andrew." Art was always bringing people to meet Jesus. He often brought someone to church or asked me to visit others whom he felt needed to know the Lord.

Our verse for the day records some of the very few words attributed to the apostle Andrew in scripture. In fact, these words were five of the twenty-six that I found in the Bible which directly quoted him. Andrew, the lesser-known brother of Simon Peter, revealed two truths by his brief statement. He quickly put his faith in Jesus as the Messiah, and then went and found his brother to tell him the good news.

We might not have great abilities to preach or evangelize for God, but there is one thing that we can all do in spite of any deficit that we feel we may have. We can invite people to church. I am glad that at the church I attend, a salvation message and invitation is given every week during our Sunday morning services. If you want a friend or loved one to hear the gospel, all you have to do is invite them to come.

Art will receive many crowns in heaven, not because of any great ability that he had, rather, for his willingness and obedience to bring others to Jesus.

Thought for the Day

Don't worry about what you think you can't do, just invite others to where you know they will hear.

DAY 110

No one can come to Me, unless the Father who sent Me draws him.

—John 6:44a

Adjustments

In my position as a chaplain for the Newport Beach Police Department, I am occasionally called to conduct weddings and funerals for the law enforcement community. Several years ago, I was asked to assist with a memorial service for the mother of a retired officer who lived out of the area, but who wanted the remembrance at a beach city hotel. Services like these are a little different than those we conduct at church where we have time to meet with those requesting the memorial and properly vet the family situation. I went into the service with minimal knowledge of the family dynamics. In short, I was flying blind.

Everything started off well. I gave my normal welcome and opening prayer. When it came time for a family member to give the eulogy and say a few words about the deceased, things changed. The son of the woman who had passed proceeded to reveal secrets of family abuse, and then accused those in attendance for their ill treatment of his mother, ending his time at the podium by saying, "You all owed her an apology, but you never gave it to her." I was glad that I had a pen with me as I started to cross out and rewrite some of the content of my memorial message. I thought that the line "When a loved one dies it is a time of memories, beautiful memories of the past as we join together to remember a loved one who has left this earth" wouldn't go over too well. I made the proper adjustments and was still able to deliver a gospel message in spite of a difficult beginning.

When we tell others about our faith in Christ, we have to be ready to make last-minute adjustments that will be dictated by the person we are talking to. There is no "one message fits all" type of testimony that will fit with every person we are talking to. Everyone has their own specific hurts and past difficulties that require a tailor-made message.

Fortunately, our verse in John assures us that our Father will do all the heavy lifting when it comes time for us to share our faith. He will bring to us those specific people He wants us to talk to after having done all the preparation and groundwork Himself. God goes even further in assuring us in Acts 1:8 when He tells us, "*You will receive power when the Holy Spirit comes upon you. And you will be my witnesses telling people about me everywhere.*" So, all we have to do is be prepared and flexible to be used as the Holy Spirit directs us.

Thought for the Day

It might take some last-minute alterations and message adjustments, but God will use us if we are ready.

DAY 111

You shall walk after the Lord your God and fear Him,
and keep His commandments and obey His voice;
you shall serve Him and hold fast to Him.

—Deuteronomy 13:4

When Should We Be Afraid?

I once had a person say about me, "He's not afraid of anything!" Well, nothing could be further from the truth. I will say that because of my law enforcement training and experience, it might be true that I am not fearful of many things that others are. It is also true that I am afraid of some things that others are not. For one thing, I hate grasshoppers! The way they look, the way they jump, in what seems like random directions, and the way they cling to you if they get anywhere near you. How can I confront a combative suspect in the street with no fear, and jump up on a chair like a schoolgirl when I see a grasshopper? I think that people perceive our courage through the filters of their own fears. If they are deeply afraid of something, they view others as courageous, if they are not afraid of that same thing.

The above verse in Deuteronomy calls for us to "fear Him" in reference to our heavenly Father. I have often heard Christians say that the fear mentioned in verses like these only refer to a great "respect" for God. I absolutely agree that we should have a respect for the Lord, but I would like to float another idea as to the definition of fear in God's word. The word fear in the above verse means "fear!" Not as in we should be scared to death of a terrible and vengeful deity, but rather we should be afraid of the repercussions in our lives for not following God's will.

So, what are the possible consequences for the failure to obey the holy and righteous God? The loss of His blessings in our lives for one thing, the failure to be able to claim His promises for us, the removal of the wisdom and peace that accompanies obedience to him, and, at times, a direct chastening from God to turn us from our error.

In C. S. Lewis's book *The Lion, the Witch, and the Wardrobe*, the little girl character, Susan, upon discovering that Aslan was a lion, asked Mr. Beaver, "Is he safe?" Mr. Beaver answered, "Who said anything about safe? Of course, he isn't safe. But he's good. He's the King, I tell you."

If we live in direct opposition to God's will for our lives as outlined in His word, we are not in a safe place. If we do not fear God, we have a reason, whether we know it or not, to be afraid. But God is good and will lovingly try to guide us back to a right place with him. But we cannot count on God's restraint in our lives indefinitely if we live without any care of our disobedience to Him.

Thought for the Day

If we strive to obey God we have nothing to fear. HE IS GOOD!

DAY 112

*I saw the dead, both great and small, standing before God's throne.
And the books were opened, including the Book of Life. And the dead
were judged according to what they had done, as recorded in the books.*
—Revelation 20:12

Big Pants

As police officers, we often hear one outlandish excuse after another that can, over the years, become comically repetitive. I can't tell you how many times I heard a defendant claim that he had accidently put on his roommate's pants, and that the cocaine I found in his pocket did not belong to him. His "friend" was six inches taller than he was and weighed forty pounds more, but somehow, he magically wore the exact same-size pants as the defendant. Either he was lying, or his roommate had some pretty goofy-fitting clothing. I often told a defendant that he was being arrested for the "possession" of the contraband and not its "ownership." In truth, he was guilty of both.

People give one excuse after another about why they are not ready to give control of their lives to Jesus Christ. There is nothing wrong with having legitimate questions about God and what a personal relationship with Christ looks like. But many times, their questions and doubts are obvious dodges designed to generate excuses so that they will be able to maintain control of their own lives. "The Bible is full of contradictions, Christians are hypocrites, and organized religions are all the same." These are just a few of the frequently repeated excuses that people give for not believing in God. They just don't want to surrender their lives to Him because they think that if they admit He exists, they will have to dramatically alter their lives.

Just like the excuses made by earthly criminal defendants, the excuses that will be given by those who have not accepted Jesus Christ as Savior and Lord will fall short at God's throne of judgment. The real tragedy will be that they will have believed the lie that a life lived for Christ would have been restricted, boring, or unfulfilled. The excuses they thought would give them reasons to hold on to their lifestyles will be what will have kept them from God's plan and purpose in this life as well as an eternity with Him when this life is over.

Thought for the Day

Are you tired of making excuses? Why don't you put on your own spiritual pants and take a stand for Jesus Christ! You will never be sorry in this life or the next!

DAY 113

Now may the God of hope fill you with all joy and peace in believing,
that you may abound in hope by the power of the Holy Spirit.

—Romans 15:13

Unlimited Power

I've noticed that new cops are in the habit of turning their radios on at the beginning of the shift and keeping them on at low volume until the end of the watch. I'm from the old school where we had weaker batteries and had to turn our radios on and off as we entered or exited our police units.

No matter what the routine, sometimes we have all had the same problem with our communication devices. When we hear that dreaded bonk (the sound the radio makes when it is about to go dead) we know that our battery has run low and our communication with Dispatch will soon end. Lasting power sources have always been a challenge, and it has only worsened with the addition of video systems, computers, and other electronics in our patrol cars.

When we give our lives to Jesus Christ, the Holy Spirit comes to reside within us. That power can give us wisdom, peace, and hope at times in our lives where having those things will make no earthly sense. Because God is the source of that power, we don't have to worry about a spiritual energy shortage.

If we ask the Holy Spirit to fill us, He promises to do so on a continual basis. Since that power is there for the asking, we never have to be concerned that our energy source from God will come to an end. Just ask Him to fill you each day, and He will be faithful to do so.

Thought for the Day

We never need to fear a bonk that signals a shortage of the Holy Spirit's power and presence in our lives.

DAY 114

I call heaven and earth as witnesses today against you, that I have set before you life and death, blessing and cursing; therefore, choose life, that both you and your descendants may live;
—Deuteronomy 30:19

Choices

When I played football, it was a yearly ritual for me to go to the sporting goods store to buy my cleats for that season. When I was recruited to play at USC, that ritual changed.

After I arrived on campus, the equipment manager asked me to come into the underground locker room at Heritage Hall (USC's old locker/training facility). When I went inside, I was shown a large display of shoes (all black, USC's mandatory color at the time) that contained a variety of cleat sizes and styles. I was then asked, "What kind do you want?" This was a shock to me because for the first time, I realized that they were going to **give** me whatever I wanted. I picked a pair that I knew would be good for the grass in the Coliseum, and the equipment guy then said, "Okay, now which ones for Astroturf [the old name for synthetic grass]?" I had never played on that kind of surface before, so I picked another pair that had a smaller molded cleat bottom. I had another surprise coming when he then asked me, "Those are for the games. What kind of shoes do you want for practices?" I was given the three pairs of new cleats to take to my locker. As I went to leave, the equipment man said, "Where are you going?" and pointed to several new football helmets and face masks of different styles and manufactures. I almost lost consciousness at that point. I was a small-town guy who had no idea until that moment that God had brought me to a larger stage than I was used to. I wasn't in Kanas anymore!

God gives all of us free choice in this life. Some are smaller and seemingly insignificant, while others can greatly impact our futures. In the above passage in Deuteronomy, God told the Israelites that the choice they were about to make was a serious one that could decide between their life and death and that of their descendants. They had come to a fork in the road.

As followers of Jesus Christ, we have many of those decision points in our lives. The first was our decision to turn over our lives to Him, but after that, we have daily choices to make that can either bring us closer to or further away from Him. Will I read God's word? Will I fellowship with other believers (church)? Will I choose to obey His commands for my life even when I don't fully understand or agree with them? All are choices that we will make every day in our walk with Jesus Christ.

The world offers us so many alternatives that we are sometimes overloaded by the choices we seem to face. God's word will always help us to narrow down those options so that we can see what is good from what is evil in our lives.

Thought for the Day

Don't get overwhelmed by the variety of selections that present themselves. Follow God's word and "choose life."

DAY 115

Then I heard a loud voice saying in heaven, "Now salvation, and strength, and the kingdom of our God, and the power of His Christ have come, for the accuser of our brethren, who accused them before our God day and night, has been cast down.
—Revelation 12:10

The Accuser

As police officers, we are often subpoenaed to court to testify in a variety of proceedings. We are usually challenged by defense attorneys whose job is to bring doubt to our testimony. Unfortunately, they usually attempt to create that doubt by falsely accusing us of negligence or untruthfulness in order to get a favorable verdict for their guilty clients. It isn't much of a stretch for us to see the connection between some defense attorneys and "the accuser of our brethren" mentioned in the above verse.

Our adversary Satan never rests and is constantly accusing us before God. When his target is a follower of Jesus Christ, he has two big problems. Firstly, God's word says, *"As far as the east is from the west, so far has he cast our transgression from us"* (Psalm 103:12) and *"If we confess our sin He is faithful and just to forgive us our sin and to cleanse us from all unrighteousness"* (1 John 1:9).

When we accept Christ's death on the cross for our sin and confess that sin to Him, He stands for us between our accuser and a righteous God. We are still guilty, but Jesus has paid the price for our sin, making us technically "not guilty" in the sight of the Lord. Secondly, Satan's accusing days will soon come to an end, and he will be "cast down" to the hell that has been prepared for him, his angels, and anyone else who chooses to go there.

If you are feeling unsettled today by condemning thoughts about your past or your present imperfections, don't. God's word says that, "*There is now no condemnation to those who are in Christ Jesus, who walk not according to the flesh, but according to the Spirit*" (Romans 8:1). You can have peace that He stands as our advocate and has paid the ultimate price for our imperfections.

Thought for the Day

Our accuser may never rest, but isn't it a relief to know that we can!

DAY 116

In the body of His flesh through death, to present you holy,
and blameless, and above reproach in His sight.

—Colossians 1:22

Divine Eyesight

I arrived at the University of Southern California in the spring of 1977. As a new player on the football team, I was provided with a practice uniform which included a pair of generic white practice pants and a plain cardinal-colored jersey. That is what I wore during spring training as did everyone else on the team.

In the fall of that year, the regular season started, and we went to the LA Coliseum to play our first game. I remember unpacking my uniform and suiting up in the locker room at the north end of the stadium. As we prepared to go out on to the field to warm up, I passed a mirror in the shower area. When I walked by, I looked up at my reflection. I was stopped dead in my tracks. I had never seen myself in the official Trojan cardinal and gold. I had watched that uniform so many times before on TV, but it wasn't until that moment that I fully realized who I had become and what a great team God had put me on!

Isn't it strange that we as Christians can sometimes work our way through life without truly knowing what we really look like to God? The above verse in Colossians tells us that through Christ's death on the cross for our sin we are now "holy and blameless in His sight." It doesn't matter what we think of ourselves or how we see ourselves. If we have made Jesus Christ the Lord of our lives, He has covered us with His righteousness. When God looks at us He only sees Jesus and His perfection. It is nothing we deserve or have earned; it is God's free gift to us *"for He hath clothed me with the garments of salvation"* (Isaiah 61:10).

Thought for the Day

Next time you look into the mirror of your life and don't like something you see, focus instead on the holy and blameless way that God views you. You couldn't be wearing a better uniform!

DAY 117

Beloved, do not believe every spirit, but test the spirits, whether they are of God; because many false prophets have gone out into the world.
—1 John 4:1

Sales in Lieu of

Some might be surprised to find out that you can get arrested for selling laundry soap. Believe it or not, dope dealers are not very honest. Sometimes they will cut the drugs they sell with fillers or dangerous chemicals in order to make more product and, in turn, more profit. Some will even sell substances that have no drugs in them at all. Laundry soap can look a lot like narcotics if it is selected and packaged correctly.

The law has made provision for the sale of such false contraband by making it a crime in what is termed as sales in lieu of. This violation only has to do with the sales of false drugs, not the possession of it. I can imagine the jailhouse scene if mere possession was arrestable. One inmate would ask the other, "What are you in for?" The answer, "Tide possession," would not bring them much credibility on the cellblock.

John warns us that we will encounter false prophets in this world. There will be those who try to sell us incorrect doctrines that will attempt to derail our faith. In the field, we have a simple presumptive test kit that can tell us if a drug is authentic or not. God also gives us a test that can help us to determine if we are experiencing spiritual sales in lieu of. In 1 John 4:2–3, we can read our spiritual presumptive test, "*By this you know the Spirit of God: Every spirit that confesses that Jesus Christ has come in the flesh is of God, and every spirit*

that does not confess that Jesus Christ has come in the flesh is not of God."
This means more than believing that Jesus existed or even that God
sent Him. Christ is not Jesus's last name, but rather His title, the
Christ, the Messiah, God with us. So, any person or religious system
that denies the deity of Jesus and that he is literally God the Father
with us in human form is false.

Thought for the Day

Don't get fooled by a false religious product. Jesus is LORD.

DAY 118

*Even if we feel guilty, God is greater than our
feelings, and he knows everything.*

—1 John 3:20

Feelings, Nothing More than Feelings

In 1974, Morris Albert wrote a popular song called "Feelings." If
you have ever spent any time counseling others, you'll understand
how that song title is true for many people you talk to, and how often
people's feelings will dominate the conversation. Whether it is regret
over past actions, an inability to accept God's forgiveness, or doubt
about a person's salvation, a person's feelings about issues in their
lives often control their emotional state. Some even use feelings as
the go-to barometer for determining God's will in their lives. But the
truth is feelings can be error filled and theologically incorrect.

Many times, the feelings we have come solely from our own
minds and have no basis in truth. They are ghosts that make the past
failure focused, the present insurmountable, and the future fearful.
Feelings make us unable to accept God's forgiveness, fear the dark
when there is no danger present, and dread our future for the what-
ifs that seem to lurk there. Proverbs 28:26 tells us, "*Whoever trusts in
his own mind is a fool, but he who walks in wisdom will be delivered.*"
And what is wisdom? Proverbs 2:6 makes it clear, "*For the Lord gives
wisdom; From His mouth come knowledge and understanding.*"

Wisdom is God's word as found in scripture. We are to rely on
it and the truth of what it says over any feeling or emotion we may
have. If we are worried about the future, we go to Philippians 4:6–7
which exhorts us to not be anxious, pray, give thanks, and receive

peace. If we are troubled about our finances, we go to Philippians 4:19 which assures us that God will provide for all our needs. If we fear what is to come, Jerimiah 29:11 tells us of God's plan for our future!

Our verse in 1 John states that even if we have incorrect feelings, God is greater than those negative emotions, and can overcome them through His forgiveness.

In short, feelings can be fickle, and we are not to depend on them as followers of Jesus Christ. We are, instead, to rely on God's word and what He says, and not our own minds and the incorrect unbiblical imaginings we can conjure up.

Thought for the Day

If our feelings don't match God's word, they are nothing more than temporary inaccurate thoughts!

DAY 119

All Scripture is given by inspiration of God, and is profitable for doctrine, for reproof, for correction, for instruction in righteousness.
—2 Timothy 3:16-17

Pigeon Scriptures

My father was born and raised on the island of Oahu in Hawaii. As a child, we made several trips to his birthplace to visit our relatives. While there, I became somewhat familiar with the dialect of English used, to a lesser or greater degree, by some inhabitants of the islands. Hawaiian Pigeon, as it is referred to, is mostly understandable as English with some special words and phrases mixed in. I have a New Testament Bible written in Pigeon English that is entitled Da Jesus Book. I looked up our scripture for today in "Da Letta Numba Two From Paul Fo Timothy (2 Timothy), and it reads as follows:

> Eh, everything inside da Bible stay dea, cuz God wen put um inside da guys heads dat wen talk fo him befo time. Dass why everything inside da Bible, can use um fo teach, an fo show wat stay wrong, an fo help peopo pau do da bad kine stuff an comeback an stick wit da good kine stuff, an fo teach peopo fo do was right.

I don't know about you, but in a strange way, that seems clearer to me than the New King James Version I used above. God did inspire men by putting His words in their heads so that they would teach them to stop doing what was wrong, and to help them do what was right. What a great translation this is for the King James "instruction in righteousness!"

In the foreword to Da Jesus Book, it states that the authors received help from Wycliffe Bible Translators in preparing this paraphrase. Wycliffe has been world-renowned for many years for translating the Bible into many foreign languages across the globe. Because of Wycliffe and others, people from many parts of the world have learned of God's plan of salvation for them in their own native tongue, people who might have been overlooked because of the obscurity of their language.

But whether it is in standard English, Spanish, French, Swahili, or Pigeon, God's word is true and can be used with certainty to teach, correct, and lead people to what is right in the gospel of Jesus Christ. And what is the gospel? Some of our friends in Hawaii would say:

Thought for the Day

> God wen get so plenny love an aloha fo da peopo inside the world, dat he wen send me, his one an only Boy, so dat everyone dat trus me no get cut off from God, but get da real kine life dat stay to da max foeva. (John 3:16)

Amen!

DAY 120

In those days there was no king in Israel: every man
did that which was right in his own eyes.

—Judges 21:25

Godly Suggestions?

In the law, there are codified statutes and regulations that gov-
ern criminal behavior. This is just a fancy way of saying that we
write down our laws so they can be referenced and applied later. As a
police officer, I was constantly looking through different code books
(Penal, Business and Professions, Welfare Institutions, Vehicle, and
Municipal) to find the exact section and subsection for a particular
crime or violation. I may have had some latitude to enforce a law or
not, but I was never given the ability to change the definition of a
law so that it fit the circumstances I was presented with. And if there
was any doubt as to the correctness of my interpretation of a specific
law, I had my supervisors or the district attorney's office to let me
know about it.

The above verse in Judges refers to a time in Jewish history
when Israel had no king and appeared to follow no documented law.
Everyone did what was right in their own estimation. I saw that same
thing during my law enforcement career, and unfortunately, I can see
it happening in the church today.

As pastors, we counseled people using the ultimate codified law,
the Bible. It amazes me how some will pick and choose from God's
commandments which passages they will decide to follow. Whether
they are a believer who dates a non-Christian (2 Corinthians 6:14),
couples who decide to divorce with no valid biblical reason (Matthew

19:9), those who have sex outside of marriage (Hebrews 13:4), people who live together without being married (1 Thessalonians 5:22), those who refuse to forgive others (Matthew 6:15), refuse to attend church (Hebrews 10:25), refuse to pray (1 Thessalonians 5:17), or those who simply choose not to read God's word regularly (Joshua 1:8), all have chosen to do so in direct violation of God's commandments, and usually with the full knowledge that their actions are wrong. In their lives, they have decided to do what is right in their own eyes and do not care (or don't care enough) about what God says. They seem to treat God's word, the Bible, as the great book of "suggestions" for their lives.

As I write this devotion, I have been a follower of Jesus Christ for fifty-seven years. I can tell you something that I have found to be an absolute truth in my life. Every time I did what God's word said to do, things turned out well for me, and every time I disobeyed Him, they did not. It might not have been immediately apparent to me that my actions would turn out to have a positive or negative result, but eventually I was either glad I obeyed Him or so sorry that I didn't.

God's word contains many promises to us that are encouraging and give us hope and peace. But God's word also contains many warnings for us that keep us from harm and despair. The difference between the two outcomes is found in our obedience to that word.

Thought for the Day

There is no dimmer switch to obeying God. If we turn the switch on, we will receive all He has for us, and if we don't, we will find ourselves afraid in the dark.

DAY 121

*Now that I am old and gray, do not abandon me, O
God. Let me proclaim your power to this new generation,
your mighty miracles to all who come after me.*

—Psalm 71:18

Old Man

Recently, I had a vivid reminder as to how quickly time passes. I was driving to Home Depot to pick up some items for a do-it-yourself job I was working on. I had put on a T-shirt that morning, and as I drove down the road, I looked at it for the first time. It was a shirt that had been given to me at the forty-year reunion of a national championship football team I had played on as a freshman in college. It read, "1975 National Champions." As I continued to the store, I started to think about how much time had passed and, specifically, what a current college player would think if he saw this shirt. It would be like me, in 1975, seeing an old guy with a shirt that read, "1930 National Champions"! Wow, they wore leather helmets with no face masks back then. I am sure a young man now would be thinking the same thing that I would have thought, "How is this old guy still alive?"

Much has happened to me in the last forty-five years, some good, some exciting, some hard, and some difficult. I, too, can lament with King David, as in the verse above, about the fact that I am getting old and, in my case, completely gray. But I can also see that I have a great mission in the life that is still in front of me. It is an assignment that would not have been possible for me before I had learned the lessons that God has taught me through time and experience. I have the great opportunity to proclaim to others in this new generation the mighty miracles of God.

We read of many accounts in the Old Testament that tell of how the Jewish people's obedience to God disappeared quickly. In fact, it was the great sin of Israel that they forgot God and started to worship idols in the span of just one generation. One generation, forty years!

If you feel that you are old and on the downward slide to the end of your life, take heart, your true life's ministry might just be starting.

Thought for the Day

Let's use what we have learned to proclaim God to this new generation.

DAY 122

*For it is God who works in you both to will
and to do for His good pleasure.*

—Philippians 2:13

Heading Down the Road

The photo I have on my computer desktop is that of a tree-lined road. It is a simple stretch of pavement with a white dotted line running down the middle. The green trees on either side of the road have grown large enough to meet at the top, forming a foliage tunnel that covers the street. The density of the vegetation is not thick enough to block out the sunlight as it filters through the trees. Because of the deep green colors of the leaves, I would assume that the picture was taken during the spring months. The pathway is completely empty with no cars, pedestrians, or animals of any kind. It gave me a sense of peace when I first saw it which was not present in my circumstances at that time.

I imagined the road as my life, and I was walking on it without a care in the world knowing that when I reached its end, I would be home with the Lord. Not very theological. After all, 2 Corinthians 5:6–8 promises us that when we are absent from this body, we will be instantly present with the Lord. I don't see a sunny walk down a tree-lined road promised there. Nonetheless, to me, it represents what is left of my life.

God has a plan for your life. You might have just started down the highway of your journey, or you could be cresting the rise that will reveal your final destination on the other side. No matter the length of journey you have left, God still wants to use you for His glory. As long as your heart is still beating, God can employ your talents and abilities in such a way as to impact those around you. Even the thief on the cross described in Luke 23 was used by our Lord in the last few minutes of his life. By calling Jesus Lord and acknowledging that He had a kingdom, he made a simple confession that gave him the assurance of paradise. His story has been read by millions of people over two millennia, giving hope to countless others as to God's grace and mercy. A crucified criminal did more for the cause of the gospel in a few minutes than some others have done in a lifetime.

It doesn't matter what you feel about your lack of possible contribution, or what you may think disqualifies you due to wasted opportunities in the past. God can use you in a mighty way for His kingdom. Just get back on the road of service and start to walk in the direction of obedience to Him. And when you come to the crest in the road that signals the end of your life, you will leave this world a follower of Jesus and hear Him say, "Well done, my good and faithful servant."

Thought for the Day

It has been said that the journey of a thousand miles starts with just one step. Step out today.

DAY 123

But as many as received Him, to them He gave the right to become children of God, to those who believed in His name.

—John 1:12

Swearing In

When I became a police officer, I had to take an oath. I stood in front of the chief's desk, raised my right hand, and solemnly swore to support and defend the constitution of the United States and the constitution of the state of California against all enemies, foreign and domestic. It was at that point that I crossed over the line from being a civilian to being a sworn police officer, with all the power, duties, and responsibilities given to that position. I did my best over the next twenty-one years to uphold that oath in every situation I found myself in. My effort was not unique. Recent statistics show that there are over three-quarters of a million men and women in United States law enforcement who have taken that same oath. If you multiply that number times the amount of citizen contacts that occur on a daily basis, it makes the few negative reports you hear about the police, no matter how much publicity they may get, seem small in comparison. I am not saying that police officers never make mistakes, or even purposefully violate their oaths, but the number who do are infinitesimal when compared to the amount who get it right day in and day out.

Several years ago, I had the privilege of being part of the Harvest Crusade at Angel Stadium in Anaheim. We had a total attendance of ninety-two thousand over the three-day event, and we saw nine thousand people come forward to make a profession of faith in Jesus

Christ. As I stood in the crowd in the outfield at the stadium and listened to them pray to receive Jesus into their lives, I couldn't help but compare that pledge to the oath I took when I became a police officer. I heard thousands of people, in unison, promise to follow Jesus Christ, and invite Him into their lives. It was, and always will be, an incredible event to behold.

The truth is that despite that Christian "swearing in," there will be some who say those words who will never make that profession real in their lives. There were follow-up counselors on the field who contacted everyone who came forward in an effort to encourage them, give them a Bible, and keep that future, falling away number, as low as possible. The oath is of no effect if the life that follows doesn't prove its validity.

If you know someone you suspect is at that tipping point between devotion to Christ and the life they had been living before, do your best to encourage them in their new commitment. Just a simple word, phone call, email, text, or invitation to church could make all the difference.

Thought for the Day

Let's help others solidify their new lives and oath to Jesus.

DAY 124

*Trust in the Lord with all your heart, And lean not on
your own understanding; In all your ways acknowledge
Him, And He shall direct your paths.*

—Proverbs 3:5–6

Life Audibles

In football, audibles are a regular part of any offensive play scheme.
The quarterback has the option to change the play at the line of
scrimmage when he sees a weakness in the opposing defense's lineup.

At USC in the late 1970s (no, we didn't wear leather helmets!),
we would establish a hot color that let us know if a play change was
coming. Our normal snap cadence would be a color, followed by a
number. That phrase would be repeated twice before we were told
to set, and then were given the snap count. So, if the play were on
one, the following signal sequence would be called on the line: "Blue
22, blue 22, set, hut." If the quarterback wanted to change the play
call, he would just change the color and number in the verbal signal
phrase. From the line of scrimmage, he would then say, "Red 28, red
28, set, hut." We would all know that he now wanted to change the
play he had called in the huddle to 28 Pitch (USC's old Student Body
Right). No matter how tired we were, you had to listen carefully and
place our trust in our quarterback so that we wouldn't miss the play.

Sometimes God has audibles for us in our walk with Him. We
may think we have our life plan settled, but God may change things
at the last minute to better serve His purposes and give us a positive
outcome in our lives. The above verse in Proverbs calls on us to trust

God, not to rely on our own understanding of a situation and to put His will for us first. He then promises that He will direct our paths.

When our quarterback changed a play at the line of scrimmage, no one ever stood up and called for a time-out so that we could confer with him about what he saw in the defense, or to ask him if he was really sure he wanted to alter the call. We had to trust that what he was doing was right and gave our best effort in the new direction that he took us. Some of our greatest plays and eventual victories came as a result of those last-second audibles.

Thought for the Day

Has God changed things up at the line of scrimmage in your life? Trust Him and go with it! A great victory is just around the corner.

DAY 125

Beloved, do not believe every spirit, but test the spirits, whether they are of God; because many false prophets have gone out into the world.
—1 John 4:1

It Looks Real

My oldest daughter, Kara, has developmental challenges and lives at home with her mom and me. She likes to sit in front of the TV and watch her favorite shows. Kara loves romantic comedies. They have the two things she wants to see most, people moving around doing funny things, and boys and girls interacting with each other. Kara is a joy addict who likes to see happy people doing happy things.

I recently saw Kara sitting on the floor very close to her new wide-screen TV. As I watched, I saw her slowly reach her hand out and carefully touch the screen with her index finger. I observed her for some time before I realized what she was doing. Kara had never seen life-size people on TV before, and she was touching them to see if they were real! After all, they looked like the real thing.

God's word exhorts us not to believe everything we see and hear, but to test them against God's word. Acts chapter 17 records the account of the people of Berea and their reaction to the gospel. In talking about the people, it reads in verse 11, "*They listened eagerly to Paul's message. They searched the Scriptures day after day to see if Paul and Silas were teaching the truth.*" The people of Berea did the right thing. They didn't just mindlessly believe what they were told. They went to God's word to find out if what they were hearing was correct. We should do the same today.

I have seen many Christians get off track because they followed their pastor and whatever he said rather than comparing the information to the truth of the Bible. The best pastor/teacher will read directly from God's word and invite you to read along and to verify for yourself if what he is saying is true.

I guess my daughter Kara had the right idea when she reached out to touch the TV to see if the people were real or not. She didn't just take what she thought she saw at face value.

Thought for the Day

Just because it looks real doesn't mean that it is. Reach out and test it to make sure.

DAY 126

For we do not have a High Priest who cannot sympathize with our weaknesses, but was in all points tempted as we are, yet without sin.
—Hebrews 4:15

Life Experience

Departments consider many things when evaluating a recruit for a position as a full-time police officer. They consider the candidate's work record, education, financial history, criminal history, and any past drug use. They also contact their family, friends, and neighbors to see if there are any ethical or character issues which do not normally show up on a standard background inquiry. It is a strenuous hiring process in which only one out of one hundred applicants successfully make it through to the job offer stage.

Background investigators also consider a recruit's life experience in general when considering how successful they will be as a police officer. If the applicant has experienced some of the challenges this life can offer, it could be a good indicator of how well they may handle the difficulties that present themselves in a law enforcement career. The department wants to know if the candidate will be able to relate to others in a variety of situations that they will be exposed to.

Jesus was exposed to every temptation and difficulty that we may face. The above verse in Hebrews tells us that He was "in all points tempted as we are." When the scripture says "all points," it really means all points! The New Living Translation paraphrases the same passage as "He faced all of the same testing as we do." The New International Version says, "Who has been tested in every way, just as we are," and the Message Bible puts it, "He's been through weakness and testing, experienced it all!"

When God became a man through Jesus Christ (John 1:14), He put to rest any notion we may have that the almighty God of the universe could not possibly relate to the problems and weaknesses we are subjected to. He proved that He has the life experience required to do the job as it relates to understanding our problems. But unlike us, there is one big difference between His experience and ours, as described in the last three words of the verse. He experienced our weaknesses and temptations "yet without sin." That is great news for us because only a perfect, spotless offering would be accepted by God as our payment for the sin in our lives.

Thought for the Day

Do not be tempted to think that God doesn't understand what you are going through. His one-word answer to that thought is "Jesus."

DAY 127

*And if some of the branches were broken off, and you, being a
wild olive tree, were grafted in among them, and with them
became a partaker of the root and fatness of the olive tree.*
—Romans 11:17

Adopted

I was not recruited to play Division 1 college football out of high
school. Despite some decent recognition, I did not receive a scholarship offer and had to go to junior college (now called community
college) for two seasons.

Some four-year schools do not take junior college transfers, but
many found it to be a great way to get immediate seasoned players at
a particular position. Fortunately for me, USC needed that kind of
help at center when I was recruited. It is a different experience coming onto a team as a junior when your fellow teammates have already
been playing together for years. You must prove yourself and find
your place in the group. This must be what it feels like to be adopted
into an already well-established family.

The above verse in Romans speaks to the condition of gentiles
(non-Jews) in God's plan of salvation. They have been adopted, or
"grafted," into God's family which originally consisted of only the
Jewish people. As adopted children, gentiles have been given the full
rights and privileges as children of God, which includes access to the
Father through Christ, the fullness of the promises in God's word,
and an eternal life in heaven when this life is over.

Now that I am many years on the other side of my football
career, I can say I am a Trojan through and through. It didn't matter

that I was a JC transfer, and by my senior year, I was a member of the squad with the full rights and acceptance of any other player. Because I have accepted Jesus Christ as my Savior and Lord, I have been grafted into God's family and have the full rights and acceptance of any other child of the King.

Thought for the Day

I am so grateful to have been adopted.

DAY 128

But strong meat belongeth to them that are of full age, even those who by reason of use have their senses exercised to discern both good and evil.
—Hebrews 5:14

Where's the Meat?

Many years ago, I was with three other officers in an El Pollo Loco restaurant on our dinner break. As the four of us sat waiting for our food, my partner left the table to use the restroom. The food was delivered while he was gone, which was unfortunate for him. We could not let this golden opportunity for a practical joke go by. He had ordered a chicken sandwich that had come wrapped in a foil covering. We opened the wrapper, took out the chicken that was inside, and neatly rewrapped the item so that it looked as though it had not been tampered with. We then placed the chicken in a napkin and hid it under some other food items on the table.

When the officer came back, he unwrapped his sandwich and took a bite. As he continued to consume his meal, it got to the point where we were laughing so hard (or trying not to) that we could not look him in the eyes as we sat there. After several minutes, he finished the sandwich without saying a negative word. I asked him how his meal had been, and he replied, "Okay, it was a little light on the chicken!" At that point, we almost fell out of our seats with laughter when we revealed that the sandwich was not just light on the chicken, it had none in it! It was just a bun, lettuce, mayo, and some meat juice. Of course, we then dubbed the meal the "aroma de pollo" sandwich from that point on.

I think that there are many churches that are just like that sandwich when it comes to God's word. They have all the trappings of a house of worship, the building, the choir, a great topical sermon, and a big cross out front. They may talk a lot about God and do many great social works in the community. However, when it comes to the meat of God's word that can only be found in the Bible, they come up short. Their services may have the aroma of God's word, but none of the nutrition that is required to keep a healthy body going.

If you are attending a church that talks about spiritual things but does not advocate the study of the Bible as the inerrant word of God, I would suggest that you find a new church! We can't grow physically without an adequate amount of protein in our diets. We also cannot grow in our relationship with Jesus Christ without the meat of God's word in our lives.

Thought for the Day

Don't settle for a church that takes the meat out of your spiritual growth.

DAY 129

❖

For everyone has sinned; we all fall short of God's glorious standard.
—Romans 3:23

Bull's-Eye

When I left the Newport Beach Police Department, I was given an ID that clearly states "RETIRED" on the front of it. The back of the card shows my physical description, ID number, blood type, and my official retirement date. It also has a printed section that allows me, as an honorably retired peace officer, to carry a concealed weapon (CCW).

When I recently examined my retirement ID, I was surprised to see that the expiration date for my department CCW was only a few months away. I knew that I needed to go back to the gun range and requalify so that I could get a new department ID and CCW clearance. I called the Newport Beach range and made an appointment to shoot, which I did a few days later. I qualified and was able to place all my rounds into the target. But I noticed that in spite of my good grouping, I was never able to hit the absolute center of the bull's-eye.

The Greek word for sin is *hamartano*. It is literally translated, "I miss the mark" or "I sin." The above verse in Romans tells us of our spiritual condition. We have all sinned and fallen short, or missed the mark, of God's standard of perfection. According to God's word, no matter how hard we try, we will never be able to hit a dead center bull's-eye when it comes to perfection in our lives. First John 1:10 covers those who claim that they have not sinned and have been able to hit that mark when it says, "*If we claim we have not sinned, we are calling God a liar and showing that His word has no place in our hearts.*"

God's word is clear about the penalty for sin in Romans 6:23 when it says, "*For the wages of sin is death*," but then finishes the verse with the great news of the gospel. The wages of sin are death, "*but the gift of God is eternal life through Jesus Christ our Lord.*"

Jesus was the only one with the ability to hit the bull's-eye of perfection and allow us to use His score to enter into heaven. Through our faith in Him, we can all become perfect marksmen, an ability that is impossible on our own.

Thought for the Day

We will always have to say, "I missed the mark," unless we let Jesus qualify for us.

DAY 130

Come to Me, all you who labor and are heavy laden, and I will give you rest. Take My yoke upon you and learn from Me, for I am gentle and lowly in heart, and you will find rest for your souls, For My yoke is easy and My burden is light.
—Matthew 11:28–30

Unnecessary Burdens

I have written before that cops can be accomplished practical jokers. Another such stunt was carried out by members of the bicycle patrol unit on an unwitting fellow officer. On the back of every department mountain bike was a canvas gear bag that was attached to the frame. In it were cite books, reference materials, and first aid equipment. At the beginning of one shift, this officer's partners slipped a flat twenty-pound weight into the canvas case and hid it under the contents of the container. Bike officers usually have to ride out to their beat from the station and must climb what can be steep inclines in the roadway in order to get there. Of course, the officer with the newly "weighted down" bicycle could not understand why he was having so much trouble climbing hills that day. His fellow officers took that opportunity to rib him about his poor conditioning as they rode past him with relative ease. It wasn't until several days later that the officer discovered the extra weight was the cause of his "recent decline" in cardiovascular condition. He had been carrying a burden that he did not need!

Isn't that a lot like many of us in our Christian walk? We struggle under worries and concerns of this world. Jesus tells us in the above verse in Matthew that we are to go to Him with our burdens and He will give us rest. He does not want us to strain under the unnecessary weight of our problems and promises us that He will make our burdens light. In 1 Peter 5:7, God's word tells us exactly what to do with those worries and struggles as they come along, *"Casting all your care upon Him, for He cares for you."*

Thought for the Day

Are you struggling up a hill in your life with a heavy weight? Give it to Him and breathe easier.

DAY 131

*And if it seems evil to you to serve the Lord, choose for
yourselves this day whom you will serve, whether the gods
which your fathers served that were on the other side of the
River, or the gods of the Amorites, in whose land you dwell.
But as for me and my house we will serve the Lord.*

—Joshua 24:15

Choose Wisely

In the movie *Indiana Jones and the Last Crusade*, the protagonist,
Dr. Jones, had a life-or-death decision to make. In competition
with a Nazi collaborator, Indiana had been searching for the Holy
Grail (the cup Christ used at the Last Supper) throughout the movie.
When they found the location of the Holy Grail, they had to choose
between many cups in order to obtain eternal life. The evil collaborator made his choice and drank from a cup that he thought was
befitting of a king. Of course, the outcome for him was disastrous.
He chose poorly. Indiana, on the other hand, made the right decision
and drank from the true Holy Grail. He chose wisely.

The above verse in Joshua documents the leader's last statements to the people of Israel at the end of his life. He talked them
through their heritage and reminded them of some of the mistakes
their forefathers had made. He then made a declarative statement to
the people which follows us to the present day, thousands of years
later. *"Choose for yourselves this day whom you will serve."* He followed
that with his response to his own statement, *"But as for me and my
house we will serve the Lord."*

The lyrics to Bob Dylan's song "Gotta Serve Somebody" says it best, "It may be the devil, or it may be the Lord, but you're gonna have to serve somebody."

There are all kinds of things we can serve in this world. It may be money or relationships or even activities. It may be position or knowledge or power. We will give our time and effort to the thing or person we serve. Whom we choose to follow now will have eternal consequences for us when we stand before God. When we are asked the question, "Whom did you serve?" If the answer is anything other than "You Lord, by accepting your death on the cross for me," we will have made the wrong decision.

Thought for the Day

Choose wisely.

DAY 132

Then I looked, and I heard the voice of many angels around the throne, the living creatures, and the elders; and the number of them was ten thousand times ten thousand, and thousands of thousands, saying with a loud voice: "Worthy is the lamb who was slain to receive power and riches and wisdom, and strength and honor and glory and blessing.
—Revelation 5:11–12

The Crowded Throne

The largest crowd I ever played football in front of was 105,526 spectators at the 1980 Rose Bowl in Pasadena, California. I can't explain the sound that is generated from that many people, but it is awe-inspiring. There is a completely different audio quality if you are standing on the field than if you are sitting in the stands. The sound hits you in 360-degree waves and can be anything from exciting to intimidating. I have never heard anything like it since.

The above verse in Revelation tells us of a future heavenly scene as recorded by John. If I am reading the passage right, he saw 100,000,000 (10,000 x 10,000) angels and elders around the throne of God, with at least 4,000,000 (2,000 x 2,000) of them saying with a loud voice, "Worthy is the lamb who was slain…" Now that is crowd noise the likes of which I can't imagine!

I am looking forward to seeing heaven someday. God's word tells us, "*But as it is written: Eye has not seen, nor ear heard, nor have entered into the heart of man the things which God has prepared for those who love Him*" (1 Corinthians 2:9). I am sure the sights, sounds, and experiences will be beyond anything we can comprehend. I am so thankful that my place in heaven has been guaranteed to me not by my works but by Jesus's work on the cross for me.

First John 5:13 tells us, "*These things I have written unto you that believe in the name of the Son of God, that ye may know that ye have eternal life, and that ye may believe in the name of the Son of God.*" The word "believe" used here does not mean the simple head knowledge that Jesus was a real person who existed on this earth. It means a belief that He was God the Son and the turning of one's life over to His lordship.

Thought for the Day

Heaven is my eternal destination, and all of its sights and sounds will be the reward because of the free gift given to me, as undeserving as I am. I can't wait to stand surrounded by that crowd.

DAY 133

*At that time you won't need to ask me for anything. I tell
you the truth, you will ask the Father directly, and he
will grant your request because you use my name.*

—John 16:23

Dial Direct

When I first became a cop, cell phones where not yet in use. If I wanted to call home, I had no way to receive a phone call while in my police unit. If my wife needed to speak with me, she would have to call our Dispatch. I would receive a radio transmission that asked me to "10-21 your B," which I knew was the code for "call my home." I would then go to a pay phone, call 911 (our Dispatch would answer), and have them connect me to my home phone.

In Old Testament times, the people of Israel had to go through a similar laborious process to talk with God. In fact, they were only allowed to talk to and receive messages from God through the high priest.

The above verse in John documents Jesus's words to His disciples toward the end of His ministry. The "time" He is speaking of here would be after His departure from this earth and the arrival of the Holy Spirit in the lives of believers. They would then not need to ask Jesus (or a priest) for anything but would be allowed to ask God directly in Jesus's name. What a departure from the law that required a formal procedure to talk with God. Imagine, talking to the almighty directly!

I think we take for granted our ability to petition God for our needs and requests. After all, unless we are over two thousand years old, we have never needed to go through a middleman to access God our Father. And what a great privilege that is! Now because of Christ's death on the cross, and our acceptance of that sacrifice for us, we can go directly to the creator of the universe with our fears, concerns, requests, and even our complaints about our lives.

Thought for the Day

Thank you, Lord, for the gift of Your Son and for allowing us to dial direct to You.

DAY 134

Lest Satan should take advantage of us; for
we are not ignorant of his devices.

—2 Corinthians 2:11

Satan Likes Cover

There are all kinds of reasons that burglars choose a specific residence to target. If they feel that no one will be home, that it will be easy to get into the house, or that they won't be seen by a neighbor or anyone on the street, they will select that residence over others that don't have those qualities.

Burglars love large bushes that have been planted in front of windows or at other access points into the house. They can hide behind the plants and take their time defeating any lock or other security measure that has been designed to keep them out. Sometimes witnesses have passed a location without ever knowing that a burglar was applying his trade only feet from where they were walking.

Satan is a fallen angel who has been around watching and learning since the world was created. He is definitely the master of all criminals who hates us and knows exactly how to best attack us. One of his favorite tricks is to tempt us to sin and then accuse us of that sin after we have failed. He hides behind our own voice and makes us believe that his attacks are our thoughts. He also loves the fact that many don't believe that he exists at all. Can you imagine how successful any criminal would be if no one believed they were there or if victims didn't recognize the sounds the crook made while committing the crime? They would be free to walk in anywhere and commit any offense without being caught.

It is never to our benefit, as believers, to spend too much time focusing our thoughts on Satan. It is a good idea, however, to acquaint ourselves with his tricks and subterfuge in order to be able to resist his temptation and attacks. We need to read God's word, confess our sins, and rest in His love and forgiveness. Those are the things that can eliminate Satan's influence.

Thought for the Day

Cut down the bushes that give Satan a hiding place where he can attack us and provide the time he needs to break into our lives.

DAY 135

*Now therefore, if you will indeed obey My voice and
keep My covenant, then you shall be a special treasure
to Me above all people; for all the earth is Mine.*

—Exodus 19:5

Feelings versus Obedience

As police officers, we receive training that simulates possible calls for service. When school shootings became more frequent in our nation, active-shooter simulations became a part of many departments' quarterly training scenarios. This prepared responding officers to take down shooting suspects who are loose on school campuses.

As part of an active-shooter response team, each officer has a specific responsibility that requires their complete focus no matter what is going on around them. If an officer's assignment is to cover the rear of the team, they need to be facing in the direction behind the group no matter what they hear going on at the front of the formation. The hard part is to not react to the feelings you have about turning around and returning fire to the front, but to maintain your assignment no matter how you may feel about it. You must have faith that your partners who are facing the frontal attack will be doing their job.

God's word calls on us to keep His commandments no matter how we may feel about them. God's word says that "*all Scripture is given by inspiration of God, and is profitable for doctrine, for reproof, for correction, for instruction in righteousness*" (2 Timothy 3:16). Since **all** scripture is God inspired, all of it is true, and our requirement to follow it, all of it, is nonnegotiable.

I've often heard Christians say that they don't feel that God's word is right for their particular situation or that they have received a leading from the Holy Spirit to follow a course of action that is not backed by the Bible. They are wrong in both situations. If we are asked about what we do when we read things in the Bible that we disagree with, our only answer should be, "I change my opinion."

Thought for the Day

Don't get caught facing the wrong way in an attack. Follow God's word no matter what.

DAY 136

*For if we live, we live to the Lord; and if we die, we die to the
Lord. Therefore, whether we live or die, we are the Lord's.*

—Romans 14:8

Pink Slip

Several years ago, my wife and I bought a new wheelchair-accessible van for our child with physical challenges. OUCH! We were
at their mercy as far as price was concerned, due to the necessary
conversion and the lack of a low-cost alternative. In order to help pay
for the new vehicle, we sold our old van to a local wholesale buyer.
I went into their office, we agreed on a price, I signed the pink slip,
and I turned over the title/ownership of the car to them. It was then
their property to do with as they pleased. In fact, if I had tried to
take the van back or enter the car to drive it away, I could have been
prosecuted for theft.

We are all in possession of our own life's pink slips. Sure, God
made us, and He owns everything, but He has given the titles of our
lives to us. It's called free will. It is now up to us to decide whom we
will give that title to. We can give it to work, pleasure, money, drugs
and alcohol, or a relationship. We can even decide to hold on to it
ourselves and stay self-focused for the rest of our lives. It is often said
that it is not "who" we are, but rather "whose" we are. We all serve
something or someone.

In truth, if we have accepted Jesus Christ as our Lord and Savior,
it might be a tug-of-war for the rest of our lives as we, at times, try
to pull that pink slip back and take control. We will never win that
battle if God truly owns us.

If you have given your life to God, practice letting go of those ownership papers every day as you submit to Him. If you have never turned your life over to His lordship, sign off on that today and receive a plan and purpose in this life as well as a certain eternity with Him.

Thought for the Day

Who holds your pink slip?

DAY 137

For my thoughts are not your thoughts,
neither are your ways my ways, declares the Lord.
As the heavens are higher than the earth, so are my ways higher
than your ways and my thoughts than your thoughts.
—Isaiah 55:8-9

God's-Eye View

I had the opportunity to fly in the police helicopter as a passenger several times during my career. The view from overhead is very different from what it is on the ground. I knew Newport Beach pretty well from the street level, but I could hardly recognize the city from above. I had no landmarks, building architecture, or landscape configurations to help me know where I was. It takes quite a while for the helicopter pilots to become used to the city from their heightened point of view.

The above verse in Isaiah tells us that we will never be able to see things or think of things the way God does. He sees time from an eternal perspective. It is like watching a parade from an elevation of two thousand feet. From that vantage point, you can see the parade's beginning, middle, and end, while those on the ground just see one float at a time as it goes by. God knows our future as well as He knows our past.

Since God's perspective and knowledge are infinitely greater than our own, it would be a good idea to let Him call the shots in our lives. He can see things much better than we can and has a clear view of what lies ahead of us. God's word says, *"Trust in the LORD with all your heart, and lean not on your own understanding; in all your ways acknowledge Him, and He shall direct your paths"* (Proverbs 3:5–6).

Thought for the Day

Let's not rely on a limited ground-level view when we can be directed by God's elevated viewpoint.

DAY 138

All Scripture is given by inspiration of God, and is profitable for doctrine, for reproof, for correction, for instruction in righteousness, that the man of God may be complete, thoroughly equipped for every good work.

—2 Timothy 3:16–17

One Fin

I used to scuba dive. One of the requirements for passing an advanced certification was a dive at night. I was off the coast of Catalina in a boat on a pitch-black evening when it was my turn to complete my night dive. As I lowered my legs over the side of the boat to enter the ocean, one of my fins slipped off my foot and sank into the inky water. Considering the "no light" conditions and the depth of the water, it was safe to assume that my fin was gone. I looked at my instructor and asked what I should do now, and if I could complete the certification. His answer was "Well, you still have one fin, go down with that!" I did the dive that night, but I have to say it was the most uncomfortable, awkward, unbalanced dive that I had ever been on. I was able to function adequately but not efficiently. I made it back to the boat alive, but the loss of my fin had made the dive more of a trial than an anticipated event.

Second Timothy tells us that the Bible is inspired by God and is good for our instruction and correction in this life. With such a valuable resource available to us, why is it that some don't take the time to read or memorize the very word of God? One of the questions we always asked someone when they came in for counseling at the church was "How often do you read your Bible?" They are given three choices to answer that question: often, occasionally, or never. It is amazing how there seems to be a direct correlation between the severity of the problem and the answers occasionally or never to the Bible reading question.

If we do not read God's word and place it in our hearts (i.e., memorize it), we will not have a vital Christian life and will be thrown down hard by many of the trials that come our way. It would be a lot like trying to swim with one fin, uncomfortable, awkward, and unbalanced. It will make life more of a trial than an anticipated event and will not allow us to comfort others with God's word.

Thought for the Day

Don't dive into this life without being properly equipped with God's word. You might be able to swim around a little, but as a believer in Jesus Christ, you will not enjoy the trip.

DAY 139

For we do not wrestle against flesh and blood, but against principalities, against powers, against the rulers of the darkness of this age, against spiritual hosts of wickedness in the heavenly places.
—Ephesians 6:12

Suspicious Attack

I am not normally a spooky Christian. By that, I mean that I don't always view everything negative in my life as an attack directly from the Devil. Sometimes it is the Holy Spirit's corrective influence. Sometimes it is a result of my own stupid actions. But sometimes it really is oppression from the enemy.

When I was a pastor at Harvest OC, I noticed something that I can't deny. Every year as we approached our crusades (Harvest America and the Anaheim Harvest Crusade), I saw the incidents of aggressive accusations toward our church increase. They came from those who claim to be believers, but for some reason, they picked the crusade season to voice their concerns about our leadership, fairness, and theology. We seemed to get accused of everything from heresy to racial discrimination, none of which had any validity. Of course, we always took a hard look at our practices to ensure that we were not drifting from the truth or presenting ourselves in an unintended manner. It wasn't that we got complaints, I am sure that all churches do, it is the timing of the complaints that I found interesting. They always came just when we were working to put together events that usually resulted in seeing thousands make professions of faith in Jesus Christ.

During that time, I needed to remind myself what Ephesians 6:12 tells us. We are not fighting against flesh and blood, but against spiritual hosts of wickedness in heavenly places. Satan is working overtime to distract, discourage, and derail our efforts to put together these large events. The good news is that the enemy's tactics are the same each year, and God's word also remains the same, *"You are of God, little children, and have overcome them, because He who is in you is greater than he who is in the world"* (1 John 4:4).

We should not be surprised when we experience opposition in our lives. In fact, that is a good sign that we are doing something right!

Thought for the Day

If you are doing God's will and experiencing difficulties, rejoice! *"These things I have spoken to you, that in Me you may have peace. In the world you will have tribulation; but be of good cheer, I have overcome the world"* (John 16:33).

DAY 140

But be doers of the word, and not hearers only, deceiving yourselves.
—James 1:22

Hearers Only?

As police officers, we are married to our radios. Through them, we receive beat information, make requests for assistance, and receive calls for service. I can't tell you how many times I was out with a suspect and received some vital information about them that helped me safely conduct the call, or that allowed me to provide some sort of life-saving medical attention. You could make a compelling argument that a police radio is probably one of the most important pieces of equipment that a law enforcement officer can carry. The radio would be of no use to us if we were to listen to what Dispatch had to say but did not respond to the information we received from them.

God's word, the Bible, is our radio for the Christian walk. Through it, we receive instruction on how to safely conduct our lives, how to recognize and avoid danger, and how to encourage others toward a relationship with Jesus Christ. I've counseled many people, however, who seem to pick and choose what parts of the Bible that they will follow. They seem to hear all that God has to say, but only choose and act on what fits best with what they want for their lives.

The above verse in James says that we deceive ourselves when we become "hearers" of the word, and not "doers." A person might be so impatient for a romantic relationship that they will date an unbeliever even though God's word strictly forbids it (2 Corinthians 6:14). A Christian husband might divorce his wife in violation of

Mark 10:11–12 because he says he "fell out of love with her." A businessperson may decide to become involved in unethical financial practices and choose to forget "Thou shalt not steal" (Exodus 20:15). Or it might be as simple as the committed believer who decides to worry about a problem even when God's word says that He is in control of the situation (Philippians 4:6–7).

Thought for the Day

If we have given the ownership of our lives over to God, we need to not only **hear** what He says, but also **do** what He says as well.

DAY 141

*Therefore, to him who knows to do good and
does not do it, to him it is sin.*

—James 4:17

Missed Opportunities

When we think back on our police careers, there are many specific calls and incidents that will come to mind. Some will be exciting, some will be rewarding, while others will be disturbing or quietly painful. All of them can affect us in ways that we will never fully understand.

I had been on duty for about four years when I was dispatched to contact a local transient who was a regular "call generator" in the area of the West Ocean Front Lot. He was known as the aborigine to the locals due to his appearance, which was just like that of Australia's native inhabitants. I don't remember the exact nature of the call, but I handled the problem as quickly as I could and asked the subject to move on his way. There was a senior officer at the scene who felt that something additional needed to be said. He walked up to the subject and talked with him out of my earshot. I don't know exactly what he said, but I could tell from the officer's demeanor and the subject's reaction that it wasn't kind. The male then walked away. I never questioned that senior officer as to what he had said to him. I did not see the transient in my area over the next several weeks and had no idea where he had moved on to.

When we were in briefing a month later, we received word that the transient had stepped in front of a train in a neighboring city and committed suicide. I have often thought about what that officer had said to him and what part it played in his death. I have also felt anguish when I wondered if I could have stepped in and done more to make a difference in that man's life. I think the things that I regret most in my career were more about what I didn't do, rather than what I did do.

The above verse in James tells us that if we don't do something that we know we should, it is a sin, just as it is when we do things that we know we should not do.

We all can play an important part in the lives of others, whether we realize it or not. We never know what a kind word or seemingly insignificant action will mean to someone else.

Thought for the Day

Let's work as hard at doing the things we should do, as we do the things that we should not. We never want to miss the opportunities that God brings our way.

DAY 142

*For the love of money is a root of all kinds of evil, for
which some have strayed from the faith in their greediness,
and pierced themselves through with many sorrows.*

—1 Timothy 6:10

It's All Going to Burn

As an accident investigator, I responded to traffic collisions (TCs) to document the incident for both violation and insurance purposes. Most accidents involved minor to moderate vehicle damage while the drivers sustained no injury. At those scenes, I would usually console the parties involved who had just damaged their cars (usually expensive ones in Newport Beach) by telling them that the most important thing was that no one was hurt. I would then tell them that the property loss was just stuff, and then I would add, "It's all going to burn someday anyway." They usually agreed with that assessment and were glad to have made it safely through the accident. I say "usually" because I remember one time when that statement wasn't well received.

I responded to a report of a TC in the Westcliff parking lot. A vehicle had hit a parked car, leaving minor damage to its bumper. The owner of the parked car had called the police department to request a report. The car that was damaged was not an expensive one; it was just an older well-kept four-door sedan of no real note. The owner of the car was someone whom I knew. She was the widow of a famous industrialist who was well-known in Southern California. As far as affluent citizens in Newport Beach go, she was probably near the top of the list. She seemed overly upset about the minor damage to her vehicle, and when I laid the "It's all going to burn" line on her, she scowled at me and continued to angrily provide me with her license and vehicle information. She was probably the most well-heeled registered owner I had ever contacted who really had nothing to lose but a little time due to the accident.

Having worked in a wealthy city during my law enforcement career, I had the opportunity to see firsthand how money doesn't seem to bring happiness to those who have it. The above verse in 1 Timothy tells that "the love of money is the root of all kinds of evil." This doesn't mean that having money is wrong; it just warns us against putting riches above our love of God.

The funny thing about money is that we don't need to have a lot of it in order to be guilty of loving it. If we are constantly thinking about making it, or continually lament over our lack of it, we can allow material things to become the focus of our lives. *"But seek ye first the kingdom of God and His righteousness, and all these things shall be added to you"* (Matthew 6:33).

Thought for the Day

If you focus on things other than God, even a minor incident can put you over the edge.

DAY 143

And whatever you do or say, do it as a representative of the Lord Jesus, giving thanks through him to God the Father.

—Colossians 3:17

Life Keys

Your key ring tells a lot about your life. I was looking at mine as I drove to work. Some of the keys are gold and some are silver. There are several different shapes and sizes of keys on my ring, but most of them look pretty much the same. They may look similar, but each has a different purpose and represents a specific aspect of my life. I have a house key that reminds me of my home and those I love who live with me there. I have keys that represent the church where I worked, and others that are for various miscellaneous locks that I use.

I would say that the keys on my ring have completely changed over time to the point where there is not even one that was there three years ago. And of course, there is almost always one key that I have no idea what it unlocks. I am sure it was important to me at one time, otherwise I would not have kept it, but for the life of me, I cannot remember what it was used for.

When it comes to the various aspects of our lives (church, family, work, hobbies, relationships, etc.), we sometimes compartmentalize things. It is like we have a different key to every part of our lives, but we only choose to give God a selective few. It is fine that we give our spiritual lives to God on Sunday, but we are not sure we really want Him in our business dealings or our personal relationships. I think we are sometimes ashamed of our choices and would not want God to unlock the door to that personal space and walk in unexpectedly.

The truth is that if Jesus Christ is truly our Lord, He should have the master key that opens every lock that we think secures our existence. He should be involved in all the spiritual, financial, relational, and recreational parts of our lives. We should have no problem if Jesus were to enter in and check out what we are up to at any time. Of course, He does not need to unlock a door to find out what we are doing, He knows anyway. But the thing about Jesus is He will not enter our lives unless He is invited in. That is true when we accept Him as our Lord for the first time and continues to be true as we attempt to live for Him.

Thought for the Day

Do not lock God out of your life. Give Him full access to every secured area that contains all the things you do. Only then will He unlock the full blessings that He has for you.

DAY 144

How great is our Lord! His power is absolute! His understanding is beyond comprehension!

—Psalm 147:5

All In?

When I was a rookie cop, I didn't always understand why my FTOs (field training officers) would treat some people the way that they did. Sometimes I would see them be relaxed and conversational with citizens, and at other times, they would be short and direct. At first, it seemed a little arbitrary and unfair to me, but as I became more experienced, I learned the purpose behind their actions. Their years of experience had given them a better ability to read people, and they had a much better sense about whom to trust than I did. When I became an FTO years later, I had to laugh at myself when my trainees had puzzled looks on their faces as I went from zero to sixty in the sternness category with a suspect. I had gained enough wisdom over the years to instinctively know what was up in most situations and who posed a real danger.

Sometimes, God's actions might not make much sense to us and seem totally arbitrary. We cannot understand why He allows things to happen in our lives the way that they do. But part of surrendering our lives completely to Him is to embrace the fact that He is all knowing, and we are not.

God's word says that *"without faith it is impossible to please Him"* (Hebrews 11:6). As believers, we all want to live a life of faith in our Lord. To have an effective faith, we must start with the unshakable belief that God knows all things. Not only must we believe in that fact, but also, we must make decisions in our lives that are consistent with that belief. Many people claim to believe in an all-knowing God only to refuse to follow His clear commandments as seen in scripture. It doesn't really matter what we may think or feel about a situation. If it is covered in His word (and almost all things are), then we need to go His way, not our own.

I have counseled couples that are living together outside of marriage. They claimed that it made more financial sense to share expenses as they saved for their future life together. They said they believed in God's word but somehow felt that the commandments that disagreed with their personal living arrangements and financial plans were more like suggestions rather than rock-solid directions from God. They are not. If we are really followers of Jesus Christ, we must commit to following His word even if it does not make sense to us.

Thought for the Day

Are you all in or not when it comes to God's commandments for your life?

DAY 145

Your ears shall hear a word behind you, saying,
"This is the way, walk in it."

—Isaiah 30:21

Which Way Is Up?

It might sound strange to those who have never been scuba diving, but sometimes you can get so turned around underwater that you don't know which way is up. When you are diving at night or in a low-visibility situation, you can actually get confused as to where the surface is. That is why you are trained to watch for the air bubbles that are released from your regulator to get reoriented. Air will always rise to the surface; it is just simple science. So, if you will follow those bubbles, no matter which way you think is up, you will always be able to find the correct way to the surface.

God speaks to us through His word, the Bible. Sometimes His directions may not make sense, and we may even feel that it would take us in the wrong direction if we were to submit to it. But He always knows what is best and will lead us to a good and safe place if we will only follow Him.

I've talked with many people who have told me that the Bible is hard to decipher and that it is full of contradictions. They could never really name a passage that was troubling them. They just "believed" that God's will for their lives could not be understood. I've found that their statement usually had more to do with their reluctance to follow His will rather than an inability to understand it.

The Bible does have some complex areas, but the vast majority of it is fairly straightforward and easy to comprehend, even in the

King James English. I've counseled many individuals whose lives are out of sync with God's word and are wondering why things have gone wrong for them. I usually find that their major problem is that they have taken His commandments for their lives as general "guide-lines" or "good suggestions." They are following His word only if it agrees with their life choices or personal opinions about things.

If you feel confused or unsure of which direction to take, retreat to the surety of God's word and do your best to simply do what it says.

Thought for the Day

Don't get caught swimming in the wrong direction. Follow God's path for you as described in His word, no matter how you may feel about it. You will always be led to the surface of His will.

DAY 146

But the day of the Lord will come as a thief in the night, in which the heavens will pass away with a great noise, and the elements will melt with a fervent heat; both the earth and the works that are in it will be burned up. Therefore, since all things will be dissolved, what manner of persons ought you to be in holy conduct and godliness.

—2 Peter 3:10–11

Burned Away

When my wife and I were first married, we lived in a small apartment in Costa Mesa. I drove a VW Bug at the time that I parked outside behind our apartment complex.

As my wife left for work one morning, she remembered that she had all of our cash for the week in her purse. Knowing that I would be left lunchless, she decided to put a $20 bill in the unsecured engine compartment of my car. She did not have a key to the Bug and thought it would be a nice hiding place. Her intent was to call me when she arrived at work to inform me of the money's location. We did not have smartphones or even computers in those days, so a phone call from her car, an email, or text was not possible. Well, she forgot to make that call until after I had already driven to work. I went out to look in the engine compartment and found that the money was gone without a trace. It was either torn up, burned up, or had somehow worked its way out of an opening in the engine area. In any case, there was no lunch for me that day.

The above verse in 2 Peter tells us that the things of this world will someday pass away. This earth will be burned up in an instant and gone without a trace. Romans 1:25 speaks of those who "*exchange the truth of God for a lie, and worshiped and served the creature rather than the creator.*" It makes you wonder about the time and effort that some people put into our environment and the animals in it. I am for a clean world and have compassion for the creatures that God has made, but I choose not to put that concern in front of the God who made them.

Second Peter 3:11 then poses the question, "*Therefore, since all things will be dissolved, what manner of persons ought you to be in holy conduct and godliness?*" I think that we can get so wrapped up in recycling, our carbon footprint, and the humane treatment of animals that we forget God and His great commission to us to "*go ye therefore, and teach all nations, baptizing them in the name of the Father, and the Son, and the Holy Spirit*" (Matthew 28:19).

Thought for the Day

How much sense would it make to invest in expensive upgrades for a house that has been condemned and scheduled for destruction?

DAY 147

But no one can tame the tongue. It is restless and evil, full of deadly poison. Sometimes it praises our Lord and Father, and sometimes it curses those who have been made in the image of God.

—James 3:8–9

Untamable

Police officers are continuously affected by the 1967 Supreme Court decision in Miranda v. Arizona. After we arrest a suspect and begin to interview them about a crime, we are required to read them what has become known as their Miranda Rights. They include an availability to counsel and a right to remain silent. I was always amazed over the years as to a suspect's talkative nature even after having been carefully advised that he was not required to tell me anything. A famous comedian in his act tells of a drunken encounter he had with the police when he was detained for public intoxication. He claimed, "I had the right to remain silent, I just didn't have the ability."

God's word says that the tongue is *"restless and evil."* One minute, it is praising God, and the next, it is cursing others.

Police work is a very critical profession. We are often critiqued by supervisors, peers, attorneys, and the public. Some of those criticisms are justified and necessary in order for us to improve our performance, and many are nothing more than products of jealously self-motivated agendas, or an attempt to cover guilt. It is human nature to lash back when our self-esteem is threatened by what we perceive as a negative attack. That is when our tongues go into overdrive in order to justify our actions or to find fault with whomever we feel has wrongly accused us. This type of response can get us into trouble both professionally and personally.

God's word says that it is wiser to be *"quick to listen, and slow to speak"* (James 1:10–20) and *"it is wiser to keep silent and be thought as wise"* (Proverbs 17:28). I can remember many times in my career when I wish I had just said nothing.

Thought for the Day

It's easy to appear wise. Just say less and listen more. (Sam Levenson)

DAY 148

Even though I gave them all my laws, they act
as if those laws don't apply to them.

—Hosea 8:12

Choose

The above verse in Hosea pretty much sums up my law enforcement career. We were constantly chasing people around who decided that the law of the land did not apply to them. Whether it was driving under the influence of alcohol, stealing property that wasn't theirs, or physically injuring someone due to their own anger or personal agenda, all suspects followed one simple rule, "the law does not apply to me because I don't want it to." Of course, their personal interpretations usually resulted in an arrest despite what they thought.

Unfortunately, our passage in Hosea applies to many believers today also. I can't tell you how many counselees have told me that they know what God's word says, but they have decided not to do it because it would be inconvenient or because they simply don't want to. Believe it or not, I don't usually get much of an argument on the interpretation of a passage, just the willingness to do what it says.

Deuteronomy 11:26–28 says it all: "*Behold, I set before you today a blessing and a curse: the blessing, if you obey the commandments of the Lord your God which I command you today; and the curse, if you do not obey the commandments of the Lord your God, but turn aside from the way which I command you today, to go after other gods which you have not known.*"

We have a choice in this life to follow God's will or not. He will not force us to do either, but the outcome of each is clear in His word. Obey God and be blessed or disobey Him and take the consequences. I am thankful that God does not necessarily directly punish us when we disobey Him. But I would say that the absence of His blessing in my life is a curse, and the possibility of His chastening due to my disobedience becomes more real.

So, let's do the wise thing and let our actions acknowledge that we believe His laws apply to us.

Thought for the Day

Let's do the wise thing and let our actions acknowledge that we believe His laws apply to us.

DAY 149

That if you confess with your mouth the Lord Jesus and believe in your heart that God has raised Him from the dead, you will be saved.

—Romans 10:9

The Eternal Code

Police stations are secure places. Not just anybody can walk in. There are digital keypads all over the building that require a specific numeric code to enter. There are even some rooms inside of the building that have their own individual keypads whose combinations are given to only a select few. These numeric security numbers are changed on a regular basis, making it even more difficult to gain unauthorized entry.

The word "gospel" is translated from a simple term in the original Greek that means "good news." So, what is this good news that the Bible is speaking of? It is God's simple plan of salvation through our faith in Jesus Christ and his death on the cross for our sin. Through this faith, we can discover God's plan and purpose in our present lives and will be given an eternity with Him when this life has ended. That is good news!

The above verse in Romans tells us of the code that is required to gain access to these great blessings. We must confess Jesus Christ as the Lord of our lives, acknowledge that He died for our sin, and believe that He was raised from the dead and is our living Savior. Seems like a pretty simple three-digit code to gain access to eternity. And the great news is that the combination to eternal life never changes. It always takes nothing more than a true one-time simple step of faith in Christ to acquire. It is rare when something in our lives, that sounds too good to be true, really is true!

The combination for personal blessing and eternal security is simple, but specific. We have to decide to push the buttons on that faith keypad ourselves. We must use God's combination for eternal life as written in His word. No matter how hard we try to push our own code numbers, we will never receive access to what God has for us unless we submit to Him.

Thought for the Day

If you have not, why don't you use God's simple code to invite Jesus Christ into your life? Heaven is a secure place, not just anyone can walk in, but He loves you and has invited you to enter. Won't you?

DAY 150

*May the day perish on which I was born, And the night in which
it was said, 'A male child is conceived.' May that day be darkness
and the shadow of death claim it, Nor light shine upon it.*

—Job 3:3–4

Disappointed People

As police officers we come across people who are hurting every
day. Some people, like Job, have lost everything and wish that
they were never born. Sometimes it's hard to see their pain through
the abrasive, confrontational facade they put up as a defense against
our contact with them. They make it easy to forget that they are
hurting, disappointed people, especially if they are trying to punch
us in the face!

When I was a brand-new probationary cop, I came across a
transient male staggering northbound on McFadden Avenue at
Twenty-Second Street. He had all the objective symptoms of drunk-
enness and was carrying a large open container of beer in his coat
pocket. I arrested him for public intoxication and placed him in the
back of my unit. As I was filling out the booking slip, he leaned forward toward the glass to say something to me. I was expecting the
usual verbal assault, "You think you're a pretty big man, don't you"
or "Don't you have anything better to do?" But instead what he said
surprised me. "You must not think much of me, this isn't the way
I wanted my life to turn out." Even after all these years, I still get
choked up by the memory of this completely honest statement made
by a truly dejected man.

Sometimes we forget that no matter what they may say, disappointed people's lives, like Job in the above verse, have not turned out the way they expected. I'm sure that when they were children, they never said to themselves, "When I grow up I want to be a drunk, or a thief, or a prostitute!" I also realized that day that no matter what I may think of myself, I know that but for the grace of God, I'm just a few bad choices or circumstances away from finding myself in a similar position.

Thought for the Day

I have never forgotten that transient and how he changed the way I view the difficult people I met on the job. I pray that now you won't forget him either.

DAY 151

And there is no creature hidden from His sight, but all things are naked and open to the eyes of Him to whom we must give account.
—Hebrews 4:13

Say What?

As a police officer, I was always amazed to hear what people would say to each other when they didn't know I was standing nearby listening. Whether it was a threat, a lie, or some ridiculous brag, people often changed their tune when I walked out of the shadows in full uniform. Some would even deny they had said what I just heard them say. In any case, I found that people would seem to speak to each other with greater restraint when I was present as compared to when they didn't know I was there.

Individuals who normally appear to be prim and proper church-going folk have admitted in counseling that they often use profane and demeaning language toward each other when in an argument outside the church. They seem to have trouble restraining their speech when they have allowed themselves to become overwhelmed with anger toward their spouse. I have often used a particular word image when counseling couples who are having a hard time speaking civilly to each other. I tell them, "Next time you feel about ready to say something negative to your wife/husband, picture that Jesus is standing right next to them with His arm on their shoulder, looking you straight in the eyes. Would you say the thing you are about to say if He were there?" The answer is overwhelmingly "No, I wouldn't."

Well, the truth is Jesus is always there with us. Our above verse in Hebrews tells us two things. First, there is no person, place, or thing that is not known by God. Secondly, we must give an account for the things we say and do on this earth. Jesus Himself stated in Matthew 12:36, "*But I say unto you, that every idle word that men shall speak, they shall give account thereof in the Day of Judgment.*"

Fortunately for the believer, all our transgressions are forgiven through Jesus's death on the cross and His payment for our sin. But just because we are forgiven doesn't mean that the purposeful and idle words we say are not grievous to God. Scripture tells us, "*Indeed, we all make mistakes. For if we could control our tongues, we would be perfect and could also control ourselves in every other way*" (James 3:2).

Thought for the Day

So, next time we are about to say something that we know we shouldn't, remember that Jesus is standing there watching and encouraging us to say the right thing in kindness.

DAY 152

I have fought the good fight, I have finished the race, I have kept the faith. Henceforth there is laid up for me the crown of righteousness, which the Lord, the righteous judge, will award to me on that Day, and not only to me but also to all who have loved his appearing.
—2 Timothy 4:7–8

Fight On!

If you are at all familiar with the University of Southern California athletic world, you know that their fans are loyalty and tradition driven. Whether it is in the LA Coliseum, the Galen Center, or on the Cromwell track field, it is routine to observe a sea of the Trojan faithful, right hands in the air with two fingers extended in victory gesture as the USC band plays "Conquest." The standard greeting two USC alumni use when passing by each other is a nod of the head, followed by the phrase "Fight On!"

God's word has the same suggestion for believers as they struggle through this world. In the above verse, Paul encourages the young pastor Timothy by this statement about his life. Paul writes, "I have fought the good fight, I have finished the race, I have kept the faith."

That is exactly what we are called to do. It is becoming harder and harder to be a believer in Jesus Christ. The latest statistics indicate that 80 percent of the religious persecution found in the world today is against Christians. We need to fight the good fight in our homes, in our schools, in our businesses, and in our communities like we never have before. And at the end of our individual life races, may it be said about us that we fought the good fight, we have finished the race, and we have kept the faith.

The USC faithful often joke that "God is a Trojan." Well, I doubt that, but I am sure that Paul would have been, or at least he would have agreed with the modern-day Trojan fighting philosophy as it applies to the Christian life.

Thought for the Day

FIGHT ON!

DAY 153

For since the creation of the world God's invisible qualities—his eternal power and divine nature—have been clearly seen, being understood from what has been made, so that people are without excuse.
—Romans 1:20

Plain Evidence

As a police officer, I was always looking for or collecting evidence. Sometimes this evidence was very clear, as in the video recording of a crime. Other times it was more circumstantial and required me to gather various items to put together a clear picture as to what had occurred. Either way, the string of evidence that led to the arrest and conviction of a suspect was usually straightforward. Generally, only in films and made-for-TV movies is the evidence, or the suspect's identification, convoluted and mysterious. Things are usually just what they appear to be.

The evidence for the existence of God is found in the same way. The above verse in Romans tells us that the responsibility for the belief in God's existence is placed on us. His power and divine nature can be clearly seen and understood by this world that He has made. So clear is this chain of evidence that according to God, those who reject it are "without excuse."

Many times, in my career, I saw people reject overwhelming evidence based on their own personal bias, beliefs, or slanted worldview. But when God is the judge, individual opinion does not matter, especially when He says the evidence is clear.

Thought for the Day

The verdict is in! God exists, and we can see Him through the world that He has created.

DAY 154

Stand therefore, having girded your waist with truth,
having put on the breastplate of righteousness.

—Ephesians 6:14

God's Kevlar

Every day I wore a uniform during my law enforcement career. I put on a bulletproof Kevlar vest. When I was a rookie, our department's policy did not require for us to wear one. Some of the salty dog veterans opted not to, but I thought it would be a good idea to get used to a vest as part of my regular uniform attire. After many years on the job, I got so used to it, I didn't even notice I had it on. The only time I felt odd was when I wore a uniform for ceremonial purposes that did not require me to wear a vest. I always felt kind of naked and out of place while in uniform without my Kevlar protection.

In the above verse in Ephesians, God calls us to put on the breastplate of righteousness. Armor in the Roman era was for essentially the same purpose as it is today. To protect the vital organs of the body, mainly the heart. The breastplate was a vital part of a warrior's armor and could mean the difference between a glancing blow and a fatal strike.

Proverbs 4:23 tells us, *"Guard your heart above all else, for it determines the course of your life."*

In our battle with Satan, we, too, must arm ourselves so that any attack from our adversary is a minor hit rather than a fatal blow. The Kevlar vest that I wore only protected me against handgun rounds and shotgun blasts. High-powered rifles, however, could pass through. It would be the same circumstance for our spiritual breastplates if they were made by our own righteousness. It would provide pretty spotty protection.

Fortunately for us, we are covered by God-made armor purchased by Christ's death on the cross. Romans 4:24 states, *"But also for us, to whom God will credit righteousness—for us who believe in him who raised Jesus our Lord from the dead."*

Now we can put on the whole armor of God that includes a God-designed breastplate of righteousness that is impervious to any attack from the enemy. If we equip ourselves with the protection afforded us in the name of Jesus, our hearts can be guarded above all else as the verse in Proverbs admonishes.

Thought for the Day

Don't go out into the world unprotected. Choose to wear the attack-proof vest that God has provided you as part of your Christian uniform. Your spiritual life might depend on it.

DAY 155

*Jesus said to him, "I am the way, the truth, and the life.
No one comes to the Father except through Me."*

—John 14:6

One Way

One of my favorite adventure movies is *The Mummy*, which came out several years ago. I have always liked films with ancient Egyptian themes, and this one was well-made.

One of the characters in the movie is a self-serving, slimy individual named Benny. In one scene, Benny was confronted by the regenerating mummy of the evil priest Imhotep. As the mummy advanced in a menacing manner, Benny started to try a variety of prayers and chants in an attempt to ward off the attack. He held up different religious symbols that were on chains around his neck and chanted a prayer in the foreign language that corresponded with each medal. He finally lucked upon a Jewish Star and said a prayer in Hebrew. Understanding the language was that of the slaves during his time, the evil Imhotep decided to spare Benny and use him in his plan to regain power.

I have seen this same belief in the lives of many people over the years. They give a nod to a wide variety of religions in an effort to cover all their eternal destination bases. They think that there are many ways to get to God and that if they acknowledge any, or all of them, they will be all right. The best example of this is the "Coexist" bumper stickers that I see on cars nowadays. They contain about every religious symbol that there is. And while their call to live peaceably with others of different faiths is good, it still makes a statement that all those belief systems are equal in truth and in their access to eternal life with God. The truth is that there are many ways to get into the presence of God and His judgment, but only one way to enter into an eternity with Him. We will all live forever; the only question is where.

In the above verse in John, we have the answer to that question made by God the Son Himself. There is only one way to the Father, and that is through submission to the Lordship of Jesus Christ. All the prayers, religious symbols, good thoughts, or efforts toward a righteous cause will be meaningless when we stand before God on the Day of Judgment. The only question that will be asked is "Do you know Jesus?"

He is the way, the truth, and the life. No one can get to an eternity in heaven except through Him alone.

You can't attend the right church, wear the right medal, say the right chant, or have the right good thoughts to get into heaven. The only way is by confessing Jesus Christ as your Lord and Savior.

Thought for the Day

Says who? Says Him!

DAY 156

*Who comforts us in all our tribulation, that we may be able
to comfort those who are in any trouble, with the comfort
with which we ourselves are comforted by God.*
                                                    —2 Corinthians 1:4

Heavy Lifting

As a football player, I lived in the weight room. I would train reli-
giously with the objective of increasing my speed and strength. I
didn't experience much success with the speed part, but I did get con-
sistently stronger throughout my athletic career. It took long hours
of effort in order to accomplish that goal. I couldn't just walk into
the weight room, put my hand on the weight stack, and get stronger
through osmosis. I had to do the heavy lifting required in order to
improve.

God's word tells us that we will go through trials and tribulations in this world. The good news is that these difficulties will not
be wasted or without meaning in our lives. With each trial, we will
increase our spiritual strength and our ability to comfort others who
are going through similar troubles.

Nothing is more rewarding than being used by God to help others. We need to remember that no matter what we are going through,
there will be a time when God will allow us to use that experience
to intervene for Him in the lives of others. It can put a whole new
perspective on our current situation.

Thought for the Day

You can't develop a strong faith unless you do some heavy lifting along the way.

DAY 157

*I saw the dead, both great and small, standing before God's
throne. And the books were opened, including the Book of Life.
And the dead were judged according to what
they had done, as recorded in the books.*

—Revelation 20:12

Missing Evidence?

Most people have never had the opportunity to stand in a law
enforcement property room. The shelves are lined with boxes
and envelopes that contain evidence from crimes that may have
occurred over many decades. I was always saddened by the silent
witness that these items gave and the amount of pain and sorrow they
represented. Each box contains physical confirmations of the loss,
abuse, or death of victims. They also, many times, hold the proof of
guilt for those who had caused all that sorrow. The property room is
a place where evidence is securely held until a case could be tried in
court. But unfortunately, it is also a place where unsolved crimes sit
dormant, waiting for a justice that may sometimes never come.

The above verse in Revelation speaks of the Great White Throne
of Judgment that will someday be held in God's court. This will not
be the judgment that believers in Jesus Christ will stand before but
will be for those who have rejected God's offer of forgiveness and
grace. At that time, all the evidence shelves will be cleared and all cases
justly adjudicated. The property room of heaven will be completely
empty, all injustice and sorrow will be addressed, and all defendants
will be found guilty because the evidence will be indisputable.

The only people that will be at the Great White Throne of Judgment will be those who have chosen to be there. We will never have to stand before God in judgment with our eternity on the line if we have made Jesus Christ the Lord of our lives. All evidence against us will have been erased due to Christ's atoning work on the cross on our behalf.

Thought for the Day

When God goes to locate your case evidence, will He find an empty shelf? Only if Jesus is the last signature on the chain of custody.

DAY 158

For by grace you have been saved through faith. And this is not your own doing; it is the gift of God, not a result of works, so that no man may boast.

—Ephesians 2:8–9

It's Not That Hard

I have found that many younger police officers work a lot harder than they have to. One day, we responded to a welfare check on a subject who was reported to have taken an overdose of illegal drugs while inside his own residence. We knew that the subject was in his house, but he refused to answer our telephone calls and our repeated knocks at the front door. Some of our newer officers had gathered on the porch and were, frankly, a little excited to kick in the door due to the exigent circumstances of the call.

We knew that it could come to that, but a senior officer at the scene decided to try something different. He stood in front of the house and called out to the subject inside by his name. From an upstairs window, we saw a curtain move aside and observed a male looking down at us. The officer then motioned to him to come down, and he walked out of the front door about thirty seconds later, much to the surprise of those gathered for the door kick. Sometimes things are just not that hard.

The above verse in Ephesians tells us that there is no way that we can earn our own salvation. It is a gift from God that cannot be obtained by our good works. He knew that no one could ever live the sinless life that would be required, so He came to the earth in human form in the person of Jesus Christ. Jesus lived the perfect life that we could not, and He died on the cross to pay the price for our sin. All we need to do is to accept that payment by asking Him to take control of our lives.

Jesus will never kick in the door to your life. He is motioning to you now to either accept His free gift of salvation for the first time, or to rededicate your life to His plan and purpose for you.

Thought for the Day

Won't you just walk out to Him now? It's just that easy.

DAY 159

Beloved, now we are children of God; and it has not yet been revealed what we shall be, but we know that when He is revealed, we shall be like Him, for we shall see Him as He is. And everyone who has this hope in Him purifies himself, just as He is pure.

—1 John 3:2–3

Like Father, Like Son

Years ago, I was writing a male subject a marijuana citation on the beach late at night. It had always been our practice to book into evidence not only the drug, but also the device that was used to smoke it. Even though in California a marijuana pipe was not illegal in and of itself, it was evidence that speaks to the possession, ownership, and active use of the drug. Some of these pipes were quite elaborate and expensive. A defendant was often more concerned that I took their pipe than they were with the fact that they were cited for illegal drug possession.

On that night when I confiscated the glass smoking device from the subject on the beach, he said to me, "Oh, man, don't take that, my dad gave it to me for Christmas!" I could see the true nature of this kid's problem; he was just like his father.

The above verse gives us the great hope that we will someday be just like our heavenly Father. But it offers us more than that! Verse 3 states, *"And everyone who has this hope in Him purifies himself, just as He is pure."* If we put our faith in God, we can have the assurance, today, that we can be forgiven. Not because of what we do, but because of who and what He is. God is pure and holy and can help us get started on the process of becoming more like Him every day by our simple faith in Him.

Thought for the Day

As believers, we have the great hope that someday, when the Lord comes again and reveals Himself to us, we will be made like Him. Now that's a dad that we will be proud to be like!

DAY 160

*A man's steps are of the LORD; How then can
a man understand his own way?*

—Proverbs 20:24

All Turned Around

At the Newport Beach Police Department, we always used true compass directions in reports and radio communications. This might not seem like a big deal, but it sometimes caused confusion, especially if you grew up in the area that I did. I had been driving for many years before I became a cop, so I was used to the roads and directional traffic signs in Southern California.

One of the more famous roadways through Newport Beach is the Pacific Coast Highway. All signs indicate that PCH travels north and south. If you want to go to Malibu, you go north. If you want to go toward San Diego, you travel south. The problem is that the road actually runs east and west per the true compass directions. If you go true south, you drive toward the ocean, and if you want to go north, you travel the opposite way. As a police officer, I was constantly fighting my old training. If I got into a pursuit or was involved in some other type of stressful call, I had to concentrate in order to advise of my correct direction of travel using true compass readings. It was something I dealt with throughout my career.

God's word says, "*Trust in the LORD with all your heart. And lean not on your own understanding; In all your ways acknowledge Him, And He shall direct your paths*" (Proverbs 3:5–6). I'm so glad that I have a God that I can go to when I don't know which way to go. I can't tell you how often I have traveled in the opposite direction from

His will for my life. There were times when I did not seek God and went the way I thought was best. That never turned out well for me.

We need to follow God whether it feels right to us or not. We need to follow Him no matter what our previous training and experiences have taught us. We need to follow our heavenly Father even if it appears that doing so will lead us to a dead end in our lives. God's word says that "*for My thoughts are not your thoughts, Nor are your ways My ways, says the LORD*" (Isaiah 55:9).

When you seem all turned around and uncomfortable with the direction in your life, it is time to get on your knees and seek His will. He promises to lead you on a good path no matter how odd that direction may seem.

Thought for the Day

Follow the true compass of God's word and not the faulty one that we were born with.

DAY 161

Though your sins are like scarlet, they shall be as white as snow; though they are like crimson, they shall be as wool.

—Isaiah 1:18

White as Snow

We just bought a new rug for our living room. We had it special ordered and bound to a specific dimension. My wife and I have talked in the past about what colors we should avoid. Having kids, and now grandchildren, I thought we had agreed to stay away from light shades due to the inevitable staining issues. That's what I thought. Somehow, I was talked into getting a white (well, off-white) carpet. It looks great for now, but I am almost certain that it won't stay that way for long. Despite our best efforts to keep it clean, accidents will happen that will challenge the immaculate condition of the rug. Maybe then I will be able to talk her into "no more white" from this point on. Yeah, right.

We are a lot like that carpet. Despite our best efforts, our sin ruins the hue of our lives. In a short time, we can create stains that will take a once pristine landscape to an ugly condition with spots that can never be removed. But God's word tells us that "*things which are impossible with men are possible with God*" (Luke 18:27).

The above verse in Isaiah documents the power God has to forgive sin and turn a stained life back to a state that is even better than the original condition. The color scarlet mentioned in verse 18 would have been well-known to people in biblical times. It was a brilliant red color worn in temple ceremonies that was very pronounced in nature. Taking a scarlet fabric and making it white as snow would have been a striking word picture for those who first heard these words.

It doesn't matter how dark and stained the fabric of your life has become. Even though our sins have put what seems to be permanent stains on our lives, God can clean them completely due to the sacrifice Jesus made on the cross for us. The scarlet of our sin, past, present, and future, can only be cleaned by the scarlet of His blood.

Thought for the Day

Only Jesus can make our lives spot free.

DAY 162

O God, You know my foolishness; And my sins are not hidden from You.
—Psalms 69:5

Useless Hiding

As police officers, we saw just about every trick that could be used to cover unlawful activity. I worked in a beach city where illegal alcohol consumption was a regular occurrence.

One day at Corona Del Mar State Beach, one of our officers was out on foot when he heard a conversation between several subjects who were unaware of his presence around the corner of a building. One of the males was bragging to the group about how he routinely emptied a soda can and refilled the container with alcohol. He then proudly stated, "You can walk around all you want, and the cops will never catch you!" That prediction was soon to be proven untrue when the subject received a citation in front of his friends for the alcohol he had in his possession. The truth is that we were already well aware of the soda-can ploy as well as the red-cup dodge and the water-bottle-refill gimmick. None were very creative, nor did they avoid the strong odor of an alcoholic beverage that came from the drinker's breath.

God knows the truth about everything in our lives. We might be successful in concealing it from others by the image that we project, or by the look of the container we pour ourselves into, but nothing is hidden from Him. It is a waste of time for us to believe that we can whitewash things or make God believe that we are better than we both know we are.

That might sound like bad news, but it is not! Romans 5:8 tells us, *"But God demonstrates His own love toward us, in that while we were sinners, Christ died for us."* That means He loved you and sent Jesus to die for you even when He knew everything about your past, present, and future. Nothing you have done, are doing now, or will do is a surprise to Him; He loves you and **wants to use you for His glory anyway!** Just ask for forgiveness (1 John 1:9), pick yourself up, and start moving toward His will.

God hates sin, but He will never hate you.

Thought for the Day

You don't need to change the containers of your life to hide the sin that God already knows about. Just pour it out and let Him fill you up anew.

DAY 163

Confess your trespasses to one another, and pray for one another, that you may be healed. The effective, fervent prayer of a righteous man avails much.

—James 5:16

Christian Actors

As an undercover police officer, I had to take on an entirely altered persona. I had a different name, job, and personal history that I used to identify myself to suspects whom I was seeking to arrest. It was sometimes difficult to keep everything straight in my head, but as time went on, I became decent at it, and I made the suspects believe that I was the fictitious person whom I claimed to be.

Over the past decades, I have also been on the security teams for several well-known pastors in the Orange County, California, area. In those positions, I became aware of specific intelligence about members of the church as it related to security concerns. I was never surprised by what I found out about these individuals that was very different from the smiling spiritual talking people that I saw on Sundays. They had developed an incredible spiritual persona that seemed to have nothing to do with their lives away from the church.

I think we are all guilty of that to some degree. We tend to place our best foot forward when it comes to the Christian presence we show to others in the church. The above verse in James tells us to *"confess our trespasses to one another."* Now I don't think this is a calling to go around and unload all of your personal failings on anyone who will listen.

I believe God is encouraging us to be authentic in our Christian walks and to be willing to share our true selves with others. I can't tell you how many times God has used my weaknesses in a counseling setting to give hope to a person who was experiencing a similar problem. We are not without precedence here. The apostle Paul wrote that he asked three different times for the Lord to take it away. Each time he said, *'My grace is all you need. My power works best in weakness.' So now I am glad to boast about my weaknesses, so that the power of Christ can work through me"* (2 Corinthians 12:8–9). God will be able to use you more if you are sincere with others and quit the Christian show.

Thought for the Day

Let's quit the act and get real for God.

DAY 164

The heart is deceitful above all things, and
desperately wicked: who can know it?

—Jeremiah 17:9

The Wicked Heart

I always tried to teach my girls that when you want to find out the truth about people, watch what they do, don't listen to what they say. It has been my experience that the old adage is true, actions do speak louder than words. I saw the truth of that statement reveal itself many times over my twenty-one years in law enforcement. I came across many bad actors during my career as well as some good people. Unfortunately for me, I was paid to find the former and not the latter. That meant I spent most of my time looking for evil.

We all know that evil people are capable of good (Luke 6:33), just as good people are capable of evil (Ecclesiastes 7:20), but actually, the good and evil balance of our hearts is not in question. Our verse today tells of the heart's true condition. It is "*deceitful above all things, and desperately wicked.*" We also read in Isaiah 64:6 that "*all our righteousness is as filthy rags*" to God. Wow, if that is the condition of our hearts and our works before the Lord, then who can have a relationship with Him?

Our salvation is not dependent on the condition of our heart, but rather the action of God the Son, Jesus, when he paid the price for our sin on the cross. God's word says, "*Though your sins are like scarlet, they shall be as white as snow*" (Isaiah 1:18). God's word promises us that even though we are evil, that even though our actions don't match our words, and even though we deserve eternal death for our sin and rebellion against God, we can be forgiven and justified through our faith in Jesus Christ.

My favorite verse on forgiveness is Micah 7:19 which says, "*He will again have compassion on us, and will subdue our iniquities. You will cast all our sins into the depths of the sea.*" One thing cops know about is evidence recovery. If they throw a gun in the lake, the divers can find it. If they throw it in the river, it can wash up somewhere. But if they throw contraband off a boat between here and Catalina Island, in the depths of the sea, it is gone forever.

Thought for the Day

I am so grateful that God doesn't decide the truth about me by my actions, but by Jesus's actions on the cross for me on my behalf.

DAY 165

*This is to my Father's glory, that you bear much
fruit, showing yourselves to be my disciples.*

—*John 15:8*

Disciple Litmus Test

As patrol officers, we were often called upon to find suspects, witnesses, or victims. If Dispatch provided an address, we would go to that location in an effort to find the subject of our search.

One trick some used to determine if anyone had recently arrived at the residence was to feel the hood of a car parked in the driveway. The theory was that if the metal of the hood was hot, the engine had been recently running. If it was, it was a good bet that someone had just arrived at the house in question.

Due to the heat of the sun near the beach, I never trusted the "hood heat" method especially during the day. I would, instead, feel the tailpipe of the car. It was usually covered and not in the direct rays of the sun. If the tailpipe was hot or even warm, I knew that the vehicle had arrived at the location in the past hour. It was a quick and easy litmus test to determine the recent activity of the vehicle just prior to my arrival.

God's word tells us that there is a quick and easy test that we can use to see if a person is a follower of Jesus Christ. The above verse in Matthew records the words of Jesus as he told His followers how to determine if someone is His disciple. They must bear fruit! A fruit-filled life is not a rock-solid indicator of salvation, but it may cause doubt if that fruit does not exist.

God's word tells us what the fruits of the Spirit are, love, joy, peace, patience, kindness, goodness, faithfulness, gentleness, and self-control. That is quite a list, isn't it? I know I don't always show these attributes in my life, but I am working on it. If we don't show any of these qualities, or rarely show them, we are not bearing much fruit and our faith is in doubt.

Thought for the Day

Will the world feel cold metal when they come into contact with your life? Or will you be hot to the touch from recent, active discipleship?

DAY 166

When he lies, it is consistent with his character;
for he is a liar and the father of lies.

—John 8:44b

Scam Artist

One of the sickest phone scams I routinely investigated involved elderly people. A suspect would call a victim and claim to be their grandchild. Their voice would sound different, but they would blame that on the poor phone connection from where they were calling. The suspect would then tell their "grandparent" that they were in jail in Mexico and that they needed bail money in order to be released. The suspect might even use the possibility of pending physical abuse by their captors to heighten the fear in the elderly victim. Most older people were astute enough to immediately call someone to check on the whereabouts of their grandchildren. But for the con artist, these types of frightening phone calls were a numbers game. They would make numerous calls until they came across someone who was diminished enough to be fooled by their scam. I never understood the depths that one would have to sink to make their living frightening defenseless people.

Our adversary Satan is that kind of individual. He is the father of liars, whose stock and trade is to frighten people so that they will make bad decisions and, in doing so, hurt themselves. He might scam you about your future, attempt to take away the assurance of your salvation and forgiven status with God, or even try to make you believe that your life is without hope and worth. Just like earthly con artists, Satan's scams will take many forms that are variations of the same intent to steal your peace in God from you.

The smart follower of Jesus Christ will verify the con as it comes to them. We can do that by comparing it to God's word. You see, when you became a follower of Jesus Christ, all the promises in the Bible belong to you. When you are lied to about your future, Jeremiah 29:11 counters that by telling you that God has a *"future and a hope"* for you. When the enemy tells you that you have gone too far and that God has rescinded His gift of salvation to you, John 10:28 records Jesus's word on the subject when He said, *"And I give them eternal life, and they shall never perish; neither shall anyone snatch them out of My hand."* And when you feel that your life is no longer worth living, 1 Corinthians 6:20 tells you that you are important and that *"you were bought at a price."*

Thought for the Day

All scams are uncovered by the truth. Don't listen to the pathetic lies of the enemy. Verify the truth by reading and believing in God's word.

DAY 167

As he spoke, he showed them the wounds in his hands and his side. They were filled with joy when they saw the Lord!

—John 20:20

Finally in Touch

I recently purchased an 1882 English halfpenny on eBay. This might seem like an oddly specific thing to buy, but it did have a significant meaning to me. For my entire childhood, I had heard the old Christmas carol "Christmas Is Coming" sung during the holiday season. The words to that song are "Christmas is coming, the goose is getting fat, please put a penny in the old man's hat. If you don't have a penny, a halfpenny will do. If you don't have a halfpenny, then God bless you."

As a child, I always wondered, "What is a halfpenny, what does it look like, and how poor do you have to be to not have one?" I recently discovered that the words to the song "Christmas Is Coming" are centuries old and had been repeated as an unofficial rhyme throughout the years in England. It wasn't until 1882 that the song was officially published and sold as sheet music. So, by purchasing a coin that only cost $4, I was not only able to finally hold a halfpenny in my hand, but also one that was in use when the song was published!

The above verse in John tells us that the disciples saw the wounds in the hands of Jesus after He had been resurrected from the dead. So, we know that His new body, which is like the one we will have some day (Philippians 3:21), still bared the scars of His death on the cross for us. We don't know exactly what Jesus looked like, but we do know that when we see Him face-to-face per 1 Corinthians 13:12, *"we shall be like Him, for we shall see Him as He is"* (1 John 3:2).

What an unbelievable day that will be when we see Jesus. All those years of wondering who He is and what He looked like will be over. For the first time, we will be able to hold the nail-scarred hands of Jesus and feel for ourselves the wounds he suffered on our behalf.

Thought for the Day

Someday, we will hold in our hands the answer to the questions we have wondered about our entire Christian lives. I can only imagine what that will be like.

DAY 168

And whatever you do, do it heartily, as to the Lord and not to men.
—Colossians 3:23

Take a Play Off?

There are some newer terms used in the evaluation of football players when coaches are deciding whether or not to recruit them at the college level. When I heard about them, they were new to me and were not used when I played. One question is "Does he have a high motor?" That one I understood right away as an inquiry into a player's level of energy and determination on the field. But another, even though I instinctively understood what it meant, I couldn't believe was possible. Coaches will ask, "Does he take plays off?" Take plays off! Can that really mean that if a player determines his assignment is not essential to a play on the field, they will not give their full effort against their opponent? I find that almost impossible to believe! I played with some great players who had long NFL careers. I don't remember any of us taking a play off for any reason. We learned that every battle was important, even if it were only to dominate your opponent in order to make a future play more productive. I was not always successful as a football player, but there is one thing I can say for myself: I never took a play off.

God wants us to do the same in our everyday work lives. The above verse in Colossians exhorts us to do everything "*heartily, as to the Lord.*" As Christians, we should have the ultimate reputation as hard workers, not just because we want to be promoted or receive pay increases. There is nothing wrong with those things, but our ultimate goal should be to honor God by our effort and not the people around us. Of course, if we put God first, the result will usually be that those we work for will respect our dedication and work ethic. Many people have been drawn to ask questions about God by the hardworking Christians they work with who set themselves apart with their honesty, effort, and integrity on the job. Whether it is at work, home, school, church, we should never take a play off, but should do everything as unto the Lord.

Thought for the Day

All our efforts of value are seen by God even if it might appear not to be important at the time.

DAY 169

"For My thoughts are not your thoughts, Nor are your ways my ways," says the LORD.

—Isaiah 55:8

God's Lens

God sees things a lot differently than we do. While earning my scuba certification in the 1990s, we were taught about the magnifying properties of the ocean and how everything looks about 25 percent larger underwater. This fact was proven true to me many times when I would bring an object up from the depths to discover that it was a lot smaller than it had first appeared. The lens in my mask had given me a distorted view of the object. Some of the dangers I encountered while underwater (i.e., eels, small sharks, metal pieces, etc.) also appeared to be a lot bigger and more ominous than they really were.

Many of the problems that we face can seem larger than life if we choose to look at them through the lens of our own perspective. Our view is almost always inaccurate. God's thoughts are not the same as ours, and He can see our present and our future with great clarity. There is no magnification or distortion in God's view. He knows our fears, and He is able to help us no matter what the situation may look like. The Bible describes God's ability to act in our lives, *"Now unto him that is able to do exceedingly abundantly above all that we ask or think, according to the power that works in us"* (Ephesians 3:20).

Thought for the Day

When our problems seem too big for us to handle, we just need to look at them through God's lens rather than our own.

DAY 170

Jesus replied, "'You must love the Lord your God with all your heart, all your soul, and all your mind.' This is the first and greatest commandment. A second is equally important: 'Love your neighbor as yourself.' The entire law and all the demands of the prophets are based on these two commandments.

—Matthew 22:37–40

Only Two Things

After I graduated from the Orange County Sherriff's Academy, I was placed into a field training program at my department. One of my field training officers (FTO) was a veteran cop named Charlie. He was about to retire from the PD, and I think I might have been one of the last officers he trained (sorry to all my past partners, don't blame Charlie). Charlie was one of those experienced straight-talking guys who had seen everything. He was a great cop that knew the difference between what was important in law enforcement and what was not. I rode with him for a month as I learned his take on police work and how to be a successful law enforcement officer.

One day as we patrolled the city, Charlie said to me, "Do you want to have a good career," referring to my newly chosen job as a police officer. He then told me, "You only have to remember two things, make your sergeant happy and go home alive every night. Nothing else matters." Wow, that sure put everything into perspective. Could it really be that simple? Over the next twenty-one years, through my career successes and failures, I often thought of that statement given to me by a wise old cop. I concluded that no truer words had ever been spoken. I always tried to do those two things, and I did finish my law enforcement race alive and with a decent reputation.

I think the same kind of advice can be given to all Christian first responders. Make God happy and go home ALIVE every night. The "make God happy" part seems straightforward and easy to define. Jesus said, "*If you love Me keep My commandments*" (John 14:15). It will always make God happy if we follow His will for our lives. The "going home emotionally alive every night" part can be harder to not only define, but also to accomplish. The things we are forced to see and hear can sometimes bleed the life out of those whose job it is to face the evil and tragedy of this world on a daily basis. But God's word covers this emotional drain with hope. 2 Corinthians 4:16 tells us, "*Therefore we do not lose heart. Even though our outward man is perishing, yet the inward man is being renewed day by day.*" Through our faith in Christ we can have the great promise of renewal that will help us stay alive in Him.

The above verse in Matthew records Jesus's response to the Pharisees who sought to trip Him up with the question, "*Teacher, which is the most important commandments in the Law of Moses?*" Jesus's answer contained just two things, love God (make Him happy) and love your neighbor (be alive in the lives of others). It really is that simple.

Thought for the Day

Do you want to live your life for God? It only takes two things, nothing else matters.

DAY 171

Whereas you do not know what will happen tomorrow.
For what is your life? It is even a vapor that appears
for a little time and then vanishes away.

—James 4:14

Here Today, Gone Tomorrow

I can remember the last play of my football career as if it were yes-terday. On January 1, 1980, I was standing on the twenty-yard line at the Pasadena Rose Bowl. We were playing Ohio State and had just finished a running play that gained minimal yardage. That was okay because the clock was quickly ticking down and we were ahead 17–16. As I stood there, I looked up at the scoreboard that was located in front of me at the end of the field. I watched as the clocked ticked down, 5, 4, 3, 2, 1, and I then heard the gun sound that signaled the end of the fourth quarter (that's when they actually used blank gun rounds at athletic events). In a few brief seconds, the game of football that had consumed the last fourteen years of my life had come to an end. I knew my chances to play in the pros were minimal and that my life was about to change from that day on. No matter how well I thought I had prepared for that moment, it came too quickly.

The above verse in James calls our lives "a vapor" that shortly evaporates away. Some will know when that end is nearing while oth-ers will be caught by surprise. This world might not come to an end tomorrow, but your world might. Those who have put their faith in Jesus Christ are covered either way. Are you ready?

Thought for the Day

Don't get caught unprepared as your world's existence counts down to the final gun.

DAY 172

*And I saw the dead, small and great, standing before God, and
books were opened. And another book was opened, which is
the Book of Life. And the dead were judged according to their
works, by the things which were written in the books.*

—Revelation 20:12

MVS

I was in traffic court years ago on a stop-sign violation. The defendant had run the sign at about 20 miles per hour without making
any attempt to slow down. I had now been subpoenaed to court so
that she could challenge the ticket before a judge. I gave my testimony about the incident, and when it was the defendant's turn to
testify, her version of the event was 180 degrees opposite of mine. She
stated that she had come to a complete stop at the intersection before
driving into a nearby liquor store parking lot. The defendant said
that she had parked her car, exited the vehicle, and entered the store
where she stayed for about ten minutes. She told the judge that she
had come out of the location, gotten into her car, and drove from the
lot onto the highway. She stated that I stopped her for the supposed
violation a short time later. The defendant told the court that "the
officer must have mistaken my car for the one he saw run the stop
sign" and added that the time delay between the violation and my
contact with her had caused the confusion.

The only problem with her story was that I had recorded the
entire event on my mobile video system (MVS). The judge looked at
me and asked if I had any additional testimony. I said, "Well, Your
Honor, I recorded the violation if that would be of any help." He

answered, "Why, yes, it would." He then had the bailiff roll out the viewing monitor. The "oh no" look on the defendant's face was priceless. As the entire court watched the uninterrupted video, it became clear that she had not only failed to come to a stop, but that she had also not gone into the liquor store for one second, let alone the "10 minutes" that she had testified to under oath. The judge looked at her over the top of his glasses and asked, "Well, do you have anything else to say?" The defendant hung her head in shame and said a simple no right before she was found guilty.

Someday, we will all stand before God and have our entire lives played back to us. For those of us who have accepted Jesus as our Lord and Savior, it will be at the Judgment Seat of Christ where our works for God will be evaluated before we enter into an eternity with Him (2 Corinthians 5:10). We will not have to pay the price for our sin because Christ will have done that work for us by His death on the cross. The above verse in Revelation shows that for the nonbeliever, their lives will be played back at the Great White Throne of Judgment. That is where all of their sins will be revealed, and their rejection of Jesus Christ will be shown in uninterrupted detail. There will be no more excuses, lies, or explanations that will cover their actions. All that will be left for them will be to hang their heads in shame and admit their guilt before God.

There is no reason for anyone to have to appear in God's court unrepresented. Accept Christ now; give the control of your life to Him. He will keep you from the Great White Throne of Judgment and declare you "not guilty" before the Father at the Judgment Seat of Christ.

Thought for the Day

The MVS of your life can be an event of great joy or the final defeat in your eternity, it's up to you.

DAY 173

You will know them by their fruits. Do men gather
grapes from thorn bushes or figs from thistles?

—Matthew 7:16

Jersey Label

I never played for a football team that had our names printed on the back of our uniforms. Not in junior All-American, high school, or college football. While I played at the University of Southern California, the question of putting our names on our jerseys came up from time to time. Our coach would always say, "Score twenty touchdowns or make ten sacks, and people will know who you are! The only difference here will be the size of the uniform and the number on it!"

Whether we realize it or not, Christians are scrutinized closely by the world. If we make a stand for Jesus Christ, people will examine our lives to see if our actions match our words. It won't make any difference to them if we have identified ourselves as believers if our faith does not actually work in tough times. We might have given ourselves the label of a Christian but have no actual working evidence to show for it.

The above verse in the book of Matthew tells us that as followers of Jesus Christ, we will be known by the "fruits" in our lives. Our conduct will either identify us as believers or confuse others due to the lack of congruency we show between our actions and stated beliefs. It couldn't be any more obvious if we held a sign or had it printed on the back of our clothing.

Thought for the Day

What will people see when they look at us? Will it be our actions for God or just our name?

DAY 174

Now when Daniel knew that the writing was signed, he went home.
And in his upper room, with his windows open toward Jerusalem,
he knelt down on his knees three times that day, and prayed and
gave thanks before God, as was his custom since early days.
                                                    —Daniel 6:10

Lion Chow

The "writing" that this verse speaks of was a proclamation by King Darius which stated that no one could make a petition to any man or god except to him during the next thirty days. The law was inspired by those who were jealous of Daniel and knew that he regularly prayed to God. They wanted a reason to accuse him. Daniel decided to follow God even though he knew of the law and that its violation was punishable by death.

My first small taste of persecution for my faith came while I played college football. I had a coach who did not think that Christianity and football belonged together. He would go out of his way to make things difficult for me. I would get blamed for others' mistakes, and my good plays would be overlooked altogether. It was a difficult time for a twenty-one-year-old whose athletic dream was ending partly because of my beliefs. That was nothing compared to what Daniel faced. He was eventually thrown into a den of hungry lions because of the stand he made for God, but God delivered Daniel, and his accusers became the lion's next meal.

Following Christ is not without its difficulties. If you stand up for your faith, you will be persecuted. You can count on it. Anyone who says that Christianity is a crutch for the weak does not know what they are talking about. God's word says, "*Blessed are you when they revile and persecute you, and say all kinds of evil against you falsely for My sake. Rejoice and be exceedingly glad, for great is your reward in heaven, for so they persecuted the prophets who were before you*" (Matthew 5:11–12).

First responder professions can be hard on people of faith. It is tough to follow God's will for our lives in the face of the hard drinking, partying, and carousing culture. The courage it takes to make a stand for Jesus Christ is not for the faint of heart.

Thought for the Day

At least we do not have to face a den of lions for our beliefs.

DAY 175

Therefore I say to you, whatever things you ask when you pray believe that you shall receive them, and you will have them.

—Mark 11:24

Answered Prayer

Faith is an important aspect for answered prayer. But according to God's word, faith is not the only requirement. First John 5:14 tells us, "*Now this is the confidence that we have in Him, that if we ask anything according to His will, He hears us.*" And Matthew 6:33 says, "*But seek ye first the kingdom of God and His righteousness and all these things will be added to you.*"

Sometimes we try to make deals with God or even threaten Him to get our prayers answered. A young Catholic boy prayed for a bicycle. When he didn't receive it, he went to his family's living room and took a statue of Mary that was located on the mantel. He took the figure to his bedroom and placed it under his bed. The boy then prayed again and said, "Lord, if you don't give me that bicycle, you will never see your mother again."

God's word is clear about how to get your prayers answered. We must pray in faith, according to His will, and live a life that seeks that will first. We can't deal or threaten our way to answered prayer. In order to pray according to God's will, we have to accept the fact that we might get no for an answer.

I wish that getting a positive answer to prayer was an exact science. As long as we are not perfect, we may pray outside of His will and get "no" answers. I have to say that the older I've gotten, the more thankful I am that I didn't get everything I asked for anyway.

Thought for the Day

All we can do is read His word, seek His will, and continue to accept that the answers He gives us will be in our best interest in the long run. That is what true faith in Him is all about.

DAY 176

And we know that all things work together for good to those who love God, to those who are the called according to His purpose.
—Romans 8:28

Why Me, Why This, Why Now?

Many times, I have wished that this verse in Romans read, "And we know that all things will turn out the way we want them to, for those who love God, to those who are called according to His purpose." Unfortunately, God makes no such promise. Matthew 5:45 reads, "*For He makes His sun to rise on the evil and on the good, and sends rain on the just and on the unjust.*" The simple truth is that we will experience tough times in this world. Things will not go as we planned, and we will, at times, find ourselves shouting the words that are written across the wall of time, "Why me, why this, why now?"

I've done my share of fist shaking at heaven which was always a waste of time on my part. Even though God does not promise that all things will work out the way we want them to, there is great hope in Romans 8:28. He is in control and has a plan for our lives despite the difficult or impossible odds that you may be facing today.

There is a condition to this promise of God. It only applies to "*those who love God, to those who are called according to His purpose.*" If we have accepted Jesus Christ as our Lord and Savior, we have the assurance that He will be actively involved in whatever situation comes our way and He will be working it out for the good.

Thought for the Day

I cannot imagine what it must be like to face the inevitable problems of life without a Savior who hears my prayers, can intervene on my behalf, and has a plan for my life.

DAY 177

*That night the king could not sleep. So one was commanded to bring
the book of records of the chronicles; and they were read before the
king. And it was found written that Mordecai had told of Bigthana
and Teresh, two of the king's eunuchs, the doorkeepers who had sought
to lay hands on King Ahasuerus. And the king said, "What honor
or dignity has been bestowed on Mordecai for this?" And the king's
servants who attended him said, "Nothing has been done for him."*
—Esther 6:1–3

The Forgotten

Mordecai had thwarted a murder plot. Two eunuchs had con-
spired to kill the king but were stopped by Mordecai when
he revealed their plan. And what recognition had Mordecai received
for his heroic effort? NOTHING! It was not until many years
later, on a sleepless night orchestrated by God, that the king heard
of Mordecai's life-saving intervention. God had waited until then
to honor Mordecai so that it would fit into His plan to use Queen
Esther to save the Jewish nation.

God has a plan for your life that not only includes direction
in life's choices, but also in its rewards. During my law enforcement
career, I have seen many officers honored for their heroic deeds. I
have also seen many overlooked for the same kind of effort performed
at a different time. It made absolutely no sense why one would be
honored and another would be ignored. But for God's people, it all
makes sense, even if we cannot understand it at the time.

You may feel overlooked, forgotten, and unappreciated for your
work. God has seen your efforts and has a plan to use them for His

glory. Nothing goes unnoticed by God. Remember, your whole story has not been told yet.

I don't know if God plans to honor you on this side of glory, but for those who have accepted Jesus Christ as their Savior and have given the control of their lives to Him, that day will come.

Thought for the Day

As nice as it might seem to have men honor us now, it always works out better to be recognized by God, in His perfect timing.

DAY 178

And the peace of God, which surpasses all understanding,
will guard your hearts and minds through Christ Jesus.

—Philippians 4:7

Video Vault

As first responders, we experience things that drain us both phys-ically and emotionally. Our minds are like video cameras that record everything we see and hear. Unlike the electronic devices, our minds also record everything that we feel.

Some view it as a door, some see a curtain, and others imagine a light switch. It is the image and psychological device that we use to close or turn off our emotions while we are en route to a difficult call. This ability allows us to function well in the traumatic situations we are often exposed to. I have taken many ride-alongs out for an evening of police work only to find out from them later that they experienced things during the shift that will impact them for the rest of their lives. The funny thing is that I usually can't remember anything special about the night that I wouldn't typify as routine. It's amazing what we can get used to.

We, as first responders, start to experience problems when we fail to reengage our emotions and go home in a "switch down, turned off" state. The above verse promises that if you trust in Him, He will give you peace and *"will guard your hearts and minds through Christ Jesus."* It's comforting to know that we can count on our Lord to help us counteract the negative things that we will experience as part of our job.

If you are a believer and feel stuck in a closed emotional state, you can have a new start by claiming God's promise to guard your heart and mind through Jesus Christ.

Thought for the Day

If you have not yet placed Him in the center of your life, you can "turn on" the light switch today and experience that peace that surpasses all understanding.

DAY 179

Let your light so shine before men, that they may see your good works and glorify your Father in heaven.

—Matthew 5:16

Christian ID Badge

It has been said, if Christianity were a crime, would there be enough evidence to convict you?

Officers who were dispatched to investigate an armed robbery at a local bank asked the teller to describe the suspect. She did so and then much to their surprise, she provided them with the robber's name and place of employment. When they asked if she knew the suspect, the teller said, "No, but he was wearing an identification badge on the front pocket of his shirt that contained his name, his picture, and the name of the company he worked for." He had apparently come straight from his place of employment to commit the crime and had forgotten to remove the badge. The suspect was arrested at his workplace a short time later. The money taken in the robbery and the gun used in the crime were found in his vehicle which was parked close by.

The defendant in this case didn't win any "brilliant criminal of the year" awards. He was easy to identify just by looking at him. The above verse in Matthew challenges us to live our lives in such a way that others will easily know of our faith in God by our actions. The Bible also calls us to be "doers" of the word, not "hearers" only.

Thought for the Day

Would others find you guilty of following Jesus Christ?

DAY 180

*Then said I: "Ah Lord God! Behold, I cannot speak, for I am
a youth." But the Lord said unto me: "Do not say, 'I am a
youth,' for you shall go to all whom I send you, and whatever
I command you, you shall speak. Do not be afraid of their
faces, for I am with you to deliver you," says the Lord.*

Jeremiah 1:6–8

They Can't Eat You

As police officers, we are called upon to speak (sometimes yell) in
public. When the Lord told Jeremiah, "*Do not be afraid of their
faces, for I am with you to deliver you*," the thought of a jury, a packed
courtroom, and a slimy defense attorney came to mind. We always
told each other a simple truth when we were faced with a difficult
public situation, "Well, at least they can't eat you!" I guess when compared to that, everything else didn't seem so bad.

Jeremiah was concerned that he didn't possess the ability
he needed to stand up in public and speak effectively for God. I wonder that myself sometimes. If you are at all like me, talking to large
groups does not come that easily. Many studies list public speaking
as the number one fear for most people.

It seems like our job is full of uncomfortable situations that we
will be called upon to endure. It is good to know that if we have given
the control of our lives to God, He will be there to help us in all the
difficult incidents we may face in life. When we invite Jesus Christ
into our lives, God's word tells us that the Holy Spirit comes in, fills
us, and gives us the wisdom and courage that we need to do things
that we never thought were possible for us.

Thought for the Day

Next time you find yourself in a difficult public situation, remember two things: they can't eat you, and God is right next to you to give you the courage and ability you need to get the job done.

DAY 181

If you had known Me,
You would have known My Father also;
and from now on you know Him
and have seen Him.

—John 14:7

Do You Know Who I Am?

I worked in a very affluent city and came into contact with many of the world's rich and famous. I can't tell you how many times I was asked the question, "Do you know who I am?" I would usually hear this statement when a defendant was about to get a ticket or be taken into custody. As police officers, we are not allowed to make gratuitous statements, but there were many times when I was tempted to answer the above question with "Yes, I know who you are, you're the guy wearing handcuffs who is under arrest!"

Jesus asks us the same question, "Do you know who I am?" The difference is that He is the only one who has the right to ask that question. He paid for that right by dying on the cross for our sins. He was perfect and blameless, yet because of His love for us, He took on the sin of the world so that we might have eternal life. If we acknowledge His death on the cross for our sin and make Him the Lord of our lives, He will give us not only a plan and a purpose in this life but also an eternity with Him when this life has ended.

It doesn't matter if we are rich, beautiful, talented, intelligent, famous, or none of those things, no one is perfect, and we cannot earn our way to heaven.

Thought for the Day

Someday, Jesus will ask you the question, "Do you know who I am?" What will your answer be?

DAY 182

*"Behold My hands and My feet, that it is I Myself.
Handle Me and see, for a spirit does not have
flesh and bones as you see I have."*

—Luke 24:39

Scarred Up

In the bookcase located in my office was the football helmet I wore when I played at USC. It is well-worn and full of scratches and dings. The gray rubber-coated facemask has numerous chunks taken out of it, and the bar at the top is bent in a little. It comes from a different era of NCAA rules where we were taught to strike with our faces and not our shoulders. You can tell by looking at my helmet that it has been through many collisions both in practice and on game day. It is visual proof that I was in the trenches.

In the above verse in Luke, Jesus asked his disciples to examine His hands and feet which had the scars of His crucifixion. He had a resurrected body of flesh and bone that contained the proof that He had been in the battle and had come out victorious. This evidence left no doubt that Jesus was our risen Lord, who had paid the ultimate sacrifice for our sin by the shedding of His blood for us. Just like my old helmet that still contains the proof of my battles, Jesus's hands and feet still showed the scars of His.

We will have many spiritual challenges in our lives as we seek to follow Christ. It is what comes with the "pick up your cross and follow me," territory. I could always tell if someone had played in a football game by the condition of their uniform after the event. If they were sweaty, bloody, and grass stained (maybe not so much now with artificial turf), I could tell they had been out on the field.

Thought for the Day

What does your spiritual uniform look like? Clean and unmarred, or dirty, sweaty, and stained? Get in the game, follow Him, tell others about Jesus, and work through the trials and tribulations that are inevitable. Only then can you truly look like our Lord.

DAY 183

*I have fought the good fight, I have finished
the race, I have kept the faith.*

—2 Timothy 4:7

Finish Well

When my two daughters were in high school, they started to wrestle with where they would attend college. The fight was mostly over the cost of the institutions and our lack of any scholarship assistance to help pay for the tuition. I asked them which college I had graduated from, and as proud daughters of Troy, they said, "USC." I then told them that was true, that is where I ended up, but that was not where I started.

After my senior year in high school, I received only one football scholarship offer from a college of no real note. I was just too small as an offensive lineman to gain the attention of any Division 1 team. I decided to go to community college to see if I could do better. That turned out to be a good decision, and after my sophomore year, I had scholarship offers from several Division 1 schools as well as other smaller schools, all of which were better than the one offer I had originally received after high school.

Both of my girls ended up attending Saddleback Community College, which is sometimes jokingly called UCLA—University of California Left at Avery (i.e., the school is on Avery Parkway in Mission Viejo, California). They had "scholarships" due to the lower tuition cost as compared to a four-year school. Both went on to transfer to USC and graduated with bachelor's degrees a few years later. So like Dad, it wasn't where they started that mattered, it was where they ended up.

The above verse was written by the apostle Paul near the end of his life to the young preacher Timothy. Paul rested in the fact that he had fought the good fight and finished the race well. It didn't matter where he had started, as a persecutor of Christians and an enemy of the faith. He had turned his life over to Jesus and had given it all to Him.

Are you troubled by where you started before coming to Christ? Or have you been discouraged by where you are, and think that He doesn't want you the way you are? Don't be! It doesn't matter to Him where you began; it only matters where you end up! Philippians 3:13 tells us, "*Forgetting those things which are behind and reaching forward to those things which are ahead.*"

Thought for the Day

Commit your life to Him every day, and you will finish well.

DAY 184

*Great peace have those who love Your law, And
nothing causes them to stumble.*

—Psalm 119:165

Policy Protection

Police work is all about codified laws, policies, and procedures. We have Penal, Business and Professions, Health and Safety, as well as Welfare and Institution codes that are used to identify state crimes that can result in an arrest. Our department manual, on the other hand, is used to inform us of internal policies that we must adhere to as police officers. They don't represent violations of any criminal code, but if we don't follow them, we open ourselves up to civil liability and the loss of our jobs. In short, following the policies and procedures set forth in the department manual will protect our careers and personal assets.

God's word is full of commandments which He wants us to follow for our own best interests. They are not there to make our life difficult, but to protect us from harm and the evil of this world. Just think if we followed God's laws according to theft, alcohol and drug use, marriage and divorce, sexual practices, and the general treatment of others. I wouldn't have had a job as a law enforcement officer unless I responded to traffic accidents and medical assists. AIDS would not be an issue, and there would be no need for theft insurance, door locks, or self-protection devices.

As long as we live in a fallen world that refuses to obey God's commandments, we will always experience sin, loss, and peril. This doesn't diminish the fact that if we keep God's commandments, our lives will be protected from many of these dangers.

Thought for the Day

The Bible is God's penal code and policy manual for our lives. Following His commandments will protect us.

DAY 185

*The power of the Lord came on Elijah and, tucking his cloak
into his belt, he ran ahead of Ahab all the way to Jezreel.*

—1 Kings 18:46

God's Power

We have all heard stories of how people were given superhuman strength when confronted by a frightening situation.
This kind of power, sometimes called hysterical strength, has allowed
mothers to lift cars off their trapped children, or for someone to fight
off a wild animal that is much bigger and stronger than they are.

The above verse in 1 Kings talks about a miraculous temporary
strength that was given to Elijah the prophet. This happened just
after Elijah had confronted the 450 priests of the false god Baal on
Mount Carmel. In front of King Ahab and the people of Israel, Elijah
had challenged these prophets to a BBQ contest. They would both
pray, and whoever brought down fire from heaven onto the altar,
the Lord or Baal, would prove to be the one true God. Despite all
their dancing and gyrations, Baal never answered the false prophet's
requests. Of course, once Elijah prayed to the Lord God, the altar
was consumed with fire from heaven. Elijah then prayed for rain,
ending a long drought, and clouds soon began to appear in the sky.

This is where another unbelievable event happened. In verse
44, Elijah told King Ahab to "climb on your chariot and go back
home. If you don't hurry, the rain will stop you!" This set the stage
for another, often overlooked, miracle to occur. Verse 46 says that
the Lord gave Elijah power, and he "ran ahead of Ahab all the way
to Jezreel." Do you get what the text just said? Elijah ran ahead of

a galloping horse all the way to Jezreel, which is twenty miles away from Mount Carmel. A horse can run at about twenty-five miles an hour. If we do the math for a man running faster than a horse, we can calculate that Elijah ran a near marathon in about forty minutes. According to the Internet, the average male runs a marathon in about four hours and twenty-one minutes. Elijah must have been flying! I am sure if a modern-day shoe manufacturer had been present, Elijah would have been signed to a sandal endorsement contract for his world record performance.

We serve the same God today that Elijah did in his day. Whether you need the fire of passion back in your life, or a soothing healing rain, or just power to run the race set before you, God is able. He is able to do things *"above and beyond anything we can ask or think, according to the power that works within us"* (Ephesians 3:20). No matter what the obstacle, God is able to provide us with the strength we need to get to our destination.

Thought for the Day

Let's run our race with faith in God's power to help us by any means that He sees fit.

DAY 186

*But the Helper, the Holy Spirit, whom the Father will
send in My name, He will teach you all things, and bring
to your remembrance all things that I said to you.*

—John 14:26

Open to Suggestions?

Cops are expert practical jokers. Apparently, this ability has
spanned the years of past law enforcement generations. My
father, a thirty-year police officer who retired in 1980, tells me of one
such event that had a positive outcome, at least for him and those he
worked with.

There was a certain supervisor on his department that no one
liked to work with. They knew that if he was on their watch, they
were in for a long, hard micromanaging "dog years" shift. That is,
every one hour would seem like seven hours to them. The only good
news for them was that this supervisor was known as an extreme
hypochondriac.

So here is how their plan went. As this supervisor sat in his
office, one officer would walk by and start up a casual conversation
with him. During their talk, the officer would at some point look at
him and say, "Do you feel all right, you look a little flush." He would
then end the conversation and leave the area. This same discussion
would be initiated by another officer a short time later. By the time
the third officer had told this supervisor that he did not look well,
he had decided to go home sick for the day and had been effectively
talked into the imaginary illness. Problem solved!

We are all open to suggestion. It is just a matter of whose suggestions we are influenced by. The above verse in John tells us whom we should be listening to. God sends the Holy Spirit into our lives to direct us and give us the counsel we need in agreement with His word. The Bible tells us of the one who will make negative suggestions in our lives that will lead us down the wrong path. When speaking of Satan, John 8:44 states, "*When he speaks a lie, he speaks from his own resources, for he is a liar and the father of it.*"

Thought for the Day

Don't get talked into a state of spiritual sickness. Read God's word and rely on the fact that as a believer in Jesus Christ, all that it promises belongs to you and that the Holy Spirit will be present to guide you in the right direction.

DAY 187

*Also I heard the voice of the Lord, saying: "Whom shall I send,
And who will go for Us?" Then I said, "Here am I! Send me."*

—Isaiah 6:8

Heroes

The last eleven months of my police career, I worked at the front desk of my department due to an injury. This was the first time I had ever been on light duty, and I learned the truth about what has always been said of this assignment, "the front desk cures cancer." We were looking to hire several recruits, and I saw numerous candidates come into the station for their initial interviews. It was interesting to see these freshly scrubbed hopeful faces arrive with their intent to start a law enforcement career. This was especially nostalgic for me since I was quickly coming to the end of mine.

Law enforcement has become an increasingly dangerous job in the thirty-plus years since I became an officer. Department of Justice statistics reports that in 2020, there was a 28 percent increase in police officer line of duty deaths since the previous year. And still the recruits keep rolling in. One might argue that the desperation generated by a poor economy keeps the candidates coming, but I think that line of thought is insulting.

All first responders endure long hours, poor work schedules, sleep deprivation, physical danger, emotional trauma, and injuries as routine parts of their job. They will miss family gatherings, their kid's events, and will have to wrestle with the stresses of a job that can result in an increased occurrence of suicide, as well as a divorce rate that is significantly higher than the national average. They will have to deal with internal politics, federal and civil litigations, and city governments who are increasingly eager to reduce their benefits for philosophical or political reasons. To say that anyone would sign up for this simply because they need a job is a little crazy.

The above verse in Isaiah speaks of the type of person who chooses to become a first responder. When the call comes out to serve, they are the ones who step forward and say, "Here am I, send me!"

Thought for the Day

God sees your service and is proud that you are the type of person who is willing to answer that call.

DAY 188

Behold what manner of love the Father has bestowed on us, that we should be called children of God! Therefore, the world does not know us because it did not know Him.

—1 John 3:1

Named

As a football player, I was affiliated with many names. As a nine-year-old, I was a Comanche. I then became a Caballo for two seasons before joining the Eagles for four years. From there, I was a Pirate and finally a Trojan. I tried to become an Oiler and a Ram after that, but due to injury, it didn't work out. As a police officer, I was also known by many names. Well, actually, I was called many names, most of which we won't mention here.

The above verse in 1 John tells us that the Father has given us a new name. His love for us and our acceptance of Jesus Christ as the Lord of our lives have allowed that "we should be called the children of God." This is unbelievable, isn't it! No matter what we have been called in the past, good or bad, we can now be known as a child of the Most High God.

God's word goes even further in Romans 8:17 where it says, "*And if children, then heirs—heirs of God and joint heirs with Christ, if indeed we suffer with Him, that we may also be glorified together.*"

Thought for the Day

It is time to take on your new name! If you already have, it is time to live as an heir to the King.

DAY 189

Let us hear the conclusion of the whole matter: Fear God, and keep his commandments: for this is the whole duty of man.

—Ecclesiastes 12:13

Just Obey

Do you remember the old EF Hutton TV commercials? They always had two people talking in a social situation surrounded by a room full of strangers. While discussing a financial investment opportunity, one would say to the other, "My broker is EF Hutton, and EF Hutton says." At that point, everyone in the room would stop their conversations and lean over in an attempt to hear the EF Hutton investment advice. The commercial announcer would then say, "When EF Hutton talks, people listen."

The above verse in Ecclesiastes records the words of Solomon at the end of his life. God had given him great wisdom that was sought after by people all over the known world. If Solomon spoke, people listened! He starts verse 12 with the phrase, "*Let us hear the conclusion of the whole matter.*" We know that what he is about to say next will be wisdom accumulated over an entire lifetime. And what was most important to him above all other learning and achievements of his life? After all that Solomon had been through, all the experiences and knowledge he had obtained, the most important thing he had learned was to "*fear God, and keep his commandments.*" Those are pretty simple marching orders aren't they? Just two things to remember, respect God and do what He says.

I was recently in a meeting where the people in attendance were asked to recite their favorite Bible verse. All of them, mostly millennials, came up with some wonderful verses about the love, forgiveness, and mercy of God. All the scriptures were infused with the passion you would expect, and hoped for, from the next generation of believers. But being a baby boomer, I have already been through some of the ups and downs that life will eventually bring their way. I have come to the same conclusion that the aging Solomon had. Passion in life is wonderful, but there will be times when all that is left is obedience to God that is required apart from any feeling we may have. That might seem like a frightening statement to the young, but once you have been through the trials of life, you realize the great comfort gained from these simple, clear directions of God.

Thought for the Day

My God is the Lord of the universe, and when God talks, we should listen and obey.

DAY 190

But let all who take refuge in you rejoice;
let them sing joyful praises forever.
Spread your protection over them, that all who
love your name may be filled with joy.

—Psalm 5:11

God's Protection

As a police officer, I responded to numerous domestic violence calls over the years. Many times, when I arrived on scene, the male half of the altercation was gone. The fact that I once played football and was still a little larger in stature was always a plus in these situations. I can't tell you the relief that many of the victims expressed when they saw a "bigger" cop at their front door. Many times, they had been physically beaten and were afraid that their abuser would return at any moment to continue the assault. They believed that I had the ability to keep them from being hurt further if he should return.

If you are a follower of Jesus Christ and have given the control of your life to Him, then all the promises found in God's word are yours to claim. Romans 8:31 says, *"What shall we say about such wonderful things as these? If God is for us, who can ever be against us?"* The bottom line is that God is bigger than anything that can come your way in this life. No person, situation, circumstance, or event can overpower God's ability to protect His children. The above verse in Psalms says that we can rejoice, take refuge, be filled with joy because of our Father's protection over us. What a great promise!

Thought for the Day

Today we face a new "abuser" in COVID-19. Always remember that our God is bigger than any situation that we may find ourselves in, and He can arrive in our lives just when we need Him most.

DAY 191

When He comes, He will convict the world about
sin, righteousness, and judgment:

—John 16:8

Are You Listening?

O ne afternoon, we were dispatched to a burglary alarm at a business in a local upscale strip mall on the east side of town. Our quick response had surprised the suspect who was still in the building. A witness had seen him crawl into the ceiling space above the business to hide. We had positioned ourselves around the store and knew that the suspect was still inside. We then took turns talking to the suspect over our unit loudspeakers, notifying him that we had the place surrounded, and that there was no way for him to escape. We encouraged him to come out and surrender. I think the combination of our repeated requests and the sound of our canine barking over the loudspeaker finally convinced the suspect to give himself up. He later said that even though he could not see us, he had heard every word we said to him during the incident.

The above verse in John 16 tells us of the Holy Spirit's function in the world. He has been sent to inform us of our sin, to instruct us in righteousness, and warn us of the judgment to come. For the non-Christian, He is not here to condemn you, but to encourage you to accept Christ's payment for your sin. For the believer in Jesus Christ, the Holy Spirit desires to work in your life to lead you, correct you, and to bring you back to God when you fall. Even though we cannot see Him, we can hear His voice in our hearts as He encourages us to surrender to His will.

Arguably, the most famous verse in the Bible is John 3:16, "*For God so loved the world that He gave His only begotten Son, that whosoever believes in Him shall not perish but have everlasting life.*" Not as famous but equally as powerful is the next verse, John 3:17, which states, "*For God did not send His Son into the world to condemn the world, but that the world through Him might be saved.*" It is the Holy Spirit's job to convince people of that truth with the great hope that "*all should come to repentance*" (2 Peter 3:9).

The Holy Spirit is talking to you today. He either wants to bring you into a relationship with God through Jesus Christ, or if you already have that relationship, He wants to guide you through a God honoring life.

Thought for the Day

God is attempting to talk to you through the loudspeaker of the Holy Spirit. Are you listening?

DAY 192

Don't be deceived. My beloved brethren. Every good gift and every
perfect gift is from above, and comes down from the Father of
lights, with whom there is no variation or shadow of turning.
—James 1:16–17

Winning?

When I worked in Vice, I had a supervisor who was well-known for his practical jokes. One such joke was carried out against my partner on his birthday. My sergeant got him a card that wished him well on his special day. Inside the card, he placed two lottery tickets as a gift. He got one ticket at a local market, and the other was purchased from a joke shop in the area. The joke document was designed to look like a winner. When you scratched off the numbers on the front of the ticket, it appeared as though you had just won $10,000.

As I looked out of the second-story window in the Vice and Intelligence office, I saw my partner standing in the parking lot of the department. I watched as he opened the envelope that contained the card and the lottery tickets. After he quickly read the card, he scratched off the numbers on the real ticket, and I saw no reaction. When he started to scratch off the numbers on the second ticket, I knew what was coming next. I watched my partner start to jump up and down and raise his right hand to the sky with the ticket still clutched in his fingers. He then pumped the winning ticket in the air several times as if to thank the lottery god for his good fortune. Of course, that joy changed to total disgust as he turned the ticket over and learned that he was to redeem his prize at "Yo Mama's house." It was then that he knew he had been duped.

The world seems to have a lot to offer us that at face value looks like a real winner. I have counseled many who have chosen money over integrity, promiscuity over faithfulness, and fame over honor. When they scratched off the covering of those choices, they thought they had a sure bet to bring them happiness. It wasn't until later, when their lives had been turned over by time, that they saw they had been duped. What they thought was a winner had turned out to be a false hope that had run their lives into a ditch.

There is only one sure way that we can find success and happiness in this life. We need to follow God's word and make it our goal in life to be more like Him. We need to care about what He cares about, value what He values, and do what He does. If we do, we can never go wrong.

Thought for the Day

Don't get caught jumping up and down over a false hope only to find that you have been duped. Turn your life over to God's will and become a true winner.

DAY 193

*The refining pot is for silver and the furnace
for gold. But the Lord tests the hearts.*

—Proverbs 17:3

The FTO

After the police academy, every officer enters a departmental training program where they are tested and evaluated for a number of months. This is a time where their field training officers (FTOs) have the opportunity to see how the rookie cop will translate what they have learned in their academy experience to the situations that they will face on the street. The trainee's strengths and weaknesses are soon revealed when their decision-making abilities are tested against real suspects, with real weapons, during real life-or-death events. The FTO will determine if their trainee has the character, discretion, temperament, and knowledge it takes to be a successful law enforcement officer. Not all new officers make it through training, and some are asked to leave early based on their poor performance in the program.

Unlike an FTO, God does not test us to discover how we will react. God is omniscient, which means He knows everything and cannot learn anything. He already knows what we will do in any given set of circumstances and is not surprised by our actions. The tests that God allows in our lives are there so that we will learn what our reactions will be. His purpose for these trials are for us to see our own deficiencies so that we can work to correct them. Our goal during these times of testing should not be to ask God why this is happening, but rather what does He want me to learn by it.

The great thing about God's FTO program is if you have invited Jesus Christ into your life, He will not throw you out due to poor performance. The Holy Spirit will keep working with you, nudging you back on to the correct path as long as you let Him. He loves you and will only put trials in your life if they will bring you closer to Him or allow you to grow.

Thought for the Day

Any training program can be difficult. Don't give up, keep moving forward, and you will come out stronger and better through the process.

DAY 194

Then the Lord your God will restore your fortunes.
He will have mercy on you and gather you back from
all the nations where he has scattered you.

—Deuteronomy 30:3

Classic Restoration

I love classic cars! My favorites are from the mid-1950s. The size, the lines, and the shapes are true works of art that we don't see much of today. I used to own a 56 Ford Fairlane when my girls were young. I had to sell it, but I hope to get another classic someday.

I love to watch those car restoration shows on TV. It is always amazing to me the talent people have for turning old beat-up wrecks into perfect time capsules that look as though they have just been driven off the showroom floor. They do frame-off restorations which require a complete disassembly of the car, down to the frame and a refurbishing of every part before reconstruction. Having restored a vehicle of my own, I can tell you that the skill it takes to bring these cars back to life is really amazing.

God is also in the restoration business. The above verse in Deuteronomy documents a promise God made to the Jewish people describing the blessing He would give if the nation returned to Him. He would restore their fortunes, give them mercy, and bring them back together. He would refurbish them so that they would, in a sense, look like the shiny new blessed nation that they once were.

God is making that same offer to you today. Second Chronicles 7:14 tells us that if Christians will "*humble themselves and pray and seek my face and turn from their wicked ways, I will hear from heaven and will forgive their sins and restore their land."* God is eager to restore us back to our former spiritual glory if we will just humbly turn back to Him.

Thought for the Day

No paint or chrome or reupholstery can match the renewal that God can do to the human heart. Start your frame off restoration today.

DAY 195

*Whoever guards his mouth preserves his life; he
who opens wide his lips comes to ruin.*

—Proverbs 13:3

Think Before You Speak

I recently took an online critical incident stress management course. The International Critical Incident Stress Foundation (ICISF) offers numerous stress intervention courses and is the leading organization in the world for those seeking to assist individuals and groups during times of trauma and disaster. I have a certification from ICISF and have used what I learned from their instruction numerous times as a police officer, chaplain, and pastor. My goal in taking the class was to renew my certification which had expired. I finished the online course and printed out the certificate that documented my completion of the class. To my surprise, I saw that the course credit was not enough for me to obtain my renewal. I have to admit that I was a little upset that I had paid my fee, done the work, and completed the course without being informed that the class would not help me meet my goal. I was not able to contact the Certificate of Specialized Training Program Department via telephone that day, so I wrote an email that strongly worded my displeasure with the ICISF staff for not informing me of the deficiency during our recent phone and email communication. Something told me, however (Holy Spirit), not to push "send" on the email, and to wait until the next day when I was able to speak with the program coordinator. After all, I could send the email after our conversation.

The next morning, I was able to contact the staff member in charge of the program. Before I could even get out my complaint, the coordinator offered a solution and was very kind and allowed me a path to my certification renewal. After we spoke, I looked again at the renewal requirements. It appeared that the real issue was mostly an operator error on my part for not reading the fine print on the course description. This made the ICISF staff member's accommodation to my situation all the more generous. I was glad that I had not shot off that angry email the night before. I'm sure they would have solved my situation with the same professionalism, but I would have looked like a real jerk, especially since all my emails had "Brad Green, Associate Pastor" and Matthew 6:33 automatically signed on the bottom!

The first responder's job is filled with stressful people and difficult situations. We are tempted to say what we think and let our mouths get us into trouble. I can't tell you the number of times I wish I could have reached out and pulled back the words that just came out of my mouth.

Proverbs tells us that an unguarded mouth (or fingers for an email) can bring us to ruin. The old adage "Count to ten" before responding might be a wise thing to do. I've often asked people in counseling if, right before they said that unkind thing, there was a split second when they knew that what was about to come out of their mouth was wrong. The answer is almost always yes.

Thought for the Day

You can't un-ring the bell. Think before you speak.

DAY 196

*However, he did not kill the children of the assassins, for he
obeyed the command of the Lord as written by Moses in the
Book of the Law: "Parents must not be put to death for the sins
of their children, nor children for the sins of their parents. Those
deserving to die must be put to death for their own crimes."*
—2 Chronicles 25:4

Don't Pass It On

As a police officer, I had a chance to see some pretty bad family dynamics in the course of my career. It was sad to see that some children followed the same immoral paths that their parents had before them. But I also saw interesting generational opposites when it came to lawless behavior. Some of the best parents I ever met had prodigal sons and daughters who broke away from their sincere attempts to teach these children right from wrong. I also saw some truly great kids whose parents were poor examples in their lives, and who either purposely attempted to teach them evil or had simply modeled wicked behavior in their formative years.

The above verse in 2 Chronicles tells of the actions of King Amaziah who reigned in Jerusalem for twenty-nine years. When Amaziah was established as the king, he executed the court officials who had assassinated his father Joash. But in doing so, he did not kill their entire families, a practice that was common for monarchs in those days. Scripture tells us that King Amaziah followed the law of Moses and did not hold the criminal's children responsible for their father's sin. The law made it clear that children were not to be blamed for the lawless acts of their parents, or the other way around!

In counseling, we often see adults with issues that have been passed on within their family. I believe that these are the generational curses that the Bible talks about.

One of the biggest motivations I can give parents in counseling for a troubled marriage are their children. If I can make them see that their children will someday model their behavior in their future relationships, it can be a giant wake-up call for them. Their children will not be held accountable for their parents' selfish actions, but they will for their own. I will often ask a father, "Do you want your daughter to be treated by the men in her life the same way you are treating your wife? And, Mom, do you want your son to look for a future spouse who will treat him the same way you are treating your husband?"

Thought for the Day

It is great to know we can be set free from our past, but free to do what? Let's not create a bad future and set a poor example for the ones we love by our actions.

DAY 197

Know that the LORD, He is God; It is He who has made us, and not we ourselves; We are His people and the sheep of His pasture.
—Psalms 100:3

Schooled

I officially retired from the police department on January 28, 2012. I was no longer a sworn police officer and would once again join society as a civilian. This represented quite a change in my life, but I looked forward to the next chapter that God had planned for me.

Actually, I was relieved to be stepping down from a job that I was always thankful to have, but that never quite fit my personality type. Government statistics profiled me as the kind of officer most likely to be killed in the line of duty. I've always been somewhat nonconfrontational, slow to use physical force, and eager to trust and believe in people. I had to work hard to suppress those tendencies over the years in order to do my job and survive on the street. I looked forward to getting back to normal in the way that I related to people.

So why did God bring me to a job that seemed ill-suited for me in so many ways? I definitely gained an expertise in a field that may open many ministry doors for me in the years to come. If God had not directed me to become a police officer, I might have never been ordained or become involved in police chaplaincy. I will always be thankful that He placed me in that position because it has given me immediate credibility in the law enforcement community. I don't have to struggle with that connection as some of my fellow chaplains say they do. I can now continue to serve others (sworn and civilian) in a way that I never could have before I was involved in law enforcement.

If you are having a hard time understanding God's plan for you and the reason for your current position or assignment, take heart in the fact that you might be in school now to prepare you for an exciting future. God loves you and knows your strengths and weaknesses. He wants to use you in a way that will not only be best for you but will also best serve His purposes in the lives of others.

Thought for the Day

God's curriculum for your life may not always make immediate sense to you. Stay in school, and the day you graduate, you will see His continued plan for your life.

DAY 198

*He only is my rock and my salvation; He is
my defense; I shall not be moved.*

—Psalm 62:2

Fires?

In Newport Beach, we had a continual flame that burned off excess underground sulfur deposits. The mechanism used was a pipe that was several stories high. The pipe was located just off Pacific Coast Highway in a utility area near Hoag Hospital. At night, you could see the flame burning out of the top of the pipe from quite a distance away.

From the street level, the pipe would blend into the hillside, and all you could see was the flame. At certain angles, it would appear that the fire was lined up with the houses on the hillside behind it. Dispatch would routinely receive calls from panicked citizens driving through the area who were convinced that the homes were on fire. We would know what to expect when the dispatcher would say, "Fire reported in the area of Superior and the Highway, probably just the flame again."

Sometimes from the way we see things in our lives, we can feel that all we value is about to be taken from us. We are convinced we can see the flames of danger right before our eyes. Sometimes the danger might be real, but other times, it is just an illusion or a trick of the enemy to panic us.

King David wrote the above verse in Psalms. Tradition tells us that it was penned during a particularly ugly time in his life. David's son Absalom was attempting to overthrow the kingdom and install himself as its ruler. Can you imagine the betrayal and anguish he must have felt? It is also called the "only" psalm not because there is just one, but because he uses the word "only" several times in its twelve verses. Even in this dark time, David clung to God as his only refuge and hope. That is one of the reasons why God called David a man after his own heart.

Do you see flames around you? Whether or not the danger is real, God should be your only go-to place. He alone can help you to decipher what is real from what is imagined, and either way, He is your only hope.

Thought for the Day

Flame or fiction, turn to Him.

DAY 199

And let us not grow weary while doing good,
for in due season we shall reap
if we do not lose heart.

—Galatians 6:9

God's Reward

I think that every first responder can relate to this verse. God recognizes that people in our position can grow tired of doing the right thing especially when it seems that there is no positive outcome for doing so. It might be that ridiculous court decision, that unfounded complaint, or that unappreciative citizen that drives us over the edge. The consequences of their mistakes can be great. We can take people's freedom, livelihood, and even their lives from them. No other job has greater scrutiny, second-guessing, media coverage, Monday morning quarterbacking, and negative civil ramifications than that of the law enforcement officer.

God promises that you will eventually reap the rewards of doing the right thing if you "do not lose heart" and continue on. No matter what you may think, you did not become involved in law enforcement by accident. God called you to this difficult career because you have a strength that is greater than the normal person. God's word says, "*Greater love has no one than this, than to lay down one's life for his friends*" (John 15:13). That's true, and the fact that you may be called upon to lay down your life for others you don't know, don't agree with, or sometimes don't even like makes you an incredible hero.

Thought for the Day

Don't give up! Keep doing what is right! God knows all, sees all, and will reward you.

DAY 200

There is a way that seems right to a man,
but its end is the way of death.

—Proverbs 14:12

Optical Illusion

I love optical illusions. If you grew up in Southern California, you might remember the Mystery Shack at Knott's Berry Farm. It was built in such a way that when you went inside, things that were actually level seemed slanted and out of kilter. The illusion made it difficult to walk through the building. You just couldn't trust objects as they appeared.

Many things in the Christian life are the same way. The world has set out a standard for what should appear level in its estimation. Following God's word for your life can make you feel as though you are walking unbalanced and out of kilter. As believers in Jesus Christ, we need to reset our optics to God's definition of "level" in our lives, and not the world's.

God's word says that we should love those who persecute us. The world says seek revenge. God says to tithe and give your first financial fruits back to Him. The world says hoard as much money as possible for yourself. God says for us to watch what we say to others, and the world tells us that it is okay to say whatever we want in any profane manner we wish. God says, "Them first," the world says, "Me first."

The best that the world can give us is the illusion that things are even and right. We don't usually find out until we have fallen over that what we thought was normal was actually crooked all along.

Thought for the Day

We need to reset our lives through God's word. It is the only source we can count on to keep level and balanced in this life.

DAY 201

The LORD looks from heaven; He sees all the sons of men. From the place of His dwelling He looks On all the inhabitants of the earth; He fashions their hearts individually; He considers all their works.
                                                        —Psalm 33: 13–15

The Watcher

Many years ago, I was on a break at Lifeguard Headquarters with several other officers. A class occupied the downstairs meeting room, and we found ourselves seated in the observation area that overlooked the pier. The room had plate glass windows on three sides that allowed the lifeguards to see not only the pier, but also the ocean and beach areas adjacent to the building. The glass had a heavy tint on it, which during the day acted as a one-way mirror. We could see out, but no one could see in. This fact was unfortunate for a pair of individuals whom we could clearly see on the sand beneath the pier. As we watched, they took out a glass pipe, filled it with an illegal drug, and started to take turns smoking it. It is not often that we as police officers get to watch such unrestricted criminal activity from such a short distance. Two officers went down to contact the pair. The looks on their faces were priceless as one of the officers pointed to the large plate glass window and informed them that their activity had been closely monitored from only a few feet away.

God sees all that we do, and there is nothing that goes unnoticed by Him. That can be either good news or bad news for us. It can give us great comfort to understand that He knows all about the difficult situations in our lives and is right there when we need Him. It can also be hard for us to realize that He has a front row seat to our sin. I think we might act differently if God were standing right next to us as we conduct our day-to-day lives. The truth is that He is right there, we just can't see Him.

God loves us more than we can possibly understand. There is nothing we can do to surprise God or separate us from that love. Romans 8:38–39 tells us that, *"for I am persuaded that neither death nor life, nor angels nor principalities nor powers, nor things present nor things to come, nor height nor depth, nor any other created thing, shall be able to separate us from the love of God which is in Christ Jesus our Lord."*

Thought for the Day

Let's conduct ourselves with the knowledge that the Lord not only loves us, but that He is an active, caring observer of our every-day activities.

DAY 202

There is a way that seems right to a man,
but its end is the way of death.

—Proverbs 14:12

Hidden Danger

Many years ago, I was scuba diving on the leeward side of Catalina Island (the coast that faces back in the direction of the California mainland). I was on the end of the island, east of Avalon, in a place we called the Quarry. There was not much to see down there since the entire submerged terrain was made up of large rocks. There were, however, a lot of openings and crevasses for animal life to hide. As I swam along the rocks, I saw many large lobsters tucked in about two feet back into the rock openings. Even though I was not there to get any lobster, I thought how easy it would be for someone to just reach in and grab one of these crustaceans. It seemed simple enough until you took a closer look at the hole they were hiding in. Almost always, I discovered that they were not in there alone. When I peered inside the opening, I usually saw the head of a large black moray eel silently biding its time for something (or someone) to enter the rocky cavity. They were motionlessly waiting to sink their razor-sharp spiked teeth into whatever crossed their path. I guess what looked like a great idea, an easy catch, would have turned out to be a colossally bad decision!

Many times in our lives, we can be tempted to grab at something that looks good at first glance. Whether it is a decision involving a job, a relationship, or financial commitment of some kind, what might seem like a perfect fit could eventually lead us to disaster. That is why it is important to always seek God's guidance for the major decisions of this life. God's word says, "*If any of you lack wisdom, let him ask God, who gives to all liberally and without reproach, and it will be given to him*" (James 1:5). This verse makes sense to us when we don't know what to do, but I think it also holds true if we think we do know! It is never a bad idea to ask God if the direction we plan to take is what is best, and if there are any hidden dangers lurking just beyond our field of vision.

Thought for the Day

Let's not get bitten by the danger of a bad decision when we have an always correct answer there just waiting for the asking.

DAY 203

Who exchanged the truth of God for a lie,
and worshiped and served the creature
rather than the creator
who is blessed forever Amen.

—*Romans 1:25*

Nature Worship

I often see the incredible effort and dedication that environmentalists will put into their beliefs. Whether it is global warming, animal rights, or tree preservation, the individuals in these groups show great zeal as they fight for what they believe in. Many of them state that they have no formal spiritual belief system, but the truth is that they are members of one of the world's oldest religions, nature worship.

Dictionary.com states, "Common to most forms of nature worship is a spiritual focus in the individual's connection to the natural world and reverence towards it." I'm not saying that it is wrong to love animals or to conserve this world that we live in. God wants us to be good stewards of all the beauty He has given us on this earth. People can be guilty, however, of worshiping the creatures that the Lord has made without giving any reverence to the God who created them. The above verse in Romans speaks of the nature worship religion and states that they have "*exchanged the truth of God for a lie, and worshipped and served the creature rather than the creator.*"

God made this earth and everything that is in it. He is worthy of our praise and should take first place in our lives. There is no created thing that should be more important than our relationship with our Lord.

Thought for the Day

Don't get caught up in any faith system that does not give God the credit He is due.

DAY 204

*Bend down, O Lord, and hear my prayer; answer me, for
I need your help. Protect me, for I am devoted to you. Save
me, for I serve you and trust you. You are my God.*

—Psalms 86:1–2

Just Talk

I once owned a yellow-naped Amazon parrot named Coco. He was quite a character and had a decent vocabulary. We were not his first owners, so he came to our home with several ready-made words and phrases. When someone walked into the room, he would say, "Hello, Coco, whatcha you doin', huh?" He would also laugh hysterically and whistle the USC fight song. The last one was my doing. Coco sounded like he was talking, but due to the random nature of his words, I never felt that he understood what he was saying. He just kept repeating phrases that he had heard.

Have you ever heard people who pray like that? They repeat Christian words and phrases without any real connection to what they are saying. They seem to be more concerned about what others will think of their ability to pray than their actual connection with God in prayer. I know I have been guilty of that before.

I love the prayers of King David. If you read his words as recorded in the above verse, you get a sense that he was a no-nonsense petitioner. His words are straightforward and simple. "Hear my prayer," "I need your help," "Save me!" Those are not the words of a man who is trying to impress anyone, but of one who is genuinely attempting to communicate with God. They sound like words that someone might say in a normal conversation with a regular person.

If we redefine prayer as a simple conversation with God, we can relax a little. God wants to hear from us. I know that the parents of toddlers love to hear their little ones talk. The sentences are not always perfect or coherent, but we always appreciate the effort and honesty they put into their attempts. Of course, that can change over time, and we do not always appreciate the communication style of a teenager once they have a better mastery of the English language.

Thought for the Day

If you are asked to pray, try to relax, and just say what is on your heart, as if God is right there with you and you are having a normal conversation with Him. I know He would love to hear from you!

DAY 205

✦✦✦

And whosoever was not found written in the
book of life was cast into the lake of fire.

—Revelation 20:15

Locker Assignment

When I was recruited to play football at the University of Southern California, I had no idea how different it would be to play on a national stage. I was from a normal suburban sized city, and played in front of regular crowds. Fast forward to three years later, when the final play of my football career was in front of a television audience of millions in a packed stadium with attendance of over 104,000 spectators. Wow, what a way to go out!

I first knew that something was up about my new football home at USC when they took me to the locker room upon my arrival on campus. As I walked down the rows of lockers, I immediately noticed something that I wasn't expecting. Each locker had a gold rectangular sign attached to it with cardinal letters (USC colors). I then realized that the players did not have locker numbers as I had always been accustomed to. They had their names engraved on personalized plates that were attached to their lockers! At the beginning of the following season, it was still quite a moment for a semi-small-town guy to stand in front of a locker that had been personalized for me. I kept that nameplate when I graduated after my senior year. Below is a picture of that actual plate.

God's word tells us that when we confess Jesus as Lord, our names are put into the Lamb's Book of Life and that we then belong to Him. John 10:28 records the words of Jesus as He spoke on this subject, "*And I give them eternal life, and they shall never perish; neither shall anyone snatch them out of My hand.*" But we can see from our verse for today that God's word also tells of the final destination for those who do not commit their lives to Christ.

You might say that I earned my way to USC through sacrifice and hard work. But the fact that my name is written in the Lamb's Book of Life has nothing to do with my effort, and everything to do with Christ's sacrifice on the cross for me.

You see, because my name was on that locker, I knew I belonged on that team.

Thought for the Day

Where is your eternal nameplate?

DAY 206

And take the helmet of salvation, and the sword
of the Spirit, which is the word of God.

—Ephesians 6:17

Assault Bible

As police officers, we spent a considerable amount of time train-ing with a variety of firearms that we either carried on our per-son or were secured in our police units. We had handguns, AR 15 rifles, shotguns, as well as several less-than-lethal options available to us. Our range master oversaw our training in how to use all of these weapons in a safe and effective manner. He would put us through shooting scenarios in various lighting conditions, shooting positions, and "shoot, don't shoot" confrontations. No one looked forward to firing our weapons at anyone, but in the event of a possibly lethal attack, we were ready to meet force with force and stop whoever would threaten the life of another.

The above verses in Ephesians begins by telling us to "put on the whole armor of God" to protect ourselves against our adversary, Satan, who is constantly mounting attacks against our physical and spiritual lives. Make no mistake about it, the enemy's aim is to destroy us and will stop at nothing to accomplish his goal. As Christians, we should always "bring out the big guns" in our attempt to fight the Devil's always-lethal attacks.

In the ancient world in which the Bible was written, a sword was the cutting edge of weapon technology. It was the go-to arma-ment of choice for any soldier in battle. Today, we would liken an AR 15 to the sword of centuries ago. Guns don't do us much good in a spiritual battle, but Ephesians 6:17 tells us what our ultimate weapon is against Satan's attacks. In modern-day terminology, it could be rewritten, "And the assault rifle of the Spirit, which is the word of God."

God's inerrant word, the Bible, is our first and best defense against the attacks of the enemy. I purchased a spiral-bound paperback book called the *Calvary Chapel Scripture Reference Guide*, which I feel is one of the best topic scripture references I have ever used. The table of contents covers numerous subject questions that I use almost every day in counseling sessions. In fact, I used it for scripture references as I prepared this devotional!

It does not matter which guide you use, but it does matter that you go to God's word first to defend yourself, look for guidance, and seek His will in your life. Second Timothy 3:16–17 tells us that "*all scripture is given by inspiration of God, and is profitable for doctrine, for reproof, for correction, for instruction in righteousness.*" Not some, not most, ALL! That even means the scriptures we don't like, don't agree with, or don't fully understand. We have been given the biggest weapon available in our fight against the enemy, God's word! So, let's use it.

Thought for the Day

Always choose the best weapon available, the word of God, when fighting our dangerous enemy.

DAY 207

These things we also speak, not in words which man's
wisdom teaches but which the Holy Spirit teaches,
comparing spiritual things with spiritual.
—1 Corinthians 2:13

Wisdom to Say

As first responders, we are called upon to comfort distraught people during the lowest points of their lives. We often search for just the right words to say. It is hard when we realize there is nothing we can tell them that will make their pain go away. If a mother just found her teenage son hanging from a rafter in the garage, is there really anything I could come up with that will make her say, "Thanks, I feel better now?" Sometimes the best I can do is to make sure I don't say the wrong thing, or just shut up and say nothing at all! When I am confronted with a difficult situation like this, I pray for wisdom.

The apostle Paul told the church in Corinth that the Holy Spirit spoke to him, revealing things that are above the conventional wisdom of man. Jesus said in John 14:26, *"But the Helper, the Holy Spirit, whom the Father will send in My name, He will teach you all things, and bring to your remembrance all things that I said to you."*

We need that wisdom when we are called upon daily to settle civil disputes, take people's freedom from them, and make life-or-death decisions.

Thought for the Day

It is good to know that if we have made Jesus Christ the Lord of our lives, we can count on the Holy Spirit to provide us with the knowledge that we need to say and do the right things on the job.

DAY 208

You saw me before I was born. Every day of my life was recorded in your book. Every moment was laid out before a single day had passed.
—Psalms 139:16

The Future

I had to repeat the second grade. The term used then was "held back," but it basically meant I had to go through the second grade twice. I had progressed too slowly that year, and my teacher felt that I was not quite ready to move on. I remember feeling badly about myself and wondered why this had happened to me.

Fast-forward a decade to my last year in high school. I was an eighteen-year-old senior, which was not uncommon. CIF rules stated that if student athletes turned nineteen before the start of the school year, they were not eligible to play that season. I was a full year under that restriction and was able to participate in both football and track without an issue. I had a great senior year, junior college career, and went on to receive a full-ride scholarship to the University of Southern California.

I often thought about the year I was held back. As much as I protested at the time, I realize where I would have ended up athletically if I moved that timeline back only one year. My freshman year at Orange Coast College would have been my sophomore year. I did not have the size I needed at that time to move on to a quality Division 1 school. I would never have been offered a scholarship at USC, I would have never had the privilege of being part of the 1978 national championship team, and I would have never participated in two Rose Bowls.

As much as I didn't understand what had happened to me when I was younger, God knew what He was doing! He knew my future and what was possible for me before anyone else could. I will always be thankful that He didn't listen to the immature demands of that eight-year-old child and allowed me to go through what I thought was a difficult circumstance at the time.

God knows you. He knows what is best for you, and He knows where He wants to take you in your life. It might not make much sense to you now, but that doesn't make His plan for you any less valid. When speaking of our lives, the above verse in Psalms tells us that *"Every moment was laid out before a single day had passed."*

God knows what he is doing in your life. He has a plan for your future. It doesn't matter if it is your relationship future, your career future, or your health future. It doesn't matter if that plan happens quickly or if it takes years to come about. It doesn't matter if we understand or like the direction that God is taking us in. He is in control and knows the end as well as He knows the middle and the beginning. The omniscience of God is complete and without error.

Thought for the Day

What great thing is God planning for you through your current circumstance? Trust Him, He knows your future!

DAY 209

Whose minds the god of this age has blinded, who do not believe, lest the light of the gospel of the glory of Christ, who is the image of God, should shine on them.

—2 Corinthians 4:4

Clear Vision

I have early-onset cataracts, or I should say I had them. Over a two-week period, they were removed and replaced with permanent lens implants. I went from having cloudy, impaired vision, to twenty-twenty overnight. I no longer need glasses or contacts! The doctor could not tell me why I developed cataracts so early, and I was definitely the youngest person in the waiting room. It could have been due to my exposure to the sun during my athletic and police careers, which was probably exacerbated by the use of computers and smart devices. For whatever reason, they developed, and the fact that they are gone is a miracle. I am stunned by how vivid colors seem now. Whites are really bright, and greens are darker and lusher. I had gotten so used to the slowly developing yellow filter that was on everything that I never realized the decline.

Our adversary Satan is a lot like a cataract. He can blind us to the point of almost total sightlessness. Sometimes it happens suddenly, but most of the time it is a dimming that occurs at such a slow pace that we are not even aware it is happening.

The above verse says that the "light of the gospel" can "shine on them," revealing the truth of Christ. The Holy Spirit can perform eye surgery on us that will take out the dull lens created by Satan's lies, and replace them by giving us a clear vision through God's word. You can go from spiritual blindness to twenty-twenty overnight!

Thought for the Day

Everything can look new and fresh when we submit to His word.

DAY 210

*He will again have compassion on us, And will subdue our
iniquities. You will cast all our sins into the depths of the sea.*
—Micah 7:19

Ticket Black Hole

I wrote thousands of citations during my law enforcement career.
The route that these "greenies" took after they were issued was
predictable. I would turn them into a supervisor who reviewed them
before they were sent to the Records Section. After the cites were
coded and processed by Records, they were sent to the court where
fines were determined and defendant notifications were made. Every
once in a while, a citation disappeared before it got to the court and
was never logged into the system. This happened very rarely, but a
ticket "black hole" did exist. If you were one of those lucky few whose
citation documentation was lost, you didn't have to pay for the ticket
and there would be no record of your violation in the court system.

God's word says that *"For all have sinned and fall short of the
glory of God"* (Romans 3:23). There is not one of us who is perfect
and have not broken God's law. The good news is that Jesus Christ
paid the price for our imperfections by His death on the cross. We
will all appear before the Father in judgment someday. If we have
accepted Jesus Christ as our Savior and Lord, and have given Him
the control of our lives, then our violation documentation will, for all
intents and purposes, be lost. Our cases will be thrown out of court
due to a lack of evidence because of the cleansing blood of our Savior.

But we don't have to wait until our lives on this earth are over to
experience this debt forgiveness. He promises to "lose our citations"

every day if we confess our flaws to Him and do our best to follow his commandments. God's word says that "*If we confess our sins, He is faithful and just to forgive us our sins and to cleanse us from all unrighteousness.*" (1 John 1:9).

Thought for the Day

We don't have to close our eyes, cross our fingers, and hope that our sin documentation will be lost before it gets to God's court. God's "ticket black hole" is His greatest promise to us.

DAY 211

*Behold I stand at the door and knock: If anyone
hears my voice, and opens the door I will come in to
him and dine with him, and he with Me.*

—Revelation 3:20

Door Kick

I kicked down many doors in my career. Whether as a result of exigency, a fresh pursuit, the destruction of evidence, or as part of a legally issued search warrant. I was given the right by law, under specific circumstances, to enter a building against the wishes of those inside. Of course, there was always a way to get in that did not require a door kick: consent of the resident.

When it comes to God's wish for a relationship with us, He will never force His way into our lives. The above verse in Revelation documents that our consent is the only requirement. If anyone hears my voice, and <u>opens the door</u> I will come in. God came to this earth in the form of a man, Jesus Christ, lived a sinless life, and paid the price for our sin by dying on the cross. He did this so that we might not only have a plan and purpose in this life, but also an eternity in heaven with Him when this life is over. Jesus did all the work for us because He knew that we could not do it for ourselves. But we still have to do our part. Whether it is when we first accept Christ as our Savior and Lord, or when we desire a continuing relationship with Him, we must **ask** Jesus into our lives.

Thought for the Day

If you are waiting for God to kick down the door to your life, stop! It is not going to happen. You must open the door and invite Him in. A relationship with Jesus Christ is always the result of a consent search into our lives.

DAY 212

"I, even I, am He who blots out your transgressions for
My own sake; And I will not remember your sins.

—Isaiah 43:25

Selective Memories

As a police officer, I was involved in thousands of incidents in the city where I served. Some were calls for service from citizens, but many more were due to self-initiated activity based on the things I observed on patrol. The end result of these contacts varied depending upon the call itself. Some ended in assists, some in reports, some in arrests, and still others in all of those things.

As I drive around the city today, there is almost no street or building I can go by that does not contain a memory for me. That can be a good thing as I remember an incident that led to a successful conclusion. But it can also be a sad thing as I recall some of the hard and gripping things I was exposed to that are still, to this day, a little hard to wash from my mind.

Sin can be a lot like that. Sometimes we are reminded of our past and the things we have done that are hard to cleanse from our memories. That is the way we see our past, but not the way God does!

The above verse in Isaiah records the words of God Himself on the subject. He will blot out our sins for His own sake and forget them forever. What an incredible promise! He will not only forgive us; He will totally forget that the incident ever occurred. And He will do this not for our own sake, but for His own!

Of course, like all unbelievable deals, there is a catch. God's word says, "*That if you confess with your mouth the Lord Jesus and believe in your heart that God has raised Him from the dead, you will be saved*" (Romans 10:9). *The* only thing we must do to obtain this permanent sin amnesia is to accept Jesus's death on the cross for our sin and turn our lives over to Him.

If you are a believer in Jesus Christ and have accepted him as your Lord and Savior, you can stand on God's promise to forget your sin forever. So, the next time you are driving around and a particular thing triggers your memories of your own failures in life, stand on the promise of Isaiah 43:25 and say to yourself:

Thought for the Day

HE HAS BLOTTED OUT MY TRANSGRESSIONS FOR HIS OWN SAKE! HE DOES NOT REMEMBER MY SIN ANYMORE!

DAY 213

I will cry out to God Most High, To God who performs all things for me.

—Psalm 57:2

First Things First

One afternoon I was working patrol on the east side of town when I was dispatched to a bank robbery that had just occurred. When I arrived on scene, I started to gather details from the bank employees in an effort to get the suspect information out as quickly as possible. I asked the bank manager how long before my arrival had the suspect fled the area. To my surprise, she told me, "Thirty minutes." I had arrived at the bank within one minute from when Dispatch had received their 911 call. My next question was obvious, "Why did you wait so long to call the police?" Her answer was stunning. She said that before she called us she was on the phone with her corporate headquarters to report the robbery. It wasn't until after she had talked with them that she contacted Dispatch to report the crime. I had to educate her on the order of things when reporting a crime. She needed to call the police first! Calling the corporate office in Duluth would not help us catch a bank robber who, after thirty minutes, was probably halfway to Los Angeles by then.

The above verse in Psalm tells us three things. It says we are to cry out to God in our times of trouble. Next, it says that our God is the "Most High," telling us that there is no greater authority other than our God. Lastly, it says that our God is able to do all things for us, nothing is too hard for Him (Jeremiah 32:17). If we are in trouble, the first place we should go is to our Lord. Not to a friend, a self-help book, or any other teaching or philosophy. We should cry out to Him first before getting any other counsel. We often had people come in for counsel about a difficult situation they were facing. One of the first questions we ask is "Have you prayed about it?" You may be surprised by how many have not!

Thought for the Day

Cry out to God first! He is the only one with the unlimited knowledge and power to help us.

DAY 214

*Then you will call upon Me and go and pray
to Me, and I will listen to you.*

—Jeremiah 29:12

Prayer

Recently I read an article in my hometown paper that posed the question to children, "If you could make one wish, what would it be?" The answers these little ones gave were priceless. Ruth, age five, wrote, "I would make a horse appear out of thin air. I would name it Horsey and she could stay in my backyard." Maxwell, age seven, stated, "I would make all the candy in the world appear in my bedroom and I would eat it all myself." Madeleine, age nine, said, "I would make a pool appear inside my house along with a pile of tacos." And finally, Sariah, age six, wrote, "I would put some Yogurtland machines in my house and have it for breakfast, lunch, and dinner." It was funny how most of the answers had a food component to them, something I could definitely relate to!

One thing is for certain, God wants to hear from us and advises us to "pray about everything," (Philippians 4:6). But not all the things we want in this life are in our own best interest. Fortunately, we serve a God who will not give us everything we ask for. First John 5:14 states, "*Now this is the confidence that we have in Him, that if we ask anything according to His will, He hears us.*" God will hear and grant us our petitions to Him with one great caveat: the request has to be in accordance to His will. Since God loves us so much, I know one thing about His will that is absolutely true. God will never affirmatively answer a prayer that is not in our own best interest.

We might smile at a child who prays for a horse, candy, tacos, or a never-ending yogurt machine, thinking of the immaturity of those requests. But are we any different in our petitions sometimes? We often make childlike requests of God that must seem shallow and immature to Him. It is never wrong to make personal requests to God about anything that is on our hearts, but we must always pray with the qualification that we only want our request if it is in God's will for our lives. If we think that way, it makes the "no" answers a little easier to understand.

Thought for the Day

It is never wrong to add "if it is Your will" to our prayers.

DAY 215

A friend loves at all times, and a brother is born for adversity.
—Proverbs 17:17

Gone and Forgotten

One afternoon, our officers were dispatched to a welfare check at a residence on the east side of town. The male subject they were looking for lived at the location but had not been seen for some time. In fact, no one had spoken to him in six months! The few who knew him thought that he had gone to rehab for a substance abuse problem. He, in fact, had not gone to rehab, but instead had died due to complications from his alcohol addiction.

When our officers entered the residence, they found hundreds of empty vodka bottles (his drink of choice). At first, there was no indication of a dead body inside the house. But, as they went into the living room area, they found out otherwise. The subject had died on his couch, and due to the lengthy passage of time, his body had decomposed, dried up, and mummified. I wondered how isolated and alone an individual would have to be to not have been missed for six months.

At Harvest OC, we have Bible study small groups for men, women, and couples. They provide opportunities to study God's word and fellowship with people who will pray for you, hold you accountable, and be there for you in tough times. It's what makes a large church smaller and more intimate for those who take part. The enemy does not want you to develop close, personal friendships with other believers. He wants you so isolated and alone so that if you were to disappear, no one would know you were gone.

Don't let that happen to you. God's word commands us to *"for-sake not the assembling of ourselves together"* (Hebrews 10:25). This means not only at church on Sunday, but also in fellowship with other believers on an intimate, personal level, people who will lift you up, pray for you, hold you accountable, and be there for you in difficult times.

Thought for the Day

Who will come looking for you if you spiritually disappear?

DAY 216

"When you go out to fight your enemies and you face horses and chariots and an army greater than your own, do not be afraid. The Lord your God, who brought you out of the land of Egypt, is with you!
—Deuteronomy 20:1

Outnumbered?

As police officers, we never wanted to be outnumbered. Whether during a vehicle pursuit, or responding to a fight in the street, we always try to have more of us than there are of them. Notice I didn't say, "As many of us as there are of them," but "more." We were under no obligation to fight fair when confronting criminal activity. Our only duty is to win and protect the citizens who we are sworn to serve.

There are times in our lives when we feel outnumbered by people, circumstances, or the overwhelming condition we find ourselves in. If we scan the battlefield and count the number of obstacles confronting us, the situation may look hopeless. But with God backing us, we can become an undefeatable army of one.

In the above verse in Deuteronomy, Moses spoke to encourage the nation Israel on the plains of Moab shortly before his death. He told them that if they obeyed God, they would not have to worry about the vast enemies that would confront them as they went into the Promised Land. No matter how many soldiers, chariots, or weapons the enemy had, or no matter how insurmountable the circumstances appeared, they would be victorious. He then reminded them that the same God who brought the plagues on Egypt, parted the Red Sea, fed them with manna, and had been leading them around via pillars of smoke and fire would come to their aid. If He could get them out of Egypt, He could help them win a battle.

You might be facing a person, situation, or circumstance today that seems undefeatable. If you use conventional wisdom provided by the world, it appears you will certainly lose. But if you serve the Lord and place your faith in Him, you do not have to be afraid. He will fight the battle for you and help you to come out victorious in the end.

Thought for the Day

When it comes to God, overwhelming backup is just a prayer away. Cry out to Him and don't be afraid.

DAY 217

"Am I only a God nearby," declares the LORD, *"and
not a God far away? Can anyone hide in secret places
so that I cannot see him?"* declares the LORD. *"Do not
I fill heaven and earth?"* declares the LORD.

—Jeremiah 23:23–24

Hiding in Plain Sight

One afternoon while on duty, I met my daughter at a local shopping mall for lunch. As she arrived, she had a little trouble
finding me at first. When I saw her, I called out from the location
where I was standing. She walked over to me and asked, "Dad, why
are you hiding over here?" I had to laugh because I hadn't realized
that I was standing against a wall behind a tall bush. I was exhibiting that paranoid cop mentality that can sometimes unconsciously
overtake those of us in law enforcement. The truth was that despite
my unconscious attempts to hide, a six two cop in full uniform was
pretty obvious to anyone.

The Bible says that *"all have sinned and fall short of the glory of
God"* (Romans 3:23). We may try to explain away, justify, or hide our
sin from God, but we cannot. God sees all, and nothing is hidden
from Him. The good news of the gospel is that He loves us anyway
and is eager and willing to forgive us at a moment's notice. God's
word says, *"But God demonstrates His own love toward us, in that while
we were still sinners, Christ died for us"* (Romans 5:8). He already
knew exactly who and what we were before He sacrificed Himself on
the cross for us.

Thought for the Day

It doesn't make any sense to attempt to hide from God when we are actually in plain sight. Confess your sin to Him now and be forgiven!

DAY 218

It is He who sits above the circle of the earth, And its inhabitants
are like grasshoppers, Who stretches out the heavens like a
curtain, And spreads them out like a tent to dwell in.

—Isaiah 40:22

Needless Fear

A practical joke was played on an officer at our department by
those who will remain unnamed, and it involved a bag of broken glass.

One night, an officer responded to a call and parked his patrol
vehicle on the street. He secured the marked unit before walking to
the residence that had been the location of the call. While he was
gone, his beat partners entered the vehicle, removed the unit's shotgun and assault rifle from their locked racks, and placed them in the
trunk of the car. They then rolled down the driver's side window and
dumped a bag of broken glass on the driver's seat. When the officer
returned to the vehicle, it appeared to him that someone had broken
in the window of his patrol unit and had stolen the weapons inside.

As he paced around on the street trying to organize his thoughts
and determine just how he was going to call this in and report it to
the watch commander, his "friends" hid in the bushes a short distance
away and filmed the entire incident with a video camera. The red dot
on the camera and their failed attempts to hold back their laughter at
the distraught officer's situation soon gave away their location. When
the officer realized that he had been fooled and that his actions had
been recorded, a short foot pursuit ensued as documented by the
jumbled bouncing video camera footage.

We all have things happen in our lives that seem so bad that we don't know if we will be able to get through them. We have no idea what to do or how to fix the problem. The good news is that we serve a God who knows exactly what to do. Things that are insurmountable to us are simple for Him. If we believe in Him, we can receive the answers to our prayers about our predicaments if we will only trust that He always has our best interests at heart. We might even look back and smile at ourselves about the way we worried when God was so in control of the situation.

Thought for the Day

Things are never as hopeless as they may seem because God is always in control!

DAY 219

My brethren, count it all joy when you fall into various trials,
knowing that the testing of your faith produces patience.
—James 1:2–3

High Stress

In 1990, I attended the Orange County Sheriff's Academy, which at the time offered the last high-stress training environments in the state. We were daily exposed to inspections and various training exercises which included screaming tactical officers who found fault with just about everything we did. It was much like the Army basic training that you see in movies and on television. This high-stress treatment continued for the entire six months that I was in the academy.

At first, I had a hard time understanding the purpose behind the actions of my training officers. It seemed that I could do nothing right no matter how hard I tried. I soon realized that it was their job to expose us to this stressful environment to test us and weed out those who didn't have the emotional makeup necessary to be in law enforcement. We started with sixty people in our class and finished with only thirty. The training had done its work, which resulted in half of our class quitting on their own accord. In the years that followed, I grew to appreciate my academy training and how it had helped me handle the volatile, emotionally trying situations that I would be exposed to on a regular basis.

The above verse in James tells us that we are to *"count it all joy"* when we go through trials in our lives because they have a positive outcome. So many times in my life I didn't understand why things were happening to me, only to see years later that they had produced a character and patience in me that I didn't possess before.

Thought for the Day

Are you going through life's academy right now? Hang in there, God never wastes a trial!

DAY 220

No, dear brothers and sisters, I have not achieved it, but I focus on one thing: forgetting the past and looking forward to what lies ahead, I press on to reach the end of the race and receive the heavenly prize for which God, through Christ Jesus, is calling us.
—Philippians 3:13–14

Long-Term Memories

Several years ago, I responded as a chaplain to a fatal traffic collision involving a nine-year-old boy. Unfortunately, scenes like the one I encountered upon my arrival are a normal part of the law enforcement experience. I have to say that due to the age and innocence of the victim, this one was particularly difficult for the police and fire personnel who were on scene. Almost all of them have or have had children who were that age. This tragedy hit the community hard and affected the boy's classmates and their parents in a personal way.

I have conducted critical incident stress debriefings for first responders after specific events. They see a lot of terrible things during their careers that do not rise to the level of a stress debriefing. Scenes like the one involving this boy are above the "horrific normal" that police and fire have come to expect. Some studies indicate that stress debriefings are hard on everyday civilian types. I believe that is because regular folks believe that they won't have to see anything like that again, and the CISD process makes them relive the incident and adds to their trauma. First responders, on the other hand, know that they will see this type of thing over and over again during their careers. This creates in them the need to process the incident knowing that it is a certainty that they will see similar, or worse, events in the future. I can tell you from firsthand experience that the in-control, calm demeanor exhibited by first responders at the scene belies the true emotions going on inside them. It is a hard job for the heroic men and woman who have volunteered to place themselves in that position.

We all have things in our past that we want to forget. Sometimes hurts, disappointments, and failures haunt us to the point where our lives seem to be stuck in neutral. As pastors, we often counsel people who can't seem to let go of the things they have experienced. I liken it to driving a car with our full concentration on the rearview mirror. If we continue to look back with the narrow focus of where we have been and not forward through the wide "windshield" view of what is ahead of us, we will crash. In our lives, we will always have a rearview mirror that we glance at occasionally to remind us of where we have been. If we didn't, we would not be able to help others by giving them the same comfort we received from God (2 Corinthians 1:4). The problem isn't one of recollection, it is one of focus.

In the above verse in Philippians, Paul talks about this forward focus as a matter of choice. Paul had a lot of terrible things to forget that could have dragged him down, as well as great things to remember that could have puffed him up with pride. In either case, he chose to forget the past and focus on the future so that he could finish his life race well.

I know it isn't always as easy as simply forgetting the past, but we can become what we focus on.

Thought for the Day

God promises that the windshield of our lives will get bigger and clearer if we focus on Him for our future.

DAY 221

But indeed, O man, who are you to reply against God? Will the thing formed say to him who formed it, "Why have you made me like this?"

—Romans 9:20

Average?

When I walked off the field at the Rose Bowl on January 1, 1980, the one thing that I could claim as an extraordinary talent ended, I was no longer a scholarship football player for the University of Southern California. The knee injury I sustained my junior year had reduced my ability to play at the level that was required by a professional football team. I was now a regular guy with no burning talent of any kind. As the years passed, I had a number of jobs, none of which gave me the kind of success I had experienced as a young man. I became the "decathlete of average" in just about everything I did. The bar had been set so high for me due to football that I expected similar success in everything else that I did. I often wondered, "Lord, why have you made me like this?" My problem was that I judged myself by the world's standards of success and failure, and not by God's.

The above verse in Romans states that we have no right to question the way God has made us or the talents and abilities He has given to us. We need to be the ultimate team player even if our purpose in the kingdom might seem of little worth in a world that usually only values money, fame, and position.

As I look to where God has led me in my life, I can now truly say that I am happy with the purpose He has given me to fulfill. I might not have the position or fame, and I definitely don't have the money, but I love knowing that I am doing exactly what God has called me to do.

Thought for the Day

It takes above-average people to embrace their worldly mediocrity so that God can accomplish great things through them in His name.

DAY 222

*Who will transform our lowly body that it may be conformed
to His glorious body, according to the working by which
He is able even to subdue all things to Himself.*
—Philippians 3:21

Worn Out

The ice maker in our refrigerator recently stopped working. The appliance was only about two years old and should not have given out so soon. Fortunately, the manufacturer decided to stand behind their product even though its warranty had just expired. We have ice again, for now. There is no guarantee that the new ice maker will last any longer than the old one did. In the past, we have had ice makers that lasted a decade. I guess it really is true that they just don't seem to make appliances the way they used to.

Originally our bodies were designed to last forever, but Adam and Eve took care of that one for all of us. Now because of their sin, and our own, our bodies will slowly (sometimes not so slowly) wear out. There is no guarantee that we will have another day to live. Some of us might have many years left on this earth, while others are unaware that their end will come soon. We will do our best to "get repaired" and extend our lives for as long as we can. But sometimes our equipment will just give out without warning, with no repair possible.

The great hope of the gospel (good news) is that if we have put our faith in Jesus Christ, we can look forward to new bodies that will never break down. The above verse in Philippians tells the believer what is in store for us after we leave this world. Jesus will transform our bodies to be just like His glorious one. What a great promise! The older I get, the more that guarantee means to me, and the more I look forward to it.

If our bodies give out sooner than expected, or if we are blessed enough to live many more years, it really doesn't matter. Our time in eternity will erase the short period we spent on this earth no matter how long that span was.

Thought for the Day

The believer has the ultimate warranty against death. All we need to do is ask.

DAY 223

*We are confident, yes, well pleased rather to be absent
from the body and to be present with the Lord.*

—2 Corinthians 5:8

Sudden Death

One afternoon, I was dispatched to a dead body call on the east side of town. A male subject was discovered dead on the side yard of his residence. The man was lying on his back at the base of a ladder with a pruning saw clutched in his right hand. The ladder was placed up against a tree, and when I looked up, I noticed a partially sawed through branch. It was apparent that the man had been cutting the limb when he had a heart attack and suddenly died. I have found many bodies which from their placement and contortion, it was obvious they died in fear and had been in a lot of pain. It was not the case with this man. It looked as though he was happily doing yard work when his world came to an unexpected end. It was the way that we all would like to go (other than in our sleep), busily working without fear or dread of what would happen soon.

For the Christian, God's word is clear on what will happen to us when we die. The above verse in Corinthians states that if we are absent from these earthly bodies, we will be present with our Lord. There are no in-between stops, no coming back to earth as another person or life-form, and certainly no black void where life just ceases to exist.

We will live forever either with God or without Him. Either this is the greatest news we have ever heard, or the worst news we could possibly think of.

For those of us who have accepted Christ as our Savior, we can live a life free from the fear or dread of the unexpected. Paul wrapped it up perfectly when he wrote, "*For to me, to live is Christ, and to die is gain*" (Philippians 1:21).

Thought for the Day

We don't need to fear our end if our future is assured.

DAY 224

Be diligent in these matters; give yourself wholly to them,
so that everyone may see your progress. Watch your life
and doctrine closely. Persevere in them, because if you
do, you will save both yourself and your hearers.

—1 Timothy 4:15–16

The Gallery

While working patrol by the bay, I was dispatched to a possible dead body call. When I arrived, I found a subject kneeling on a dock with his left arm in the water. He pointed down to the bay, and I saw, for the first time, what he was holding with his submerged hand. It was a fully clothed male who, from his appearance, had been dead for several days. The man holding him was a retired Royal Mountie rescue diver who had been in this situation many times before. What made this incident different was that he knew and worked with the deceased. The dead man was known to have had a drinking problem and had been missing from the dock area for the past three days. I grabbed the deceased by the leg as the retired Mountie took hold of his jacket. Together we pulled him out of the water and up on to the dock. The three days in the bay had taken their toll on the man's body due to the salt water and the hungry marine life.

As I stood on the dock, I turned around and looked up at the building located next to us. It was a local seafood restaurant that had large plate glass windows which faced the dock. Lined up at the windows were a number of restaurant customers who had horrified looks on their faces. Unknown to us, they had been watching our actions the entire time. My guess was that the chowder sales dropped off sharply that afternoon.

In the above passage, Paul encourages Timothy to "*watch your life*" because he knew that others would be. Paul wanted to make sure that Timothy was a good example for Jesus Christ in everything he did, said, and believed.

As first responders, we are very familiar with the concept of having our actions observed and evaluated by others. As Christians we need to practice the same due diligence in our lives so that we will not cause others to question the validity of our faith. The world is watching to see if a relationship with Jesus Christ can bring meaning and purpose to their own lives.

Thought for the Day

If we could look into the thoughts of those around us, would we see horrified faces or would we see a longing to have the peace that a relationship with Christ can bring?

DAY 225

*And whosoever was not found written in the
book of life was cast into the lake of fire.*

—Revelation 20:15

Worse than Death

I have had many conversations over the years about the death penalty and its appropriateness as a punishment. I have found good
people of conscience on both sides of the issue, and I support their
right to the personal beliefs that they hold. Many who are opposed to
the death penalty state that no one can be absolutely sure of the guilt
of the defendant, so they just don't want to take that chance.

One thing I have found for certain, no matter what side of the
question you are on, people feel that the death penalty and its application is the worst punishment that a human being can be given. The
above verse in Revelation shows us that it is not.

Revelation 20:15 shows the end result after the Great White
Throne of Judgment for all those who have not accepted Christ as
their Savior and Lord. This is an eternal punishment for those who
have chosen to reject God's free gift of love and salvation as described
in John 3:16: *"For God so loved the world that He gave His only begotten Son, that whosoever believes in Him should not perish but have everlasting life."*

Through a belief in Jesus Christ, anyone can have instant forgiveness that doesn't depend upon anything that happens in this
world. This truth lessens the fear of a possible mistake that could, on
a rare occasion, be made in the trial by jury system that we have in
this country.

All of us will stand before the perfect and righteous judge who knows the complete truth about every detail of our lives. If an injustice has been done, and if that person has accepted Jesus Christ as Lord, God will have an eternity to make right any wrong that has occurred in this vapor we call a life. One second into eternity, none of what has gone before will matter to us unless we have not prepared for that final court appearance.

Thought for the Day

There is something worse than physical death, an eternity apart from God.

DAY 226

Likewise the Spirit also helps in our weaknesses. For we do not know what we should pray for as we ought, but the Spirit Himself makes intercession for us with groanings which cannot be uttered.

—Romans 8:26

Code Breaker

As law enforcement officers, we use radio codes for everything. The purpose behind this practice is to shorten our transmissions and to protect our conversations from those who might be listening with a scanner. There are so many codes that sometimes we have a mental block as to which one to use for a specific situation. I find that the older I got, the more that happened to me.

Sometimes when we pray, we have trouble coming up with the right words to say that accurately expresses our desires, requests, or praises to God. The above verse in Romans gives us the assurance that the Holy Spirit will assist us at times like this when we are at a loss for words. He knows our hearts and will translate our prayers so that the finished product will be a perfectly worded request to God. I'm so thankful for that!

Don't let the fear of a weak prayer keep you from communicating with God. He wants to hear from you so badly that He has given you the Holy Spirit to translate your prayers to Him.

Thought for the Day

Do not worry if you don't know the codes to a perfect prayer, the Holy Spirit owns the codebook!

DAY 227

And when you pray, you shall not be like the hypocrites. For they love to pray standing in the synagogues and on the corners of the streets, that they may be seen by men. Assuredly, I say to you, they have their reward.
—Matthew 6:5

Too Many Words

As a field training officer (FTO), I tried to instill good habits in the rookie police officers under my supervision. One very important skill that they needed to master was radio transmission restraint. After each call, a specific disposition had to be radioed in to close out an event. The dispatcher just wanted to hear a simple preset phrase so that they knew what action was taken to solve the reported problem. Ten-eight advised, 10-8 with report info, 10-8 unfounded, or 10-8 arrested were all examples of appropriate dispositions. Every time I rode with a trainee and we heard some long drawn-out transmission that included what the officer did, what they thought, or what they had for lunch, I would point at the radio and tell the new cop, "Don't ever do that!"

As a chaplain, I often officiate at weddings. I've never had anyone say to me after the ceremony, "Man, Padre, that would have been better if you had just gone on a little longer." People seem to appreciate a succinct ceremony with greater meaning.

Purposeful brevity can be a real gift in our public prayer lives too. In the above verse in Matthew, we read about a certain type of person who liked to pray aloud and thought that they could impress others by how spiritual they sounded. I think we've all had to endure that long-winded or holier-than-thou prayer at a meal or special occasion that was delivered by this type of individual. They don't seem to realize that they are not impressing anybody, including God.

There is an old saying about prayer, "Keep your prayers short in public and long in private." This is good news for those who feel that public prayer is not one of their strengths.

God appreciates your heartfelt words to Him, even if they are not in KING JAMES ENGLISH! Just relax and talk to God about what is on your heart. He will appreciate it, and so will those who hear you pray. They just might be drawn to God due to your authentic communication that demonstrates what a real personal relationship with Him sounds like.

Thought for the Day

Keep your public transmissions to God meaningful and concise.

DAY 228

I have taught you in the way of wisdom; I have led you in right paths.
—Proverbs 4:11

Driving Directions

As police officers, we were regularly called upon to direct traffic at accident scenes. It was our job to not only assist those involved in the collision, but also to keep traffic safely moving so that no other life or property would be endangered. This often included temporarily blocking a turn lane or other path of travel until the wreckage, debris, or fluid spills could be cleaned.

It was inevitable that a driver will pull up to the blocked-off area, point just past the wreckage, and yell, "But I live right there!" They often angrily speed off, frustrated over having to use a different way home that was not on their usual route. We didn't redirect them for the fun of it, but if they took the path they wanted, it would destroy evidence or place their lives in danger. They got frustrated because they didn't understand the entire situation, and frankly, we didn't have the time to explain it to them. They just had to believe that in this instance, we knew best.

God calls on us to follow His directions in this life even if we don't understand why. I can't tell you how many times I have questioned God's plan for me, only to later ask for His forgiveness when the purpose for His direction was revealed. Whenever I don't understand God's will, one thing has been made clear to me. He is always right, and if I doubt Him, I am always wrong!

Are you trying to turn in to a destination that God has blocked? You might be right there within sight of your plan, and for some reason, you just can't make that last turn. God knows all things, and He can see the dangers that lie ahead and might be invisible to you. Trust Him. Follow the path He points you toward even if it seems to take longer or makes no sense to you at the time.

Thought for the Day

Remember, He sees our future with greater clarity than we see our present. He will never point you in the wrong direction.

DAY 229

Such is the destiny of all who forget God; so perishes the hope of the godless. What they trust in is fragile, what they rely on is a spider's web.
—Job 8:13–14

Shatterproof

We have a fourteen-inch-diameter hanging globe light at the entrance to our home. Since we are midcentury decor enthusiasts, it fits right in with our front door and the furnishings inside. Several years ago, I saw that the globe was dirty and needed to be cleaned after months of exposure to the elements. I took down the globe very carefully, knowing that it was made of extremely fragile glass. In fact, I was proud of myself for getting it out of its fixture without breaking it. I took the globe in my left hand and opened the front door with my right hand in order to enter the house. I apparently did not open the door quite enough, and as I walked in, I barely tapped the glass against the front door handle. Well, that small tap was enough to break the fragile globe in my hands. My wife was sitting inside with a visitor from our church. I did not react the way I wanted to, but instead it took all I had to come up with the correct pastoral response of "Oh well, these things happen." Of course, that was not what was going on inside my head! I immediately went to Amazon.com and was able to find a replacement globe. This one was made out of Lucite that would not break during my next cleaning attempt, at least, I hope not.

The above verse in Job records a statement made to Job by one of his "friends," Bildad, the Shuite who visited him during his suffering. This statement had one big problem. It did not apply to Job, as God would later point out to Bildad. Even though Job had not forgotten God, it does give us some truth as to the state of those who do. They have no real hope, and what they do trust in is as fragile as a spiderweb, there one second and gone the next.

We as believers in Jesus Christ, on the other hand, have the greatest foundation for our hope imaginable. Jeremiah 29:11 tells us, "*For I know the thoughts that I think toward you, says the LORD, thoughts of peace and not of evil, to give you a future and a hope.*" Psalm 42:5 states, "*Why are you cast down, O my soul? And why are you disquieted within me? Hope in God, for I shall yet praise Him for the help of His countenance.*" If the hope of the world is as fragile as a spider's web, the hope of God is stronger than the highest tensile strength cable known to man.

Thought for the Day

Put your trust in him. No hit that the world strikes you with will cause your life to shatter in His hands.

DAY 230

Though you grind a fool in a mortar with a pestle along with crushed grain, Yet his foolishness will not depart from him.

—Proverbs 27:22

Foolishness

While working a light-duty front-desk assignment due to an injury, I realized something as I never had before, there is a lot of foolishness in the world! And it seemed like almost all of it either showed up at the station or called in during my shift. Word to the wise, if you keep receiving phone calls from your ex in violation of a valid restraining order, contacting the police every half hour and stating "They called again, I want another police report" might be an abuse of the system. The answer to your problem is very simple, CHANGE YOUR PHONE NUMBER! We are also not there to tell your teenage children to stop fighting in the car, threaten your three-year-old with arrest if they don't stay in their car seat, listen to complaints about citations issued to you by another city because all cops are "jerks," or hear how unfair it is that your car was towed just because you had twenty outstanding parking cites!

All of us can act foolishly, not just those who come to the PD front lobby. Sins are foolish acts that God's word says we are all guilty of. The Bible tells us, "*For all have sinned and fall short of the glory of God*" *(Romans 3:23)*. But there is only one foolish sin that can keep us from an eternal life with Him, blasphemy against the Holy Spirit. God's word says, "*But he who blasphemes against the Holy Spirit never has forgiveness but is subject to eternal condemnation*" (Mark 3:29).

So how do we blaspheme the Holy Spirit? If we do not have a relationship with Jesus Christ, the Holy Spirit is currently nudging and encouraging us to do so. When we refuse the Spirit's leading to accept God's free gift of eternal life purchased for us by Christ's death on the cross, we blaspheme Him. That is the only unforgivable sin. I'm so glad that the list is just one item long. God makes it so simple!

We all need to listen to the Holy Spirit's leading whether it is to turn the control of our lives over to Christ for the first time, or to renew our commitment to Him.

Thought for the Day

Don't be a fool, listen and receive all that God has for you here on this earth and in the eternity that will follow.

DAY 231

But He said, "More than that, blessed are those
who hear the word of God and keep it!"

—Luke 11:28

Preprogrammed

Several years ago, my wife and I bought one of those vacuuming robots as an early Christmas gift to each other. COSTCO had one on sale, and since we have wood floors throughout our home, we thought we would give it a try. I immediately named it Robbie after the robot that appeared in the movie *Forbidden Planet* and who was the first well-known cinematic android of the modern era. Robbie turns on every morning at 7:00 a.m. and starts his automatic sweeping pattern around the house. My wife is very happy with him and his ability to keep the floor dust free.

The other day, I was outside doing yard work when I heard a mechanical sound to my left. I looked over and saw Robbie heading down the driveway toward the street. I picked him up before he rolled out into traffic and immediately looked around to determine how he had been able to get outside. I discovered that we had left the kitchen door to the garage open. Robbie had jumped the threshold and cruised down my daughter's wheelchair ramp to the garage floor. From there, he headed out the open garage door and down the driveway to the point where I ended his journey. The poor guy was just doing his job on what he must have thought was a pretty big house. I had to admire how he followed his cleaning program despite some fairly unusual obstacles. It would have been sad, and funny really, if we had lost Robbie due to being run over by a car!

Robbie can teach us all a valuable lesson when it comes to following God's word. There are many times when we don't understand where our lives are taking us, or what the eventual outcome of a situation may be. That is when we need to follow our program, God's word, whether or not we recognize the end result of His plan for us. If we keep busy obeying him, we will be successful in whatever direction He chooses to take us. And just like in Robbie's case, God will pick us up before we get into any real danger. I have been a Christian for a long time. I can tell you that I have never come across a believer that complained that their life took a bad turn because they followed God's word.

Thought for the Day

Keep focused on following God's word wherever it takes you.

DAY 232

Therefore I urge you, imitate me.

—1 Corinthians 4:16

Good Imitation

When I was a new police officer, I rode with different field training officers (FTOs) for several months before I was released to solo patrol. During that time, my goal was to learn from these veterans and to, in many ways, emulate their actions and decisions. How well I did that had a lot to do with passing the initial part of my training.

The above verse was written by Paul in his letter to the church in Corinth. He spent some time, in chapter 3, admonishing those in the church for some of their un-Christian-like practices and attitudes. He then tells them in verse 16 to "imitate me." Wow, that is something Paul might be able to say, but I would be very hesitant to suggest. How does my life measure up? Am I an example for others to follow that is so Christlike that I can say, "Do what I do?"

So, are we to follow Paul, a mere man? Well, the apostle himself clears this up later in the book (1 Corinthians 11:1) when he wrote, *Imitate me, just as I also imitate Christ.* And there it is. We might as well cut to the chase and direct our imitative efforts toward the only One who is truly qualified, Jesus Christ. First John 2:6 states, "*He who says he abides in Him ought himself also to walk just as He did.*" So, Paul's urging to "imitate me" was not based on his own inflated sense of self, but on his assurance that his life had been dramatically altered by his encounter with Jesus and the strength God had given him to change his life.

While in training, I often admired my FTOs for what I thought was an endless supply of knowledge and experience. It wasn't until later when they became my peers and partners, and when I became an FTO, that I realized we all have limited knowledge. I am thankful that I have a written record in God's word of the only One, Jesus Christ, I can always emulate in His every thought, word, and deed.

Thought for the Day

They say that imitation is the greatest form of flattery, but with Jesus, it is not only the wisest thing to do, but also the greatest form of obedience.

DAY 233

No man shall be able to stand before you all the days
of your life; as I was with Moses, so I will be with
you. I will not leave you nor forsake you.

—Joshua 1:5

Never Alone

I remember many incidents from my police career. Some were big, violent, and graphic; others were small, routine, and seemly insignificant. For some reason, it is the insignificant events that bother me most in the post-career period of my life.

One night while on duty, I contacted a young woman who had marijuana in her possession. At that time, possession of cannabis was a detainable offense for a juvenile. We never "arrested" a juvenile, we "detained" them for their own safety, pending parental notification. We would hold them in a separate area of the jail until a parent or legal guardian could come retrieve them. It was the officer's duty to contact someone who could come take responsibility of the young person.

When I asked this young lady for her parents' phone number, she told me she did not have anyone who lived in the area she could refer me to. I don't remember the particulars as to why she was so alone, other than all my attempts to find someone to pick her up failed. I remember her slumped-over countenance and the defeated look on her face that told me she felt completely abandoned and unwanted. I had three teenage daughters at the time, and I did my best to treat her as kindly as I could considering I was the one responsible for her detainment. I wanted to tell her she wasn't alone, that

God loved her, and that he had a future plan for her, but I didn't. I should have spoken up even if it went against our prohibition to discuss religion with people we contacted unless they asked about our faith first. Little did she know that the big cop who had brought her in was sitting across the room praying for her, doing his best to hold back his tears. I went off shift before her situation was resolved, and I never heard how she was released. I am not ashamed of anything I did as a cop (acts of commission), but the things I should have done (acts of omission) stay with me.

I have thought of her in the years since, hoping that she is doing well and that she had found a relationship with God despite my silence that night. My suggestion to those whom God puts in a situation to tell others about Him is do it! It's the lost opportunities that haunt you.

Unlike earthly parents, God will never leave you alone or stranded. The above verse in Joshua tells us that He says, "*I will be with you. I will not leave you nor forsake you.*" You might feel dejected, deserted, unwanted, or without help, but God says that is not true. Psalm 55:22 tells us, "*Give your burdens to the Lord, and he will take care of you. He will not permit the godly to slip and fall.*"

Thought for the Day

No matter what you may think or feel, God will always be there to pick you up. You are never alone.

DAY 234

*He who covers his sins will not prosper, but whoever
confesses and forsakes them will have mercy.*
—Proverbs 28:13

How to Get Out of a Ticket

I wrote thousands of citations for various violations over my law enforcement career. I have often been asked, "What is the best way to get out of a ticket?" Well, there is no surefire way to avoid a ducat, but I can certainly tell you a way to get one. LIE!

I wrote numerous stop-sign violations when I was in patrol. I can't tell you how many times I observed a defendant drive their vehicle through a posted sign at about fifteen or twenty miles per hour. When I initiated the car stop and approached the driver, I often got the exact same response. They would say to me, "What do you mean, I made a complete stop!" They would continue their denials all the way to traffic court where the video recording of the violation ended their objections.

But when the driver told me the truth and confessed that they had committed the violation, they passed what we called the integrity test. More times than not, I would either write them a warning cite or just give them verbal counsel before sending them on their way. I'm not promising that if you tell the truth you will always avoid a ticket, but at least it will give you a fighting chance.

Unlike the uncertainty of getting out of a ticket, God promises us that if we confess our sins to Him, we will receive mercy.

We don't have to wonder how to receive forgiveness from God. His ticket avoidance procedure is set in stone and will work every time. If you have given your life to Jesus Christ and have made Him the Lord of your life, all you must do is confess your sin to Him and you will be forgiven instantly.

Thought for the Day

Confessing to Him is always the way to avoid a sin ticket.

DAY 235

For in this we groan, earnestly desiring to be clothed
with our habitation which is from heaven,
—2 Corinthians 5:2

Longing for Home

When I retired from the police force, we moved to Irvine, which I thought would be a great change of pace after having lived so many years in one area. During that time, we had often returned to South Orange County for one reason or another, and I had to admit something, I missed it! We raised our girls in Mission Viejo, and we had fond recollections of those times. All the markets, schools, businesses, and streets have such good memories for us, driving our girls around to their activities and watching them grow. Whenever we went to our old home area and had to start back northbound on the Santa Ana Freeway, I had this aching feeling that I was driving away from my home. After having spent so many years living south of the El Toro Y, my internal beacon had become reset without me knowing it. I guess I just have a desire to go home.

When we became believers in Jesus Christ, we were filled with the Holy Spirit. We received many blessings which included direction, wisdom, peace, and faith that can only come from God's indwelling. But we also received something that is not as tangible as the previously mentioned gifts, an internal beacon for our new heavenly home.

The first phrase of the old hymn written by Albert Edward Brumley says it best, "This world is not my home I'm just passing through, my treasures are laid up somewhere beyond the blue. The angels beckon me from heaven's open door, and I can't feel at home in this world anymore."

Someday I will get to go home where all the wrongs and injustices of this world will be made right. I will no longer have the feeling that I am moving away from where I should be to an unfamiliar place. I will finally be where I belong, and where I was made to be.

God created each of us with the great hope that we would all make heaven our final destination (2 Peter 3:9). We will all have to move someday, but where will our new home be?

Thought for the Day

I pray that you will not choose to travel in the wrong direction. Just go home.

DAY 236

The righteous perishes, And no man takes it to heart;
Merciful men are taken away, While no one considers
That the righteous is taken away from evil.

—Isaiah 57:1

The Great Escape

Some of the most difficult calls for me were those involving babies and young children. Whether it was by a traffic collision, crime, or a SIDS death, the loss of these young lives always seemed particularly unfair. They had their entire lives ahead of them and had done nothing to contribute to their early departure from this world.

During my POST chaplain certification course, we watched a filmed interview of a man who had lost his wife and young children in an unexpected flash flood that struck the vehicle he was driving. He had made it out of the car and had attempted to open the driver's side door in order to save his family. The current was so strong that it washed him away from the vehicle. The last thing he saw were the faces of his wife and two young children as they submerged beneath the rapid water. The vehicle was swept away, and all inside were found dead several miles downriver. The resulting trauma, grief, and survivor's guilt affected not only the father, but also the first responders who had arrived at the location and had seen the entire event as it happened. It is hard to even imagine.

As I watched the interview, it became apparent that the father was a believer and that he had a strong faith in God. When he said that he read a scripture verse that helped him make it through this unimaginable event, I immediately picked up my pen to write it down. This was going to be a great one! It was the above verse in Isaiah which states, *"The righteous is taken away from evil."* What gave him the most comfort was the knowledge that his children were in the loving arms of the Father and that they would never have to experience the pain and evil that become our frequent companions in this life. I read the verse over several times before I understood how right he was.

The Bible calls this life a "vapor" (James 4:14) that is here and gone. It is nothing when compared to the eternity we can spend in heaven. When I think of all the dead children that I have seen over the years, the verse in Isaiah gives me great comfort. They are in the loving arms of our heavenly Father and will only know peace and joy. They will not be exposed to the worst that this world has to offer. Frankly, it doesn't take away all the pain, but it helps.

If we have accepted Jesus Christ as our Savior and Lord, we have the promise of heaven. One second into eternity, we will forget about the vapor that was our life on this earth.

Thought for the Day

How wonderful it is for those innocents and believers who have made this great escape!

DAY 237

Having abolished in His flesh the enmity that is, the law of
commandments contained in ordinances, so as to create in
Himself one new man from the two, thus making peace.
—Ephesians 2:15

Wrecking Ball

Many residences in Newport Beach have not changed since the turn of the century. That's the twentieth century, not the twenty-first! Some houses on the west side of town are originals that were built in the early 1900s. As a police officer, I had to search in and around those dwellings for a variety of reasons throughout the years. Some were in such poor shape that I was amazed they were still standing. The land they were on was worth many times what the structure was. I seriously could have made a run at some of the interior walls and broken through to the adjacent room. Not only were they old, but the building codes of a hundred years ago, if they had any, were not what they are today. It was just a matter of time before the owner would tear down the residence and build a new structure in its place.

Our spiritual bodies are a lot like those old houses. Before we accepted Jesus Christ as our Savior and Lord, we were "built" under the law and the perfection that it required. But because of our inability to keep these codes, our walls are thin, and our foundations are crumbling.

When we give the control of our lives to Him, we allow God to build a new structure, one that has a foundation in Jesus Christ. This building is constructed under a code that He has purchased for us by

His death on the cross. We no longer have to put our faith in a structure that is poorly built, and we can now have peace by becoming the new person that God will help us to be.

Thought for the Day

Don't cling to the decaying ruins that will eventually be torn down. Let God build you anew.

DAY 238

Does not rejoice in iniquity but rejoices in the truth.
—1 Corinthians 13:6

The Unusual Truth

If you have been a cop for more than one shift, there is something you can count on, you have been lied to. Over a twenty-one-year career, I couldn't count the number of times I was not told the truth by the people I contacted. That is why I always respected those who were completely honest with me, even though they were few and far between.

So who did I find to be most truthful over the years? Believe it or not, it was the homeless people I interacted with. I found that they either avoided me entirely, or they told me mostly the truth about whatever situation they were involved in. These people had lost any pretense in their lives and seemed to have nothing left to hide.

The above verse in 1 Corinthians tells us that true love "*rejoices in the truth.*" Since we know that "*God is love*" (1 John 4:8), we also know that He loves the truth over a lie. I know that God appreciates the truth even more than we do.

When we pray to Him, we need to drop the pretense in our lives and just tell Him the truth about what we are feeling. There is no need to pretty it up or talk around the situation when He already knows everything about it. He is our heavenly Father, He loves us, and He is waiting for us to be truthful with Him about our fears and shortcomings. This takes the pressure off us because we don't have to say the right thing, use the right terminology, or repeat the correct phrases in order to connect with Him.

Thought for the Day

Drop the pretense and let God know what is on your heart today!

DAY 239

*For just as we share abundantly in the sufferings of
Christ, so also our comfort abounds through Christ.*

—2 Corinthians 1:5

Comfort That Abounds

As the parent of a child with developmental challenges, and
another who was medically fragile at birth, we had our share
of difficult times. Holidays were the toughest for us. Everyone else
seemed so happy and trouble free in comparison to what our family
was going through. One thing that hurt us were some of those "great
news only" holiday letters that families sent out to recap their previous year. We read about the academic and athletic achievements of
their children, the purchase of their new home, the dream vacation
they had taken, and about another year of good health, happiness,
and financial success. We were happy for their accomplishments, and
we never wished anything different for them. But it was still hard to
read when our financial and health situations were dim and seemed
to be growing darker every day. My wife and I have never sent out
a recap letter like that in all the time we have been married. As God
blessed us over the years, we could have. We always remembered that
others might be going through tough times, and we never wanted to
bring them pain in the midst of their struggle.

God's word has many promises for us, not only in this life, but
also in the eternal life to come. As Christians, we often claim those
promises that when provided by God would bring rescue, restoration, and provision. God's word also promises us that we will have

trials and tribulations in this world (John 16:33). Anyone want to claim that promise?

The above verse in 2 Corinthians tells us that as we share in the sufferings that Christ experienced on this earth, we will also have His promise of comfort. John 14:27 says, *"Peace I leave with you; My peace I give to you; not as the world gives do I give you. Let not your heart be troubled, neither let it be afraid."* The world has an idea of what it means to have peace and joy. It usually centers on good health, financial security, and family success. But what happens when you can't put any of those things in that yearly holiday recap?

The good news is that if you have accepted Jesus Christ as your Lord and Savior, you can still have peace and comfort in the face of the worst that this world has to offer. You can focus on the plan and provision promised you now, as well as the eternity guaranteed to you through your faith in Christ.

Thought for the Day

If you are going through one of those valleys in life, trust in Him, and your comfort will abound in time.

DAY 240

You saw me before I was born.
Every day of my life was recorded in your book.
Every moment was laid out before a single day had passed.
—Psalm 139:16

Total Control

I recently had an interesting health issue that took me completely by surprise. I have always eaten well (no red meat, cheese products, or foods high in saturated fat). I have also kept my cholesterol low and exercised at least three times a week for the last fifty years. When I developed a slight pain in my chest during a workout, even my cardiologist felt it had to be from some minor cause. She said that statistically, it was highly improbable for someone like me to have a heart issue. After some tests, it was finally decided that we should settle the matter and do an angiogram (minimally invasive look into heart's coronary arteries). We were stunned to discover that in spite of all my best efforts to take care of myself, I had a 95 percent blockage in my LAD, commonly called, the widow-maker (yikes!), and an 80 percent blockage in another major artery. Two stents later, they corrected the blockages without any complications. When they told my wife that they had put stents in my heart, her response was, "No, my husband is Brad Green." She thought they had gotten the patient information mixed up. It was hard for her to believe, considering my eating and exercise habits, that I had developed heart blockages. I thank God that they found and corrected the problem before I had a heart attack which could have been fatal.

My issue was not that I had failed to take care of myself, but that I thought my efforts would guarantee a perfect cardiac future. I am glad that I lived such a healthy lifestyle, otherwise I might have been one of those who died suddenly in their early fifties. God wants us to live heathy lives, and exercise combined with a good diet is very important. But I had been lulled into believing that I was ultimately in control of my own health future. You could say that my health-care efforts had become an idol in my life, and I was replacing God's rightful position of total control, with confidence in my own self-control. His "gentle" reminder has helped me to do the best I can in all areas of my life, but to know that He is in control, and my days upon this earth are ultimately up to Him. Believe it or not, this had helped me to worry less about my future.

For those who have given the control of their futures over to God through accepting Jesus Christ as their Savior and Lord, we can rest in the assurance that He knows all our days before we have even lived them. He can intervene in any circumstance and change any outcome He wishes to as long as it will be what is best for us (Romans 8:28). But for those who live without God's control over their lives, and depend upon their own direction and self-control, there is no guarantee that He will intercede in their lives for the good. He will know their future but will not intervene without their invitation. It has been said that we have two choices in life when talking to God, "*Thy will be done*" or "*My will be done.*"

Thought for the Day

Let's choose to do the will of the one who knows all the days of our lives before they even happen!

DAY 241

Therefore, just as sin came into
the world through one man, and death through sin,
and so death spread to all men
because all sinned.

—Romans 5:12

Drunk with Sin

I made hundreds of driving under the influence (DUI) arrests in my law enforcement career. The series of events that led up to the arrests were usually very similar. I would make a routine car stop for a simple vehicle code violation. I would talk with the driver and notice the symptoms of alcohol intoxication (red/watery eyes, thick/slurred speech, and the odor of an alcoholic beverage on their breath). I would then request that they exit their car so that I could talk with them further.

Sometimes the field sobriety tests (FSTs) were comical. At one point, early in my career, we had suspects say the alphabet as part of the test. I would give a clear set of instructions that they were NOT to sing the letters, and that they were to say each one clearly starting with A and ending with Z. Many times, what followed was a rendition of the childhood ABCs song. I had to stop them, remind them NOT to sing and start over. Often, they would look straight at me and say something like, "A, B, C, Q, O, P, T, Z, there!" They would defiantly act as if they had nailed it, and would be eager for the next test to prove to me that they were not intoxicated. They usually performed the following tests with equal skill resulting in their arrest. I found that alcohol certainly does impair judgment and diminishes the awareness of one's actions.

Sin is a lot like an intoxicating substance. The more we get into us, the less we seem to realize just what it is doing to us. Sometimes we even arrogantly believe that we have gotten past our ability to sin and have now reached a place or a plateau of righteousness. If we believe that, we look just as stupid as that intoxicated driver claiming victory over a poorly said alphabet.

Here is the straight scoop. We all have sinned, we are all sinning now, and we will all sin in the future. But the good news is that we can be forgiven then, now, and in the future. All we have to do is continue to ask and let God take sin's influence and intoxication away from our lives.

Thought for the Day

We all need to sober up from sin through the power of Jesus's death on the cross for us.

DAY 242

Brethren, I do not count myself to have apprehended; but one thing I do, forgetting those things which are behind and reaching forward to those things which are ahead, I press toward the goal for the prize of the upward call of God in Christ Jesus.
—Philippians 3:13–14

Short-Term Memory

One of the greatest talents an athlete can have is a short memory. This ability demonstrates itself best on the football field at the position of quarterback. I have seen many signal callers throw an interception and then lose all their confidence from that point on. This lack of belief in himself, if allowed to continue, can then affect his future performance in not only that game, but the entire season as well. The great quarterbacks are those who are able to make a mistake and come back during the next series of plays with the confidence to attempt a difficult throw. They don't let their past issues ruin their future potential.

The above verse was written by the apostle Paul in his epistle to the church in Philippi. I can't think of anyone who had as much to put behind him or who had a past he regretted more than Paul. Before his conversion, he was responsible for hunting down and persecuting Christians, a job he was very good at. But Paul did not let himself get mired down by the mistakes of his past. Instead he chose to focus on his future calling in Christ.

Many of the problems we encounter in pastoral counseling deal with people who are unable to believe they are truly forgiven. Once you have asked God to forgive you, you are forgiven. Micah 7:19 tells us that he has thrown our *"sins into the depths of the sea."* The one thing that God does not want you to do is get bogged down by your past to the point where you cannot see the future He has for you.

Instead of staring into the rearview mirror, God wants you to look forward out of the windshield of your spiritual car to see all that He can still accomplish through you. This doesn't mean you must completely forget the past. That is impossible. He just wants you to choose to focus on the future He has for you, whatever that might be.

Thought for the Day

Let's do our best to forget the past, accept His forgiveness, and focus on our future in Christ Jesus.

DAY 243

*When I first came to you, dear brothers and sisters, I didn't use
lofty words and impressive wisdom to tell you God's secret plan.*
—1 Corinthians 2:1

Foreign Language

The comedian and actor Steve Martin had a great line that he delivered while he was still doing his standup act. He did a bit about visiting France which centered on how different the Parisians were from the people of the United States. The self-deprecating comedian quipped, "I don't understand the French, it's like they have a different word for everything!" Well, of course, they do. After all, it is their national language.

Sometimes, we as Christians talk in a language that is foreign to those in the world. We use terms and phrases like "born again," "salvation," "ask Jesus into your heart," "fellowship," "gospel," "sanctification," and, my favorite, "travel mercies." I'm not even sure what that last one really means. It's like those Christians have a different word for everything.

When telling others about Jesus Christ, it is important for us to remember we are talking to people who do not share our same Christian cultural context. The level of biblical reference education today is far different than when I was a child. Back then, most people were familiar with the basic stories and characters of the Bible, even if they were not regular church attenders.

So, when we tell others about our faith, work to use regular vernacular that doesn't confuse or put off our audience.

Thought for the Day

Let's not use Christianese as a foreign language. It may keep us from reaching a hurting world.

DAY 244

Dear friends, do not believe every spirit, but test the spirits to see whether they are from God, for many false prophets have gone out into the world.

—1 John 4:1

Presumptive Test

Whenever I arrested a suspect for the possession of a controlled substance, I had to conduct a presumptive test in the field to determine if the drug was real or not. I would put a small sample of the contraband into a prepared plastic container and break the chemical vial that was inside. The reaction would turn a specific color that would verify the authenticity of the drug.

The above verse in 1 John tells us that we will find false spirits and prophets in this world. It warns us that we are to *"test"* these spirits, *"to see whether they are from God."*

The only reliable presumptive test for the Christian is God's word. First Thessalonians 5:21 advises us to *"test all things; hold fast to what is good."* God's word is good and has all that we need to see the truth in every circumstance.

One big problem for many Christians is that they pick and choose what parts of the Bible they will believe. When someone becomes this type of "cafeteria Christian" (i.e., selecting to obey only those commands in God's word that they like and/or agree with), they allow the enemy to nullify the Bible to the point where it is of no use at all. It then becomes impossible to accurately test anything by the standard of God's word.

Second Timothy 3:16 tells us that *"all scripture is given by inspiration of God, and is profitable for doctrine, for reproof, for correction, for instruction in righteousness."* We need to put our faith in His word, all of His word, whether or not we agree with it, understand it, or like it!

Thought for the Day

The word of God is the only true presumptive test for our lives! Neither God nor His word will ever let us down.

DAY 245

*And do not be conformed to this world, but be transformed
by the renewing of your mind, that you may prove what
is that good and acceptable and perfect will of God.*

—Romans 12:2

GPS

God has a perfect will for our lives. We can often start to believe, however, that this will has only one set of possible circumstances. We wrongfully think that if we mess up at all, we will have to settle for a lesser, second-rate plan. If that were true, there wouldn't be a person in the world who could ever realize God's perfect will. We all make wrong choices at some time in our lives.

I have navigation software on my cell phone. It talks to me in a woman's voice and gives me driving directions. Now I have two women in the car telling me where to drive! The computer program uses a GPS to guide me to my destination without making any commentary of my directional deficiencies. No matter how many times I make a wrong turn, it calmly informs me of the mistake by simply saying, "Recalculating route." It then gives me the information I need to get back on the right path.

My GPS is a lot like God. When I have made a wrong decision (sin) and admit my mistake to Him, He is there to patiently create a new plan for me without making a commentary on my mistake. He loves me and is always more than willing to help me start over. Romans 8:1 tells us, "*There is therefore now no condemnation to those who are in Christ Jesus, who do not walk according to the flesh, but according to the Spirit.*" When I'm driving, I don't spend much time feeling guilty about the GPS corrections that my cell phone made for me on my trip. I just listen to its voice and follow the new directions.

Thought for the Day

God has a plan for your life that is greater than you can imagine and is not dependent on the mistakes you have made. He is able to create a new perfect plan for you if you admit your sin. Ask Him for direction.

Recalculating route!

DAY 246

He saved us, not because of righteous things we had done, but because of his mercy. He saved us through the washing of rebirth and renewal by the Holy Spirit.

—Titus 3:5

Never Empty

My daughter recently gave me an old-fashioned quill pen and inkwell set for my birthday. It was a fun gift that demonstrated how hard it was for our founding fathers to write things by hand. I have a new respect for Timothy Matlack, who most historians believe handwrote the final copy of the Declaration of Independence from Thomas Jefferson's initial draft. When I wrote with my quill, I was surprised that the ink lasted for about five words. I guess I always assumed that it would run out of ink more quickly. But it did run out, which required that I dip the pen in the inkwell in order to write several more words. It made me appreciate the throwaway ballpoint pens we have today.

The above verse in Titus tells us we have been saved, not because of what we have done, but by God's mercy in our lives. When we first accept Jesus as Lord, we are saved by the washing and rebirth given to us through His sacrifice on the cross. At that time, we are also renewed by the Holy Spirit who resides in us and continues to regenerate us throughout our Christian lives. We can ask for that Holy Spirit indwelling over and over again after initially receiving Him. Just like a quill pen, the ink may run low in our spiritual lives, but we can dip it back into the well at any time and get a fresh indwelling of the Holy Spirit's power. All we need to do is ask.

If you feel that you are running a little dry in your life, just ask the Holy Spirit to renew you through His power. All the comfort, wisdom, and direction we need is there waiting to be dipped into.

Thought for the Day

You never need to be empty when the Holy Spirit's well is always available.

DAY 247

Jesus turned to Peter and said, "Get away from me, Satan!
You are a dangerous trap to me. You are seeing things
merely from a human point of view, not from God's."
—Matthew 16:23

Human View

S ometimes citizens would question our actions as police officers
because they could not find a reasonable explanation in their
minds as to why we did things. I remember one individual asking me
why officers always held their flashlights out away from their bodies during a nighttime traffic stop. From the way the question was
framed, he seemed to insinuate that we were either showing some
sort of false bravado by the action, or that we just didn't have the
"intelligence" to hold the light in front of us like he would. I gave
him a five-word answer that stopped him in his tracks. I told him,
"They shoot at the light." You see, when I approached a car at night,
I would purposefully point my flashlight directly at the driver of the
vehicle, usually at the back of their head. If they were to turn around
to look at me, all they would see would be the blinding light of my
halogen torch. If they decide to shoot a gun at me, the only frame of
reference they would have, as to my position, would be the location
of my light. They would be counting on me holding the flashlight
in front of my body. The original question asker realized that he was
viewing the situation from a civilian's point of view, and not that of
an officer, who wanted to go home alive every night.

The above statement in Matthew was made by Jesus to the
apostle Peter. It came on the heels of Peter's Holy Spirit–inspired

declaration that Jesus was the "Messiah, the Son of God." But when Jesus told His disciples that he would be persecuted and killed by the religious leaders and rise again three days later, Peter reprimanded him for saying such negative things. Jesus's statement went against the commonly held beliefs about the Messiah's purpose on this earth. Peter was looking at Jesus's words from a "human point of view, not from God's."

We often do the same thing when dealing with God's plan for our lives. We look at His will from an earthly, human standpoint, and not from a godly one. We seem to think that God is the head of a democracy where the majority vote decides a course of action in our lives. God's will for us is not determined by any human point of view. He is our King and the sole ruler of our lives. What He says is the only voice we should listen to, and His decisions for us are final. I have often told people that obeying God is like a light switch that has two positions, on and off. We either obey Him, or we don't. There is no dimmer switch on keeping God's commands.

If we are believers who take the view that God's words are merely great suggestions for our lives, we will always find ourselves at odds with our creator.

Thought for the Day

The only view that matters is the one from the top.

DAY 248

They will act religious, but they will reject the power that could make them godly. Stay away from people like that!
—2 Timothy 3:5

Look-Alike Christianity

In my office, I had a wall of bookshelves that had an espresso brown finish to them. They looked great and gave the appearance of real wood. The truth is that they were pressboard with a vinyl covering. If I were to scratch them with a sharp object, it would reveal the sawdust and glue composite that lied beneath the surface. They gave the appearance of wood without the true depth of material found in the real thing.

I have come across many people who say they are Christians but are really similar to those bookshelves. They look great, attend church, worship enthusiastically, and may even know God's word. But when you scratch the surface of their lives, you find that just underneath is an unbelief that is revealed through adversity or selfish desire.

Our verse in 2 Timothy tells of people who act like they have accepted Christ but reject the work of the Spirit in their lives which could give them victory over their circumstances. They talk a good game when being a Christian suits them, but when the going gets tough, they decide to redefine God's word and place their own wants in front of His will for their lives. God's word says for us to stay away from people like that.

The only thing more important than avoiding these "look-alike" Christians is to not be one! When the trials of this world scratch the surface of our Christian lives, what will be found underneath? Will we see a composite of sin and pride glued together to form a substance that can temporarily support a thin veneer? Or will we see a depth of character that is consistent with the surface of our lives, not perfect, just consistent?

Thought for the Day

Let's build our lives from the solid material found in His word and not accept a thin temporary veneer of false faith.

DAY 249

*"This is the new covenant I will make with my people
on that day, says the LORD: I will put my laws in their
hearts, and I will write them on their minds."*

—Hebrews 10:16

Written Covenant

Police officers spend much of their time writing. When it came to writing materials while out in the field, we got very creative. If I needed to take down some information (i.e., suspect name, license plate number, phone number, address, etc.), I would often write it on my hand. This did two things for me. First, it allowed me to transcribe the information quickly as Dispatch provided the critical data. Even the few seconds it took me to get out a pad of paper could have been vital and caused me to miss the broadcasted information. And second, I would never lose that name/number in the course of the call. I would have to lose a hand in order for that to happen! My wife would often look at me strangely when I came home from a shift with names and numbers written on the palm and the back of my left hand.

In the above verse in Hebrews, Paul repeats Jeremiah's prophecy made in Jeremiah 31:33 that foretold of the new covenant God would make with His people. The old covenant was based on the law of Moses and the sacrifice of animals as a covering for one's sin. The new covenant, as described by Paul, was based on the atoning blood of Jesus Christ and His forgiveness of our sin. Our transgressions were no longer "covered over," but could now be paid for.

God promises us that He has given us a new covenant. I find it interesting that He did not say, "Write on their hearts and minds," but instead made a distinction between "*I will **put** my laws in their hearts, and I will **write** them on their minds.*" God's word and His promises to us are not just a thing of feeling for the believer, but also a rational choice of the mind.

We choose to accept this new covenant, this free gift given to us, because God's word says it is true and available to us. We might not always feel it is there, but it will never leave us all the same. It is like that writing on my hand, I took it with me wherever I went.

For the followers of Jesus Christ, the ones who have given their lives to His Lordship, God has written His promise of salvation in their minds and put that peace of the new covenant in their hearts.

Thought for the Day

Let God write His promise on your life today.

DAY 250

But it is written: "Eye has not seen,
nor ear heard, nor have entered into the
heart of man the things which God has prepared
for those who love Him."

—1 Corinthians 2:9

The Joyful Ending

I love happy endings! The older I get, the less interested I am in any movies or shows with unsettling conclusions. I guess I saw enough of that as a police officer to last me a lifetime.

One of the greatest things about being a follower of Jesus Christ is our promise to the ultimate joyful ending. God's word contains many promises for us about exactly what we can expect at the end of our time here on this earth. The above verse in 1 Corinthians lays it out pretty well, I think. If we have accepted Christ as our Savior and Lord, then we can expect the unbelievable when we leave this earth and go to our new address in heaven. We will not believe our eyes and ears when we see eternity for the first time. It will be beyond anything that our hearts and minds can imagine.

I can usually tell at the beginning of a movie if it will be one of those "happy ending" types. God's word promises us that when it comes to eternity, we can count on it. First John 5:13a says, *"These things I have written to you who believe in the name of the Son of God, that you may **know** that you have eternal life."*

Thought for the Day

Isn't it wonderful to know how the story will end, especially when it comes to our eternity! I can stop worrying about if things will end well, and think more about how unbelievable that great ending will be.

DAY 251

My son, if you receive my words, And treasure my commands within you, So that you incline your ear to wisdom, And apply your heart to understanding; Yes, if you cry out for discernment, And lift up your voice for understanding, If you seek her as silver, And search for her as for hidden treasures; Then you will understand the fear of the LORD, And find the knowledge of God.
—Proverbs 2:1–5

Treasure

It is amazing what some people treasure. I worked in a beach town which was a destination spot for transients. Standard gear for these individuals was a shopping cart filled with their personal belongings. I often had to contact these subjects due to criminal violations that resulted in an arrest. Sometimes when that occurred, I had to book their property into safekeeping at the station. I would find food wrappers, spoiled food, small broken appliances, receipts, old newspapers and magazines, broken glass, clothing, cigarette butts, plastic bags, and many other items that we would normally view as trash. But to these people, they were valuable personal possessions and insisted that every scrap be returned to them after their release.

The above verse in Proverbs tells us what we should treasure above all else in our lives, wisdom. It promises that as we value God's word, listen, concentrate on understanding, and seek wisdom as if it were a precious metal, then we will gain the knowledge that only God can provide. Psalm 19:7 states that *"the instructions of the LORD are perfect, reviving the soul. The decrees of the LORD are trustworthy, making wise the simple.*" I'm so grateful for that promise. It means that if I follow God's word, even I can be wise!

So besides wanting it and seeking after it, how do we get this wisdom? James 1:5 says, "*If any of you lacks wisdom, let him ask of God, who gives to all liberally and without reproach, and it will be given to him.*"

Do you want this insight? Seek after it as if it were of great value and ask for it from God who will never rebuke you for your request.

Thought for the Day

Don't fill your basket with junk, seek the treasure of wisdom that is found in God's word.

DAY 252

Train up a child in the way he should go, and
when he is old he will not depart from it.

—Proverbs 22:6

Sight Training

When I went through my field training program as a rookie cop, I was trained by some real veteran (salty dog) field training officers. They never had me wear a seat belt because they felt it might have hindered my quick emergency exit from the police unit. I guess if I had made it a habit to put on and take off my seat belt each time I entered or exited my unit, it would have become part of my automatic muscle memory. The only problem was that not using my seat belt became part of my routine, even when I was in my personal vehicle.

Whenever I drove in the car with my youngest daughter, I would notice that she didn't have her seat belt on. I then tried an experiment. Without saying a word, I would put my seat belt on. Immediately she would, without any prompting, reach over, grab her seat belt, and snap it in place. I tried this on several different occasions with the exact same result. I then realized that in order for me to make her safe, I would have to lead by example and put on my seat belt whenever I was in the car. I think that was the first time it really connected with me how much of my children's behavior (good or bad) was my responsibility.

The above verse in Proverbs tells us of our responsibility to train up our children in the *"way they should go."* For the Christian, this includes reading God's word, attending church, loving others, giving tithe back to God, being honest, and following His commandments. Whether we completely realize it or not, they are watching our every move. We are not only seen as infallible by them; we are also representations of God in their lives. If we are untrustworthy, undependable, or our integrity compromised, they may view God in the same way. It takes a lot more than good intentions to raise children. We must have success in our own personal walks with God.

Thought for the Day

We need to train up our children in the way they should go. Not the way we went, or the way we are allowing ourselves to go now.

DAY 253

*Not forsaking the assembling of ourselves together, as is
the manner of some, but exhorting one another, and so
much the more as you see the Day approaching.*

—Hebrews 10:25

Forsake Not

At the beginning of each of my shifts as a uniformed cop, I spent
thirty minutes in briefing, and sometimes more depending
upon the long-windedness of the supervisor running the show. It
was a time when we learned what our area assignment would be for
the day, heard crime bulletins for cities throughout the Southern
California area, discussed department policies, and were trained on
specific topics that affected our jobs. As much as I did not like briefings, I had to admit that they were an essential part of police work
and they enhanced my ability to function on the job.

In addition to the important information provided, briefings
also gave the officers on each shift a feeling of comradery as part of
a team. We brought that esprit de corps out into the field, and it
helped us to be better partners and police officers. It could be argued
that this team-building process was the most important part of the
entire briefing experience.

As believers in Jesus Christ, He commands us to do many things,
all of which are for our own good. After accepting Jesus Christ as our
Savior and Lord, there is nothing else that is necessary to obtain eternal life (Romans 10:9). But there are many things that God asks us to
do that are in the "for the good of ourselves and others," categories.
Attending church is one of those things.

We gain many things from our consistent fellowship with other believers. Just like in a police briefing, it is a place where we can learn our ministry assignments from the Lord, hear updates about the church, and get sound biblical teaching that can help us to follow God's will more closely. And just like in police briefings, we can develop a comradery with other believers that can be a cure for our loneliness and help us through the toughest times of our lives.

The above verse in Hebrews commands us to assemble and exhort (encourage) one another, so much more as you see the "day approaching." This is not a "should do" from God, this is a "shall do" that we need to follow unless we have a compelling reason (i.e., illness or other situations beyond our control). We must admit that this is God's will for us and that it is an essential part of our Christian walk. It will enhance our ability to serve Him whether we understand it or not.

Thought for the Day

Forsake not the assembling of ourselves together.

DAY 254

Then He will also say to those on the left hand, Depart from Me, you
cursed, into the everlasting fire prepared for the devil and his angels.
—Matthew 25:41

Prison Avoidance

As a law enforcement officer, I spent a significant amount of time
in jail. Not that I was incarcerated, but I had to transport prisoners to that destination. I guess I don't have to tell you this, but
jail is not a nice place. It is full of anger, depravity, hopelessness, and
pain. Whenever I entered the jail complex, I imagined that it was
a foretaste of what hell is like. I have the greatest respect for those
deputies who must work in that environment every day. I was always
relieved to exit the building and get back to my normal beat.

As Christians, one of the most frequent questions we are asked
is "Why would a loving God send someone to hell?" The above verse
in Matthew records the words from God the Son Himself as He
spoke on the subject. Jesus tells us that hell was not made for man
but was prepared for the devil and his angels. But hell, just like our
prison system, which was not prepared for law-abiding citizens, will
be the final destination for those who, of their own free will, chose
to go to there.

I used to patrol the streets looking for individuals who were
either about to, or had already, chosen to break the law and reap
the punishment that they now qualified for. I didn't encourage or
force them to do so, they had chosen that for themselves. The jail or
prison I then took them to was not made specifically for them, but it
became their new home earned by their actions.

The question mankind has for themselves is not "Will I live forever?" It is "Where will I live forever?" It is our choice of a free will that is given to us by a God who loves us. The Bible says, "*The Lord is not slack concerning His promise, as some count slackness, but is longsuffering toward us, not willing that any should perish but that all should come to repentance*" (2 Peter 3:9).

God loves you and wants nothing more than to have you with Him for all eternity. He will not, however, force you into a personal relationship with Him. Just like the fact that obeying the laws of man will keep us out of prison on this earth, so will obeying the word of God keep us out of an eternal prison. And what does the word of God command us to do? *"That if you confess with your mouth the Lord Jesus and believe in your heart that God has raised Him from the dead, you will be saved"* (Romans 10:9).

Thought for the Day

Do you want the ultimate "get out of jail free" card? Bow your knee to Jesus now and have your eternity secured.

DAY 255

*I thought, "Those who are older should speak,
for wisdom comes with age."*

—Job 32:7

Gray Wisdom

One of my favorite movies is *Shawshank Redemption*. It is the story of a wrongly incarcerated inmate, his experiences with prison life, and the cultivation of friendships while behind bars. My favorite scene from the movie is the parole hearing of Red, a main character in the film who was rightly jailed for murder when he was a young man. Now advanced in years, Red speaks to the parole board about his feelings regarding his crime and the regret he feels every day. He explains his desire to be able to talk to the young man he once was.

> I want to talk to him. I want to try and talk
> some sense to him. Tell him the way things are.
> But I can't, that kid's long gone, this old man is
> all that's left, I gotta live with that.

I would love to talk to the young me just for a while to "tell him the way things are." But just like Red, I can't because he is gone, and I am all that's left. God's word tells us that wisdom can come with age, or at least it is supposed to. I think wisdom is about having a good memory for the mistakes you have made and the ability to warn others away from those mistakes.

So, what would I tell the young me? Don't worry, it is a waste of time and God is in control; read and study God's word more, it really does contain all you need in this life; pray more, God wants to hear from you just because He loves you; be a better example to your wife and children, it will make a difference for them in the years to come; and God is not mad at you, rest in His grace and mercy. I know that these are simple, straightforward suggestions, but my life and ministry would be better now if I had done these things early and often.

If you are older and reading this, start now. If you are young, listen to this old man and change your direction in this life. Rest in God, read His word, pray more often, lead your family, rest in His grace, and receive His mercy when you fail to do any of these things.

Thought for the Day

Forewarned is forearmed!

DAY 256

I lie awake thinking of you,
meditating on you through the night.

—Psalm 63:6

Never Talk Alone

When I first became a cop, cell phones were not in use. I can still remember one day when I was on patrol, I saw a woman leaning against the wall of a building. She was yelling and flailing her arms around violently, talking with no one else present. To that point, such a person engaged in that kind of solo animated conversation was usually in need of medical assistance, or at least a thorough psychiatric evaluation. When I stopped to talk with her, I discovered that she had a new cell phone complete with an earpiece that contained an in-line mic. The conversation she was having was with a friend on the other end of her call, and she was not in need of any assistance at all. I had to readjust my thinking from that point on to accept the numerous future individuals whom I would see "talking to themselves" throughout the city.

Isn't it great that we can talk to God at any place and at any time! Our above verse in Psalms tells us that we can even have a conversation with Him as we lie awake in bed. Due to Christ's sacrifice for us on the cross, we now have full access to the Father at any time. And even better than this direct contact with God are the limits to the topics we can discuss. THERE ARE NONE! We can completely unburden ourselves, the good, the bad, and the ugly, before our Lord, without the fear of repercussion.

Next to an eternity guaranteed us through our faith in Christ, I think unfettered access to the Father is one of the greatest gifts of salvation. God's word also promises us that He will not only hear us but will also act on our behalf. Isaiah 41:13 tells us, *"For I hold you by your right hand, I, the LORD your God. And I say to you, 'Don't be afraid, I am here to help you.'"*

Thought for the Day

You never have to be alone when God is always on the line, ready to listen to your concerns.

DAY 257

But He gives more grace. Therefore He says: "God
resists the proud, but gives grace to the humble."

—James 4:6

Humility

October is Pastor Appreciation Month. When I was a pastor, one of the Children's Ministry staff brought a gift to me along with handwritten thank-you notes from the second-grade Sunday school class. Each one of the notes thanked me for being a pastor (they all had the same wording), and I was thankful for the crayoned messages. One of the notes caught my attention due to its interesting spelling. Instead of being written to "Pastor Brad," it was written to "Pastor Brag." I'm sure it was an innocent mistake from a child who was still learning to spell (I hope), but it did make me think about how I might come across in my conversations at church. I would sure hate to have the moniker Pastor Brag represent my ministry life.

The above verse in James promises us that God will give grace to the humble and resist the proud. I don't know about you, but I would rather be on the grace side of that equation rather than put myself in a position where the God of the universe "resists" me. Sounds like a pretty good motivation to remain humble.

It has been said that true humility is not thinking less of yourself but thinking about yourself less. I know that going forward, it would be a good thing for me to remember that statement.

Thought for the Day

If we want God's unmerited favor in our lives, let's practice thinking less about ourselves, and more about others.

DAY 258

*For the Lord gives wisdom; From His mouth come knowledge
and understanding; He stores up sound wisdom for the
upright; He is a shield to those who walk uprightly.*
—Proverbs 2:6-7

Look Out!

During my senior year in 1979, we played UCLA in the LA
Coliseum. I was a center for USC, and I was playing in the
final home game of my college career. An ex-teammate of mine from
junior college was playing outside linebacker for the Bruins. We were
on their ten-yard line and were threatening to score at the tunnel
end of the stadium. Our quarterback called the play in the huddle,
28 Pitch, which was otherwise known as Student Body Right at the
time. As I ran to the line of scrimmage, I glanced to my right and saw
my friend positioning himself on the strong side of the field. I knew
that the play was going to be run directly at him. The whole world
was about to come his way which at that time consisted of a future
Heisman Trophy–winning tailback and a group of linemen, all of
whom would later go on to star in the NFL. There was a small part
of me (a very, very small part) that wanted to warn my friend of his
impending doom. We scored on that play and went on to a decisive
victory. After the game, my ex-teammate walked up to me, shook my
hand, and said, "Man, you've got some big guys!"

Unlike me, who kept my silence about the dark future of a specific football play, God goes out of His way to warn us of the problems we may face in life. If we have made Jesus Christ our Lord and
Savior, He promises to give us wisdom through the gift of the Holy

Spirit. He has also given us His written word, the Bible, which lays out an endless amount of direction that can lengthen our lives, keep us safe, and protect our relationships. But in order to get this knowledge, we have to read His word, ask for His guidance, and obey Him even when it does not seem to make any sense.

I don't know if my friend would have believed me if I had warned him that day on the floor of The Coliseum. To tell you the truth, with the quality of players we had, it might not have made a difference. Is God trying to warn you about something today? Please listen to Him, He loves you and will never let you down. The Bible says that "*if God be for us who can be against us?*" (Romans 8:31).

Thought for the Day

There is no need for you to be trampled today by overwhelming odds. Listen to His warnings.

DAY 259

Do not get drunk on wine, which leads to debauchery.
Instead, be filled with the Spirit.

—Ephesians 5:18

Wrong Cars

As police officers, we have seen thousands of intoxicated individuals during the course of our careers. The worst examples are those who are so drunk that they "hail" our police car thinking we are a taxi. They would then get in the back of the unit and ask us to take them to a specific location. The defendant usually got their wish, but the destination was a little different than the one they had expected.

God's word has little to say about drinking, but it has a lot to say about getting drunk. If we remember that God is on our side, and only wants the best for us, we won't be tempted into thinking that He is some sort of cosmic killjoy who doesn't want us to have any fun. God's warning for us is to not lose control of our common sense and get into the "wrong cars" of our life.

I think this warning goes a little further than having too much alcohol on board. If we let anything intoxicate us to the point where we are not thinking clearly, we can get into trouble. It doesn't matter if it is drugs, alcohol, money, power, prestige, sex, TV, video games, family, or recreation; all of them have the potential to lead us away from God.

The solution is simple. Replace those temporary things with the Holy Spirit. If we ask God to fill us daily with His power, read His word, and make prayer a regular part of our daily routine, we will have the strength and wisdom we need to stay away from the things that can hurt us.

Thought for the Day

It is our choice whose car we get into. Only God's has a sure destination.

DAY 260

Then the angel showed me a pure river with the water of life, clear as crystal, flowing from the throne of God and of the Lamb. It flowed down the center of the main street. On each side of the river grew a tree of life, bearing twelve crops of fruit, with a fresh crop each month. The leaves were used for medicine to heal the nations. No longer will there be a curse upon anything. For the throne of God and of the Lamb will be there, and his servants will worship him. And they will see his face, and his name will be written on their foreheads. And there will be no night there—no need for lamps or sun—for the Lord God will shine on them. And they will reign forever and ever.

—Revelation 22:1–5

The Happiest Place

On my desk, I have a vintage Disneyland child's ticket book that was printed in October of 1963. You must know where to look on the book for the printing date. It predates the Haunted Manson ride by six years, and Pirates of the Caribbean ride by four years. It is the exact kind of ticket book that my parents would have purchased for me when I was seven years old. Oh, and by the way, the price on the book is a whopping $3.95. Now wouldn't that be nice!

As a child, I lived exactly 10.5 miles from Disneyland. I was a frequent visitor to the magic kingdom from ages three to adulthood. I would visit the park several times a year and was as excited for each trip as a boy could possibly get. My first date with the girl who would someday become my wife was at Disneyland. The park holds many special memories for me.

A trip into the magic kingdom always started and ended with a walk down Main Street. The sights and sounds of that stroll only served to get me even more excited for the wondrous lands that lay beyond. But as wonderful as, "the happiest place on earth" appeared to have been, things were not always what they seemed. As an adult, I discovered that most of what I saw was just a grand illusion made by man. But I still liked it, and I looked forward to each visit.

The new earth described in Revelation 22 will not be an illusion made by man but will be a real place created by almighty God Himself. There will be nothing disappointing to discover behind the scenes. The above verse in Revelation gives just a glimpse of Heaven and some of its attractions. Crystal rivers, healing fruit trees, and the throne of God sounds like a pretty incredible beginning to what we will experience. These amazing things will be only the start as we stroll down Main Street with expectations of the spectacular lands ahead.

The entrance fee into Disneyland has changed significantly over the years, to the point where it is prohibitive for some to even think of going. Not so with the admission price into heaven. That debt was paid once and for all by Jesus when He died on the cross for our sin and rose again on the third day. Now all we have to do is accept his payment for us by confessing Him as Lord to gain entrance into the heaven's new earth and all the wonderful attractions it will hold, not the least of which will be the Lord God Himself!

Thought for the Day

Accept Jesus's payment for your admission price to receive a ticket to the happiest place on the new earth.

DAY 261

Against You, You only, have I sinned, And done this
evil in Your sight—That You may be found just when
You speak, And blameless when You judge.

—Psalm 51:4

True Confession

Law enforcement officers devote a significant portion of their time in an effort to find the truth. Many times, we would have photographic or video evidence of a crime before we would interview a suspect. They were unaware of the mountain of evidence against them, and I have to admit, it was entertaining to listen to them lie for an hour before I finally laid down the proof of their actions. What is even more amazing is that some would continue to lie even in the face of irrefutable evidence!

God called King David "a man after My own Heart." This wasn't because he was perfect. In fact, He had a list of sins that included adultery, murder, and lying. But he did have a zeal and love for God that was unmatched by those around him. He also had the strength of character to completely admit when he was wrong.

The above verse in Psalms shows this ability after the prophet Nathan confronted David with his sin. David didn't make excuses, he didn't minimize what he had done, he didn't compare his sin to others, or blame anyone else. He got on his knees before God and fully confessed that he, and he alone, was the only one responsible for his sin against God.

First John 1:9 tells us, *"If we confess our sins, He is faithful and just to forgive us our sins and to cleanse us from all unrighteousness."*

When we confess our sin to God, He promises to forgive us and cleanse us from ALL unrighteousness. Not some, not just the big things, and not only those things we have never done before. There is no limit on God's forgiveness, but we must do what David did and come before him with a truly repentant heart.

Thought for the Day

Call out to the Lord with the truth about your sin and experience His forgiveness that can only come when we have accepted Christ's sacrifice on the cross for us.

DAY 262

"What sorrow awaits those who argue with their Creator.
Does a clay pot argue with its maker? Does the clay dispute
with the one who shapes it, saying, 'Stop, you're doing it
wrong!' Does the pot exclaim, 'How clumsy can you be?'
—Isaiah 45:9

Control Holds

O ne of the reasons that I love to watch MMA (mixed martial
arts) bouts are the different ways in which the fight might end.
The fighters get to use a wide variety of methods to defeat their opponents that always makes for an exciting sporting event. I particularly
like the strategy and skill required in submission holds. These moves
are quick, bloodless, and end when the opponent quits by tapping on
his opponent (tap out) before any real pain or damage can take place.
Of course, there are always those who refuse to tap out which usually
results in a serious injury.

I heard of a pastor who made a hospital visit at the request of
the family of a dying man. The man didn't really want to talk with
him about spiritual matters, and the conversation was difficult. After
a short visit, the pastor asked the man one last question before he left.
"What would God have to do to get you to turn to him?" The man
angrily replied, "He would have to kill me first!" It was then the man
realized where he was and that the end to his life was exactly what
was happening to him.

God loves us and will do just about anything to bring us to
Him. He knows that what happens in this life represents only a grain

of sand in the beach of our eternity, and if He has to, He will bring difficult situations our way if the end result is heaven.

God is not limited to the number or type of moves He may be forced to use in order to win our souls. All we have to do is choose whether we submit our lives to the Lordship of Jesus Christ. This submission will be ongoing as we continue to yield ourselves to His authority during the remainder of our Christian lives. The smart move is to tap out early and often as we serve Him.

Thought for the Day

Let's don't get hurt fighting the Lord's control of our lives.

DAY 263

For it is written: "As I live, says the Lord, Every knee shall bow to Me, And every tongue shall confess to God."

—Romans 14:11

Silence

The Bible has a lot to say about the love, grace, and mercy of God, but it also talks about His judgment.

In 1977, USC played Texas A&M in the Astro Bluebonnet Bowl at the Astro Dome in Houston, Texas. When it was full, the Astro Dome was an incredibly loud place. It was so loud that you couldn't hear someone yell who was standing right next to you. USC had just been thrown for a loss on our own five-yard line and our tailback, Charles White, was injured on the play. The A&M crowd was going out of their minds as USC sent in a replacement tailback, Dwight Ford. They didn't know who they were dealing with, but we did.

Before he injured his knee, Dwight Ford was the heir apparent at tailback. Even though he was no longer a starter, he was extremely dangerous. The ball was snapped and given to Dwight at the five-yard line. By the time he reached the fifty-yard line, something happened that still stands as one of my most enduring memories of football. The crowd went completely silent. One second, it was deafening, and a few seconds later, it was like the air had been sucked out of the building. Dwight ran the last fifty yards for the touchdown in such complete silence that you could almost hear the sound of his feet hit on the Astro Turf. It was a perfect example of "quieting the crowd," and it was the turning point in the game. We went on to win 47–28.

Someday, maybe someday very soon, Jesus will come back again. When that happens, all those who mocked Christ's Lordship and His sacrifice on the cross for our sins will bow to Him and admit he is God. The crowd will be silenced in their opposition.

Thought for the Day

The choice is ours. We can choose to drop to our knees now or be forced to them later.

DAY 264

❖

"I—yes, I alone—will blot out your sins for my own
sake and will never think of them again.

—Isaiah 43:25

Forgetfulness

I played football for fourteen years and was involved in literally
thousands of plays in both practices and games. God blessed my
time in the sport by giving me a full athletic scholarship and playing
time on a Division 1 national championship team. An injury slowed
down my collegiate career and pretty much ended any chance I had
to play in the NFL.

It would not be a stretch for me to assume that considering the
success I enjoyed on the gridiron, I did well on at least a majority of
the plays I was involved in. I don't think I could have received the
scholarship mentioned before if that were not true. So why is it that
when I try to remember the good blocks I made, I come up blank? I
have a recollection of some games and situations where I came out on
top, but I can specifically recall only a few successful individual plays
I was involved in with any real clarity. I'll tell you what I can remember well, every mistake, missed block, and failure I ever had on the
field. Why is it that our minds seem to work that way sometimes?
Remembering the bad, the problems, and the disappointments,
while blocking out the good, the successes, and the victories of life.

I am thankful God is not at all like me. In fact, He is the complete opposite. The above verse in Isaiah tells us of the unbelievably
forgiving nature of God. Not only does He forgive our sins if we

commit our lives to Him, but, He even goes further by functionally forgetting that we even committed them at all!

I often use God as the model of forgiveness in counseling sessions. When an individual says they forgive their spouse, I explain to them what that absolution will need to look like with God as our model. As humans, we will never be able to forget the offenses against us, but God requires us to at least do our best to treat the other as if they had never occurred. It is the constant struggle of successful relationships between flawed human beings. God, on the other hand, has no problem in forgiving, and is eager to do so whenever we ask.

Thought for the Day

We should never judge God's ability to forgive and forget our sin by our inability to do the same.

DAY 265

He was fully convinced that God is able to do whatever he promises.
—Romans 4:21

Promises

As police officers, we made many promises while on duty. Most of them had to do with the sure resolution to a situation if a subject chose not to follow our clear instructions. There would be times when we would be dealing with a subject, and an uninvolved citizen would feel compelled to stand close to us and provide their personal commentary on our actions. This was a distracting and unsafe situation when dealing with a potentially dangerous suspect. This would usually result in our request for them to please step back and let us do our job. When our first request was not successful, it would be followed by the same programmed response on the part of the backup officer. "Please step back or I will arrest you for obstruction of justice. I will give you two more warnings." If that was not successful, they would then issue the remaining countdown warnings, with the hope that the subject would clear the area. It was a lot like counting to three when dealing with a child. Most of the time, the subject would move on before the officer got to zero. But believe it or not, some would refuse to move away or stop their distracting banter. It was then that we would keep our promise and arrest them for their actions.

The above verse in Romans brings either great joy or great terror to its reader. I love the fact that God always keeps His promises. There are so many of them that I count on every day. But for those who have rejected Christ, or who are not attempting to walk according to His will, the above statement about God's complete ability to do whatever He promises can be frightening.

Ephesians 5:6 tells us, "*Let no one deceive you with empty words, for because of these things the wrath of God comes upon the sons of disobedience.*"

There is no doubt that our Lord is a God of love, but He is also a God of judgment who is able to keep His promises. Why not do all you can to obey Him and live in the rest He provides? Hebrews 11:6 tells us that, "*He rewards those who earnestly seek Him.*"

Thought for the Day

Don't make the Holy Spirit give you countdown warnings to His correction in your life. Obey right away, and rest in God's ability to do whatever He promises.

DAY 266

*If you then, being evil, know how to give good gifts to
your children, how much more will your Father who is
in heaven give good things to those who ask Him!*

—Matthew 7:11

Great Gifts

I got a vacuum cleaner for Christmas from my wife. Well, actually,
it was a shop vac for my workshop area. Don't get me wrong, I love
it! It works great, and I will be able to use it to clean our cars, blow
off my workbench, and keep our garage debris free.

It is funny though when I think about what the consequences
would have been for me if I had given my wife a vacuum for
Christmas. Every husband knows (or should know) that in spite of
our best intentions, giving certain "appliance type" gifts may land
us on the couch for a week. Some gifts just mean different things to
different people.

The above verse in Matthew records Jesus's words as He compared the world's ability to give gifts to their children to God's ability
to give gifts to His children. God always gives good gifts. He knows
what is best for us even when we don't. Sometimes His gifts match
what we ask for, sometimes He gives us things we didn't know we
needed, and other times, He withholds things that we are sure we
want.

In any case, we need to have faith that whatever God gives us
will be the best for us and in line with His purpose for our lives. It
is a matter of trusting God with our personal disappointments, with
the assurance that better things are coming soon.

Thought for the Day

If the world can give good gifts, how greater will those from our Father be!

DAY 267

And Jesus said to him, "Assuredly, I say to you,
today you will be with Me in Paradise.

—Luke 23:43

Never Too Late

As an associate pastor, I was asked to go to the home of a man in Santa Ana who had been given forty-eight hours to live. When I arrived, I was led to a dark room where the bedridden gentleman was surrounded by family and friends. He was wearing an oxygen mask but was still conscious enough to respond to my questions. The man was a gang member who had lived in opposition to God's will his entire life. It was odd that an ex-cop was in the room with an individual who at one time would have been "a client," so to speak. I didn't tell anyone there what I used to do for a living, but maybe they knew it anyway. Just as I could look at them and know who they were, I'm sure that I still had the posture and look of my old profession. But none of that mattered. I was there as a pastor to pray for a man who would soon be in the presence of God.

I had a simple question for him, "Do you know where you will go when you die?" He motioned to one of his family members to help him remove the mask. He then said to me, "I want to go to heaven." I told him that God's word says that "*these things are written so that you may know that you have eternal life*" (1 John 5:13). I added that if you invite Christ into your life now, you can receive forgiveness and know that heaven will be your eternal destination. I asked him if he wanted to do this, and he said, "Yes." And then, through a simple prayer, for the first time in his life, this hardened gang member confessed his sin, stated his belief that Christ had died for that sin, asked for forgiveness, and turned his heart over to Jesus. I asked him if he meant what he just prayed, and he nodded yes. I spent the next few minutes encouraging him as to the rock-solid promises of God for his future, and the fact that all those who also confessed Jesus as Lord would see him again in heaven.

One of the biggest lies of the enemy tells us that it is too late to come to Christ, that we have waited too long, or that God will not accept us because of the short time we have left. The above verse in Luke records Jesus's words on the cross to one of the men who was crucified with Him. This man had also lived in opposition to God and was in the last few minutes of his life. He, too, bowed to Jesus's Lordship through a simple statement of faith, and he received a personal promise of eternity from God the Son Himself.

It is never too late to come to God, but not many have the luxury of those last few minutes to get their eternity straight. Ecclesiastes 9:12 says it best, *"For man also does not know his time: Like fish taken in a cruel net, like birds caught in a snare, so the sons of men are snared in an evil time, when it falls suddenly upon them."*

Thought for the Day

Don't gamble on a "late in the game" opportunity to come to Christ. Put your trust in Him now and receive all that He has to give you in this life and in the one to come.

DAY 268

The Lord is good to those who wait for Him, to the soul who seeks Him.
—Lamentations 3:25

Hurry-Up Button

I used to ride my bike around the city where I lived. When I would come to an intersection, I would stop if there was a red light. I would then push the pedestrian button so that the walk / don't walk sign would change in the direction I am traveling. For some reason, I always imagined pushing that button would speed up the time it took the walk/don't walk sign to change. I know others think the same thing because I see them push the button repeatedly as they become impatient for a green light. I am pretty sure that pushing that button doesn't speed up anything at all, it just changes the walk / don't walk signage. The lights only seemed to be affected by the pressure plates embedded in the traffic lanes and not by the pedestrian button. I had to wait patiently for the sign to change in its own sweet time.

God's timing is always perfect! We might not think so, and we wish that we could hurry His answers to a situation we are facing. The above verse in Lamentations tells us to do two things to receive God's goodness in our lives. We are to seek Him and to wait patiently for Him to respond to a situation in His own time. We can push the "hurry up" button all we want, but if we are His child, He will only allow things to happen in our lives if they are what's best for us.

Psalm 27:14 encourages us to *"wait patiently for the LORD, be brave and courageous. Yes, wait patiently for the LORD."* Sometimes it takes courage to wait on God when possibilities seem dim, when we are waiting for that job offer that hasn't come, that diagnosis that seems hopeless, or the restoration of a relationship that appears unlikely. I have always had the greatest respect for those who continue to obey God in spite of circumstances that seem impossible.

Whenever I pray with someone at church, I remind them of God's word to us in Jeremiah 32:27 which states, *"Behold, I am the Lord, the God of all flesh. Is there anything too hard for Me?"* Since the answer to that rhetorical question is a resounding no, all we have to do is seek Him and wait for His answer. It is another one of those "easy to figure out, sometimes hard to do" things in our life, but the reward will be God's favor and blessing.

Thought for the Day

When we come to a crossroads, will we repeatedly push the "hurry up" button for an answer that makes us feel comfortable? Or will we simply push the button once and wait patiently for the Lord to reveal His direction in our lives?

DAY 269

Let no one despise your youth, but be an example to the believers
in word, in conduct, in love, in spirit, in faith, in purity.
—1 Timothy 4:12

Look Who's Watching Now

Several years ago, I was out to dinner with my family in Costa Mesa. Toward the end of the meal, a young man approached our table and asked if I was involved in ministry at Harvest OC. He was at the restaurant that evening with his wife and children and had seen me at the church where I served. After a brief pleasant conversation, he said goodbye and left the establishment. Since I never usually see anyone I know when I am out and about, I wondered just how many people have recognized me when I am in public but have never said anything to me.

I hold myself to a strict ministry policy as to the consumption of alcohol. I know that many Christians believe that they have liberty in this area as long as they do not become intoxicated. I believe, however, in holding myself to a higher standard. What if the young man mentioned earlier had been a recovering alcoholic and had seen me, an associate pastor at the church, imbibing alcohol in a public place? He might have been tempted to believe that he, too, could drink "just a little, after all, the staff at Harvest does." This could lead him back down the road to addiction, and I would have played a pivotal role in that decline.

As followers of Jesus Christ, we need to be an encouraging example to the lives of others. This means that we might need to give up some of our liberty if there is any chance that others could be hurt by it. You never know who is watching us and may be evaluating our lives. In the case of alcohol, you might be able to consume it in private, but you will almost always have to buy it in public.

Thought for the Day

Don't let your liberty hurt those around you. You never know who's watching.

DAY 270

So he answered, "Do not fear, for those who are with
us are more than those who are with them."

—2 Kings 6:16

The Invisible Army

Many times, citizens will call the police in the middle of the night because they hear noises and believe that someone is either in their house or on their property. In our city, officers are dispatched immediately and arrive at the residence within several minutes. The homeowner will sometimes call back to complain about the slow police response only to be told that our officers had already arrived on the scene and had been outside doing their job for some time. The caller was unaware of our presence and was needlessly worried about their safety.

In the above passage, we read about the prophet Elisha who was surrounded by invading forces. The king of Syria had sent a large number of soldiers to capture and kill Elisha because of his ability to receive information directly from God, who told him of the king's battle plans. Elisha's servant was afraid due to the size of the army, and he expressed his concerns. Elisha prayed that his servant's eyes would be opened so that he could see the heavenly host that was invisibly there to protect them. The servant saw that *"the mountain was full of horses and chariots of fire all round"* (verse 17). When the Syrian army attacked, God blinded them which allowed Elisha and his servant to escape unharmed.

If Jesus Christ is the Lord of your life, you have unseen forces that surround you. It does not matter if you can't see them, or if you don't feel their presence. God promises His protection and assures you that nothing will happen to you that is outside of His will for your life. The Bible says, "*For he shall give his angels charge over thee, to keep thee in all thy ways*" (Psalm 91:11).

Thought for the Day

No matter how bad the odds seem and how far away your backup may be, God has all the resources you will ever need to bring you safely through to the other side.

DAY 271

Test all things; hold fast what is good.

—1 Thessalonians 5:21

Wrong Voice

My daughter has a beautiful singing voice. She is a hundred-pound girl who can sing like Aretha Franklin. It is truly startling to hear those vocals come from such a little person.

One night, my wife was recording my daughter on her iPhone as she sang at church. Later that night, she reviewed the recording and was surprised to hear that my daughter was singing extremely off-key. It wasn't like her to do that, and my wife was shocked by her uncharacteristically poor performance. It wasn't until my wife listened carefully again that she realized the musical pitch violator was not our daughter, but her own voice singing along with her! My wife is such a great spouse, mother, and friend, but singing cannot be listed as one of her strong suits. She had made her assumption as to the quality of the performance by listening to the wrong voice.

The above verse in Thessalonians tells us to put everything we hear to the test and hold on to only what is true. I have had many people come in for counsel who tell me that God has spoken to them about a certain direction they were to take in life. The only problem was that the course they wanted to follow was in direct opposition to God's clear command according to His word.

Psalm 119:160 states that "*the entirety of Your word is truth, and every one of Your righteous judgments endures forever.*" So, we know that if we get any direction that we think is from God, that choice must be in line with what scripture tells us. If it is not, then we have listened to either the voice of the enemy, or our own, to make our decision.

Thought for the Day

Let's not think we are listening to God when, in truth, it is another voice creating the misdirection.

DAY 272

*For you, O God have heard my vows; You have given
me the heritage of those who fear Your name.*

—Psalm 61:5

True Heritage

All my life, I have been told that my ethnicity was a mixture of German, Scottish, Portuguese, and American Indian. My Indian blood was the only real question mark that could not be proven. My grandfather did not know anything about his father, other than he was told that he was of Native American descent. For years, my family has attempted to trace our linage back, but the official record always stopped with my great-grandfather.

I sent in a DNA sample to Ancestry.com that would tell me exactly what my genetic ethnicity was. The results came back a week later. As expected, I am 49 percent German, 23 percent Scottish, 9 percent Portuguese, and 11 percent trace countries like Scandinavian, Eastern European, Italian, Great Britain, and European Jew. If you are doing the math with me, that leaves 8 percent unaccounted for, and it is not American Indian. My remaining ancestors are from North Africa, the Congo, Togo, Nigeria, and Senegal. I am 92 percent European and 8 percent African. I can finally stop looking for that missing Native American piece of my heritage, and what a great heritage it is! Every one of my forefathers were brought together in God's great plan to make me who I am today. I am proud of all of them.

God's word talks about our greatest heritage. It is a lineage that transcends any genetic marker or international boundary. We are told that we have an eternal heritage that only comes from our faith in God and our obedience to His word. You may not know who your people are, but you can know whose people you are. If you have confessed Jesus Christ as your Lord and Savior and have accepted His sacrifice on the cross for your sin, you are a child of the almighty living God. Nothing can be more important. No genetic marker, no country of origin, and no family oral history can trump that!

Thought for the Day

Zero percent lost, 0 percent alone, 100 percent child of God.

DAY 273

For everyone practicing evil hates the light and does not
come to the light, lest his deeds should be exposed.

—John 3:20

The Light

I spent most of my time on the police force working the night watch. It was in the last several years, during the twilight of my law enforcement career, that I switched to days. I think most of us would agree that more crime occurs at night. It is not that nothing illegal happens during the daylight hours, it just seems to intensify under the cover of darkness.

One thing that criminals hate is the light. They just can't carry out their crimes or escape as easily afterward when they can be seen by others. And just as criminals hate the light of day, those who make it a practice to sin against God hate the way His word illuminates their lives.

As followers of Jesus Christ, we can use that same light to improve our relationship with Him. Instead of hating the light, we can look for it in God's word to grow in our Christian walk. God's word says, *"But if we walk in the light as He is in the light, we have fellowship with one another, and the blood of Jesus Christ His Son cleanses us from all sin"* (1 John 1:7).

Thought for the Day

We have no need to fear the light that God's word shines on our lives.

DAY 274

*These desires give birth to sinful actions. And when
sin is allowed to grow, it gives birth to death.*

—James 1:15

Simple Beginnings

I heard a story about a man who was walking by a psychiatric facility. As he passed the location, he heard a large group of people
behind its ten-foot perimeter wall shouting the number "thirteen,
thirteen" in unison. Since the wall around the building was so high,
the man could not see over it to determine what everyone was shouting about. As he continued on, the chant became louder and louder
until he finally came to a small hole in the brick that would allow
him a view of what was going on inside. When he put his face up
against the hole, a finger quickly thrust through the opening from
the other side and poked him directly in the eye. Startled and in pain,
the man fell back and immediately heard the voices again shouting
in unison from behind the wall. This time, they chanted, "Fourteen,
fourteen!

Sin is a lot like that wall. It can tempt us with unknown chants
from hidden places where we cannot see the full extent of what is
attracting us. But it is just enough to pique our interest and give us
an appetite for more. Unfortunately, when we finally place ourselves
in a position to get a full view of our desire, we get an unexpected
attack that will injure our spiritual sight and relationship with God.

James 1:15 tells us, *"These desires give birth to sinful actions. And
when sin is allowed to grow, it gives birth to death."* Sin usually starts
off as a small desire, or a fleeting interest, that can grow to the point

where it eventually leads to death. I know those who are bound by sin's grip who would have been stunned, twenty years before, if they knew where their first compromise would eventually lead them. Satan never shows you where he wants to take you, he just starts off with a small concession that you will be convinced is a one-time event to satisfy your curiosity. Then one concession after another can eventually lead you to a place where you never thought would be possible.

Fortunately, Jesus has given us the answer for our sin, no matter how far down its continuum we have allowed ourselves to go. First John 1:9 states *"if we confess our sins, He is faithful and just to forgive us our sins and to cleanse us from all unrighteousness."* It doesn't matter if we have just committed our first compromise, or if we are in bondage to the sum of numerous poor choices over a lifetime of concessions. Jesus is able to forgive us through the sacrifice He made on the cross to pay the price for that sin. All we must do is confess it and turn from it and accept His grace. But God does not leave us there. Romans 6:14 assures us, *"For sin shall not have dominion over you, for you are not under law but under grace."* You can not only be forgiven of sin but be relieved from its domination over your life.

Thought for the Day

Don't wait for the next sin casualty in your life. Turn from it now and accept God's grace.

DAY 275

The LORD keeps you from all harm and watches over your life.
—Psalm 121:7

Cover versus Concealment

In a gunfight, the concepts of cover versus concealment are two totally different things. Concealment is the visual hiding of yourself from the suspect, and cover is gained by positioning yourself behind an object that will provide you protection from the oncoming gunfire. If I were to hide behind a hollow core door or barrier made of drywall, I would only have concealment because the gunman could shoot me directly through the object. That fact is something that we as police officers often use against dangerous armed suspects. Cover, on the other hand, can be obtained by standing behind a thick tree, block wall, vehicle, or any other object that cannot be penetrated by gunfire. Concealment might make you feel safe, but only cover can truly protect you.

We often put our faith in the things of this world, falsely believing that they will protect us. Saving for retirement, being a good steward with our finances, eating well, exercising, or anything else we may do to better our position in life are all good things. God wants us to be the best we can be to serve Him effectively while we are here on this Earth. But if we start to believe that those things will truly protect us against an unknown future, we are mistaken. Only God can do that. All other efforts on our part might make us feel better but are only concealment from issues that may arise in our lives. They offer no real protective cover.

The good news for us is that through our faith in Jesus Christ, God can take on the job as our protector in a way that we never could. He has given us the greatest cover of all time by coming to Earth as a man and dying on the cross for our sins. He has provided us with the most solid shield that there is, one that nothing in this world can penetrate. God also provides for us in this life and protects us against an unknown future if we will only put our faith in Him.

Thought for the Day

Let's not get shot from a place where we only feel safe. Step behind the rock-solid wall of God's love and protection for you.

DAY 276

*Your ears shall hear a word behind you saying, "This
is the way, walk in it," whenever you turn to the
right hand or whenever you turn to the left.*

—Isaiah 30:21

Listen and Obey

Several years ago, I went to see a friend at the UCI Medical Center. After our visit was over, I walked outside of the main building on my way back to the parking structure. As I passed the oncology building, I went inside to use a restroom that I knew was there due to my previous visits to the hospital. As I left the building, I passed by the waiting room and noticed an elderly woman who was seated in a wheelchair. She was leaning forward with her face in her hands. I kept walking, but when I reached the front door, a still small voice in me said, "Go back and pray with her." I have to get back to the church, I thought as I continued out the door and onto the sidewalk. I walked on toward the parking structure and again heard the voice in my head (a little louder this time), "Go back and pray with her!" "Oh, she probably doesn't want to be bothered," I said to myself as I continued to move down the sidewalk. Then I noticed something. My feet seemed to be having difficulty going forward. It was as if they were stuck in the cement. I stopped in my tracks and heard that voice again, "If you won't obey me, how can you tell anyone else that they ought to?" Boy, good one, Lord!

I turned around and went back toward the building. I thought, She will probably be gone by now, but at least I obeyed God's leading. When I entered the front door, I saw the woman still seated in the same position with her face in her hands. I went up to her, introduced myself, and asked if I could pray with her. She told me that she was waiting for her family and that she was about to go in for a radiation treatment. She said I could pray for her, and I asked God for her healing, wisdom for her doctors, and peace during this difficult time. Then guess what happened, nothing! She thanked me for my prayer, and I went on my way. I still wonder if this entire event was for her, or for a lesson in obedience for me. Probably both, I think.

We may never know the outcome of how God uses us in this life to touch others. As a police officer, I can tell you that was usually the case for me. And it seems as an associate pastor that the same might still be true. But that does not excuse me, or you, from obeying God's voice when He asks you to do something.

Who knows what part we play in a string of events orchestrated by God to reach someone for Jesus Christ. Our part is to do what He says, not to try to figure the whole thing out.

Thought for the Day

Listen and obey that still small voice.

DAY 277

If the prophet speaks in the Lord's name but his prediction
does not happen or come true, you will know that the
Lord did not give that message. That prophet has spoken
without my authority and need not be feared.

—Deuteronomy 18:22

Fortune-Tellers

During every political cycle, we hear a constant stream of predictions about the future of our country. Some claim to know what will happen if a particular candidate is elected, a certain bill is passed, or even if a claimed right is infringed upon. I would like to see a scorecard at the end of each year where prognosticators would be held accountable for the predictions they made. That would be a show I would watch!

Over the years, there have been individuals who have made predictions about coming events. This could be as simple as someone telling us, "I have a word from the Lord for you," or a supposed spiritual leader claiming to know of the day of the Lord's coming or pending punishments on those around them.

The above verse in Deuteronomy gives us the simple formula to determine if a prophecy or a word of knowledge that predicts the future is from God or not. DOES IT COME TRUE! You see, God is never wrong, and His predictions are always true. The Lord tells us in Ezekiel 12:25, "*I will fulfill whatever I say.*" So, when any person makes any prediction that does not come true, we know that it is not from God. It is a lot like predicting the score of a football game.

People might argue back and forth, but the game will eventually be played, and there will be a final score.

Thought for the Day

Don't be fooled by those who claim to know the future. Anything short of 100 percent accuracy is not from God.

DAY 278

*But the Lord said to Moses and Aaron, "Because you did not
trust me enough to demonstrate my holiness to the people of Israel,
you will not lead them into the land I am giving them!"*

—Numbers 20:12

Great Responsibility

I was thirty-four years old when I entered the police academy. I was
one of the oldest in my class. As we approached our graduation
day, I started to see how excited my fellow recruits were about their
new law enforcement careers. They spoke of how they looked forward to the pursuits, the arrests, and the suspect confrontations that
would soon come their way. Their youthful exuberance was typical
for a group who averaged about twenty-four years old. One thing I
noticed was that the more excited they got, the more the weight of
the duty we were about to take on affected me. I kept wondering,
"Don't any of these kids realize the great responsibility that is about
to be placed on us?" We would soon have the ability to take away
people's freedoms, their reputations, or even their lives in some cases.
People would look to us for protection or to find those who damaged
their lives through assault and theft. They didn't seem to fully understand the gravity of the responsibility that was about to be placed on
them. I guess you just can't put old heads on young shoulders.

In the above passage of the book of Numbers, we find the result
of Moses's interaction with the people of Israel. When the people
were thirsty, God told Moses to "speak" to a rock in order to get
water. Moses instead struck the rock in anger, took credit for a miracle, and, in essence, misrepresented God to the people. Moses was

never allowed to enter the Promised Land due to his actions on that day.

When I was ordained as a pastor, I had the old familiar feeling of the weight of responsibility that was being placed on my shoulders. James 3:1 tells us, *"Dear brothers and sisters, not many of you should become teachers in the church, for we who teach will be judged more strictly."*

In writing this devotional, I always try to accurately relay God's sound word to others without any personal or unorthodox interpretation. Because of James 3, how I represent God and His word is always very important to me.

Thought for the Day

Please pray for all of those whom God uses to bring you commentary on His word. The weight of that responsibility can be very heavy at times.

DAY 279

*Looking for the blessed hope and glorious appearing
of our great God and Savior Jesus Christ.*

—Titus 2:13

Looking Forward?

If you want to hear an unusual answer to a question, ask a cop when they plan to retire. If you ask a normal person (i.e., accountant, doctor, real estate agent, or business executive), they will probably give you the general age they plan to stop working. I have heard people say, "Oh, I don't know, probably at sixty-five or sooner if I can get my 401(k) lined up the way I want." But for those in law enforcement, it is different. If you ask them when they retire, they will answer with an exact number of years. If you ask a cop who is closer to retirement, they will not only tell you the years, but also will have calculated the months, weeks, and sometimes even the number of days until they can "pull the pin"! Even those who have enjoyed the work still seem to know exactly how long they have until they remove themselves from the law enforcement pressure cooker. It is something they long for.

As believers in Jesus Christ, we should have that same longing for the return of our Lord. But unlike those on the force, Jesus Himself told us that there is no exact countdown for His return. Matthew 24:36 records Jesus's own words on the subject when He said, *"But of that day and hour no one knows, not even the angels of heaven, but My Father only."*

I believe that the Lord's return could be very soon. The signs of the times point to it as never before in our history. But, I have heard that same statement many times over the fifty-plus years that I have been a believer. The truth is that we just do not know if His return is imminent or if Jesus will wait just a little while longer. And the Lord's definition of "a little while longer" may be completely different than ours.

Soon or not, we should be looking forward to "*the blessed hope and glorious appearing of our great God and Savior Jesus Christ*" as if we knew the exact number of years, months, days, or even hours until his return. I have heard it said many times that you can tell a person's spiritual condition by the joy or fear they exhibit when contemplating the Lord's return. If our lives are truly in line with God's will, we should be looking forward to the event with the anticipation of a cop calculating his retirement date. If the thought of Christ's return brings fear, dread, or even disappointment due to things not yet accomplished in our lives, we need to reexamine our priorities.

Thought for the Day

Are you ready for His return? And if you are, are you truly happy about the possibility? It will be great to retire from this life into the unbelievable eternal plan that God has for us.

DAY 280

*Those who are wise must finally die, just like the foolish
and senseless, leaving all their wealth behind.*

—Psalm 49:10

You Can Take It with You

I responded to many dead body calls over the years. In fact, at one point, there were so many in my area that the detectives jokingly referred to me as Dr. Death. They quipped that they wouldn't want to live in any area that I patrolled because it upped their chances of departing this life!

Because Newport Beach is an affluent town, many people whose deaths I was assigned to investigate were wealthy. Of course, by the time I got there, their earthly possessions didn't matter anymore. Despite the multimillion-dollar home in which they had lived, the exotic cars in their garage, and the expensive jewelry they left behind, they were dead. They were just as dead as the person of meager circumstances that I had investigated the week before. What they had or hadn't earned in this life didn't matter anymore. It really is true that "you can't take it with you." Well, almost true.

In discussing personal wealth in the afterlife, I have heard many preachers say, "You can't take it with you, but you can send it ahead!" Matthew 6: 19–20 tells us, "*Don't store up treasures here on earth, where moths eat them and rust destroys them, and where thieves break in and steal. Store your treasures in heaven, where moths and rust cannot destroy, and thieves do not break in and steal.*"

So what kind of treasure can we send ahead? I can think of at least three. First, we have the treasure of our inheritance of grace.

Second Corinthians 8:9 tells us, "*You know the generous grace of our Lord Jesus Christ. Though he was rich, yet he became poor, so that by his poverty he could make you rich.*" We will have the great treasure of forgiveness given to us through Jesus's sacrifice on the cross. Second, we have the gift of eternal life because of that same sacrifice. John 3:16 tells us, "*For God so loved the world that He gave His only begotten son, that whoever believes in Him should not parish but have everlasting life.*" There can be no greater wealth waiting for us, after this life, than assurance of our eternity. And finally, we have the great riches of bringing friends and loved ones to Christ so that we will see them again in heaven. First Thessalonians 4:17 states, "*Then, together with them, we who are still alive and remain on the earth will be caught up in the clouds to meet the Lord in the air. Then **we** will be with the Lord forever.*" For the believer, heaven will be a place of great reunions with the friends and loved ones who have gone before us.

Thought for the Day

Nothing is wrong with working hard for wealth in this world as long as we don't neglect the true fortune that will last forever, that only a relationship with Jesus Christ can bring.

DAY 281

Lying lips are an abomination to the Lord, but
those who deal truthfully are His delight.

—Proverbs 12:22

True Liar

It is pretty clear from God's word that He hates lying. He wants us
to be truthful in all of our statements and actions. But this puts
police officers in an apparently difficult position as we attempt to
do our jobs. Many times, we use subterfuge during the interviewing
process in order to obtain a confession or to cover our identity. While
working undercover, I was asked many times, "Are you now or have
you ever been a police officer?" At that point, I had two choices.
Either I would say, "Man, you got me, I'm a cop," and wonder why I
never had a successful undercover encounter, or I would lie.

I settled this difficulty in my mind many years ago. People lie
for a variety of reasons. Sometimes they lie to cover their guilt, to get
something that doesn't belong to them, or to avoid an uncomfortable consequence in their lives. The ruses we use as police officers are
not done for any of these reasons. The Penal Code allows us to use
deception "in pursuit of the truth," and I believe that God does too!

God understands our unique job requirements and looks into
our hearts to discover the reason for our actions. God is truth, and
He does not count the ruses we use on the job as the lies that violate
His laws for us. The only problem we may have is if we take this "ruse
mentality" home with us after the shift. That is when we can start to
go against His admonition for us to "deal truthfully."

God has placed you in this job for a reason. Every day, you deal with situations and "gray areas" that the public cannot imagine. He has given you a special grace and mercy to deal with the evil we are forced to confront in this world. There are not many who could handle that kind of power.

Thought for the Day

You are part of a first responder chosen elect. Let's make Him proud of us as we make the daily transitions between the darkness of our jobs and the light of His truth.

DAY 282

Jesus said to her, "I am the resurrection and the life. He who believes in Me, though he may die, he shall live."

—John 11:25

The Living Dead

During the course of our first responder careers, we will see many ways in which a person can die. Drowning, hanging, gunshot, traffic collisions (blunt force trauma), fall (or jump), overdose (pills, alcohol, IV drugs), heart attack, seizure, asphyxiation, decapitation, burned, plane crash, slip and fall, crushed by a falling object, bleed out, electrocution, explosion, allergic reaction, SIDS, unknown causes, and that's the short list! I never really thought about the wide variety of ways a person could die until I got into law enforcement.

Some of those who died took their own lives, but most had no idea that the end was coming. I was especially surprised by some traffic fatalities. When I drove up to the scene, I would find one driver seated in their car injured and unconscious. The driver of the other vehicle was walking around talking with emergency responders with what appeared to be minor injuries. I later heard that the accident was to be labeled a fatal because one of the drivers had died. I was shocked to hear that the unconscious driver was going to be okay, but the one who had been walking around, talking had expired due to internal injuries, whose severity had not been apparent at the time of the collision.

The one thing that all the people whom I saw deceased had in common was that death found them, if they were ready for it or not. It will find us all one day. We might spend a lot of time wondering what means we will leave this earth, but the real question is not how we will die, but where we will go when we do?

Fortunately, for the believer in Christ, that question was settled on the cross. Jesus gave himself as a sacrifice for us to pay the debt of our sin. Revelation 1:5 tells us, "*To Him who loved us and washed us from our sins in His own blood.*" Because of this, death takes on a completely new meaning to those who have given their lives to Jesus. Now we can say, "*O death, where is thy sting? O grave where is thy victory?*" (1 Corinthians 15:55). First John 5:13 tells us, "*These things I have written to you who believe in the name of the Son of God, that you may know that you have eternal life.*"

Thought for the Day

We might not know how we will die, but we can be assured of our eternal destination by the authority of God's word.

DAY 283

If a man makes a vow to the LORD, or swears an oath to bind himself by some agreement, he shall not break his word; he shall do according to all that proceeds out of his mouth.

—Numbers 30:2

Situational Ethics

As police officers, we spend a lot of time in court with our right hands in the air promising to tell the truth. We also sign many documents in the course of our duties that serve to verify money counts, the probable cause for arrests, or the authenticity of our written reports. I am proud to have worked with a high caliber of officers during my law enforcement career. I would put their honesty and integrity on the job up against any profession that I know.

Many officers, however, seem to have no problem compartmentalizing their ethics for the different areas in their lives. They would never dream of falsifying a report, providing false testimony, administering justice unevenly due to the race of a suspect. But I've seen a few of these same officers break their marriage vows, fudge on their taxes, or not follow some other alcohol-related law while not on duty.

We all had to memorize the law enforcement code of ethics when we were in the academy. The first line of the second paragraph contains a phrase that law enforcement officers sometimes forget as they go about their daily lives away from the department.

I will keep my private life unsullied as an example to all.

God calls on all first responders to maintain our integrity on the job as well as in our personal lives. There should be no difference between what we do when we are on or off duty. We can't keep the above vow documented in the code of ethics if we fail to keep the promises in our relationships and personal dealings.

Thought for the Day

Let's be men and women of our word and commit to aligning our private lives with our public promises.

DAY 284

Blessed is he whose transgression is forgiven; whose sin is covered.
—Psalms 32:1

Covered Imperfection

Several years ago, we had the floor of our garage epoxied. It was amazing to see all the stains, cracks, and imperfections disappear during the quick four-hour process. They first etched the concrete floor and filled in any existing cracks. They then applied the epoxy base coat and sprinkled multicolored chips evenly on the surface. After all the excess chips were scraped away, they ended the process with a clear sealer coat. The result was a thick, durable epoxy floor that will last for many years. All the defects that were once so apparent in the old concrete were gone, covered over by the craftsmanship of the installer.

The above verse in Psalms 32 tells us of a similar action involving the covering up of imperfections. The psalmist rejoices in the fact that the ultimate craftsman, God the Father, can not only forgive sin, but can also cover the eternal damage it can cause.

In Old Testament times, this was accomplished by sacrifices that were brought to the temple and laid before God by the priests. Today, we can also lay our sins before God but without having to rely on the purity of animal sacrifice. We can now have our imperfection covered by the blood of our Savior who died to give us forgiveness. All the stains, cracks, and imperfections can disappear simply by making Jesus Christ the Lord of our lives. Others might still see those sins and faults, but due to Christ's blood shed for us, God the Father only sees the perfect finished product, clean, whole, and restored.

If you have not yet, let the master craftsman restore your life to perfection. If you have given your life to Jesus, rest in the finished work that has covered your sin and given you a place in eternity with Him.

Thought for the Day

Let God resurface your life through faith in Jesus.

DAY 285

Have You not made a hedge around him, around his household,
and around all that he has on every side? You have blessed the work
of his hands, and his possessions have increased in the land.

—Job 1:10

Protective Barrier

For many years, we had an employee parking lot at the police department that was not gated. Anyone could just walk onto the lot from the adjacent street. We often found that subjects, who had just been released from our jail, had walked around to the east side of the building and were wandering around the personal vehicles of the officers. I remember that I made several arrests in that lot over the years for a variety of criminal activity. Well, at least it was a short walk to the jail!

Several years ago, the city solved this problem by erecting metal fencing that secured the entire perimeter of the police station. Now you must have a special access code to get into the employee parking area.

The above verse records Satan's lament that God had placed a protective hedge around Job's life. The Devil had to ask for special permission to do anything against Job or his family. As a follower of Jesus Christ, you have been given the forgiveness of your sin, the reward of eternal life, and a plan and purpose in this life. God also provides you protection just like Job that requires permission to penetrate. The enemy can do nothing to you without God's approval.

The Bible says we will have trials and tribulations in this life, but it is great to know that Satan won't be able to add an attack to them without God's consent.

Thought for the Day

The Christian does not have to worry about being unprotected in any situation that the enemy might bring our way.

DAY 286

Looking unto Jesus, the author and finisher of our faith; who for the joy that was set before Him endured the cross, despising the shame, and is set down at the right hand of the throne of God.
—Hebrews 12:2

Forward Focus

One night while working beach patrol, I was riding an all-terrain vehicle (ATV) on the sand between the Balboa and Newport Piers. We usually drove with our headlights off so that we could sneak up on suspects after hours who were involved in illegal activity. The moonlight gave us enough illumination so that we could see anything on the sand that might be an obstacle for us. As I traveled westbound, I looked to my left at the shoreline where I thought I saw someone walking. The next thing I knew, I was flying through the air followed by a somersault in the sand that landed me back up onto my feet uninjured. It was then that I realized I had taken my eyes off the path directly in front of me and failed to see one of the small metal dumpsters lined up on the beach. I had broadsided the container, and the resulting collision had thrown me off the ATV. Due to the accident, a change was made in our policy (jokingly called the Green Rule) which required that our lights be turned on as we drove down the beach.

As Christians, we always get into trouble when we take our eyes off Jesus. Problems become bigger and our future uncertain when we get distracted by this world and its unpredictability. If we focus on His love for us and the promises found in His word, we can remain on track and avoid some real obstacles in this life.

Thought for the Day

Turn your eyes upon Jesus, look full in his wonderful face, and the things of earth will grow strangely dim, in the light of His glory and grace. (Helen H. Leamer, 1922)

DAY 287

*"Come now, let us settle the matter." Says the LORD. "Though
your sins are like scarlet, they shall be as white as snow;
though they are red as crimson, they shall be like wool.*
—Isaiah 1:18

New Car Smell

After a recent traffic accident, my old car was pronounced DOA
(dead on arrival). I received word about two weeks after the
collision that my insurance company considered my car to be a total
loss. I was glad, because the damage was so severe that any attempt
to repair it would have left me with a ride that would never function
well again. I had paid off the vehicle several years ago and had kept it
in good condition. I was not happy for the need to buy a new car and
have a payment once again, but I used the insurance check to make
a healthy 50 percent down payment on a new car and received a very
low interest rate on the new loan.

I have to say that I love the smell of a new car! Everything is
shiny, clean, and without a scratch. The combination of the aromas
generated from the new seats, carpet, and interior is something that
is hard to duplicate. I know, in the past, I have purchased a bottle
of "new car" vehicle scent in a failed attempt to keep that fragrance
alive. Nothing seems to be like that original smell.

Everything eventually deteriorates, wears down, and loses that
brand-new look, feel, and fragrance. Our lives outside of Christ are
like that. The sins we have committed over the years clings to us, and
not only ruins our innocence but also erases any chance we have of
an eternity with God. He knew our plight and that the just compen-

sation for our sin was death. So, God came to earth in the form of a man, lived a perfect life, and endured an unjust death for our sin.

The above verse in Isaiah tells of God's great power to clean up our lives. He can take the stain of our sin and make us white as snow. God is the ultimate restorer who can make our hearts brand-new. All that we need to do is bow our knee to Him, accept Jesus as our Lord, turn from our sin, and live for Him. Jesus will then step in and completely take the stain of sin from our lives.

Thought for the Day

Do you want that "new car" smell in your life? Confess, bow, repent, and obey.

DAY 288

*In God (I will praise His word), In God I have put my
trust; I will not fear. What can flesh do to me?*

Psalm 56:4

Guaranteed Safe

Several years ago, I went to visit my youngest daughter and her
husband who then lived in Hawaii. She was a crime scene investigator (CSI) for the Hawaii Police Department in Hilo. They were
great hosts during our visit and planned lots of fun activities for my
wife and me on our first trip to the Big Island. One such outing
was to a zip line adventure. I had no problem with the concept of
zip-lining. I have never been afraid of heights and have actually been
comfortable looking off tall buildings, being up in airplanes, or even
standing at the edge of the basket in a hot air balloon.

The rides start off with lower-height trips that lasted a short
time. Our final trip, however, was a 1.5-minute ride that took us over
a large gorge complete with a 250-foot waterfall that looked relatively
small from of our position of over 450 feet up. As I was gliding across
to the other side, thoughts like "I hope this cable doesn't break" and
"What would it feel like to free-fall from this height" crossed my
mind. For the first time in my life, I was bothered by the height. I
finished the ride alive, and I am glad I did it, but I have to say that I
probably won't be doing that again.

One of the best definitions for fear that I found stated it was "a
strong emotion caused by great worry about something dangerous,
painful, or unknown that is happening or might happen." I think
we can all agree that fear is not always a bad thing. It keeps us from

walking over a cliff or touching a hot burner, and fits in with the "something dangerous and painful that is happening" part of our fear definition. But fear can also be a sin, especially when it challenges God's provision in our lives. The "something unknown that might happen" perfectly defines sinful fear for the believer in Jesus Christ. A nonbeliever has the right to be afraid of many things. They do not have the promise of the assurances found in scripture. To them, God's word is merely a collection of interesting or uplifting stories that have little lasting effect on them. On their zip line ride through this life, they are hooked to a cable that has not been inspected or certified safe. But for the believer in Jesus Christ, we are given the assurance that He has a plan and a purpose for us in this life no matter what our circumstances appear to be or how we feel about them.

When I accepted Jesus as my Savior and Lord, I was guaranteed a safe trip to the other side. I might still get afraid sometimes as I pass over the gorges of this life and look down as I think about the possibility of what might happen. But what I feel doesn't really matter because in reality, I have the promise of the chief engineer of this universe that everything is in perfect working order and I will make it safely to the other side. Jesus Himself said, "*Most assuredly, I say to you, he who hears My word and believes in Him who sent Me has everlasting life, and shall not come into judgment, but has passed from death into life*" *(John 5:24)*.

Thought for the Day

Why risk a trip to the other side on a cable that is not assured safe and true or, worse yet, doesn't exist at all?

DAY 289

But Joseph replied, "Don't be afraid of me. Am I God, that I can punish you? You intended to harm me, but God intended it all for good. He brought me to this position so I could save the lives of many people.
—Genesis 50:19–20

Loose Ends

I was never able to advance beyond the officer level in my law enforcement career. Now I guess I could claim all kinds of reasons for that, but the true bottom line was that it just was not God's will that I be promoted. If He had really wanted me to, there would have been no deficiency I possessed, adversary I faced, or situation I experienced that could have stopped me.

In the above passage in Genesis, Joseph's brothers were afraid that he would kill them because of all the evil they had done to him. Joseph understood God's plan and told his brothers, "*You intended to harm me, but God intended it all for good.*" God had a plan for Joseph that took him from being sold into slavery to becoming the second-in-command of all of Egypt. God's plan might not have made sense to Joseph as he was going through it, but it did after he had come out on the other side, then all he had experienced came into clear focus for him.

I know that our current struggles can seem to make no possible sense to us as we work through them. But I am here to tell you that no matter what we think, if you are a follower of Jesus Christ, He will bring together all the ugly loose ends of your life to reveal His plan for you.

Thought for the Day

> *And we know that all things work together for good to those who love God, to those who are called according to His purpose.* (Romans 8:28)

DAY 290

But Jonah arose to flee to Tarshish from the presence of the LORD. He went down to Joppa, and found a ship going to Tarshish; so he paid the fare, and went down into it, to go with them to Tarshish from the presence of the LORD.

—Jonah 1:3

You Can't Outrun It

Vehicle pursuits usually came as a surprise to us when we attempted to conduct a routine car stop. People run from the police for a variety of reasons. They may have contraband in their car, they may feel that they have a valid arrest warrant, they may be under the influence of drugs and/or alcohol, or they may be experiencing some sort of mental breakdown. Whatever the reason, all of them have the same thought, "I think I can get away." The biggest problem that they will face after the pursuit begins is revealed in an old law enforcement saying, "You can't outrun the radio." They usually get caught.

Jonah thought the same thing. God wanted to send him to Nineveh to warn the people of His coming judgment. Jonah didn't want to go, and he decided to run in the opposite direction to Tarshish (modern-day Spain). He bought passage on a ship and hid in the bottom of the vessel as it sailed to its destination. Can you imagine trying to hide from the almighty God in the bottom of a boat? I've got to wonder about Jonah's overall brainpower on this one. It is a little like the story of the ostrich who stuck its head in the sand so that it couldn't be seen. Jonah's attempt to hide from God didn't turn out too well and ended with him being thrown overboard and earning a three-day stay in the belly of a giant fish.

If God is speaking to you today about something He wants you to do in your life, please listen to Him. You can't hide from the Lord, and it will always work out better if you follow His plan. God's word says, "*For I know the thoughts I think toward you, says the Lord, thoughts of peace and not evil, to give you a future and a hope*" (Jeremiah 29:11).

Just as police pursuits never end well for the apprehended suspect, neither does a life spent in resistance to God's will. The only difference is that God loves us and is not coming after us to put us in jail.

Thought for the Day

He has a plan for our lives that can only be realized if we submit to Him.

DAY 291

*Singing psalms and hymns and spiritual songs among
yourselves, and making music to the Lord in your hearts.*
—Ephesians 5:19

True Worship

As a father of a child with developmental challenges, I have had a
thirty-six-year introduction to the world of disabilities. I can tell
you that many of the children and adults I have met in that world are
about the happiest, kindest people I know.

At our church, we had a young man named Trevor who had
Down syndrome. Trevor always sat on the left side of the sanctuary
in the same general area. When it would come time to worship, you
would find Trevor on his feet with his hands in the air singing to
God. It didn't matter if he was the only one standing. Trevor was
determined to praise our Lord in the best way he could with every
chance he got.

Whenever I saw Trevor singing and praising the way he did, I
always thought, That's the way we should all be worshipping God
and probably would be if we weren't so messed up. When I see the
joy and reckless abandon he showed every Sunday, and when I think
about my own worries and fears, I realize that he is the blessed one.

God's word says that one of our main occupations in heaven
will be worship. Revelation 5:13 says, "*And every creature which is in
heaven and on the earth and under the earth and such as are in the sea,
and all that are in them, I heard saying: Blessing and honor and glory
and power be to Him who sits on the throne, and to the Lamb, forever
and ever!*" That level of unrestrained worship will be something new

for most of us, but not for Trevor. He will be before the King doing exactly what he did when he was on this earth, without any hesitancy or apology.

Thought for the Day

We should all worship like Trevor.

DAY 292

And when He brings out His own sheep, He goes before them;
and the sheep follow Him, for they know his voice.

—John 10:4

The Mimic

Police dispatchers are remarkable. They spend their entire shift looking at a computer screen, unable to see the actual events that they are handling. With this lack of a visual picture, their voice recognition becomes highly developed. Dispatchers can not only identify every officer by the sound of their voice, but they can also determine if the officer is under stress by the slightest change in their tone.

God's word says that His sheep (us) know His voice and follow Him. The problem we sometimes experience is that our adversary Satan mimics the voice of God in our minds. He attempts to make us think that our internal dialogue is either our own thoughts, or the voice of the Holy Spirit directing us. There are several ways for us to determine if "that voice" is from God or not. First, if the mental thought makes us feel guilty about a past sin that we have already brought before the Lord, it can't be from God. His world tells us that *"I, I am He who blots out your transgressions for My own sake, and I will not remember your sins"* (Isaiah 43:25). God's word also tells us that *"there is therefore now no condemnation for those who are in Christ Jesus"* (Romans 8:1).

Secondly, if the thought makes us fearful about the future, it can't be from the Lord. God's word tells us, *"For I know the plans I have for you, declares the Lord, "plans to prosper you and not to harm you, plans to give you hope and a future"* (Jeremiah 29:11).

And lastly, if the thought makes you question God's love and concern for you, it is a lie! His word says that *"Neither height nor depth, nor anything else in all creation, will be able to separate us from the love of God that is in Christ Jesus our Lord"* (Romans 8:39).

Thought for the Day

Are you being lied to today about your past, present, or future? Stand on God's word which promises forgiveness, peace, and provision. The more you stand on His word, the more you will be able to accurately recognize His voice.

DAY 293

I know what it is to be in need,
and I know what it is to have plenty. I have learned the
secret of being content in any and every situation, whether
well fed or hungry, whether living in plenty or in want.
I can do everything through him who gives me strength.
—Philippians 4:12–13

Situations

I once officiated at a marriage vow renewal ceremony. Renewals are far different than a first-time wedding rite. A lot of the things I would say to a brand-new bride and groom don't make much sense to a couple who have been married for ten or twenty-plus years. During a rookie wedding ceremony, I would stress that there will be "good times and hard times, times of plenty and times of want." When I am standing there looking at a renewal couple, I know that if I were to say those words I would be preaching to the choir. They know all too well that life can he filled with ups and downs, failures and successes. That is what makes their desire to recommit their lives to each other so special. They are not together for what they think they know, but rather they are still together in spite of what they do know.

The apostle Paul wrote the above words in his letter to the church in Philippi. His words speak to a follower of Jesus Christ who had been there and done that in regard to steadfastly walking in the Christian life. Paul had learned to be content in every situation by his faith in Jesus Christ as demonstrated in verse 13, "*I can do everything through him who gives me strength.*"

A passage like this might make you fearful about a future and the low points of your life that have not come yet. But fear not, you, too, will be able to do all things through Christ Jesus if you have given your life to Him. Jesus said in John 16:33, "*I have told you all this so that you may have peace in me. Here on earth you will have many trials and sorrows. But take heart, because I have overcome the world.*"

You don't have to fear the future. He will be with you in the good times and the hard times, through times of plenty and the times of want.

Thought for the Day

God will renew your strength, and you will be able to stand and recommit your life to Him in every situation.

DAY 294

*Though I walk in the midst of trouble, You will revive
me; You will stretch out Your hand against the wrath of
my enemies, and Your right hand will save me.*

—Psalm 138:7

Crash Course

As a police officer, I drove the streets of Newport Beach twelve hours a day for most of my twenty-one-year career. I was involved in several fender benders during that time, which resulted in no injuries to me or anyone else. I thank God for His protection over my career as I drove around the city with "my hair on fire" much of the time.

Several years ago, I was on my way to church in the early evening for a lay counselor training graduation ceremony. I was the first car in my lane, stopped for a red light at the limit line. When the light turned green, I entered the intersection southbound toward the church. I made it about three-quarters of the way across when a vehicle ran a four-second stale red light to my right and broadsided my car at about forty miles per hour. The impact pushed me completely across the intersection to the south curbline of the street. Thank God, no one received any serious injuries other than sprains and contusions. My car fared much worse and had to be put down.

In the days that followed the accident, I had time to think about what had happened. The other vehicle had struck my car on the right front passenger side at the engine compartment. Imagine if we moved that back only three feet and I was hit squarely in my right-side passenger door. My injury outcome could have been quite different with flying glass and a greater intrusion into the interior of my car.

We don't always know the reasons God allows difficult things to happen in our lives. Sometimes the events can be confusing, frightening, and even painful. But whatever occurs, I know one thing for sure, He is in control!

I haven't always lived like I truly believe those words. When I get anxious over the future or worried about the present, I am saying with my attitude that I am not certain that God's hand is on my life. They have said that football can be called a game of inches, referring to yardage and victories that are sometimes decided by the slimmest of margins. Life can be like that, too, but in God's economy, an inch is as good as a mile. He is in control no matter how close to disaster we may feel we are.

Thought for the Day

Trust in Him. There are no out-of-control accidents for the followers of Jesus Christ.

DAY 295

"So I will restore to you the years that the swarming locust has eaten, The crawling locust, The consuming locust and the chewing locust, My great army which I sent among you."

—Joel 2:25

Restoration

When I think back the most difficult things I saw during my law enforcement career, I have quite a large mental image library to choose from. Murder victims, fatal traffic accidents, and suicides via shotgun all come to mind. So why is it that when I think of the one incident that I would most not want to relive again, I always go to the SIDS death (sudden infant death syndrome) that I investigated? Nothing gruesome there, just a perfectly formed little two-week-old with no apparent injury or reason for their demise. I remember the zombie expression on the mother's face as she battled the fatigue from recent childbirth combined with the anguish of losing her first child. I can also remember standing in a small emergency side room with the coroner's investigator. We had been on many dead body calls together and had always found some sort of gallows humor to alleviate the tension of the incident. Not so this time. I remember that the room was eerily quiet in contrast to the rest of the busy ER. The doctors and nurses had left us alone with the baby. It was just as hard for them to see that kind of tragedy. As I looked into the coroner's eyes, I saw a depth of pain that I'm sure was only matched by my own expression. But like all first responders, we had to swallow hard, take a deep breath, and do our jobs. We owed that to the child, her parents, and our profession.

I don't know what horrific things have happened in your life, but I learned something over my law enforcement career, "hard is hard." It is senseless to compare one person's tragedy against another's, because all of it alters our lives and changes us forever.

We serve a great God who specializes in making things right when they have gone wrong. The above verse in Joel tells us of His promise to restore to us the years that have been robbed from us by the circumstances of our lives. I believe that this not only speaks to our eventual restoration in heaven when all things will be made perfect, but our lives on this earth also.

No matter what you have seen, what they did to you, or how you were made to feel, God is able to restore those lost years and give you a future and a hope in this life as well as the next. Tragedy might make you different than you once were, but not hopelessly so.

Thought for the Day

Bow to Him, give it to Him, and let Him start that restoration process.

DAY 296

Now when they had gone through
Phrygia and the region of Galatia, they were forbidden
by the Holy Spirit to preach the word in Asia.

—Acts 16:6

Oh No You Don't!

As children we were forbidden from doing many things that we wanted to do. Playing in the street, going out after dark, talking with strangers, and refusing to eat our vegetables are a few that come to mind. These things had one thing in common: we wanted to do all of them! We just didn't understand how our parents could have been so wrong in their guidance about these things which were "obviously" good ideas in our childlike minds. We might have imagined that our parents were mean or uncaring for their insistence upon these unfair restrictions in our lives.

In the above verse in Acts, the apostle Paul was forbidden by the Holy Spirit to go into an area in Asia to preach the Gospel. FORBIDDEN TO PREACH THE GOSPEL, are you kidding? Isn't that in violation of the great commandment, *"Go therefore and make disciples of all nations"* (Matthew 28:19)? There is no mention in the passage as to what Paul and Silas, his missionary companion, thought of this restriction other than them obeying God's will. Little did Paul know that he would be sent back to the region where his ministry would flourish in God's perfect timing.

God may be closing a door in your life on an activity, a ministry, or a relationship that seems perfect to you. But just like little children, we only see events through our own limited sight and experience. We might even imagine that God is unkind or out to make us miserable when He stops the plans we have for ourselves. Little do we know He might be redirecting us or putting us in a holding pattern until just the right time; He will revisit the subject with a successful outcome.

God can stop or delay events in our lives even when we are certain that they are good and in His will. It might be that they are, but the timing of His provision will make things even better. Ephesians 3:20 tells us, *"Now to Him who is able to do exceedingly abundantly above all that we can ask or think, according to the power that works in us."*

Thought for the Day

Let's yield to God's timing in our lives even when we don't immediately understand the why of the forbidden direction.

DAY 297

She said, "No one, Lord." And Jesus said to her, "Neither do I condemn you; go and sin no more."

—John 8:11

New Start

In my career as a police officer, everyone I ever arrested was guilty. At least I thought they were, or I would not have taken them into custody! Despite what some people may think, the threshold for an arrest is quite high. I had to release many suspects due to a technicality, procedural error, or some fine point in the law. It was more likely that a guilty person was set free than an innocent one was arrested.

The above passage is from one of the more famous incidents in the Bible. Some men in the town brought a woman caught in the act of adultery to Jesus. Their purpose was not to root out sin in their community, but to trap Jesus in what they thought was a no-win situation. If He said, "Stone her," as the law prescribed, they would say He had no compassion or forgiveness. If he said, "Let her go," they would say He was not from God due to His disobedience to the law. Of course, Jesus knew their plan and had the perfect response to their deception. He told them, *"He who is without sin among you. Let him cast the first stone"* (John 8:7). He placed the responsibility for her judgment, and the requirement to carry out its sentence, on them. They all eventually walked away because it seemed that none of them were up to taking on that task.

During the course of this event, there was not one word spoken by anyone, including the woman, protesting her innocence. Apparently, her guilt was not in question. She had been caught in the very act. But when she and Jesus were left alone, He asked her, *"Where are your accusers, has no one condemned you?"* Our verse for today tells us of the heart of God and His will for our lives as much as any other passage in His word. *"Neither do I condemn you; go and sin no more."*

You may feel condemned today for what you have done in the past, or by what you are doing right now. If you have received Jesus into your heart and asked Him to forgive you for your sin, He has two things for you to do. Believe in His forgiveness and repent from the sin. All He wants from you is your continuing best effort to turn from the sin in your life. I am not saying that God expects you to never sin again. That ability won't come to us this side of heaven. But He does expect all of us to get into the fight against the sin in our lives. To fight against our natural tendencies and to ask God for forgiveness when we fall. We need to come up a little bloody in the battle as we strive to obey God and keep His commandments for our lives.

Thought for the Day

God offers everyone a new start every day. Accept it and fight to stay in His will.

DAY 298

There is therefore now no condemnation to those
who are in Christ Jesus, who do not walk according
to the flesh, but according to the Spirit.

—Romans 8:1

Guilt Free

As Christians we are often bothered by guilt. We know of God's promise to us that, *"If we confess our sins. He is faithful and just to forgive us our sins and to cleanse us from all unrighteousness" 1 John 1:9.* Even though we have asked Him to forgive us, we still seem to have that nagging ach in our hearts for what we have done. Sometimes we feel guilty because of the magnitude of the sin we have committed or because of its repetitive nature. We feel that as Christians we should be past "that," by now. The truth is that we are imperfect people who will constantly struggle with the presence of sin in our lives. It is a lot like trying to plug up eleven small holes in a pool with our hands. No matter how we switch the position of our ten fingers, some water is going to leak out.

The problem lies in our tendency toward legalism. We can believe that salvation through Jesus Christ is a free gift that we cannot earn. But somehow, we take a wrong turn in our thinking about living the Christian life. We believe that living a spirit filled life has to do with the degree of success we have in avoiding sin altogether. The good news is that the only one who expects us to be perfect is us! God makes no requirement, and His word tells us that if we have confessed our sin to Him, "there is no condemnation to those who are in Christ Jesus." All that He asks from us is to agree with Him that the sin was wrong, confess it, and to do our best to turn from it. If we still feel bad after doing that, the guilt is not coming from God. There is no limit to His grace. Not the size of the sin or the number of times we commit it can tax God's ability to forgive us.

My favorite quote on the ease at which God is willing to forgive us says, "The moment I confess the transgressions in my heart, even before the words come out of my mouth, God has already forgiven me." Can you imagine that? God's attitude toward forgiving us is a lot like when my wife and I were encouraging our children to walk for the first time. The moment they took one shaky step we raised our hands in victory and praised them for what they have done. It made no difference that they fell one step later as long as they got up and tried again.

Today God is waiting for you to take that step. Don't let Satan rob you of your peace by making you believe that you have gone too far, or that the sin is too big for God to forgive. He is excitedly waiting for you to ask for His forgiveness about the sin that He knew you would commit anyway!

Thought for the Day

As you read this devotional something might come to your mind that you feel led to confess to God. You can start to form the words and it will be too late. He will have already forgiven you!

DAY 299

"So then, they are no longer two but one flesh. Therefore,
what God has joined together, let not man separate.
—Matthew 19:6

Loose Guidelines?

My wife and I have been part of the disabled community for thirty-six years now, and we know firsthand the reality of the stress brought to parents of a child with special needs. The financial, emotional, and physical pressures that accompany these children can cause the breakup rate between their parents to skyrocket. Some estimate that the divorce rate for parents of disabled children is as high as 85 percent, which is well above the national average.

The divorce rate among cops is legendary. Some estimates suggest that it is as high as 75 percent. Most cops talk about the longevity of their marriages in terms of months, not years. I took probability classes in college, but I cannot remember much more than if you flip a coin, you get a fifty-fifty chance of heads or tails. I also remember that there is a formula for determining the likelihood of a percentage for a single event considering the product of other events. In short, if you multiply the odds of the divorce rate for parents of a child with special needs with that of a law enforcement officer, the total outcome of this combination would be devastating for the likelihood of a successful marriage.

So how is it possible that my wife and I have made it to the forty-one-year mark? We both decided long ago to follow God's plan for marriage. From day one, we were determined to trust in God's word and consider His will first in our lives. We promised each other that we would keep His rules for us no matter what.

I always include the following statement in the vows portion of the wedding ceremonies that I perform. "Vows are not suggestions. Vows are not loose guidelines. They are rock-solid, etched in stone promises to God. Before your family, your friends, and the world, you are locking yourselves together and voluntarily throwing away the key. These vows are sacred promises to a holy God and should not be taken lightly. God wants you to keep your word to Him and to each other whether **you feel like keeping it or not**."

Do you want a successful marriage? The answer is simple but not always easy. DON'T MAKE DIVORCE AN OPTION. God's word says, "*But seek ye first the kingdom of God and His righteousness, and all these things will be added unto you*" (Matthew 6:33).

Thought for the Day

If He is the Lord of your life, then He needs to be the Lord of your marriage too.

DAY 300

Whereas you do not know what will happen tomorrow.
For what is your life? It is even a vapor that appears
for a little time and then vanishes away.

—James 4:14

You Never Know

I had just finished traffic collision school and was on my first shift as an official Newport Beach accident investigator. I was hoping for a routine, uneventful night to break me into my new assignment, but that was not to be. Just after midnight, one of our officers went in pursuit of a motorcycle traveling northbound on Newport Boulevard. What was initially a routine traffic stop for a simple vehicle code violation had turned into a high-speed chase. As the suspect approached the juncture of Newport Boulevard and the 405 Freeway, he attempted to take the off-ramp toward South Orange County. The area was under construction, and the ramp had been funneled down to only one lane lined by cement dividers. It was there that the motorcyclist lost control of his vehicle and struck one of the cement lane dividers. The suspect then bounced back and forth between the dividers as he was thrown off the bike and continued northbound. By the time our officer caught up with him, it was too late. The rider had been killed due to his violent collisions with the immovable barriers.

My first call as an accident investigator had turned out to be an officer-involved fatal traffic collision. The only fortunate thing for me was that the incident had occurred so close to the freeway that we were now in the California Highway Patrol jurisdiction. They took the report, and I just mirrored their investigation. It was a tough night for the suspect, his family, and the officer who had initiated the pursuit. None of them wanted the eventual outcome.

One thing I learned as a police officer was that life can be fragile. I often saw how circumstances could quickly go from the routine to the disastrous. It could happen in the blink of an eye. One minute, we are riding home from a friend's house, and the next minute, we are lying dead in the roadway.

The above verse in James refers to our lives as a vapor, here one second and gone the next. We might not know the exact number of our days on this earth, but we can all be ready if that number comes sooner than we think. First John 5:13 tells us, *"I have written these things to you who believe in the name of the Son of God so that you may **know** that you have eternal life."* God's word promises that if we have accepted Jesus Christ as the Lord of our lives, we have our eternal destination secured. It is a done deal that we don't have to wonder about, hope for, or do more to earn.

Thought for the Day

When the vapor of your life clears, where will you be standing?

DAY 301

"And I will pray the Father,
and He will give you another helper, That He may
abide with you forever; the Spirit of truth,
whom the world cannot receive, because it neither sees
Him nor knows Him; but you know Him,
for He dwells with you and will be in you."

—John 14:16–17

The Monologue

One day, while I was working at the department, Dispatch received a call about a barricaded suspect in a residence on the east side of town. A female hostage had escaped from a house and was now reporting that a male suspect was still inside. Dispatch made several calls that went unanswered which initiated a SWAT callout to the location. I was on light duty at the time and could not respond out into the field as part of the Crisis Negotiation Team. I could, however, continue to attempt to reach the suspect via telephone from inside the Dispatch center (my back was hurt, but my mouth worked fine). As I called into the residence, I could not get the suspect to answer the telephone. We discovered that the house in question belonged to the suspect's parents who were out of town at the time of the incident.

As hostage negotiators, we will often get in touch with the family of the suspect in order to obtain information about them. I was able to contact his mother by phone and spoke with her about her son. As I talked with Mom, a thought occurred to me. I asked her, "Is the volume on the answering machine in your home up loud enough so that it can be heard throughout the house? She answered, "Yes, we have it turned up so that we can hear it from almost any room inside." I then started to call the suspect and leave messages on the phone using the techniques I had learned in negotiation school. If I couldn't have a dialogue with the suspect, I would at least make him hear a monologue. As the SWAT team deployed over the next hour, I continued to conduct a one-way conversation with the suspect. In fact, I completely filled the answering machine with messages imploring him that it was in his best interest to work toward a peaceful resolution to this situation.

At about the one-hour mark, to my surprise, the suspect answered the telephone and told me that he was coming out. Apparently, he had heard everything I had said to him over the answering machine. I think he finally decided that he would rather surrender to the police than hear my voice one more time! Well, at least it worked!

In the above verse in John, Jesus tells us that the Father will give those who have accepted Jesus Christ as Savior and Lord a "helper," the Holy Spirit, who will be with us forever. The Holy Spirit will be relentless in His love for us and will continue to encourage us toward a right relationship with the Father, even if we do not seem to listen or if we refuse to respond to His leading. He will always be there, as the voice in our ear who urges us to keep God's commandments and do what is in our own best interest.

Thought for the Day

God will never give up on you. Don't let that be a one-way conversation.

DAY 302

Two are better than one,
because they have a good reward for their labor.
For if they fall, one will lift up his companion.
But woe to him who is alone when he falls,
for he has no one to help him up.
—Ecclesiastes 4:9–10

Support

I recently tried to calculate how many times I had my ankles wrapped when I played football. I never got taped in Pop Warner, or in high school, but it became a requirement at the college level. The best I could guess was near a thousand times. At first I didn't like it, but once I got used to the feel and restriction posed by the tape, I became thankful for the support it gave me. I never twisted an ankle throughout my entire college career. Of course, I blew out my ACL, but that was nothing that tape could have prevented.

Support in our Christian lives is even more important than any athletic tape or brace. Encouragement from our Christian brothers and sisters can make the difference between the success and failure in our Christian walk. God knows the importance of friendship, and we can find many verses in the Bible that demonstrate His thoughts on the subject. Romans 1:12 tells us that we are to "*mutually encourage one another.*" Hebrews 10:24–25 exhorts us to, "*Not forsake the assembling of ourselves together,* and Proverbs 27:17 likens the benefits of friendship to "*iron sharpening iron.*"

The above verse in Ecclesiastes warns us about trying to go solo in this life when it states, "*But woe to him who is alone when he falls, for he has no one to help him.*" C. S. Lewis wrote, "Friendship is born at the moment when one man says to the other, 'What? You too? I thought that no one but myself.'"

Friendships start when we realize that we have something in common. There is no greater common interest and shared experience than a mutual faith in Jesus Christ. It immediately unites people of various colors, creeds, and national origins. But in order to obtain this bond, we must actively look to others for that Christian support. We all need friends to share in our times of triumph as well as our lows in tragedy. Without the support that fellowship can bring, we risk facing our lives alone.

Thought for the Day

Get spiritually taped up through fellowship or run the risk of unnecessary injury.

DAY 303

*In him we have redemption through his blood, the forgiveness
of sins, in accordance with the riches of God's grace*
—Ephesians 1:7

Trust Me

One winter night, I was dispatched to a domestic dispute on
the east side of town. My backup was a rookie officer who was
new to law enforcement. When we arrived on the scene, we found
that the front door to the residence had been broken in. There were
numerous pieces of glass, large and small, spread on the floor inside
the entrance to the home. A female was standing just inside the
doorway, and we were quickly able to determine that she was one
half of the dispute. The frightened victim told us that her husband
was no longer at the scene, and that she didn't need our assistance.
Understanding that our entry into the home might have Fourth
Amendment (search and seizure) implications, I asked her (consent)
if it we could come in and make sure everything was all right. She
refused to give us permission to enter and asked that we leave.

The rookie officer was a little confused as to what to do next.
Can we enter the residence over the objections of the owner with
no seemingly obvious exigent circumstances? Fortunately for me, I
had been the officer involved in a precedence-setting case ten years
before that had similar circumstances. In that case, the court ruled
that we could enter over the objections of the occupant in cases
where ongoing domestic violence was suspected (*Higgins v. the State
of California*). The court ruled that victims might be afraid to tell the
truth about the presence of a suspect due to fear of continued abuse.

If the police feel that abuse had occurred and will continue if they left without taking action, exigency could be established and our entry justified. Of course, my partner was not aware of this case law and questioned me about our ability to go inside. I remember looking at him and saying, "We can enter, trust me, I will explain later."

Some of the greatest verses in the Bible deal with God's great ability to forgive our sins. If you are like me, you might have a tougher time forgiving yourself than God has forgiving you. Recently I felt this way, and something occurred to me. If I sincerely ask God to forgive me, He immediately does. But if I doubt His forgiveness and continue to act as if He has not, I have created a new sin that needs to be forgiven by not believing His word. Basically, I was saying that the promise of total forgiveness found in His word was not true. It might be accurate for me to say that I don't understand how that is possible, but not for me to act as if it isn't true. It is just one of those things we will not be able to fully grasp this side of heaven.

Thought for the Day

You can be forgiven whether or not you fully understand how it is possible. What Jesus is saying to you is "I paid for it, trust me, I will explain it later."

DAY 304

And the Lord added to the church daily those who were being saved.
—Acts 2:47b

The Playing Field

During my freshman year in college, we played a football game at Angel Stadium in Anaheim. In those days, the field was marked out in chalk directly over the baseball diamond. The problem with that was seen on the south end of the field, on the west side, from the end zone to about the thirty-yard line. That part of the field was marked over the dirt of the baseball infield. Depending on which hash mark the referee placed the ball, we would either line up on the grass of right field (good) or on red dirt between first and second base (not so good).

Cleats versus dirt were not a great situation when you were trying to get enough traction to drive an opponent off the line of scrimmage. I was always relieved when we advanced the ball past the thirty-yard line, or at least ran a sweep to the east side of the field. I spent several hours that night experiencing the various surfaces and conditions on the field.

During the years that I had worked for Harvest OC, I had the opportunity to be back down on that field for the Anaheim Harvest Crusade. It brings back some of the reminiscences I had at the stadium, but it has added many new memories which are far greater than those vague recollections of the past. Each year at the crusade, Pastor Greg Laurie gives a gospel presentation and invitation for those in the capacity crowd to give their lives to Jesus Christ. I never get tired of seeing the outfield fill up with thousands of people who have decided to make that profession of faith.

If you have not witnessed a Harvest Crusade before, you should! Where else can you get a free concert, a great message, and be allowed to see thousands of people change their lives, all in one night!

For the believer, it is an experience that you must see at least once before you leave this earth or before He comes back for you. We never know how many more chances we will get. And if you have not heard about the personal relationship you can have with God through Jesus, then it will be a night that could change your life and eternal destiny.

Thought for the Day

Be down on the field playing in a different game with a greater outcome than a winning score!

DAY 305

Don't worry about anything; instead, pray about everything.
Tell God what you need, and thank him for all he has done.
—Philippians 4:6

Small Prayers

Many years ago, I was scuba diving at Catalina Island off the shore that faced out to the open Pacific Ocean. I had dived there many times before at various locations around the island, but this was my first time on the windward side. I had seen many incredible things on my dive trips that included giant schools of fish, towering kelp forests, and large sea creatures. But, I had never found anything under the water that I could recover as a souvenir of a dive. On this trip, I remember saying a quick little prayer, "Lord, it sure would be nice to find something this time that I could take home with me." As the dive progressed, I swam up to a kelp plant that was standing alone on a rock ledge. Positioned in the middle of the plant was a beautiful large empty crab shell that looked like it had been placed there on display. From its size, I could tell it was very old and it was in a location on the plant where it seemed impossible to have gotten there on its own. I have kept that shell to this day as a reminder to me of how God answers prayer, even small ones that might seem insignificant.

Many times, I have heard people express the opinion that it is an insult to God to pray for small things, like an upcoming test, a job interview, or even a road trip free from red lights. I've heard them say, "He's too busy, He's got bigger things on His mind." Nothing could be further from the truth. The above verse in Philippians tells us to pray about "everything." God is never too busy to hear from you and wants you to talk to Him about anything that is of concern to you. If it matters to you, it matters to Him. I often remember listening to my girls when they were very small as they told me about their day. Their concerns were not really significant in the adult world, but it mattered to them, so it mattered to me. Besides, I just liked to hear them talk to me.

God feels the same way about you. In truth, there is nothing we could bring before an all-powerful and all-knowing God that could not be labeled as insignificant. Your heavenly Father loves you and wants to be part of every aspect of your life. There is nothing that Satan would love more than to make you believe that God is too busy to hear from you. Satan hates it when we make conversation with our Lord (otherwise known as prayer) a consistent part of our daily lives.

Thought for the Day

Do you have a concern or request on your mind, great or small? Then it is on God's mind too! Go ahead and ask Him. You might be surprised at what you may find on your next dive into prayer.

DAY 306

Like newborn babies, you must crave pure spiritual
milk so that you will grow into a full experience of salvation.
Cry out for this nourishment, now that you have
had a taste of the Lord's kindness.

—1 Peter 2:2–3

Cravings

When I was a new grandfather, I had the exciting experience of watching my daughter care for my grandson. She is a great mother and attended to our grandson's every need without irritation or complaint. At that point, he was very young and seemed to feed constantly. I told my wife that for some reason, I did not remember our three girls needing to eat so often when they were infants. She reminded me that our first two were in the hospital for several months before they came home, and by the time they did, they had already started to eat solid food. My youngest daughter (the mother of my grandson) was born right about the time I went into the police academy. My wife said that I was too exhausted and preoccupied to know much of what was going on around me at that time. Seeing how much work my grandson was gave me a new respect for what my wife went through with two sick babies and a newborn.

Whenever my grandson cried for food, I could see firsthand what it is like to crave milk. It seemed that there was nothing more important to him at that time, and he made his need loudly known.

The above verse in 1 Peter tells us that we are to crave spiritual milk just like a newborn desires the real thing. The result of that feeding will be the same as in an infant, growth. Having had sick children, I know that when a baby refuses to eat, it means that there is something seriously wrong. The same can be said for a Christian who has no desire to feed on spiritual things.

No growth will occur unless we pray, read God's word, attend church, serve, and tell others about our faith. We need to cry out for these things not only because they are good for us, but also because we have tasted of the Lord's kindness for ourselves.

Thought for the Day

We need to crave spiritual milk and make that need loudly known.

DAY 307

*Trust in the LORD with all your heart, And lean
not on your own understanding; In all your ways
acknowledge Him, And He shall direct your paths.*
—Proverbs 3:5–6

Pursuing God's Will

The famous humorist Sam Levenson once said. "It's so simple to be wise, just think of something stupid to say, and don't say it!" I often wish that obtaining wisdom and the knowledge of God's will was that easy. Next to accepting Jesus Christ as our Savior and Lord, determining His plan for our lives should be our number one priority. The above verse in Proverbs gives us a blueprint for knowing God's will. Trust in the Lord, don't rely on our own understanding of things, seek Him in all areas of our life, and God promises us that He will give us direction. We can use the acronym PRAYS when we attempt to determine God's will for our lives.

First, we should always **Pray** for direction about a situation. James 1:5 instructs us to *"ask of God"* if we want wisdom, and He promises to give it to us.

Then we should **Read** God's word and see what it has to say about what we are going through. The Bible says in 2 Timothy 3:16 that *"all scripture is given by inspiration of God,"* so we can count on it to give us infallible direction. Many times, our exact question will be answered in His word.

We must also be **Aware** of the open and closed doors that God places before us. Revelation 3:7 tells us about God's ability to direct us through circumstances when it says about Jesus Christ, *"He who* opens and no one shuts, and shuts and no one opens." Sometimes God reveals His plan for us by the opportunities or lack of them that come our way.

Next you should examine **Your** feelings that God has given to you about a situation. Colossians 3:15 says, "*And let the peace of God rule in your hearts.*" God can give us peace in a situation that can lead us to know His will. This is one to be careful of because human feelings are fickle and can be faked by our enemy, Satan.

And lastly, sometimes we need to **Seek** wise counsel about the situations in our life. Proverbs 1:5 says, "*A wise man will hear and increase learning, And a man of understanding will attain wise counsel.*" Wisdom is not about the level of intelligence that we possess or the amount of knowledge that we can accumulate. It is more about having a good memory for the stupid things we have done and the ability to help others not make those same mistakes. Sometimes it is wise to seek counsel from those who have greater life experience than you have.

Even if we follow the steps above, knowing God's will is not an exact science. That is where faith comes in to play as we trust in the Lord, lean not on our own understanding, and in all our ways acknowledge Him.

Thought for the Day

There is no more rewarding pursuit than that of finding God's will for our lives.

DAY 308

*And so we have the prophetic word confirmed, which you do
well to heed as a light that shines in a dark place, until the
day dawns and the morning star rises in your hearts.*

—2 Peter 1:19

From Stupid to Spiritual

When I first became a cop, I said a lot of stupid things. Some
might argue that I continued to do so over the next twenty-one years, but let's just say that it was more of a common occurrence early in my career. My use of abbreviations, acronyms, code
numbers, and phrases was sometimes comical to the veteran officers
around me as I struggled to learn my job.

The above verse was written near the end of Peter's life when he
was a veteran pastor and teacher of God's word. The beautiful words
he penned under the inspiration of the Holy Spirit told of what he
had seen and heard at the transfiguration of Christ. Here we have a
mature Peter remembering what he had witnessed when he saw Jesus
standing with Moses and Elijah, and heard God's audible voice say,
"*This is my beloved Son in whom I am well pleased. Hear Him.*" Peter's
thoughts about the importance of that event, chronicled in 2 Peter
1:17–21, stand in stark contrast to what he said and did at the actual
incident.

In Matthew 17:4, we have Peter's comments as he saw Jesus
standing with the two deceased prophets, Moses, and Elijah, who
had played such an important part in the history of Israel. Peter said,
"Lord, it is good for us to be here; if You wish, let us make here three
tabernacles: one for You, one for Moses, and one for Elijah." Wow,

I'm sure that the two prophets were looking at Jesus and thinking, "Who is this guy?" Peter was good at saying something when silence would have been the better course of action. When God said, "Hear Him," I'm sure it was a kind way of saying, "Shut up, Peter."

The above passage should give us great hope. It documents the development that is possible over time in the Christian life. If Peter could go from a comment that would cause God to ask Him to be quiet to a great apostle, teacher, and martyr of the faith, who spoke with effective boldness at Pentecost, then it is possible for us to grow too!

Thought for the Day

What does it take to go from stupid to spiritual? Time and a continuing desire to follow His will for our lives.

DAY 309

*For whoever desires to save his life will lose it, but
whoever loses his life for My sake will find it.*

—Matthew 16:25

Lose to Win

Before I became a police officer, I was involved in fitness train-ing. It was always hard working with women to help them lose weight. The problem was the amount of food they would eat. It was not that they ate too much; it was that they usually were not eating enough! I saw men do this, too, but not eating enough was usually more of a women's problem.

When the body gets too few calories, it slows its metabolism, thinking that you are going into starvation mode. This results in the retention of fat and whatever else the body thinks it needs to stay alive. You can actually gain weight by not eating enough! It seems counterintuitive, but six small meals a day results in more body fat loss than eating only two. Skipping meals is never a way to lean out and stay strong.

The above verse in Matthew may also seem a little backward to us. Jesus is asking us to lose our lives in order for us to save them. It has to do with ownership and to whom you have given your life. If we lose the control of our lives to Jesus Christ, we not only obtain God's promise and purpose in this life, but we also gain an eternity with Him when this life is over. God's word says, *"For what shall it profit a man, if he shall gain the whole world, and lose his own soul?"* (Mark 8:36).

Thought for the Day

Do you want to be a winner? Then give yourself away to the only one you can trust. What do you have to lose?

DAY 310

For the Son of Man has come to seek and to save that which was lost.
—Luke 19:10

You Are Wanted

One of the things that dominated the walls of our briefing room at the department were the wanted posters. These documents hung on the walls and contained the pictures, crimes committed, as well as other pertinent information on suspects wanted throughout the state. I could always tell when they were going to use the room for general purposes involving civilians. All the wanted posters would be turned around so that sensitive eyes would not be offended by some of the graphic information listed on them.

A wanted poster makes it clear that an individual is being actively sought by law enforcement. The suspect's information will be teletyped, faxed, and emailed all around the state, and in some cases the country, in an attempt to locate the suspect. From the amount of effort that will be placed into finding them, these individuals are definitely wanted.

You are a wanted person too! If you have accepted Jesus Christ as your Lord and Savior, He is looking to have an ongoing relationship with you. He wants to hear from you, talk to you, and be included in every aspect of your life. If you have not yet given your life to Jesus, He still has you on His most wanted list. Second Peter 3:9 tells us, *"The Lord is not slack concerning His promise, as some count slackness, but is longsuffering toward us, not willing that any should perish but that all should come to repentance."* He loves you and wants to be included in your life. Not only does He want to give you a plan and purpose in this life, but He also wants to secure your eternal destiny with Him.

None of the people on criminal wanted posters are glad to be there. But for those on God's wanted posters, it is a great joy to have our face plastered up on the wall. There is only one thing, in order to settle your account with Him, you will have to turn yourself in. God will not go out and take you in against your will.

Thought for the Day

You are wanted! Give Him the custody of your life.

DAY 311

*You will keep him in perfect peace, Whose mind is
stayed on You, Because he trusts in You.*

—Isaiah 26:3

Trust

I trusted my partners. I placed my life in their hands many times,
and as I write this devotional, I still have a pulse, so I guess we can
assume that they never let me down. Trust is vital to any organization
or relationship. In Steven Covey's book *The Speed of Trust*, he states
that trust not only raises the moral and positive atmosphere of a work
environment, but it has an economic benefit as well. Organizations
that have a high level of trust built into their culture will experience
increased productivity, resulting in a greater financial reward.

In God's economy, the word "trust" is used to encourage His
followers to have faith in Him. The Bible defines faith as "*the substance of things hoped for, the evidence of things not seen*" (Hebrews
11:1). In spite of what the situation may look like on the surface,
when we trust in God and His plan for our lives, we open up a giant
invisible realm of possibilities.

The Bible says that "*without faith it is impossible to please God*"
(Hebrews 11:6). Just like the benefit that an organization can obtain
from a high level of trust, we can experience a gain from our faith in
the Lord. If we don't place our trust in Him and His plan for us, even
in tough times, we can't experience all that God has for us.

Thought for the Day

As first responders, we trust our lives to each other's care, thousands of times during our careers. It is great to know that God has our back, both on and off the job, if we will only trust and believe in Him.

DAY 312

When the whirlwind passes by, the wicked is no more,
but the righteous has an everlasting foundation.

—Proverbs 10:25

The Problem with Staying High

Street cops become experts regarding the symptoms and effects of most intoxicating substances. Methamphetamine is a particularly debilitating drug. The look and demeanor of a meth user is pretty consistent. The drug causes them to be in a continually agitated state. They pick at their skin, leaving scabs on their arms and faces. Food becomes a secondary priority to them. You don't see many speed addicts who are overweight. In fact, the opposite is true. Normal hygiene also takes a back seat to the drug, and their teeth start to rot away. The user's pulse, blood pressure, and respiration are kept at dangerously high levels. It is not uncommon for subjects to go without sleep for several days as the drug courses through their system. That eventually comes to an end as they crash and sleep for days. The body is not designed to function at that increased level for extended periods of time. Some meth user's hearts just stop under the strain of the drug's effect on their bodies.

I have seen many believers attempt to live their spiritual lives at a similarly elevated level. Unless they are constantly undergoing some sort of miraculous event or emotional experience, they feel they are not living a true Christian life. They seek to continually have mountaintop experiences and believe that they are supposed to remain at that height in order to remain in God's will.

There is nothing wrong with mountaintop experiences, and we will all have them at times in our Christian walk. The problem is believing that there is something wrong if we don't always stay on top of that emotional mountain. In my experience, those who think that true faith means a constant euphoric Christian state seem to be the ones who fall the hardest when that false belief does not match up with the realities of their lives.

We will spend some time on the mountaintop, but we will also do our time in the valley. The joy that God's word promises us does not mean that we will always be euphorically happy. It means that we will always have hope, and be encouraged in our good times as well as our bad. God does not grow our faith by allowing us to operate at that increased level for unending periods of time. Our spiritual bodies were not designed to grow best at that elevated state. That is what heaven will be about.

The verse in Proverbs above tells us that we will go through some whirlwinds in our lives, but those times that destroy the wicked will pass by us because of our foundation in the Lord. God will allow us to have many great moments where we can't believe His continual blessings in our lives. But there will also come hard times when we feel that God has moved away from us and the euphoric mountains of the past seem distant and far away. Know that God's plan for us involves both of these extremes.

Thought for the Day

It has been said that it isn't how high we jump, but how well we land that really matters. Allow God to be there for both.

DAY 313

Even so you also outwardly appear righteous to men, but
inside you are full of hypocrisy and lawlessness.

—Matthew 23:28

Some Good News!

At about the five-year mark in my law enforcement career, the department had video cameras installed in our police vehicles to record officer activities. At first, we were hesitant about what this would mean and fearful that the recordings would be misused by defense attorneys or even our own supervision. But our worries turned out to be baseless, and we grew to be thankful for the recordings which often exonerated us from false allegations made by the public.

One place I was always glad to have a video recording was in traffic court. When I wrote a ticket where I had recorded the violation, I would always write on the bottom of the narrative portion of the citation, "Violation Recorded on DVD," and then identify the specific number of the recording. In spite of this warning, I can't tell you how many times a suspect would take me to court and, under oath, make the statement that "I completely stopped at the sign," "I never said such and such," or even "The officer got the wrong car, it just looked like mine." They would come to court looking well-dressed, respectable, and give a convincing clear statement as to their innocence that would almost have me convinced!

After I had given my testimony about the incident, I would tell the judge, "Your Honor, I have a video tape of the violation if that would help." The look on the defendants' faces were priceless when the judge would smile and say, "Yes, I would like to see that!" Of course, what followed was digitally colored video proof that the defendant had been mistaken in their earlier testimony before the court.

The above verse in Matthew tells of the true condition of the human heart. No matter how we might try to prop ourselves up, dress ourselves, or act in a respectable, righteous manner, inside we are full of hypocrisy and lawlessness. God knows the truth about us and has recorded all our deeds (Revelation 20:12). That would be a hopeless statement if it were not for the complete forgiveness offered us through Christ's death on the cross for our sin. He will not only forgive us for our past but He also is there to forgive us throughout our Christian lives as we battle the sin nature that is within us.

The word "gospel" comes from the Greek noun *evangelion*, and can be translated, "good news." And that is exactly what the gospel is, the good news that our sin can be forgiven through confessing Jesus Christ as Lord and turning the control of our lives over to Him. And what do we get for doing that? Our past sin, "NOT GUILTY," our current and future sin, "NOT GUILTY," and a plan and purpose in this life, as well as an eternal future in heaven with our Lord.

Thought for the Day

That sounds like good news to me! Let's either rest in that truth or accept it for the first time today.

DAY 314

*The LORD is close to the broken hearted and
saves those who are crushed in spirit.*
—Psalm 34:18

Crushed and Broken

As first responders, we see a lot of crushed things. We probably can't count the number of vehicles, buildings, and bodies we have seen in a smashed state over the years. But I have to say that in spite of those great numbers, we see more crushed spirits than anything else. We regularly see people who have lost everything that they own, and everyone whom they hold dear. It is the unspoken pain of the first responder to be a forced witness to every kind of tragedy over and over and over again throughout the course of a career.

We serve a God who is omniscient and knows all things. The Bible tells us that God came to earth in the form of a man, Jesus Christ, to be our ultimate example and share our experience as a human being on this earth. That is true, but I would argue that since God knows everything, He was already well aware of what our pain and sorrow felt like.

The above verse in Psalms was written centuries before Jesus came to this earth. It tells us that the all-knowing God of the universe is close to those who are broken and crushed. It not only tells of this closeness, but also, it promises an action when it says, "He **saves** those who are crushed in Spirit."

If you are crushed in spirit, God knows of your situation and He can save you if you will turn to Him. He is a God who loves you and has a plan for your life whether you can feel it or see it today.

Thought for the Day

Listen to an older man who has seen many crushed things, and personally experienced the smashing circumstances of this life. THE LORD IS CLOSE TO THE BROKENHEARTED AND SAVES THOSE WHO ARE CRUSHED IN SPIRIT.

DAY 315

*Then one of the criminals who were hanging blasphemed Him saying,
"If You are the Christ save Yourself and us." But the other, answering,
rebuked him saying, "Do you not even fear God, seeing you are under
the same condemnation? And we indeed justly, for we receive the
due reward of our deeds; but this Man has done nothing wrong."*
—Luke 23:39–41

Full Confession

One of the most rewarding activities in police work is an effective interview that leads to a confession. Taking a defendant from "I wasn't there" to "I did it" is not only personally gratifying, but also, it is often the key to a successful prosecution.

In the above passage, we read of a confession made by a criminal who was crucified with Jesus. He had come to the end of his life and saw no further need to lie or defend himself. He was guilty and he knew it. His confession was not gained through an interrogation technique or undercover operation. This man was truly sorry for his actions and knew that the punishment he was receiving was the "due reward" for his crimes. His honest confession was heard by Jesus who forgave him and promised him eternal life.

The first step in a personal relationship with Jesus Christ is the realization that we are all sinners. No more excuses, no more rationalizations, no more lying to ourselves. God's word tells us that "*all have sinned and come short of the glory of God*" (Romans 3:23). There is not a person on this earth that does not fall into that category. God knew our situation and loved us so much that He came to earth in human form to pay the price for our sin. Through Christ's death on the cross, our guilt can be wiped out and we can receive a plan and purpose in this life as well as an eternity with Him. But the first step is a true confession.

If you feel guilty today for your past or present actions, there is a good reason, YOU ARE! But stand in line, so are all of us. God's word promises to cast our sin from us as far as the east is from the west (Psalm 103:12) if we will confess it all to Him.

Thought for the Day

Are you ready to stop running? Confess your sin, recognize that Jesus is Lord, ask for His forgiveness, and give the control of your life to Him. If you have done that, then rest in the assurance of God's forgiveness and your eternal destination.

DAY 316

You must not turn away from any of the
commands I am giving you today.

—Deuteronomy 28:14a

No Discretion

As a police officer, I was given great discretion as to how I did my job. California Penal Code 4 stated that I was allowed, in many cases, to "promote justice" by my "fair import" of the law. What did that mean? In short, unless otherwise explicitly directed by the law, I could choose to arrest or not arrest as I saw fit.

One example of this was the night I stopped a man for a vehicle code violation that quickly turned into a DUI investigation. The man had the strong odor of an alcoholic beverage on his breath, and I was pretty sure he would be found under the influence of alcohol while driving his vehicle. As part of the field sobriety exam, I asked him where he had come from that night. His answer was "From my son's wake, he died last week." My suspicious cop mind thought that answer sounded a little too convenient, and I felt he might be making it up to solicit sympathy on my part.

Well, the story was easy enough to check up on. I asked him for his wife's phone number, and I called her to see if they had recently lost their son. I found out that they had. Now it might upset you to hear this, especially if you or someone you know has ever been arrested for DUI, but there was no way, no way in this world, I was going to arrest a grieving father who had just come from his son's funeral. His car was parked legally at the scene, I wrote its location on a piece of paper and stuck it in his pocket, his keys were locked in his trunk, and I called for a taxi to take him home. PC 4 allowed me to not arrest that gentleman, and based on what I saw, it was a fair import of justice that night. I can live with that.

As a Christian, one thing that we should not be able to live with is disobedience to God's word. There is no PC 4 in the Bible that allows us to skip over or make up our own minds about what God's law asks us to do. Man's law might allow for some wiggle room in its application because we are imperfect people writing an imperfect law that requires it. But God's law is perfect.

Thought for the Day

Obedience to God's word will always promote justice with fair import.

DAY 317

*Train up a child in the way he should go, and
when he is old, he will not depart from it.*

—Proverbs 22:6

Lost and Found

I committed my life to Jesus at a very young age. I really do not remember much about my relationship with God during my early childhood other than I went to church and believed in Him. I remember praying at night before I went to bed even before I had a full understanding of who God was and the extent of His power to answer those prayers.

I had a GI Joe action figure that I played with on a regular basis. In fact, it was my favorite toy. One day, I was in my room with my GI Joe when I realized that I could not find the small handgun which was one of his accessories. I looked for that tiny plastic semiautomatic for the good part of thirty minutes (an eternity for an eight-year-old boy). Finally, in total frustration, and in tears, I told my mom that I had lost the gun. This might not seem like a big deal, but it was a devastating tragedy in my young life. My mom looked with me for a short time and then said, "Well, let's pray that God will help us find it." We said a quick prayer, and when we finished, my mother reached down, for some unexplained reason, to pick up a book that was on a chair in my room. I stood there in disbelief as I looked down and saw the very toy I had been looking for resting in the middle of the chair's seat cushion. It was the first time in my life that one of the basic truths of the Christian faith struck home for me in a real way. God not only hears my prayers, but he will answer them too!

I might be tempted to reduce the importance of this simple inci-dent in my life if it were not for one immutable truth, I remember it as if it were yesterday. I might not be able to recollect many other spiritual lessons from my preteen years, but that day, God taught me that He hears me, He answers prayers, and if it matters to me, it mat-ters to Him. In the years that followed, I might not have always acted like I remembered the lesson of that day. But now that I am older, I think about it often, when I am tempted to worry or doubt God. Only God can provide such an effective life lesson that happened more than a half century ago and involved a two-cent toy gun!

As parents, it is easy to let the pressures of this life distract us from the spiritual upbringing of our children. We might take them to church, read them Bible stories, and pray with them at bedtime, but it is the practical lessons of faith that we teach our children along the way that can mean the most.

Thought for the Day

Look for opportunities to interject God into the lives of your children or grandchildren, and when they are old (like me), they will always remember. Thanks, Mom!

DAY 318

"I have sinned by betraying innocent blood." And they said, "What is that to us? You see to it!" Then he threw down the pieces of silver in the temple and departed, and went and hanged himself.
—Matthew 27:4–5

Two Choices

All 927Ds (dead body calls) must be investigated as possible crimes until the evidence shows otherwise. What looks like a natural death might turn out not to be. It is the responsibility of the police department and the Coroner's Office to determine the cause of death and to collect any evidence at the scene. I had more than my share of 927D calls in my tenure as an officer.

The method of death I dislike most was hanging (as if I like any method). The vast majority of these deaths were suicides. You can't imagine the heartbreak and distress of the victim's family, who were usually the ones who discovered the body. There was generally some sort of note left behind by the victim that apologized and tried to explain the desperation that led to their final actions. In their minds, the pain they felt outweighed any hope for their future.

In our above verse in Matthew, we see the account of Judas's actions after he had betrayed Jesus. His despair over his betrayal was so great that it outweighed his desire to go on living. He then hanged himself to escape the emotions he felt due to his actions.

But Judas was not the only one who would betray Jesus that night. Peter, three times, denied that he even knew the Lord in an attempt to escape punishment through his association with Jesus. When he remembered that Jesus had said that was exactly what he would do, scripture tells us that he went out and *"wept bitterly"* (Matthew 26:75). Two very different reactions to emotional distress caused by their own sin. We know that Peter was later forgiven and used by God in a great way. I think that the same would have been possible for Judas if he had not decided that his own will was more important than God's. He chose a permanent solution to a temporary problem, and there was no turning back.

We have all betrayed (sinned against) God. When that happens, we are left with two choices, either ask for and receive God's forgiveness, or decide that our own will is best, run from God, and experience disastrous results.

There is no reason to follow Judas's example in our lives. What we see as a hopeless situation can be turned around and made right by Jesus. Don't give up, turn to Him, and he will take care of your future.

Thought for the Day

Don't make permanent decisions on what God views as temporary problems.

DAY 319

Search me, O God, and know my heart; Try me, and know my anxieties; And see if there is any wicked way in me, And lead me in the way everlasting.

—Psalm 139:23–24

Spiritual Sobriety Exams

As a police officer, I have given thousands of field sobriety exams and made hundreds of driving-under-the-influence arrests over the years. It was sometimes comical to see the poor physical performance that some of these suspects demonstrated. As I "balanced them out," the term we used for giving them a field sobriety exam (FSE), they swayed heavily, slurred their speech, staggered, and sometimes even fell down. Almost all the suspects that I arrested for DUI had the same misguided belief at the end of the FSEs. They falsely thought that they had done better on the exam than they really had. Some were even outraged that they had been arrested and stated, "But I passed every test!" In reality, it wasn't even a close call.

Sometimes in our Christian walk, we can also have the false belief that we are doing better than we really are. We become blind to our own shortcomings and stop seeking God's wisdom and direction from the Holy Spirit to improve our walk with Him. The above verses in Psalms were written by King David and showed His true love for God. He invited the Lord to search and evaluate him in every aspect so that He could reveal any "*wicked way*," in his life. That is why despite all his flaws, God called David "*a man after My own heart.*"

Thought for the Day

Today let's ask God to "balance us out" and put us through some spiritual FSEs. He will bless us if our hearts truly seek after Him.

DAY 320

And all this assembly shall know that the LORD
saveth not with sword and spear: for the battle is the
LORD's, and he will give you into our hands.

—1 Samuel 17:47

No Failure Drills Required

As police officers, we tend to rely on our issued weapons for defense. We spend a lot of time in training to become proficient with a baton, Taser, handgun, shotgun, rifle or any other tool given to us in order to serve and protect others. It is a constant battle to keep up with a well-armed criminal element who always seems to be one step ahead of us. We also devote a lot of time to failure drills in the event that our weapons don't perform as advertised. Guns can jam, Tasers can malfunction, and pepper spray cans expire. You don't need to have been a cop for long to have a story of how one of your weapons let you down.

God does not share our problems with weapons. In the above verse, David stated his belief in God as he confronted the giant Goliath. He understood that God did not need a weapon to be victorious and truly believed that the fight was over before it had started.

I don't know what battle you are struggling with today, but you can rest in the fact that your God has all that is required for you to be victorious. God never needs to work on any failure drills. He is never at a loss for which direction to take, and there is never any problem you can experience that is too big for Him to handle. As always, there is a catch to releasing His power in our lives. *"Trust in the Lord with all your heart, And lean not on your own understanding; In all your ways acknowledge Him, And He will direct your paths"* (Proverbs 3:5–6).

Thought for the Day

God has all He needs to protect and direct our lives. He will never fail, make a mistake, or miss the mark. If we place our trust in Him, the battle is won!

DAY 321

He will again have compassion on us, And will cast our sins Into the depths of the sea.

—Micah 7:19

Lost Evidence

Every cop has experienced the lengths at which a suspect will go to destroy the evidence of their crime. I have seen them hide items so they can pick them up later, burn things, throw evidence on the roof of a house or out of a moving car. I have even seen them swallow contraband in an effort to conceal the illegal item (at least temporarily!) so as not to be held accountable for its possession.

If you work by the beach like I did, we all knew that the best way to destroy evidence was to throw it in the ocean. We can dredge a lake or pond, send scuba divers down, or use some other means to recover things from an isolated body of water. But if the suspect could get on a boat and throw the evidence into the middle of the channel in the twenty-six miles between the coast and Catalina Island, it was pretty much gone. The area was just too big and too deep to recover a small item such as a gun, stolen property, or even a weighed-down body.

First John 1:9 tells us that "*if we confess our sin He is faithful and just to forgive us our sins and to cleanse us from all unrighteousness.*" The above verse in Micah shows us just where He puts that forgiven sin in a place where it cannot be brought up and recovered for use against us. In Psalm 103:12, God says that "*He casts our sin from us as far as the east is from the west.*" That's pretty far, isn't it!

If you need God's forgiveness today either as a current follower of Jesus Christ, or as someone inviting Him into your heart for the first time, all you have to do is ask for it. He will throw that sin into the deepest ocean, never to be seen or heard from again. Sure, we may have to deal with the consequences that sin causes in our lives, but it will never be used in God's judgment against us.

God's word says, *"But one thing I do, forgetting those things which are behind and reaching forward to those things which are ahead"* (Philippians 3:13).

Thought for the Day

If God has thrown your sin into the deepest ocean, don't try to go fishing for the evidence!

DAY 322

The former account I made, O Theophilus, of all
that Jesus began both to do and teach.

—Acts 1:1

The Proper Order

Before a cop can become a field training officer (FTO), they need to have years of experience on the job. An officer must demonstrate a high level of law enforcement competence before they will be allowed to teach someone else. Teaching a new recruit policing would be ridiculous if the trainer had not proven that they knew what they were doing. It would truly be "the blind leading the blind."

In the opening verse to the book of Acts, the author Luke explains to Theophilus that his previous writing (the book of Luke) was generated to tell him of Jesus's ministry. Notice the order of Christ's actions at the end of the verse, "*Jesus began to do and to teach.*" He "did" first and "taught" afterward. Jesus lived thirty years before He started His public ministry. As he taught, He did many good works to the point where the apostle John wrote, "*And there are also many other things that Jesus did, which if they were written one by one, I suppose that even the world itself could not contain the books that would be written*" (John 21:25). Jesus would not have had the authority to teach anyone if he had not successfully demonstrated the life that He commanded others to lead. In short, He had to walk the walk before He could talk the talk.

Anyone who aspires to teach at any level should take that order of events to heart. Whether it is as a parent in our own homes, or as a pastor in full-time ministry, we will have no credibility to guide or instruct others without first demonstrating that what we tell others is working for us. "Do as I say, not as I do" never works for anyone who wishes to lead others in a certain path to a positive outcome.

Thought for the Day

Let's get things in the right order. Do first, and teach later.

DAY 323

And the sea gave up the dead who were in it, Death and Hades
gave up the dead who were in them, and they were judged,
each one of them, according to what they had done.

—Revelation 20:13

Stand Alone

Every police officer who has had to testify in traffic court is familiar with the illogical justifications given by defendants who have been ticketed for a violation. One such irrational explanation was the "other people did it too" defense. Their argument went something like this, "While the officer was giving me a ticket, I saw four other cars run the same stop sign too." Their statement insinuated that the cop had a personal grudge against them and had unfairly targeted only them for a ticket. Somehow, they felt that if others were not ticketed at the same time for the same offense, they should be released from their responsibility to obey the traffic laws.

There was only one problem with that defense. It did not address **their** guilt! You see, the judge was not there to take into consideration what anyone else did. The only issue before the court were the specific actions of the individual cited. The defendant's testimony would have to prove to the judge that they did not commit the violation they were cited for. No attempt to shout, "Olly, olly, oxen, free, free, free," on a guilty verdict could be successful by diverting the court's attention to the actions of others. Each defendant has to stand before the court based on their own deeds.

The above verse in Revelation 20 talks about the future judgment of mankind before God. On that day, those present will be judged "*according to what **they** have done.*" The actions of others, good or bad, will not be considered as they stand alone before the throne of God.

But there will be some who will not be present at this final judgment in spite of their individual guilt. They will be just as responsible for their actions in this life as those who are documented in the above verse. The only difference will be that their sin will be forgiven through their faith in Jesus Christ.

In traffic court, I saw many judges cancel tickets, reduce fines, and otherwise absolve defendants in what they referred to as in the interest of justice. Other than evidence of innocence, it was the only way you could be released from your debt. In the final judgment, there will be only one way to escape eternal punishment. Since no one's innocence will be in question, they will need a mediator, the one who will stand before God, to agree with their guilt but cancel the punishment due them and expunge their record. First Timothy 2:5 tells us, "*For there is one God and one mediator between God and men, the Man Christ Jesus.*"

Thought for the Day

Who will stand up for you when you have your day in court?

DAY 324

*Then they will see the Son of Man coming in
the clouds with great power and glory.*

—Mark 13:26

Cumulus Return

I have a friend who recently wrote in a Facebook post, "It was a beautiful day, without a cloud in the sky!" I don't get that, why is a cloudless sky so beautiful? I love clouds! You know, the great big snow-white cumulus clouds that hang majestically as far as the eye can see. The kind that brings no rain, but becomes food for your imagination as you create all kinds of animals, faces, and structures by using their irregular shapes. Some of my best memories as a child were when I used to lie on my back in my parents' front yard and stare at those magnificent billowing clouds. I guess, to each his own.

Another reason I love clouds is found in the above verse in Mark. When I see a cloudy sky, I imagine that it will be a day like that, when we come back with our Lord to this earth. It is then He will set up His kingdom and make all things right. I look forward to fulfilling one of my childhood fantasies of what it would be like to be able to fly through those clouds. It's what I think about every time I am in a plane as it passes through the cloud layer before landing.

No matter which way our culture attempts to turn us or the plans that some may have for this world, one thing is certain, Jesus is coming again to judge and to make all things right. At that time, the laws and opinions of man will fall silent. I choose to bow now, and bow often, to the unchanging will and word of the one eternal God. I plan to get as much practice as I can for that final day when "*every knee shall bow and every tongue will confess that Jesus Christ is Lord"* (Philippians 2:10–11).

Thought for the Day

Look forward to that cumulus return.

DAY 325

But God commendeth his love toward us, in that,
while we were yet sinners, Christ died for us.

—Romans 5:8

Two Drinks

As part of the investigative FSEs (field sobriety exams), I would always ask the suspect how many drinks of alcohol they had consumed that night. They usually gave one of two answers to that question. They would either say, "None," or give the most frequent response of "Two drinks." From their red and watery eyes, slurred speech, and unsteady body motions, I suspected that those answers were not true. Either they had a strange physical condition that caused them to sway as they stood and smelled strongly of alcohol, or the "two drinks" they consumed were in containers that had wooden sides and were held together with metal bands (i.e., a barrel). Either way, the truth came out when I conducted the FSE and completed a blood or breath test.

God knows the complete truth about all of us. There is nothing that we can confess to Him that He will be shocked to hear. But the amazing thing is that He loves us anyway.

The above verse in Romans states that Christ died for us when He already knew we were sinners. We don't have to clean ourselves up first in order to gain God's love and forgiveness, because that work has already been done. We also can't lie about our faults or fool Him about our past. All He requires is that we honestly confess our sin, turn from it, and give the control of our lives to Him. This doesn't mean that we are promising to never sin again. God knows that is impossible for us as human beings. He is only asking us to commit ourselves to following His word and admit to Him our mistakes as they come.

Thought for the Day

Don't look God in the eye and say that we have not sinned. Let's confess Him as Lord and let Him forgive us now.

DAY 326

This vision is for a future time. It describes the end, and it will be fulfilled. If it seems slow in coming, wait patiently, for it will surely take place. It will not be delayed.

—Habakkuk 2:3

Future Certainty

The movie documentary *Steve McQueen: American Icon* was released in 2017 as a planned one-night-only Fathom event that was shown in over eight hundred theaters across the country. It was so well received that two more showing dates were scheduled. The film chronicled Steve's difficult childhood, his rise to Hollywood stardom, and his ultimate death at age fifty from a rare form of cancer.

The movie faithfully depicted Steve McQueen's fame, relationships, as well as the disillusion he felt after he had received stardom. Steve's earthly life came to an end on November 7, 1980, but his eternal life started on the same day, due to a decision he made a short time before his death. Steve McQueen accepted Jesus Christ as his Lord and Savior months before being diagnosed with mesothelioma. He stated that his one regret was that he was not able to tell others about his newfound faith. This movie has allowed him to do so thirty-seven years later. I don't know if those in heaven can see all the activities here on this earth, but I hope that God will let Mr. McQueen know that some of the angels he hears rejoicing at the repentance of even one person (Luke 15:10) will be because of the movie about his life. He finally got his wish to tell others about his faith.

God's timing can be a great mystery to me. If I were in charge, I would do things at a different pace and in a different order. Of course, I have learned the folly of that way of thinking over the years as I have seen that my way, my order, and my timing can end in disaster. God's word says that He knows the end from the beginning (Isaiah 46:10), and every decision He makes is perfect. The above verse in Habakkuk tells us that our part in God's decision-making process is to "wait patiently!"

I am sure that those Christians who knew about Steve McQueen's new faith wondered why his death was so close to his conversion. In the documentary, Steve himself wondered the same thing, as recorded in an interview near the end of his life. I don't know the complete answer to that, but the impact of the recent *American Icon* movie might add some sense for his deferred testimony.

Thought for the Day

If you have been waiting for something to happen in your life, know this, God's timing and provision are always perfect. "*Wait patiently, for it will surely take place. It will not be delayed.*"

DAY 327

Then he said to him, "Thus says the LORD: 'Because you have sent messengers to inquire of Baal-Zebub, the god of Ek'ron, is it because there is no God in Israel to inquire of His word? Therefore you shall not come down from your bed to which you have gone up, but you shall surely die.'"

—2 Kings 1:16

No God Available?

One of the most maddening things I had to deal with as a police officer were people talking on their cell phones. I would get called to a scene only to find the victim on their cell phone talking to someone else about what had just happened. I had bank employees who had been robbed talking about the crime with their corporate managers in another state, people who had been in a traffic collision telling a friend about what had just happened, and victims of assault lamenting their condition to a relative.

As sympathetic as the person on the other end of the call could be, there was not much they could really do for them at that moment, especially compared to the uniformed police officer who was standing right there! It would have been more helpful if they would talk to me so that I could broadcast a suspect description, stolen car info, or record their property loss. Did they think there was no one there who could help them or answer their questions? I even had to threaten to leave the scene in order to get some victims off the phone.

The above passage records the stupidity of King Ahaziah of Israel. Earlier in the chapter we learned that he *"did evil in the sight of the LORD"* and *"served Baal and worshiped him."* So, it should come as no surprise that when he fell and seriously hurt himself, he sent messengers to the servants of a false god to inquire if he would recover from his injuries. The prophet Elijah was informed by an angel what was going on, and he stopped the messengers before they reached the pagan temple. Elijah was eventually brought before the king where he asked the monarch the above question contained in our verse for the day. He wanted to know why the king had sent messengers to the false god Baal-Zebub and asked, "*Is it because there is no God in Israel to inquire of His word?*" Imagine, the king of Israel did not think to ask the God of Israel for help. Well, he didn't get any help, and he died just as Elijah had prophesied.

Where should we go when we are in trouble and need direction? To our friends, a horoscope, or the latest self-help book? God should always be our first choice. Sometimes we might be lulled into believing that we can only go to God with the big issues of life. But answer me this, aren't all the issues we face small to God? When we use other sources for help or choose not to go to God at all, thinking we can handle the issue ourselves, we run the risk of God allowing us to do just that, handle it on our own. King Ahaziah sought information and help from the wrong source. He paid for that action with his life.

Thought for the Day

Go to God first and often. He wants to be involved in everything you do, and He is always available.

DAY 328

All have sinned and fall short of the glory of God.

—Romans 3:23

Lost Gun

When I was a rookie cop, I had gone to the station for a meeting and had to use the upstairs restroom in the administration area. As I went into one of the stalls, I was surprised to find a loaded semiauto handgun on the floor next to the toilet. It had obviously been inadvertently left there by another officer while he was using the facilities. I picked up the gun, wrote down its serial number, and started to walk to the Records Section in an attempt to match that number to its rightful owner before a supervisor discovered the incident. At that time at our department, leaving a weapon unattended like that would most likely result in a suspension without pay.

While en route to the Records Section, I was met by a panicked-looking fellow officer who I immediately knew must be the owner of the gun. I held out the weapon and asked, "Are you looking for this?" The relief on his face was priceless, as he thanked me over and over for my discretion and the return of the handgun. Knowledge of the incident went no further than the two of us, and he went on in the years to come to be a great officer who was promoted several times.

The Bible refers to the mistakes that we have made in our lives as sins. Romans 3:23 tells us that, "*all have sinned and fall short of the glory of God.*" And in Romans 6:23, we read that, "*For the wages of sin is death; but the gift of God is eternal life through Jesus Christ our Lord.*" So, the great message of the gospel is "*that if you confess with your mouth the Lord Jesus Christ and believe in your heart that God has raised Him from the dead, you will be saved*" (Romans 10:9).

If we accept the living Jesus Christ as the Lord of our lives, we can be forgiven for our sins and given eternal life. And the news gets even better! First John 1:9 says that "*if we confess our sins, he is faithful and just to forgive us our sins and to cleanse us from all unrighteousness.*" So, this forgiveness is not a one-time event. We can continue to receive that forgiveness as we work our way through life. All we must do is ask for it.

Thought for the Day

Jesus Christ has found what we have lost and paid the price for it by His death on the cross!

DAY 329

*But without faith it is impossible to please Him, for he
who comes to God must believe that He is, and that He
is a rewarder of those who diligently seek Him.*

—Hebrews 11:6

*"But why do you call Me 'Lord, Lord,' and
not do the things which I say?*

—Luke 6:46

Two-Sided Coin

The need for a Miranda warning (reading a suspect their legal rights) has two requirements. The person must be both under arrest and under interrogation. If both of these things are not happening at the time of the contact, no Miranda warning is required.

Our Christian lives have a similar double obligation. Two things must be happening at the same time in order to please God. First, Hebrews 11:6 tells us that without faith, it is impossible to please God. Not harder or unlikely, but IMPOSSIBLE! This doesn't mean that if we ever fail in this area, God is completely unpleased with us. We will all dip under the surface of doubt and fear at times. But if we are not living a life that shows some consistency of faith, we are not pleasing God. We are in a sense telling Him, "My issues are too big Lord, too big for You to handle." Secondly, if we want to please God, we will do what He says! In our above verse in Luke, Jesus Himself asks that question. *"If I am really your Lord, why won't you obey Me."* You see, it is kind of hard to answer that question in any other way than "I'm sorry, yes, Lord."

So, the believer has to work on two things at once in order to please God. We must develop and demonstrate our faith in God by trusting Him in all areas of our lives, and we must do what He says. We can have all the faith in the world, and it will be for naught if we don't obey God. We can also obey God to the letter but have no faith in His promises to us. It takes an effort toward both to truly please Him, an effort, but not a complete success. We won't have that kind of perfection until we see Him face-to-face. But for now, we must work, stumble, ask for forgiveness, get up, and repeat.

Thought for the Day

Pleasing God is like a two-sided coin that requires both heads and tails to be successful.

DAY 330

That which was from the beginning, which we have heard,
which we have seen with our eyes, which we have looked upon,
and our hands have handled, concerning the Word of life.

—1 John 1:1

No Hearsay

We often talk about the inadmissibility of hearsay evidence in a legal proceeding. The court will not allow a witness to testify about things that they themselves did not see or hear. In other words, a witness cannot testify to something that someone else said they heard or what was told to them. The feeling of the court is that all testimony in a criminal trial should be firsthand "best evidence" accounts.

The writer of 1 John was an original disciple of Jesus. He walked, talked, ate, and lived with our Lord. John saw the miracles that Christ performed, he heard his words of instruction and compassion to others and was present at His crucifixion. John was there! He didn't write about things that he heard someone else say, or that were passed down from generation to generation over hundreds of years. John gives us "best evidence" accounts to things he saw, heard, and handled when he was with Jesus.

I think that sometimes we get lulled into thinking that the Bible is a compilation of great stories that God just wants us to know. It is much more than that. The Bible is the inspired word of God that contains many firsthand accounts from those who lived with Jesus, heard His words, and, in many cases, died for their belief in His Lordship.

Thought for the Day

God calls on us to follow His commandments as they are documented in scripture. Isn't it great to know that we can count on the Bible to be an accurate "best evidence" account of God's words to us!

DAY 331

Therefore we also, since we are surrounded by so great a cloud of witnesses, let us lay aside every weight, and the sin which so easily ensnares us, and let us run with endurance the race that is set before us.

—Hebrews 12:1

The Race

When I was a younger officer working nights on the Peninsula, I was often involved in foot pursuits. Being a gravitationally challenged ex–offensive lineman was never a help to me as I attempted to catch twenty-year-old barefoot surfer types in board shorts. The equipment I was required to carry also weighed me down to the point where it became a true victory for me, and a real embarrassment for them, when I caught anyone.

The apostle Paul often referred to living the Christian life as a race. He warned us that sin can weigh us down and ensnare us as we attempt to run toward God's plan. We are to "lay aside" any sin in our lives that can slow us down. It would have been great if the suspects I attempted to contact waited until I took off my Sam Brown and bulletproof vest before they started to run. I think my "catch rate" over the years would have been much better.

Every day, we can choose to follow Him or not. What we need to do is admit our sin, lay it down, and move forward in our race without it. God will always be there to forgive us and give us a fresh start no matter how many times we fall.

Thought for the Day

Let's take off the duty gear, put on our spiritual running shorts, and finish the race with endurance.

DAY 332

Only I can tell the future before it even happens.
Everything I plan will come to pass.

—Isaiah 46:10

Future Telling

As police officers, we spent a lot of our time trying to determine the future. As a defensive tactics instructor, it was my job to prepare officers for the possible use of force situations that might come their way. Much of our training centered around "worse case" scenarios and were based on past recorded incidents where officers lost their lives. Our hope was to learn from others' mistakes so that they would not be repeated or copy good examples so that we could do the same in similar situations. Either way, we were thinking of the possibilities of future events.

Whenever we make plans for the future, whether they are financial, relational, or health related, we are attempting to predict what might be, and prepare for it. We save and invest our money, we look for a mate to share our lives with, and we take medication to reduce the chance of physical illnesses. All of these are current actions that attempt to reduce the possible ill effects of an unknown future.

But the truth is that despite our best efforts, we cannot predict the uncertain. The above verse in Isaiah tells us that God is not restrained by human limitation of the unknown. He can tell us with complete accuracy about things that have not happened yet, and He is never wrong. We have countless examples in God's word where He gave the prophets insight into things that would happen. Those prophecies have either already occurred or will in the future.

Our inability to know what's in store for us can be frightening as limited human beings. But if we trust in God's ability to define and guide our future, we can never go wrong. I might not know what is next, but I am glad that I serve a God who does.

Thought for the Day

God knows the future before it happens, and His plans will always come to pass!

DAY 333

This is my commandment, that ye love one another, as I have loved you.
—John 15:12

Love in Action

As police officers, we were forced to give people a lot of commands. These orders range from something as simple as "please move along" to "put your hands behind your back" just before an arrest. Most of the commands we gave were not well received, and I am sure that those we were dealing with did not want to obey our direction. They cooperated, most of the time, because we had the authority to make them comply and could use force if necessary.

In the above verse in John, Jesus commands us to love one another as He has loved us. So, is Jesus saying that we have to feel warm and fuzzy about everyone? In 1 Corinthians 13, we read the most famous definition of love found in the Bible. The passage tells us that love is patient, kind, not jealous, boastful, or proud, does not demand its own way, keeps no record of wrong, and does not rejoice in injustice. The interesting thing about these conditions which define love is that they all can be seen as actions, not feelings. We can choose to be kind, patient, and just, even if we do not really want to. When Jesus calls us to love, He is asking for our obedience whether we feel like it or not. That is the only way it would be possible for us to "*love our enemies,*" which is another commandment that Jesus gave us in Mathew 5:44. He is not asking us to feel good about those who persecute us, but to show them the actions of love that seem to be in direct opposition to their behaviors. This is no easy task, but God's word says that "*I can do all things through Christ who strengthens me.*" (Philippians 4:13).

The good news is that we can show love to others without the difficult duty of feeling love for their actions. This can work in relationships when a husband or wife states, "I don't feel anything for him/her anymore." That's okay, love them anyway by your actions. When a person is being persecuted at work by a jealous fellow employee, love them in spite of their conduct toward you by how you treat them. There is no excuse for the Christian not to love others, no matter the circumstance. It is simple obedience to God.

Thought for the Day

You don't have to feel anything to put love in action according to God's word.

DAY 334

For a person who keeps all the laws except one is as guilty
as a person who has broken all of God's laws.

—James 2:10

No Innocent Bystanders

The responsibility for some crimes can spread further than one might think. In law enforcement, we often see cases where a suspect who did not actually commit the physical crime can be found equally guilty by their simple association, knowledge, and actions in the event. A case in point is the robbery getaway car driver. This suspect can be outside of a bank waiting for his partners in crime to exit the location so that he can speed them away from the area. He is there with the full knowledge that those inside are armed and will use force to accomplish their criminal goal. He may believe that they had no intention of killing anyone in the course of the crime, but things don't always go as planned. If a guard or brave citizen tries to intervene and stop the robbery and are killed in the process, all those involved in the commission of that crime are equally guilty of that murder under the law. The defense "I didn't know they were going to do it" does not work, and the getaway driver can be found just as guilty of the murder as the one who pulled the trigger. He may only be the driver, but he is responsible for all the laws broken that day.

The above verse in James tells us of our predicament under God's law. We might not have committed the level, or amount of sins as someone else, but that doesn't matter. If we break one law, we are just as guilty as someone who has broken many.

The Bible says that "*all have sinned and come short of the glory of God*" (Romans 3:23), and that the punishment for that sin is physical and spiritual death (Romans 6:23a). God understood our dilemma, and that is why He came to earth in the form of the man, Jesus Christ, to die for that sin. By accepting His payment on the cross for our imperfection, we can be forgiven for whatever severity of wrong we have committed. I think this is the greatest news for those who feel they have gone too far for God to forgive them. That is not possible. God can wipe your slate clean through Jesus's sacrifice on the cross for you, regardless of the sin, or length of time it has been a part of your life.

Thought for the Day

It doesn't matter if you are sitting in sin's car watching other's actions against God or are actively involved in those actions, there is no level of sin He can't forgive.

DAY 335

For the good that I will do, I do not do; but the
evil I will not to do, that I practice.

—Romans 7:19

Stand in Line

You might think that the above verse in Romans was written in the generic voice for all mankind. I know it would be true of me because I often fail to do God's will. But the above verse was actually written by the apostle Paul who was arguably one of the most spiritual men of all time. Much of God's revealed word to us was written by this man under the inspiration of the Holy Spirit, and in those writings, we find some of the greatest truths in the Bible about God's grace, forgiveness, and mercy. Yet from this passage, we find that even Paul struggled with his Christian walk that led him to conclude in verse 24 of the same chapter, "*O wretched man that I am.*"

Now I know what you are probably thinking, "Yeah, right, I'm sure that those failings that Paul talked about were things like not praying a hundred times a day, reading the scripture for twenty-three straight hours, or for failing to give every cent he made as a tent maker to the work of the church." You might say, "I'm sure that his worst failings were far better than the Christian goals that I have for myself." I want to float an idea by you. Maybe Paul really did struggle and fail with the exact same temptations that we do. Yet God was able to use him in a great way for His glory.

In Hebrews 4:15, we read, "*For we have not a high priest which cannot be touched with the feeling of our infirmities; But was in all points tempted like as we are, yet without sin.*" The definition of "all points tempted" means exactly what it says, "all points tempted." If our Lord Jesus Christ was tempted by all things in the exact same way that we are, we can be encouraged that He knows exactly what we are going through. The only difference is that Jesus never sinned due to that temptation. That puts you and I, the apostle Paul, and any other person you know in the same company of imperfect sinners.

Thought for the Day

If God only used perfect people for his work, there would be no one able to stand in the line for His service. If He used Paul, He can definitely use you and me!

DAY 336

Dear friends, let us continue to love one another, for love comes from God. Anyone who loves is a child of God and knows God. But anyone who does not love does not know God, for God is love.

—1 John 4:7–8

Love Test

Anyone I arrested for DUI was required to take a test to determine their blood alcohol content. If alcohol were suspected as the inebriating agent, they could choose between a blood test or a breath test. If I suspected that some sort of drug was on board, they had one choice, blood, because drugs did not show up on a breath test.

I always liked it when they chose a blood test because it would be administered by a technician whom I called to the jail. The breath test was also very accurate, and I administered that myself. Either way, I was able to obtain a blood alcohol/drug content reading to be used in the upcoming court proceedings. These were accurate scientific tests that could verify the intoxication level of the person I had arrested, and confirm that the determination I had made in the field was true.

The above verse in John tells us one of the tests we can use to verify if a stated Christian is a true believer in Jesus Christ. It is our love for others that confirms the truth of our faith. This verse makes it very clear when it declares, *"Anyone who loves is a child of God and knows God. But anyone who does not love does not know God, for God is love."* I have seen many religious groups who claim to know God but show hatred and disdain for the lost people of this world. God does not allow me to be the judge of who is saved or not, but from the above verse in 1 John, I could have a reasonable doubt.

I felt privileged to have served at a church that placed such an emphasis on bringing people to a personal relationship with Jesus Christ. Our concern for the eternal destination of others demonstrated that kind of love that John wrote about. In addition to a person's salvation, we also place great emphasis on our attenders' spiritual development, as well as counseling, in the event things got off track. All these things showed our love for the seekers, the lost, and the hurting of this world. I was thankful to be a part of that.

Thought for the Day

Is a love for others coursing in your blood, and is it a part of every breath you take? What are your love test results? Are you guilty of loving others? This is one time where innocence would be a conviction in your life.

DAY 337

Behold, I stand at the door and knock. If anyone
hears My voice and opens the door, I will come in to
him and dine with him, and he with Me.

—Revelation 3:20

The Recruiter

As a high school football player, I had a problem that kept me from being recruited by Division 1 schools, I didn't weigh enough. At six feet and two inches, 220 pounds, I was a little light for an offensive lineman, even in the mid-1970s when I played. I went to Orange Coast Community College with the intent to gain some experience and grow. I had two great seasons at OCC, I was part of the national championship team, and I grew! After my sophomore year, I was about 245 pounds which seemed to be just big enough for Division 1 schools to take notice of me. I was recruited by Stanford, Cal Berkley, and Arizona State, and I was just happy for the opportunity to get a scholarship and play in the newly expanded Pacific 10 Conference.

One day, as I walked past the head coach's office, he asked me to step inside. Seated with him was a man I had never met. I had grown tired of the recruiting grind by that time, and I was weary of telling the lower-level college coaches that I only wanted to play in the PAC 10. Before I could say hello, the man introduced himself as the offensive line coach for the University of Southern California. He then held up his right hand, exposed a large gold Rose Bowl championship ring, and said to me, "Do you want one of these?" To say that his tactic was merely effective is a little like calling a tidal wave moist! With those few words, he caused two years of recruiting efforts by some fine universities to be immediately nullified. I went to USC, and I was not disappointed. I received three rings over the next few seasons, one of which was for membership on the 1978 national championship team.

Jesus is holding out his hand to you today with an offer far greater than a football scholarship or a gold ring. He wants to give you a plan and a purpose in this life as well as an eternity with Him when this life has ended. The best news is that you don't have to get any bigger or better to receive this gift. He wants to give it to you just the way you are.

God knew that there was nothing we could do to earn this heavenly full ride. That is why He came to the earth in human form and paid the price for our sin by His death on the cross. If you will open the door and give Him the control of your life, you will become a member of the universe's championship team. He is holding out a gold crown to you today and asking:

Thought for the Day

"Do you want one of these?"

DAY 338

There is a way that seems right to man, but its end is the way of death.
—Proverbs 16:25

Standing in the Rain

One day I was working on the Balboa Peninsula in the rain. There had just been an accident that completely blocked a small one-way street in front of the Fun Zone. I had been requested to the scene to assist responding patrol units with traffic control. My job was to divert all westbound vehicles so that drivers would not be exposed to debris, fluids and other hazardous materials that were spread across the entire roadway. As I stood at my post in the middle of the street, it began to rain heavily, and I started to put on my raincoat. At that time, a citizen passed by and said, "Well, that's not too smart, why don't you come over here to put that on," as he motioned to an awning that was keeping him dry during the thunder burst.

As police officers, we just love those kinds of "helpful" remarks that are made by citizens who don't have a clue about our job. I did not move or respond to the man's suggestion as I continued to put on my coat. I didn't have time to explain to him that if I were to leave my post in the middle of the street, a vehicle might pass by that I would be unable to stop, thus exposing the driver to potential danger down the road. He was just thinking of what he would do in his own best interest if he were me and was not considering the bigger picture of the situation at hand.

As human beings, we all have ideas as to what would be best for ourselves and others. Usually those opinions are based on our own limited knowledge. We just don't have the capability of seeing the big picture of our future.

I've often wondered what God was up to regarding certain occurrences in my life. It wasn't until much later that I realized He had saved me from dangerous situations by His directing me away from what seemed to me a good decision at the time.

Thought for the Day

God's word contains all the wisdom we need to navigate our lives. Look to Him, He loves you, and will always direct you toward the best thing for you.

DAY 339

*"But of that day and hour no one knows, not even
the angels of heaven, but My Father only.*
—Matthew 24:36

No One Knows

I recently read an article about some of the most famous end-of-the-world predictions made throughout history. In 1524, London astrologers predicted that world-ending floods would occur on February 1 of that year due to an unusual planet alignment. Tens of thousands of people moved to high ground, and some even built arks. In 1910, newspapers sparked widespread panic with supposedly scientific articles which claimed the poisonous gas tail from Halley's Comet would kill the earth's inhabitants.

In 1936, Herbert W. Armstrong told the members of his church, the Worldwide Church of God, that Christ was coming back that year and that they would be the only ones saved. Some sold their homes and liquidated their assets, believing this would happen. After it did not, he changed the date three more times before giving up on his predictions. In 1974, some astrophysicists claimed that the world would be destroyed by massive earthquakes due to the gravitational pull caused by an unusual planet alignment. They named the pending catastrophe the Jupiter Effect. And most recently, some claimed that on December 7, 2012, the world would come to an end according to the ancient Mayan calendar. All of these predictions had one thing in common, THEY DIDN'T HAPPEN!

I can usually count on one thing in life. If someone makes a prediction regarding the end of the world and gives a specific date, that day is safe.

God's word is clear on the matter. "NO ONE KNOWS the day or the hour when these things will happen." Having said that, recent events in the Middle East seem to point to an imminent return of our Lord. But then again, He could decide to wait another thousand years.

The Lord wants us to live as though He was coming tomorrow but plan as though His return is far into the future. In Luke, Jesus told a parable in which the nobleman stated to his servants, "*Occupy until I come*." That is the same thing Jesus tells us to do, to remain active, engaged, and about God's business until He comes again.

Thought for the Day

I have a prediction, Jesus is coming! I do not know when that will be, but all that really matters is that He knows.

DAY 340

But to the Son He says: Your throne, O God, is forever and ever;
A scepter of righteousness is the scepter of Your kingdom.
—Hebrews 1:8

The "Same As" Game

When my daughters were young, I used to walk them home from their elementary school which was located near our home. To pass the time as we walked, we would play the "same as" game. I would say a word, and they would give me another word that had the same meaning. When they had mastered that, we moved on to the "opposite as" game. They were smart, and it wasn't long before they had mastered the meanings and subtleties of both synonyms and antonyms.

If you have read many of my devotionals, you will find that I often speak of God the Father and Jesus Christ as interchangeable identities. The Bible has a lot to say about these two personages of the trinity. The above verse in Hebrews tells us who God says that Jesus is. He says of Him, "*Your throne, O <u>God</u>, is forever and ever; A scepter of righteousness is the scepter of Your kingdom.*" It has been said that Jesus is God with skin on. He is more than a good man who lived a good life as an example for us. He is God the Father, the creator of the universe who took on the form of a human being and suffered and died for us. Philippians 2:8 says, "*And being found in appearance as a man, He humbled Himself and became obedient to the point of death, even the death of the cross.*"

It is comforting for me to know that God is not some lofty being who is "out there" somewhere and who has a difficult time relating to our lives. He lived and died as a human being, rose from the dead, and has firsthand knowledge about everything that we are going through.

Thought for the Day

God the Father and Jesus Christ are synonyms in the universe's "same as" game.

DAY 341

For now we see in a mirror, dimly,
but then face to face. Now I know in part,
but then I shall know just as I also am known.
—1 Corinthians 13:12

Starstruck

In 1978, I was a member of the football team at the University of Southern California. The team was staying at a Los Angeles area hotel in preparation for a game at the Memorial Coliseum. I was in an elevator with a teammate of mine, and we were traveling down to the lobby to meet the other players before leaving the hotel on the team bus. The elevator stopped on our way down to pick up a guest on a lower floor. As the doors opened, I was stunned to find myself face-to-face with boxing legend Muhammad Ali. Ali had just lost his heavyweight championship title several months earlier in an incredible upset to Leon Spinks.

When Mr. Ali saw my teammate, he stepped back in surprise and said in a loud voice, "Man, I thought you were Spinks!" I looked at my teammate and had to laugh when I realized that he did look a lot like Leon Spinks, missing front tooth and all! I'm not usually very starstruck, but that one took me by surprise. The champ rode down to the lobby with us and was very gracious as he answered the questions posed to him by a large crowd of my fellow teammates who had gathered there.

Someday, we will see Jesus face-to-face. I cannot imagine what that day will be like. The group Mercy Me says it best with the lyrics of their song "I Can Only Imagine."

> I can only imagine what my eyes will see when your face is before me.
> Surrounded by your glory what will my heart feel.
> Will I dance for You Jesus or in awe of You be still.
> Will I stand in your presence or to my knees will I fall.
> Will I sing hallelujah, will I be able to speak at all.

Thought for the Day

Someday, maybe someday very soon, that question will be answered for all those who have put their faith in Jesus Christ. What an incredible day that will be when we finally see Him face-to-face.

DAY 342

*But seek ye first the kingdom of God and His righteousness
and all these things will be added unto you.*
—Matthew 6:33

Swept Along

I grew up in Costa Mesa, California, which is located a short distance from the ocean. As a teenager, I went bodysurfing at the beach on a regular basis. I was never a great swimmer, but I did learn how sets work, how to avoid getting pounded by the waves, and how to swim around riptides.

One thing that always amazed me about the ocean was its currents. I would go straight out from where my towel was located (usually next to the Fifty-Second Street lifeguard tower in Newport Beach) and attempt to catch some waves. When I got tired and came in, I was always at least one hundred yards west of the position on the beach where I had originally started. I had been quickly moved along by the ocean currents and was unaware of it.

As we strive to seek God's will for us, we can sometimes get discouraged by what we feel is a lack of movement in our spiritual lives. We are doing the right things, reading, and obeying His word, fellowshipping at church, serving, telling others about our faith. Yet it seems that we see no movement toward that ministry goal that we have been so earnestly seeking God's will about. It might be possible that He has another unrelated plan for you, or it might be that the Lord has been moving you toward your goal all along in such a way that you are unaware of the motion!

Spiritual growth, just like physical growth, educational growth, and emotional growth, is not without effort and discomfort. I have always wanted to just "arrive" in all of those areas in my life, but that never happened. Take heart, you are not alone. And the truth is that you could be making more progress than you think! You just might look up one day to see you have been moved along by God's spiritual current to a place beyond where you thought you would be.

So, keep on doing the right things in your spiritual life. Galatians 6:9 tells us, "*And let us not grow weary while doing good, for in due season we shall reap if we do not lose heart.*"

Thought for the Day

You might be almost ready to exit God's spiritual current to a place where He can use you. A place where you always hoped you would arrive. Don't give up!

DAY 343

Vengeance is Mine, and recompense; Their foot shall
slip in due time; For the day of their calamity is at
hand, And the things to come hasten upon them.
                                        —Deuteronomy 32:35

No One Would Blame Him

When I was teaching criminal justice in a local undergraduate program, I had a student who was a bailiff in the court system. He was working in the courtroom during a famous murder trial that was conducted in our area. Part of the evidence presented were video tapes that the defendant had made when he raped, tortured, and killed multiple victims. Listening to and watching those tapes were excruciatingly hard for the families of the victims, the jurors, and employees of the court. My student told me that at one point he actually thought, *If I pull out my gun now and shoot this guy in the head, no one here would blame me.* Of course, he did not do that, and he acted as any law enforcement professional would in such a difficult situation. The defendant was eventually found guilty on numerous counts of murder and was sentenced to death.

You may feel that you have been wronged in this life and that you are justified in seeking revenge for that wrong. You are probably justified in those feelings, but God calls on us to give up that right to revenge and to let Him handle both the perpetrator and the punishment.

Many families of victims have said that they did not get the full sense of satisfaction that they thought they would when the defendant was found guilty. God knows the way we work, and that anger, bitterness, and vengeance will end up hurting us more than the targets of those feelings. Some criminals are able to remotely attack people over and over again simply because of the victim's unwillingness to let God handle the situation.

If you have been wronged, listen to God's promise made in the above verse in Deuteronomy. God knows the truth of what happened, and the day of their comeuppance is at hand, He will take care of it.

Thought for the Day

Do not become a defendant by attempting to solve the problem your way. Let God handle that for you.

DAY 344

The devil, who deceived them, was cast into the lake of fire and brimstone where the beast and the false prophet are. And they will be tormented day and night forever and ever.
—Revelation 20:10

The Sentence

One afternoon several years ago, I responded to a traffic subpoena at the courthouse with a number of other uniformed police officers. The room that we were assigned was different from the usual traffic court and had a very small public seating area. The defendants were also directed there and had quickly filled up the gallery. The only seating available for the officers was in the jury box. After several minutes, the judge came into the courtroom to start the traffic trials. As he took the bench, he looked up to see the jury box filled with armed uniformed police officers. The judge then said in a loud-enough voice for all the court to hear, "Wouldn't that be nice!" He could only dream of the swift and just outcomes of every trial with us as the jury.

God sees the future with greater clarity than we can see the present or the past. The above verse in Revelation tells us about the ultimate destination of our adversary Satan. This isn't what may happen, it is what will happen.

We see so much evil that sometimes we may start to believe that Satan has control of this earth. **He does not!** Jesus, through His death on the cross, has redeemed this world from Satan and has the final word in all things. For this reason, the Devil's destination and eventual demise are certainties.

As we go about our daily lives with the struggles that will inevitably come our way, we can remember that through Christ, we can have victory because *"He who is within us is greater than he who is in the world"* (1 John 4:4). The jury is in, Satan has been found guilty, and his sentence has already been handed down.

Thought for the Day

We are just waiting for God's perfect timing when our adversary Satan will be taken into custody forever!

DAY 345

*"Do not remember the former things, nor consider the
things of old. Behold, I will do a new thing, now it shall
spring forth; shall you not know it? I will even make a
road in the wilderness and rivers in the desert.*
—Isaiah 43:18–19

Starting Over

One negative thing about working for a small police department
is the inability to escape bad past impressions. If you made
mistakes early on in your career, it is hard to shake the negative reputation that seems to follow you. I had things brought up in promotional reviews that had occurred a decade before. They never really
considered the fact that I might have changed and learned from my
mistakes over the years. Of course, there was no one to blame but
myself. I had everything to do with the creation of those bad impressions, even if they were no longer valid.

Large cities, on the other hand, have many divisions that are
like small departments unto themselves. If you have created a bad
impression in one division, you can switch to another within the city
and reinvent yourself. It is as if your past stupidity can be erased and
you are given a fresh career start.

Have you ever wanted a fresh start in life? The above verse in
Isaiah tells us that God specializes in do-overs for His people. He tells
us, *"Do not remember the former things, nor consider the things of old."*
God's command to simply, "stop it," in regard to remembering the
former things in our lives wouldn't be very encouraging if it were not
for what He says next. *"Behold, **I will do a new thing**, it shall spring*

forth; shall you not know it?" Not only are we urged to forget the past, but also God Himself tells us that He will be in charge of the new thing that He will bring into our lives! He then goes on to give two examples of what seemed difficult or even impossible in the ancient world, the creation of a new road in the wilderness, and a river in the desert. Notice, God does not say he will find us existing roads and rivers, He says, "I will make" new ones.

The same God who made the universe, this world, and everything in it can remake your life, career, and even your reputation. Our part in this process is found in my favorite verse, *"But seek ye first the kingdom of God and His righteousness, and all these things will be added unto you"* (Matthew 6:33). A fresh start is something we cannot make for ourselves, but God's word says, *"I can do all things through Christ who strengthens me"* (Philippians 4:13).

Thought for the Day

Do you want to start over? Forget the past, seek Him, and let God create new roads and rivers in your life.

DAY 346

*I, even I, am He who blots out your transgressions for
My own sake; And I will not remember your sins.*

—Isaiah 43:25

No Payback

Cops find very creative ways at getting back at other officers who have played practical jokes on them. After one of our bicycle officers unwittingly carried around a hidden twenty-pound weight in the gear bag attached to his bike (he was tired and didn't know why), we all knew that a special payback would be coming in the future.

Our victim officer found out that the perpetrator, his partner, had worked for a well-known national fast-food chain in his youth. Somehow, he was able to obtain some official-looking stationery that contained the corporate logo and address of the business. He then sent the offending officer a letter claiming that he had neglected to pick up dividends from stock he had unknowingly earned, twenty-five years prior, while working at the business. The letter said that the stock had doubled, tripled, and quadrupled in value over the last quarter century, and was now worth several thousand dollars. It was not an unbelievable amount of money, but enough to justify a drive to the Los Angeles corporate office to pick up the check. Before fighting traffic to get to LA, he even called ahead to get confirmation that the check would be waiting (I don't exactly know how that was accomplished). Of course, when he arrived, a letter was waiting for him that basically said, "Gotcha," and thus one of the best thought-out, well-executed pranks in Newport Beach Police Department history was realized.

We have all sinned against God and deserve to be paid back for our actions. The great news about the character of God is that He has no interest in getting even with us for what we have done. In fact, the Lord is ready to forgive us and completely forget our offenses. The above verse in Isaiah tells us that He blots out our sin for His own sake, because it means so much to Him to do it! And then He adds, "*I will not remember your sins.*" He forgives us and then acts as if we are doing Him a favor by letting Him do so! What a great God we serve!

If you are waiting for the other shoe to drop for God's revenge in your life, you are wasting your time. He loves you and wants to forgive you if you will just bow your knee to Him, confess Him as Lord, and ask for that forgiveness.

Thought for the Day

There is no payback awaiting those who surrender to Jesus Christ.

DAY 347

Draw near to God and He will draw near to you.

—James 4:8a

Stay Close

Whether it was in search of a suspect, in response to an alarm call, or as the result of an unsecured door, we were required to enter the location and search every room in the structure. That often took a long time due to the size of the residence or commercial building involved.

There were rules we followed when searching a location. We never went in alone, always announced ourselves before entering, had our guns drawn, and always stayed within sight of each other during the search. You can imagine it would be problematic to come around a corner with your gun drawn and be surprised by your partner who also had their gun out. You could say that we drew near to each other during a search for our own safety.

The above verse in James tells us of an unbelievable benefit for drawing near to God. He will, in turn, draw near to us! God is often depicted as an angry distant being who requires some sort of magical combination of works and praise before He will move on our behalf. But that is simply not the God of the Bible. If we want to get closer to God, all we must do is seek Him and make any simple attempt to do his will (i.e., draw near). He is then eager to meet us more than halfway.

Of course, the first step to developing a relationship with God is accepting Jesus as our Lord and Savior. John 3:16 tells us, "*For God so loved the world that He gave His only begotten Son, that whosoever* believes in Him shall not perish but have everlasting life. For He did not send His Son into the world to condemn the world, but that the world through Him might be saved." Only when we have accepted that free gift of salvation and have turned the control of our lives over to Jesus do we have the right and the ability to truly draw near to Him. From that point on, our feeble attempts to approach God will be met by His overwhelming grace and love, as the God of the universe rushes to meet us.

"The Lord is near to all who call upon Him, to all who call upon Him in truth" (Psalm 145:18).

Thought for the Day

God is the best partner you could ever have. Always keep Him in sight and draw near to Him through Jesus.

DAY 348

*Now faith is the substance of things hoped
for, the evidence of things not seen.*

—Hebrews 11:1

No Surface in Sight

One thing I remember vividly about scuba diving was the visibility of the water. Some days I could see for long distances underwater, while other days I had trouble recognizing things just a few feet away. While on a deep dive, there was always something I found a little unnerving. No matter how clear the water was, if I went deep enough, I was unable to see the surface when I looked up. That might not seem like much until you've experienced not having the surface as a frame of reference. To stare up into the undefined haze above you can be unsettling if you have not experienced it before. I was also aware that an emergency ascent (i.e., shooting straight to the surface if you ran out of air) would then not be possible without serious injury. Even though I could not see the surface, I had to have faith in my gauges as to the depth and in my training, despite the lack of evidence that I could see.

The Christian life is a lot like diving at depth. So often, our lives seem out of control with no evidence of a plan or purpose. Whether it is a health concern, financial situation, or an uncertain relationship, we can become fearful and panicked because we have no clear solution to our dilemma. And when we look up to our God, sometimes all we can see is an undefined haze as we wait for His answers and timing in our lives. If we don't rely on our training (God's word), we can panic and swim straight into that dimness, damaging our lives and relationship with Him.

The above verse in Hebrews accurately defines what faith really is. It is believing in something that we have no tangible proof of. The New Living Translation gives us some clarity in its paraphrase of the passage when it says, "*Faith is the confidence that what we hope for will actually happen; it gives us assurance about things we cannot see.*"

We cannot see the future, and we don't know the joys and difficulties that may lie ahead. But we do know that for the believer in Jesus Christ, God has a plan and purpose for our lives. We might not be able to see it, and we might not like or understand it, but we have faith that He is working for us anyway. Sometimes people have used the term "blind faith" in a derogatory sense, condemning an absolute trust that has no concrete evidence behind it. God is not asking us for blind faith, just faith that the undefinable things we can see, combined with God's past goodness in our lives, will work out for our benefit in the end.

> *And we know that God causes everything to work together for the good of those who love God and are called according to his purpose for them.*
> (Romans 8:28)

Thought for the Day

Sometimes it takes great faith to stand on that verse. Keep looking up. God will cause that haze to clear as He brings you closer to the surface of His will.

DAY 349

Then He said, "Go out, and stand on the mountain before the LORD."
And behold, the LORD passed by, and a great and strong wind tore
into the mountains and broke the rocks in pieces before the LORD, but
the LORD was not in the wind; and after the wind an earthquake, but
*the LORD was not in the earthquake; **12** and after the earthquake a*
fire, but the LORD was not in the fire; and after the fire a still small
voice. So it was, when Elijah heard it, that he wrapped his face in his
mantle and went out and stood in the entrance of the cave. Suddenly
a voice came to him, and said, "What are you doing here, Elijah?"
—1 Kings 19:11–13

The Speed of Sound

As police officers, we are often required to activate our overhead lights and siren due to emergency situations. These "code 3" runs can be extremely dangerous, and many officers have lost their lives in traffic collisions as they responded to those in need. The problem is one of sound travel. If we drive our units at speeds greater than seventy miles per hour, we can actually outrun the sound of our own siren. When we drive too fast, other motorists can enter the roadway and collide with our police vehicles before they have even heard the approaching sirens. The key is to drive at a regular speed and slow down significantly when you pass through intersections.

Fortunately for us, God will never enter our lives in a way that is too fast for us to hear His voice. But with work, family, and social obligations, we can often become overwhelmed by the noise and pace of our own lives. In the above passage, Elijah learned a valuable lesson about hearing God's voice. God sent him a great wind, an earthquake, and a fire, none of which contained His presence. It was God's "still small voice" that spoke to Elijah. Notice that when he heard God speak he went to the front of the cave and quietly "stood" before the Lord spoke with him further.

If we want to hear from God, we need to stop, stand still, and listen for His voice. Whether He communicates to us through His word or by the circumstances in our lives, we will never understand Him if we are moving so fast that our pace exceeds our ability to hear His voice. God loves us and wants nothing more than to communicate His desire to become the leader of our lives. All we need to do is slow down, listen, and give Him that chance.

Thought for the Day

Don't outrun the sound of God's guiding voice in your life.

DAY 350

*I am the light of the world. Whosoever follows me will
not walk in darkness, but will have the light of life.*

—John 8:12

The Torch

If you were to ask a civilian to identify a police officer's most important tool, the answer might surprise them. They may think it is our service weapon, handcuffs, or bulletproof vest. As important as those items are, any cop will tell you that we most often use our flashlights while on duty. If you were to inspect any night cop's torch, you would see that it is scraped, dented, and worn from constant use. It illuminates threats confronting us, uncovers evidence that we cannot see with our naked eyes, and lights our paths as we move through the darkness of night.

I think that our lives can often be compared to a zero dark thirty search without a flashlight. We can't see what's ahead of us and are constantly tripping over obstacles in our way. Fortunately, Jesus promises that if we follow Him, He will direct our paths and be our light in this world of uncertainty. Like all of Christ's promises to us, there is a condition. Proverbs 3:5–6 states, *"Trust in the Lord with all your heart, And lean not on your own understanding; In all your ways acknowledge Him, and He will direct your paths."* In order to obtain this never-ending light, we must turn the control of our lives over to God.

Never again will we need to experience that sinking feeling we get when our flashlight begins to dim just when we really need it. If we accept Jesus Christ as our Savior and Lord and give the control of our lives to Him, He will give us direction and purpose in this life as well as a place in eternity.

Thought for the Day

Jesus promises to shine a light on our lives and show us a safe path. He is a little like solar power only this "Son" never sets. Step into the light.

DAY 351

Be very careful, then, how you live—not as unwise but as wise,
making the most of every opportunity, because the days are evil.
Therefore do not be foolish but understand what the Lord's will is.
—Ephesians 5:15–17

Non-Programmable

I bought and installed a new thermostat in our home. The old one was working, but it was a programmable model that was very complicated to set. It had start times, stop times, day-of-the-week settings, and various other custom features. It was in our home when we bought it but didn't come with any instructions. We went online and was able to find the manual, but that didn't help. I am not an electronics numbskull, but for the life of me this thing was so complicated, I could not get it programmed. We ended up just pushing an override button which temporarily set the thermostat to whatever temperature we wanted it to be at any given time.

While at Home Depot, I saw a simple non-programmable thermostat that had a heating/off/cooling switch, and up and down arrows to adjust the temperature. Wow, back to the basics of letting our brains be the computer that controls the environment in our home!

Sometimes our lives become so busy and complicated that we can lose our way. With many demands that pull us in different directions, we can start to lose our sense of priorities. So many options seem good that we can't determine what is important from what is not. We can't do it all, and our lives get so overly scheduled that we end up giving ourselves over to the program and its automatic control.

The above verse in Ephesians 5 tells us to live wisely and make the most of every opening that God give us. We are to weigh our opportunities by laying them over the template of the Lord's will for us. If we do that, some of the extra things we focus on just might fall away as we learn that they were really not as important as we thought.

Thought for the Day

Let's get back to the basics and let God's will control the environment of our lives.

DAY 352

*Jesus spoke to the people once more and said, "I
have come into the world as light, so that whoever
believes in me may not remain in darkness."*

—John 12:46

Step into the Light

Several years ago, we moved back to Mission Viejo where we had
previously lived for sixteen years. We love the small place we
bought, but we were not pleased with one condition in the house.
There were no lights! Almost every room required floor lamps or
some other kind of portable illumination. We found that when the
sun went down, we gravitated toward the kitchen area that contained
the only ceiling light fixtures in the house.

A good friend of ours in the building industry lined us up with
a contractor who mounted the new LED canned ceiling lights in
almost every room. What a dramatic difference! We went from total
darkness to lights so bright that we needed dimmer switches installed
so that the fixtures did not blind us when we looked up. Living in the
light is so much better than wandering in the darkness.

In the above verse in John, Jesus said that He was the light of
the world. Until then, people were either stumbling around in the
darkness or relying on the dim flicker of future hope that was provided by adherence to the law of Moses. But when Jesus came, that
low level of illumination provided by the law, which was at best a
temporary patch job to man's problem of sin, exploded into a light
so brilliant that it was hard to stare directly at it. Through faith in
Jesus Christ, mankind never had to walk in spiritual darkness again

because the light that Jesus gave led to eternal life. Now, due to our faith in Jesus Christ, we can have our life in this world as well as the next brightly illuminated for us.

Thought for the Day

I don't like to stumble around in the dark. Flick on the switch of faith.

DAY 353

*For God bought you with a high price. So you
must honor God with your body.*

—1 Corinthians 6:20

No Return Item

I recently received a watch as a gift for my birthday. Having never worn anything above a Casio-type diver's watch, this new timepiece was pretty expensive, at least in my estimation. I was with my wife when she bought it, so I knew exactly how much it cost. When I got home, I noticed that the watch did not come with a user's manual, so I went online to find it. When I put in the model numbers, the information for several online companies came up who were selling the item for 50 percent less than I had just paid in the store! With my wife's endorsement, I returned it and purchased the same one online for a significant savings.

When we accept Christ as our Savior and Lord, we get the greatest gift we can ever imagine. Our sins are forgiven, we have a guaranteed eternity, and we receive a plan and a purpose in this life. Our "user's manual," the Bible, became activated for us when we turned our lives over to Jesus.

Now all the Bible's promises, wisdom, and cautions are ours to claim as it reveals light and truth for our lives. And the price of this great gift is free to us because it was paid in full through Christ's death on the cross and resurrection from that death for us. Now that is a great discount!

Thought for the Day

You will never have to return God's provision for your eternity. There is no place where you will find a better deal.

DAY 354

So I am writing to you not because you don't know the truth but because you know the difference between truth and lies.
—1 John 2:21

The Truth versus the Lie

As a police officer, one of the first things I had to learn was to determine who was lying to me. That was hard to do, considering that many people are good liars. Coming up with the truth of a statement became a function of the likelihood of their story, my past experience, some of the physical clues they gave off as they spoke, and the verification of their statement. I never became a 100 percent accurate lie detector, but I improved greatly as the years passed.

Just as difficult at times was to determine who was telling the truth! Believe it or not, some people are horrible truth tellers. They just look like they are lying even when they are not. Once again, determining the truth was about the story, my experience, physical clues, and verification.

John wrote the above verse when he was the pastor at the church in Ephesus in around AD 90. He was talking to the core members of his church. He knew they were true believers in Christ and that they had the ability to see the difference between a truth and a lie. Later in verse 27 of the same chapter, John stated, *"But you have received the Holy Spirit, and He lives within you."* The indwelling of the Holy Spirit is the promise of God when we accept Jesus Christ as our Lord and Savior. Ezekiel 36:27 prophesied of this promise when he wrote, *"I will put My Spirit within you and cause you to walk in My statutes, and you will be careful to observe My ordinances."*

Thought for the Day

The Holy Spirit is promised to comfort, exhort, and guide us to the truth. When He lives in us, we don't need to work so hard at telling the truth from a lie. He will be there to guide us in our lives if we seek Him.

DAY 355

The king's heart is in the hand of the Lord, Like the rivers of water; He turns it wherever He wishes.

—Proverbs 21:1

Still On the Throne

Every four years we go through a presidential election cycle which can be brutal. I love the recent quote by author Max Lucado where he wrote, "I have a prediction. I know exactly what November will bring. Another day of God's perfect sovereignty. He will still be in charge. His throne will still be occupied. He will still manage the affairs of the world." Amen to that!

The above verse in Proverbs tells us the same thing. No matter how powerful a leader might think they are, God turns them in whatever direction He wants them to go according to His will. They might think they are in charge, but they are wrong. God is still in control.

I don't always understand God's plan, but I do know one thing, He never phones to ask me, "Hey, Brad, I have an idea, is it okay if I run it past you?" He is God and I am not. We do know from God's word that things will get worse before He comes again, and that we have seen faith grow around the world in the harshest of ungodly environments. In fact, the worse the circumstances, the faster the message of salvation through Jesus Christ seems to spread. Maybe it is our turn in America to host that adverse fertile growing ground.

We can be thankful today; we are still free to worship God openly and thank Him for the many blessings in our lives.

Thought for the Day

God is in control!

DAY 356

*The man said, "The woman you put here with me—she
gave me some fruit from the tree, and I ate it." Then the
Lord God said to the woman, "What is this you have done?
The woman said, "The serpent deceived me, and I ate."*
—Genesis 3:12–13

Not My Fault

An article in the news recently published the findings of a study that identified a specific university for having more documented cases of cheating than anywhere else in the country. One student at the college, who was found to have plagiarized an essay, came up with a unique way of shifting the blame for his actions. The young scholar sued the university, claiming that he had been cheating for three years, and that it was the faculty's fault for not stopping him sooner. I guess I should sue the In-N-Out worker for not stopping me from eating those three Double Doubles. Wow, talk about grasping at straws to make someone else responsible for his own actions!

Shifting the blame is not a new concept as shown in the above Genesis account of Adam and Eve. First, we have Adam blaming God for his sin (the woman YOU put here), and then we have Eve blaming the serpent (he deceived me, and I ate). It seemed that in their minds they had been compelled to sin. Unfortunately for them, their excuse was no more successful than I suspect the previously mentioned university students will be.

King David, for all his faults, had the right idea of what to do when confronted with a sin in his life. Psalm 51:4 records his statement after his sin with Bathsheba, and the murder of her husband was revealed by the prophet Nathan. David said, "*Against You, You only, have I sinned and done what is evil in Your sight; so, you are right in Your verdict and justified when You judge.*"

It is wonderful that we serve a God who is so willing to forgive. First John 1:9 tells us, "*If we confess our sins, He is faithful and just to forgive our sins and to cleanse us from all unrighteousness.*" The first thing we must do is confess, without hesitation, just like David did.

Mankind's sin might have started with Adam and Eve, but we have kept it going. The comedian Flip Wilson had a routine that always ended with the phrase "The Devil made me do it" in justification for some misguided action. Well, Satan might be cheering us on, but he definitely is not "making" us do what we do. We decide that for ourselves. We can also decide what we do with that sin once it has been brought to our attention.

Thought for the Day

We might have trouble stopping ourselves from sinning, but we can choose to immediately confess that sin after we do.

DAY 357

*(For the Lord your God is a merciful God), He will
not forsake you nor destroy you, nor forget the covenant
of your fathers which He swore to them.*

—Deuteronomy 4:31

The Unforgotten

The Newport Beach Police Department experienced a great victory with a guilty verdict in the trial of a cold case murder investigation that occurred seventeen years prior. The investigators who were involved celebrated along with the victim's family that justice had finally been served.

On the wall in my department's detective division, there are numerous pictures of the victims in our unsolved murder cases that date back to 1970. The smiling faces in the photographs show the victims in happier times and represent a stark contrast to the condition in which they were eventually discovered. Our investigators keep those pictures posted as a reminder to themselves and as a promise to the victim's families that they will never forget these murders or stop in their pursuit to solve and prosecute these crimes.

Sometimes our circumstances can lead us to believe that God has forgotten us and that we are facing this life on our own. Nothing can be further from the truth. God knew you and loved you before the world was made.

Only a belief in Christ can solve the problem of our separation from God as a result of the sin in our lives. He loves you and will never cease in his pursuit of a personal relationship with you. However, that relationship can only be realized when you surrender the control of your life to Jesus. Whether it is to accept Him as your personal Savior and Lord for the first time, or to rededicate your life to Him, God always has you on His mind.

Thought for the Day

God doesn't need to keep a picture on the wall to remind Himself of His love for you.

DAY 358

I have told you all this so that you may have peace in me.
Here on earth you will have many trials and sorrows.
But take heart, because I have overcome the world.
                                                    —John 16:33

Stories

As a police officer, I had to listen to a lot of stories told to me by suspects who were trying to evade arrest. All these fictitious accounts had two things in common. They always portrayed innocence on their part, and were tailored to what they thought I wanted to hear. It was rare that an individual told me the truth up front, and even when they eventually confessed, they still held back part of the truth in an effort to minimize the full details of their actions.

Our culture today is a lot like that. Advertising campaigns encourage us to seek easy, happy, me-first lives, whose marketed images are tailor-made to what they think we want to hear. Unfortunately, many churches today have been sucked in by the culture around them, and promote that same easy, trouble-free life as an obtainable goal. Some have become so seeker friendly and prosperity driven that they no longer preach the gospel, and salvation becomes almost impossible under their teaching.

Let's suppose that you needed to take a private plane flight to another state. You had your choice of two pilots to get you to your destination. The first pilot offered you a perfect turbulence-free flight. On top of that, you would have the best food, music, and video entertainment possible on your trip. There was only one catch. The pilot told you that he had never made a successful landing, and that he had crashed every time he touched down. The other pilot stated that your flight might experience turbulence and some difficulty along the way. He could not promise a smooth, comfortable, entertaining ride at all times, but he did assure you of one thing. He had a perfect landing record, and always got his passengers to their destination safely. Which flight would you choose?

God does not offer us a trouble-free life. In fact, just the opposite, He promises that we will have trials and tribulations in this world. But He also assures us that through our faith in Jesus Christ, we will be guaranteed a safe landing in eternity with Him. We should be wary of any person, church, or teaching that does not tell us the truth, and promises us things not found in God's word.

Thought for the Day

Don't listen to stories that are tailor-made to what you might want to hear. Listen instead to the truth of God's word and the eternal promises He provides.

DAY 359

Casting all your care upon Him, for He cares for you.
—1 Peter 5:7

Not So Easy

When I worked as an associate pastor, I had an "easy" button on my desk. You know, the red plastic device that says "easy" in white lettering on top. When you push it down, a male voice said, "That was easy." It was a promotional item from Staples geared toward telling prospective shoppers that their company makes difficult office supply problems "easy." I didn't have it on my desk to tell anyone who came in for counsel that the solutions to their problems were easy. It was there to let them know that I understood their anxiety and how they wish they could just push a button to make it all go away. I always told them, "If that were true, I know you would push the button, tape it down and put a hundred-pound weight on it!" People's problems and the answers in God's word might be quick to define, but not always so fast to implement. It is like the weight-loss business. Burn off more than you take in, simple, right? Well, billions of dollars are spent every year proving that statement to be not so easy.

The answers to our problems can take time and dedication as we are in obedience to God's word. But they all begin at the same place. Our above verse in 1 Peter tells us to give our concerns to Jesus, because he cares for us. In fact, it advises that we "cast" those cares away. To me, that speaks of more than just handing them to the Savior, but actually throwing them onto Him. Have you ever had someone ask you to toss an item to them? It means that they want it quickly or that they don't want to make you walk across the room to give it to them.

Jesus is like that. He is so eager for you to unload your burdens that He wants you to throw them to Him. He doesn't want you to waste another second by walking over where He is to hand them over. Throw it away, get rid of it now, "cast" it to Him. And why? Because He cares for you. Once He has taken your burden, the uncontrollable, the inconceivable, the impossible, from you, He can start to give you His promises of comfort and provision. But the process doesn't start until the casting is done.

Thought for the Day

If you are troubled today, throw those burdens away. Jesus is always ready to take them from you.

DAY 360

By this all will know that you are My disciples, if you love one another.
—John 13:35

The Uniform

As police officers, we stood out in public. It is easy to identify who we are by the uniforms we wear. We didn't have to say a word to anyone for them to get a pretty good idea about what we stood for and whom we served. It was different when I worked as an undercover officer. I grew my hair long, had a beard, and wore casual clothing. In essence, I spent most of my time trying to hide who I really was from those whom I came into contact with on the job.

The above verse in John tells of how others will know that we are followers of Jesus Christ. If we demonstrate His love to one another, it will be as obvious as wearing a police uniform that we are different than those around us.

The problem that some Christians have is that they have gone undercover in their connection with God. Nothing about their lives shows a positive difference that a personal relationship with Jesus Christ can make. God's word says, *"Let your light so shine before men, that they may see our good works and glorify your Father in heaven"* (Matthew 5:16). In describing these good works, 1 Corinthians 13:13 states, *"And now abide faith, hope, love, these three; but the greatest of these is love."*

As police officers, it can be difficult to show compassion for those whom we come into contact with on a daily basis. In truth, many don't act in a manner that seems to deserve our love. But if we are honest with ourselves, we must say that we don't deserve God's love for the way we act toward Him. Romans 5:8 tells us, "*But God demonstrates His own love toward us, in that while we were still sinners, Christ died for us.*" If we want to be easily identified with our Lord, we must love others the way He does.

Thought for the Day

Are you a Christian who is working undercover?

DAY 361

For "whoever calls on the name of the Lord shall be saved."

Romans 10:13

No Background Required

Police officers go through a rigorous selection process before they are hired. It includes an application, aptitude test, physical agility test, background check, psychological test, oral interview, and polygraph examination. The background check is very thorough. It looks into their past criminal behavior as well as their financial dealings. They even interview their friends and neighbors about their attitudes and actions. And just in case they made it through all that, the polygraph (lie detector test) uncovers any other area of untruthfulness or deception in their lives.

At the Newport Beach Police Department, the process was so exacting that only one out of every one hundred candidates were actually hired. Even when they were selected, there were a number of those new officers who failed to make it through their field training programs or probationary periods.

I'm so glad that God does not require the same kind of testing in order to accept us into His kingdom. God's word says that, *"For whoever calls on the name of the Lord shall be saved."* There is no application, aptitude, agility, background, psychological, or interviewing required. Just simply call upon the Lord, believe that He died for your sins and rose again from the dead, and turn the rest of your life over to His control. He doesn't accept one out of every one hundred. He accepts **every single one**! You do not have to take a polygraph because God knows your heart and the truth of your commitment.

You also don't have to fear not making it through a probationary period as a Christian. If you were sincere in accepting Christ as your Lord and Savior, nothing will be able to pull you out of your Father's hand (John 10:28–29).

You do not have to go through a lengthy process to be accepted into God's kingdom. You can be instantly hired by placing your faith in Jesus Christ.

Thought for the Day

No background required.

DAY 362

Then I looked again, and I heard the voices of thousands and millions of angels around the throne and of the living beings and the elders. And they sang in a mighty chorus: "Worthy is the Lamb who was slaughtered—to receive power and riches and wisdom and strength and honor and glory and blessing."
—Revelation 5:11–12

Commencement

In 2010, we had the great joy of watching our two daughters graduate on the same day from my alma mater, the University of Southern California (Fight On!). I love graduation ceremonies. Commencement is the crowning achievement that represents years of hard work and sacrifice. The graduates and their families are all happy and proud to have finally received the award they worked so long and hard for.

When I was in college, I struggled through athletics and a full class schedule. It always helped for me to concentrate on my future commencement ceremony and to focus on what I knew would be a great day.

As beautiful as the college grounds, the caps and gowns, and the pomp and circumstance of a commencement ceremony are, it pales in comparison to what awaits the believer when they get to heaven.

Can you imagine hearing millions of beings singing in a chorus to our Lord? The book of Revelation goes into detail about John's vision of the heavenly scene in ways that are hard for us to accurately visualize. But the follower of Jesus Christ can be assured of one thing, it will be better than anything we can possibly imagine.

> *And God will wipe away every tear from their eyes; there shall be no more death, nor sorrow, nor crying. There shall be no more pain, for the former things have passed away. (Revelation 21:4)*

Thought for the Day

Even when we have given the control of our lives to Jesus Christ, at times we may still struggle with the "here and now" problems of today. When that happens, let's try to stay focused on our assured invitation to the greatest commencement ceremony of all time.

DAY 363

Now Cain talked with Abel his brother; and it came
to pass, when they were in the field, that Cain rose
up against Abel his brother and killed him.

—Genesis 4:8

Specialty Selection

It didn't take long in the Bible's record of man to see our first murder. Cain killed his brother Abel. This one wouldn't have been too
difficult to investigate with such a short list of possible suspects. We
would have started where we always do, with family members, and
found out who had a grudge against the victim. The account doesn't
say what weapon was used to carry out the crime, but the fact that
the suspect lured the victim to a remote location was standard. The
motive was also routine, jealousy.

God had accepted Abel's sacrifice to Him but had not approved
of Cain's. Apparently, Cain had held something back and had not
given God his best. After God confronted him about his sin, Cain
eventually turned his anger against his brother and killed him.

Jealousy can eat us alive and cause us to do some foolish things.
There will always be those around us who possess something or have
achieved something that we want. The air around the department is
thick with the smell of jealousy, especially after a specialty or promotional selection.

I've been on the losing end of that selection process more times
than I can remember. I've concluded that God is in control and if
He had wanted me to promote or to get a specialty assignment, no
person or situation could have stopped Him. I had to accept the fact

that His will for my life did not always follow the world's standard career advancement path. If I was jealous of those who advanced instead of me, I was basically telling God that He didn't know what he is doing.

If we keep giving our best to God, He will place us exactly where He wants us at the time He wants us there. Becoming jealous of those who achieve what we want can only lead us down a dangerous and sometimes irrational path.

Thought of the Day

Commit your career to Him, and He will give you true success.

DAY 364

I asked the Lord to give me this boy, and He has granted my request. Now I am giving him to the Lord, and he will belong to the Lord his whole life." And they worshiped the Lord there.
—1 Samuel 1:27–28

Give It Back

First responders usually carry a lot of equipment with them while on the job. I once weighed my duty belt that contained a handgun, two filled ammo magazines, two pair of handcuffs, a Taser, pepper spray, baton, and key ring. Those items plus the weight of their leather holders topped twenty-five pounds. Add a Kevlar vest to that group, and I was on duty with nearly thirty pounds of additional weight during a normal shift. All those items belonged to the department and were on loan to me throughout my career. When I retired, I had to give them all back. They even had a check-off form to make sure each one was returned to our property officer.

At Harvest OC, we don't perform infant baptism. We believe that baptism is an outward expression that tells of an inward commitment to God. Only a person who fully understands what that inward commitment means qualifies to be baptized in obedience to God's word. We do, however, dedicate children to the Lord on a regular basis. This consists of bringing the child and their parents in front of the congregation so that we can pray for that child and officially dedicate their lives to the Lord.

The above verse in 1 Samuel records Hannah's statement regarding her son, Samuel. She had been childless for some time and had pleaded with the Lord to give her a baby. God answered Hannah's prayer, and in an act of gratitude, Hannah dedicated her infant son's life to the Lord. It was an acknowledgment of the fact that her child was just on loan to her from God, and that even though she would be in his life, Samuel belonged to Him.

Everything we have, children, relationships, wealth, assets, health, and talent, have been given to us by God to use and enjoy in this life. Sometimes we forget that fact and start to believe that those items and abilities belong to us, but they do not. For the believer in Jesus Christ, our lives will be a continual tug-of-war between us and the Lord for ownership over the various areas of our lives. The better we get at releasing our grip, the more God will be able to bless what we have been so tightly holding on to.

At the Judgment Seat of Christ, all believers will someday be judged as to what their effectiveness was in using the talents and abilities God gave them in this life. First Corinthians 5:10 tells us, *"For we must all appear before the judgment seat of Christ, that each one may receive the things done in the body, according to what he has done, whether good or bad."* This won't be a time of punishment for believers because their eternity will have been already secured through their faith in Christ's death on the cross for them. It will be a time of reward and possible regret for how ineffectively we had been using the talents and abilities He gave us.

Thought for the Day

Whatever we have is on loan from God. Let's give back to Him what is already His and receive the blessing for it!

DAY 365

So it was, when I heard these words, that I sat down
and wept, and mourned for many days; I was fasting
and praying before the God of heaven.

—Nehemiah 1:4

Leadership

N ehemiah was given the news that the Jewish people had been attacked. The walls of Jerusalem were broken down, and its gates had been burned by their enemies. Nehemiah eventually led the Jewish people to rebuild the walls of Jerusalem in only fifty-two days! How did he accomplish this great act of leadership? Nehemiah 1:4 says that he wept, fasted, and prayed for many days. He started where all great leadership should start, HE CARED!

As police officers, we have seen all kinds of leadership styles throughout our careers. At our department, we had a mixed bag of laterals, recruits, and veterans. It would be safe to say that between us, we had seen it all as far as leadership goes. There are those supervisors whom we will always remember for their compassion and concern about our personal lives and careers, and there are those that we won't. Wouldn't it be nice if an officer's compassion for his or her peers was considered a requirement for promotion?

Regardless of whether or not you are experiencing effective supervision in your current assignment, you can practice the leadership trait of compassion in your own life. Law enforcement is a hard job with lots of criticism and finger-pointing. There isn't an officer in these trying times that doesn't need a positive word in their lives. Studies indicate that many officers who were shot on duty had a bad performance review or other negative job-related occurrence that preceded the incident.

Thought for the Day

We can become great leaders today! Let's encourage our peers, put others' needs before our own, and show compassion in our interactions with one another. Remember, you don't need an official position to lead.

ONE MORE THING

I pray this devotional book has given you direction when the road ahead seems uncertain, hope where there seems like none can be found, and peace in times of trouble. The verse that always helped me throughout my law enforcement career when the things I saw make no sense to me was Romans 8:28 which tells us, "For we know that all things work together for the good to those who love God, to those who are called according to His purpose." Romans doesn't promise us that all things work together for the good for everyone; it has a distinct caveat that must be fulfilled in order for God to work in our lives. We must love God and be called in alignment with His purpose.

Have you given the control of your life over to the one who made you, loves you, and has a plan and purpose for your life? Direction, peace, and hope are only a simple prayer away. But first you must realize that

1. You are a sinner. No more excuses. The Bible says that everyone has sinned and fallen short of God's standard.
2. Recognize that Jesus died on the cross for you. Jesus said, "There is no greater love than to lay down one's life for one's friends."
3. Repent of your sin. This means to turn away from all known sin in your life. The Bible says that God commands everyone everywhere to repent of their sins and turn to Him.
4. Receive Christ into your life. It's not just believing He is the Son of God but receiving Him into your life as Lord, Savior, and friend. Jesus said, "Look, I stand at the door

and knock. If you hear my voice and open the door, I will come in."

5. Do it now! Jesus said, "Everyone who acknowledges me publicly here on earth, I will also acknowledge before my father in heaven."

If you would like to invite Jesus into your life, pray this simple prayer and mean it from your heart.

Jesus, I know I am a sinner, and I am sorry for my sin. I repent of it and turn to You by faith right now. I thank you for dying on the cross for me and paying the price for all my sins. I ask you to come into my life right now and be my Lord, my Savior, and my friend. Fill me with Your Holy Spirit. Help me to stand for You from this moment forward. Thank you, Jesus. Amen.

If you prayed that prayer, congratulations and welcome to the family of God! Now all God's promises found in the Bible belong to you. I encourage you to start reading the Bible and pray daily. Find and attend a church in your area where they believe in and teach from God's word.

ABOUT THE AUTHOR

B rad Green grew up in Costa Mesa, California, and is a third-generation public servant. Brad accepted Jesus Christ as his Savior and Lord when he was seven years old at the First Baptist Church in Costa Mesa. His early life was centered around attending church, school, friends, and playing football. The latter served him well as he later developed into an All-CIF high school football player and his team's MVP at Orange Coast Community College in California. Brad went on to receive a full football scholarship at the University of Southern California and was a member of the 1978 national championship team.

In 1990, Brad became a member of the Newport Beach Police Department. During his service at NBPD, he worked patrol, traffic, detective investigations, defensive tactics, field training, and was a hostage negotiator for the department. Brad has a critical incident stress management certification and has conducted critical stress debriefings for NBPD officers after major incidents. Brad served as a police chaplain during the last five years of his sworn police officer career and in the years since his retirement. From 2013 to 2021, he was an associate pastor at Harvest Christian Fellowship where he worked for renowned evangelist Greg Laurie. Brad has a burning desire to encourage some of his favorite people, the first responder community.

Brad lives in Mission Viejo, California, with his beautiful wife of forty-one years, Terri. He is the proud father of three daughters and grandfather of two.